CHARLIE CHAPLIN VS. AMERICA

WHEN ART, SEX, AND POLITICS COLLIDED

SCOTT EYMAN

SIMON & SCHUSTER

NEW YORK   LONDON   TORONTO   SYDNEY   NEW DELHI

Simon & Schuster
1230 Avenue of the Americas
New York, NY 10020

First Simon & Schuster hardcover edition October 2023

SIMON & SCHUSTER and colophon are registered trademarks of Simon &
Schuster, Inc.

For information about special discounts for bulk purchases, please contact Simon
& Schuster Special Sales at 1-866-506-1949 or business@simonandschuster.com.

The Simon & Schuster Speakers Bureau can bring authors to your live event. For
more information or to book an event, contact the Simon & Schuster Speakers
Bureau at 1-866-248-3049 or visit our website at www.simonspeakers.com.

Interior design by Carly Loman

Manufactured in the United States of America

10 9 8 7 6 5 4 3 2 1

Library of Congress Cataloging-in-Publication Data is available.

ISBN 978-1-9821-7635-8
ISBN 978-1-9821-7637-2 (ebook)

For Mort Janklow, who made a difference in this writer's life.

"I have no morals in the sense that I abide with them in awe. I respect no book of rules, for they have been written by someone else. . . . My ego edits my life more than any moral code and I would never do anything to shame it for I have to live with myself.

"One thing I know is that poverty taught me nothing; but on the contrary distorted and twisted my sense of values, gave me a wrong concept of life . . . it neither gave me pity for the poor, nor a social conscience. Its general effect was a numbing of the senses as one used to see of the derelicts sleeping on the Thames embankment on winter nights. . . .

"I remember shaking an old lady and give her five bob to get a bed. She looked up, then looked at the money, and without uttering a word fell asleep again."

—From an abandoned preface to Chaplin's *My Autobiography*

CONTENTS

PROLOGUE
1

PART ONE
19

PART TWO
95

PART THREE
243

EPILOGUE
353

ACKNOWLEDGMENTS   361

SOURCE NOTES   365

BIBLIOGRAPHY   391

INDEX   395

CHARLIE CHAPLIN
VS. AMERICA

PROLOGUE

In those days, nothing important happened on the weekends.

Movie people went to parties, to Palm Springs, or to clubs on the Sunset Strip. Occasionally they paired off in a way they couldn't during the week, when they had to get up before dawn in order to get to the studio by 8 a.m. And sometimes they just rested.

What this meant in practice was that a Monday gossip column was typically filled with soft items saved for a slow news day. Hedda Hopper's column for Monday, May 19, 1952, was a case in point: "Ava had a party of 10 to put Frankie in the groove at the Grove. And [photographer] Hymie Fink covered him from every angle. . . . Phil Yordan's 'Edgar' for the *Detective Story* screenplay was stolen from the detective bringing it to him by train. So Phil's hiring a detective to find it."

Hopper's lead item seemed to fit right in: "Charlie Chaplin has his return visa and he's all set for Europe in September for the preems of *Limelight* in London and Paris. Oona goes along, but the kids stay behind in Beverly."

In fact, the item was not a space-filler so much as one of those barely perceptible tremors that precedes an earthquake. A day or two after the item ran, Hopper sent a clipping in a letter addressed to California Senator Richard M. Nixon:

My dear Dick,

The enclosed about Charlie Chaplin is very distressing. He tried
to leave the country a year or so ago and was told he couldn't get
back in. I hope that situation has not changed. And if it has been
changed and he has finagled through the State Department and has
obtained a passport with re-entry, I believe it is the duty of each
Senator to know about it.

Personally, I hope he goes and never comes back in. He is as bad
a citizen as we have in this country, as you well know.

I hope you will look into this matter and do what you can
about it.

For Nixon—or anybody else—Hopper was categorized as High
Maintenance. She wrote Nixon dozens of letters of approval, as well
as occasional scoldings when she felt that he came up short in attending to her needs. This invariably involved Nixon failing to placate
her with a soothing "Dear Hedda" letter of reassurance about her
vital contributions to their shared priorities.

On May 29, Nixon replied: "I agree with you that the way the
Chaplin case has been handled has been a disgrace for years. Unfortunately, we aren't able to do too much about it when the top
decisions are made by the likes of [Secretary of State Dean] Acheson
and [Attorney General James] McGranery. You can be sure, however,
that I will keep my eye on the case and possibly after January we will
be able to work with an Administration which will apply the same
rules to Chaplin as they do to ordinary citizens."

That paragraph aside, it's a chatty letter between old friends.
Nixon discusses the upcoming Republican convention and the tactics being deployed by Robert Taft and Dwight Eisenhower, the two
main candidates for the nomination. Hopper was ardently for Taft,
and Nixon didn't disabuse her of the notion that he was as well, even
though he would happily accept the vice presidential nomination
from Eisenhower. Nixon had a hunch that the convention would not
devolve into a destructive food fight. "I still think that we are going
to come out of the Convention united behind a good candidate.

"Pat joins me in sending our best to you."

Nixon had been a member of the House Un-American Activities Committee whose hearings had shaken Hollywood to its core in 1947, with Hopper serving as a primary cheerleader. They were devout coreligionists in the fight against the social decay represented by Communism, not to mention unchecked sexuality, and they believed Chaplin embodied both.

Hopper in particular had long regarded Chaplin as an affront to both her country and her movie industry—Hopper personalized all relationships. She had furiously sniped at Chaplin's plans to make *The Great Dictator* and greeted its great success with sullen silence. In April 1947, when Chaplin's film *Monsieur Verdoux* was meeting with critical contempt and public indifference, she wrote J. Edgar Hoover: "I'd like to run every one of those [Communist] rats out of the country and start with Charlie Chaplin. . . . It's about time we stood up and be counted."

Chaplin gave no indication that he was aware of the storm clouds forming on the horizon. On August 2, a few months after Hopper's column item, Chaplin hosted a preview of *Limelight* at the Paramount studio. The guest list amounted to about two hundred people, including Humphrey Bogart, David Selznick, Ronald Colman, and Sylvia Fairbanks Gable—the elite of old Hollywood.

The only journalist invited was Sidney Skolsky. He reported that as the end titles faded, the audience stood up en masse and shouted "Bravo." Chaplin stepped in front of the screen and said, "I thank you. I was very afraid. You are the first ones in the world to see my film, which lasts two hours and a half. I don't want to keep you long, but I care to say 'Thank You.'"

A woman stopped him by shouting "No!! No! Thanks to you!" and the rest of the crowd started shouting "Thank You."

The tumultuous response was soon confirmed by the response of the novelist Lion Feuchtwanger, who wrote Chaplin on August 8: "The film . . . arouses emotions much like Dickens' novels. It moves without ever becoming corny, and, at the right moment, the legitimate emotion is mingled with a good, sound, legitimate laugh. Your picture is deeply human and in the best sense popular. So it accomplishes the mission which Molière requires of a real work of art; it satisfies and pleases the professor as well as the cook."

The response to the preview must have assuaged some of Chaplin's fears of obsolescence. After *The Great Dictator*, he had endured years of public castigation for his support for opening a second front to aid Russia during World War II while simultaneously enduring a definitively ugly, trumped-up paternity suit. After that, *Monsieur Verdoux* had been his first critical flop and, in America, a commercial disaster.

On the night of September 5, Chaplin was having a cup of coffee at Googie's, a small café on Sunset Boulevard. Across from him sat his assistant Jerry Epstein. Some pictures turned out to be less than Chaplin had hoped (*The Circus*), and some turned out to be better than he had dreamed (*City Lights*) but he was calmly confident about *Limelight*. He was sixty-three years old, madly in love with his wife, Oona, the mother of four of his six children. He believed that his third act would be his richest, and he believed he knew why.

It was all about America.

"I could never have found such success in England," he told Epstein that night. "This is really the land of opportunity."

The next day, Saturday the 6th, he made a few last-minute trims in *Limelight*. As he left the editing room Chaplin insisted that Oona come with him to the Bank of America. He wanted her signature on a joint account. He explained that in case anything happened to him, she would have instant access to his cash and securities. Oona thought he was being silly. What could possibly happen? Chaplin insisted, and Oona did as he asked.

Later that day, Chaplin, Oona, and Harry Crocker, an old friend who had served, variously, as costar (*The Circus*), assistant director (*City Lights*), and publicity director (*Limelight*) left for New York on the Santa Fe Chief. A week later, the Chaplin children—Geraldine, Michael, Josephine, and Victoria—followed, along with two nurses.

The plan was to travel to England on the *Queen Elizabeth* for the world premiere of *Limelight* in London, and then take the family on a vacation through Europe. Chaplin wanted to show Oona his London: Lambeth, Kennington, the East End—the rooming house where he had lived with his father and his father's mistress; the workhouse where he had been interned as an indigent child; the pub where he had seen his alcoholic father for the last time. After London and the Continent, they would return to Los Angeles within six months.

Chaplin had originally planned the trip for several weeks earlier, but Oona had fallen ill, and the trip was pushed back. Then Chaplin realized he had lost his passport, which entailed applying for a duplicate, wherein he asserted that the passport "might have been lost during rebuilding of my house." That rebuilding was necessary because of the birth of his and Oona's fourth child. The house at 1085 Summit Drive, just up the road from Pickfair, had been expensively expanded and reconfigured for his growing family.

Upon arriving in New York City, the Chaplins checked into the Sherry-Netherland. Oona called their friend Lillian Ross of *The New Yorker*, and invited her to go for a walk with Chaplin the next day. At eleven the next morning, Ross picked up Chaplin at his suite.

"Walking around the city is a ritual with me," Chaplin explained. "I love to walk all over New York."

Out on the sidewalk, Chaplin took a deep breath. It was close to autumn, but the day was warm. "I like this kind of day for walking in the city. A sultry, Indian summer September day. But do you know the best time for walking in the city? Two a.m. It's the best time. The city is chaste. Virginal. Two a.m. in the winter is the best, with everything looking frosty. The tops of the automobiles. Shiny. All those colors."

Chaplin began walking briskly, taking it all in. "You come along this avenue and you meet the world. In Hollywood, you walk for miles and you don't meet a single friend. Sometimes when I have a whole day here I walk a whole day. I just go along and I discover places. . . . I used to go to Grand Central—to the Oyster Bar. I'd get a dozen clams, and all you'd want besides is the lemon. You'd get a dozen clams for eighty cents. . . .

"You know, in 1910, when I first arrived in New York, it was just this kind of a day in September. Indian summer. Funny thing. We got off the boat and had our luggage sent to the theater—to the

Colonial Theatre, at 62nd and Broadway. The theater is gone now. I can conduct you on a tour. Tell you all about New York in 1910 and in 1912. I've outlived it all."

On 42nd Street, Chaplin stopped and looked around. "There used to be a Child's restaurant around about here. That Child's was wonderful. It was all *very* white. They used to make hotcakes right in their window. Forty-second street was *very* elegant then. *Very* elegant. . . . What a meal you could get at Child's for a quarter, plus dessert. Or two eggs, hot biscuits and wonderful coffee, all for fifteen cents."

The day before Chaplin and his family were scheduled to leave for London, he called Richard Avedon. The photographer had been chasing him for years, but Chaplin hadn't answered his letters. It wasn't personal—Chaplin rarely answered letters. Avedon thought the call was a joke and hung up, but Chaplin was used to that response and immediately called back. "I'm coming over right now," he told Avedon, who promptly sent all of his assistants out of the studio—he didn't want any distractions.

At first, Avedon shot a few pictures straight on, "almost as though I was doing a passport picture." When Avedon thought he had his shot, Chaplin asked, "May I do something for you?" He lowered his head, and came up grinning in extreme close-up, with his index fingers forming horns on the side of his head—the Great God Pan. Or, if you believed Hedda Hopper, Satan incarnate. Chaplin did it once more, and the second time was the keeper.

"I can't take responsibility for this picture," Avedon would write. "It was one of those perfect moments when the light was right, and I was there, and the sitter offered the photographer a gift . . . the kind of gift that arrives once in a lifetime."

That night, Chaplin and Oona went to dinner with Lillian Ross and James Agee and his wife, Mia, at the Stork Club. Later, they went to 21.

On the evening of September 17, Chaplin and his family left for London on board the *Queen Elizabeth*. Years later, Chaplin remembered watching the Statue of Liberty recede into the distance as the ship sailed out of the harbor. "I thought to myself what it had meant to me when I first saw the statue. It filled me with tremendous joy. It meant freedom and progress in America. But when I looked at it that day on my way out to sea, I found myself wondering how accurate a symbol it really was."

ONE DAY OUT of New York, Chaplin and his wife were having dinner with Harry Crocker, Adolph Green, and Arthur and Nela Rubinstein when a steward told Crocker there were four radio telephone calls for him. Crocker left the table to attend to the problem. The calls had come from newspaper reporters. They read Crocker a cursory press release from the Department of Justice: "Attorney General James P. McGranery announced today that he had issued orders to the Immigration and Naturalization Service to hold for hearing Charles Chaplin when he seeks to re-enter this country.

"The hearing will determine whether he is admissible under the laws of the United States."

An accompanying statement said that McGranery had taken the action under a provision permitting the barring of resident aliens on grounds of "morals, health or insanity, or for advocating Communism or associating with Communist or pro-Communist organizations."

The reporters wanted a response from Chaplin.

Crocker sent a note to Chaplin, asking him to come immediately to Crocker's cabin. Chaplin knew something was radically wrong as soon as he walked through the door—Crocker's face had gone dead white.

Chaplin remembered that, as Crocker read the communiqué, "Every nerve in me tensed. Whether I re-entered that unhappy country or not was of little consequence to me. I would have liked to tell them the sooner I was rid of that hate-beleaguered atmosphere the better, that I was fed up with America's insults and moral pomposity, and that the whole subject was damned boring. But everything I possessed was in the States and I was terrified they might find a way of confiscating it. Now I could expect any unscrupulous action from them. So instead I came out with a . . . statement to the effect that I would return and answer the charges, and that my re-entry was not a 'scrap of paper,' but a document given to me in good faith by the United States government—blah, blah, blah."

Chaplin's statement: "Through the proper procedure I applied for a re-entry permit which I was given in good faith and which I accepted in good faith; therefore I assume that the United States Government will recognize its validity."

By the time Crocker returned the first four calls, there were nine more waiting.

In chaotic circumstances, it was hard to get much information about what was being said in the newspapers back home. Chaplin and Crocker did find out that the Department of Justice refused to state specific grounds for revoking the reentry permit because, said one official, "It might prejudice our case."

Despite being suddenly hurled into limbo, there wasn't really much Chaplin could do other than continue with the routine of shipboard life for the rest of the crossing. Passengers saw him walking around the deck, reading, eating, and dancing with his wife after watching a movie.

The morning after the attorney general's announcement, the *Los Angeles Times* page one banner headline read "U.S. BARS CHAPLIN: INQUIRY ORDERED." The *Chicago Tribune* page one headline read "MOVE TO BAN CHAPLIN IN U.S." with a heavily slanted accompanying story that said Chaplin "had scorned citizenship in this country," that Congress had denounced him as "left wing and radical," and that he had been declared the father of an illegitimate child. The fact that blood tests had proved Chaplin wasn't the father was not mentioned.

As always, Chaplin's automatic response to a crisis was to seek solace in work. At some point during the crossing, Chaplin took out a yellow legal pad and began outlining an idea for a film in his rapid, sprawling hand:

"An immigrant arrives in America and owing to the fact that he cannot be understood by the U.S. authorities, who try to discover him . . ."

He broke off. Flipping the page, he began again: "Arriving in America, an immigrant who speaks a strange language which the

U.S. officials cannot understand, passes the immigration authorities, because of not being understood and, therefore, he does not come under the quota of any foreign nation.

"When he discovers that he is at last in America, he tries his best to get a job. He eventually gets a job. He eventually gets one as a [blank space] and gets into all sorts of complications because he does not understand the American language. Everybody tries to make him understand by pantomime and, of course, he only understands what he wants to understand."

The idea harks back to the animating principle underlying Chaplin's films as the Tramp: a well-meaning outsider at perpetual cross-purposes with his surroundings, doomed to isolation because of a basic imbalance in the relationship between an individual and conventional society.

When the *Queen Elizabeth* stopped in Cherbourg, reporters stampeded on board to talk to Chaplin, who tried to lower the temperature. He "was very surprised at the action, of course. I don't know exactly in what circumstances it was taken." He had, he said, "millions of friends" in America, and noted that "the government of the United States does not usually go back on such a thing as a re-entry permit. I am sure it is valid." Furthermore, he said that the Immigration Department in New York had wished him bon voyage and "said they hoped I would soon return."

And then he focused on what he believed to be the crux of the matter. "I am not political. I have never been political. I have no political convictions. I am an individualist and believe in liberty. That is as far as my political convictions go." When a reporter asked him why he had never become an American citizen, he replied, "That has come in for a great deal of criticism. Super-patriotism leads to Hitler-ism. I assume that in a democracy one can have a private opinion. During the war I made several speeches sponsored by the government and several people took exception to what I said. I said nothing subversive in my opinion. I don't want to create revolution. I just want to create a few more pictures."

Over the next few days, the roster of American columnists who had been assaulting Chaplin in print for years weighed in all over again: "A menace to young girls." (Westbrook Pegler). "Good riddance to bad rubbish." (Hedda Hopper). "Maybe you'll miss us, but I don't think we'll miss you." (Florabel Muir).

Only Bosley Crowther of *The New York Times* and the columnist Dorothy Thompson stood up for Chaplin.

Crowther: "There is no way of knowing what evidence the Justice Department may have with which to challenge Mr. Chaplin when he seeks to re-enter the United States. But it would seem fairly reasonable to imagine that, if any evidence sufficiently strong to prove him a dangerous alien had been uncovered by now, it would already have been brought against him in a formal deportation suit. The basis for the Justice Department's action remains to be disclosed."

Thompson: "Judge him in the only way an artist can be judged—by his art—and he emerges as one of the most effective anti-Communists alive."

Ed Sullivan, already fronting the television show that would banish memories of his reliably right-wing newspaper column, shot back at Crowther, scoffing at his assertion that Chaplin's films had comforted and allayed the loneliness of first-generation Americans. Sullivan wrote that "what most Americans resented was non-citizen Chaplin's loud interference in U.S. policy, plus his extension of the 'little tramp' role to his private life and dalliances. Crowther's portrait of Chaplin as the right-hand man of U.S. naturalization officials is laughable."

On September 21 the *Los Angeles Times* headlined a story "GOVERNMENT HINTS NEW FACTS IN CHAPLIN CASE." Attorney General James McGranery took ten days to issue a statement elaborating on his reasons for the rescinding of the reentry permit. He asserted that Chaplin had "a leering, sneering attitude" toward America.

On October 3, McGranery held a press conference during which he referred to the banishment as a question of "morals" and called Chaplin a "menace to womanhood." McGranery also said that the Department of Justice planned to deport one hundred "unsavory characters," and included Chaplin in a roster that was otherwise made up entirely of mafiosi. In the same issue of *Variety* that reported McGranery's remarks, Assistant Secretary of State Howland Sargeant contradicted the attorney general by saying that Chaplin "has every State Dept. paper he needs to get back into the country," and that it was the Defense Department that believed him to be a security risk.

Confusion reigned.

Again, *The New York Times* stood up for Chaplin, this time in an editorial: "Those who have followed him through the years cannot easily regard him as a dangerous person. No political situation, no international menace, can destroy the fact that he is a great artist who has given infinite pleasure to many millions, not in one country, but in all countries. Unless there is far more evidence against him than is at the moment visible, the Department of State will not dignify itself or increase the national security if it sends him into exile."

The back-and-forth continued for months, for years. And none of it made any difference.

Charlie Chaplin had been canceled.

NEITHER THE REPORTERS nor Chaplin were aware that, in the opinion of the Immigration and Naturalization Service, there would have been nothing the government could have done if Chaplin had demanded his reentry permit be honored. On September 29, ten days after the reentry permit was rescinded, in a meeting attended by INS deputy commissioner Raymond Farrell, it was noted that, "Mr. Farrell stated bluntly that at the present time INS does not have sufficient information to exclude Chaplin from the United States if he attempts to re-enter."

They could, Farrell thought, make it difficult, perhaps even embarrassing, "but in the end, there is no doubt Chaplin would be admitted," if only because he had never been found guilty of any crime. Furthermore, if the INS attempted to delay Chaplin's reentry, the result "might well rock INS and the Department of Justice to its foundations." A year or two later, the solicitor general of the Eisenhower administration, Simon Sobeloff, would say that the government had no grounds to ban Chaplin, let alone enforce a deportation.

Armed with this knowledge, the INS had to be able to counter with something devastating or risk looking foolish if Chaplin forced the issue. And so Lita Grey, Chaplin's second wife, whose divorce complaint had charged him with adultery, as well as what the complaint characterized as degrading sexual acts, was questioned in an attempt to build a case against her ex-husband. On October 20, 1952, the FBI questioned Grey, but she steadfastly refused to help:

"They were desperately trying to build a case of moral turpitude because [my divorce complaint] contained intimate details of my sex life with him. I said, 'I'm sorry gentlemen, but I am an adult now and I didn't draw the complaint. It is true that most of the content is correct. However, the way it is presented, the words used, the description of sex, was all drawn up by my attorneys. I can't cooperate with you. Besides, I have two wonderful children by Charlie and I don't want to be responsible for keeping him out of this country.' "

At the end of the interview with Grey, the FBI had no more on Chaplin than they had before September 1952. Had Chaplin wanted to come back to America, neither the FBI nor the INS could have stopped him.

But Chaplin would make no attempt to resume his life in America. Not then, not ever.

In a sense, it was all Sydney Chaplin's fault. Charlie's half-brother had a profound understanding of money and of comedy, but something of a blind spot about politics. On April 22, 1952, Sydney had written his brother suggesting he "take a run over to England for the opening [of *Limelight*] . . . in London & I don't think you will have much trouble in obtaining a return permit & one that will be honored [*sic*] on your return."

That same day, Sydney wrote a friend: "Regarding [rumors of] Charlie coming to live in Europe, I don't place any value on that report. He has spent a lot of money having his house transformed to accommodate his larger family. However, I would not be surprised to see him make a trip to England for the showing of his picture and if he applies for a return permit, I think it will be granted & no obstacles in the way of his return. He has an American wife and 6 American children, two of which have fought for America in the last war. I think, except for the Catholic element, prejudice against Charlie has died down & from the government point, they know he has never been connected with any Communist organizations & for a period of 40 years he has been an asset & not a liability to America."

Less than a month later, Chaplin began filing paperwork for the family jaunt through Europe. Sydney reported in a letter to his brother on May 2 that he had read in the papers that his name-sake nephew, Charlie's son Sydney, was going to play Shakespeare in Stratford. Sydney the elder thought Sydney the younger was wasting his time: "With his name and ability, he should now be earning big money either in the movies or on the TV. Look at some of the big salary boys, past & present. . . . Valentino was a dish washer, Clark Gable worked in a boiler factory, Cary Grant walked on stilts & gave away hand bills outside the New York Hippodrome. Harry Lauder came from the coal mines, the Chaplin Bros came from the gutter & Sir Henry Irving went broke playing Shakespeare. I am grateful that I learned to . . . do a cut-up fall.

"The years are fleeting & . . . as Doug Fairbanks used to say, 'Life is a room with several doors & the problem is to know which door to open.' "

BY THE TIME the *Queen Elizabeth* docked in London, Chaplin's mood was markedly less conciliatory. The more he thought about it, the angrier he got. He vowed to return to America and fight the charges.

But reality forced him toward circumspection. Everything Chaplin possessed was in America. Not merely his home, his cash and securities, but the negatives of his films and his studio on La Brea Avenue. It wasn't hard to imagine a scenario where he could become an elderly reconfiguration of the Tramp—stateless, impoverished. In the fall of 1952, it was once again clear that Charlie Chaplin's life had an eerie way of prefiguring—not to mention explaining—his art. First psychologically, now literally.

So Chaplin once again opted for bland pronouncements: "I do not want to create any revolution. All I want to do is create a few more films. It might amuse people."

A month after the revocation of the reentry permit, the FBI issued a massive internal report documenting more than thirty years of investigations focused on Chaplin, a copy of which was dispatched to the attorney general. The report revealed that, besides the FBI, Army and Navy Intelligence, the Internal Revenue Service, the Central Intelligence Agency, the Department of State, and the U.S. Postal Service had all been surveilling Chaplin at one time or another. In short, the entire security apparatus of the United States had descended upon a motion picture comedian.

The report's ultimate verdict was that Chaplin was not and never had been a Communist, nor had he donated a dime to the cause. Nevertheless, the implicit conclusion was that the revocation of his reentry permit was justified for reasons evenly divided between sex and politics.

It was all very strange. For more than thirty years, Chaplin's Tramp had navigated the perilous no-man's-land situated between the way things are supposed to be and the way they actually are.

Early in his movie career, Chaplin's social conscience had generally been limited to occasional jabs in otherwise apolitical contexts: the sharp, savage little moment when the immigrants are roped off like cattle just as the Statue of Liberty hoves into view in *The Immigrant*; the Bible Belt's hypocrisy in *The Pilgrim*; the alcoholic millionaire in *City Lights* who sees the Tramp as his best friend when drunk and needy but doesn't know him when sober—more or less a behavioral analogy for capitalism at its predatory worst.

America's right wing sensed a heretic. *The Pilgrim* resulted in a formal protest from the South Carolina Ku Klux Klan, while the Evangelical Ministers' Association in Atlanta called it "an insult to the Gospel."

The overall tenor of Chaplin's films began to shift with *Modern Times* in 1936, when Chaplin made rampant instability in a newly spawned age of anxiety wrought by a worldwide Depression the motivation for the entire film. The Tramp is forced into an incessant round-robin of survival strategies, all of which prove useless. Despite his focus on just getting by, the Tramp can't avoid the stigma of Communism when he helpfully picks up a red flag that has fallen off a truck just as a mob of strikers comes around the corner. Result: arrest as a dangerous radical.

Chaplin's disavowal of Communist politics could hardly be wittier, or more pointed.

Other than the huge success of *The Great Dictator* in 1940, the ensuing decade had been a largely dreadful period for Chaplin. The paternity suit confirmed suspicions that he was not merely politically subversive but sexually subversive as well. Despite the exculpatory results of the blood test, he was found guilty in court and, far more damagingly, in the court of public opinion. The speeches he had made on behalf of opening a second front to aid Russia, America's ally at the time, had served as prima facie evidence of Communist sympathies. "I don't want the old rugged individualism," he had proclaimed. "Rugged for a few, ragged for many."

In 1948, the FBI began perusing reports gathered over the previous twenty-six years to "determine whether or not CHAPLIN was or is engaged in Soviet espionage activities"—an investigation focused on the intrinsically absurd idea that a multimillionaire was plotting to overthrow capitalism.

James McGranery's action was the culmination of years of a concerted campaign targeting the private sexual behavior and public political sympathies of the most dangerous brand of dissident—a beloved popular artist. The result was excision from the body politic as if he was a collection of malignant cells.

The action would disrupt both Chaplin's career and recently stabilized private life—this decade also brought the emotional security he had sought his entire life in his 1943 marriage to Oona O'Neill, which lasted the rest of his life and produced eight children.

THIS BOOK IS a social, political, and cultural history of a crucial period in the life of a seminal twentieth-century figure—the original independent filmmaker who gradually fell into mortal combat with his adopted country precisely because of the beliefs that formed the core of his personality and films.

At a time when political and cultural paranoia converged, the FBI did not restrict itself to the collection of facts, but actively proselytized for the image of Chaplin as subversive, freely disseminating a steady stream of largely unsubstantiated disinformation to Chaplin's political adversaries. Chaplin became the most prominent victim of what amounted to a cultural cold war—a place where art always loses.

America lost a lot in this period. So did Chaplin. *A King in New York* and *A Countess from Hong Kong*, the two films he made after his forced exile, are a precipitous decline from *Monsieur Verdoux* and *Limelight*.

This is the story of one of the earliest junctions between show business and politics, of how a theoretically liberal Democratic administration capitulated to a Red Scare made up of what Dean Acheson called "the primitives," a phrase that in its aloof condescension predates Hillary Clinton's "basket of deplorables."

In the twenty-first century, Charlie Chaplin remains popular but is no longer fashionable. Most modern critics prefer the apolitical, slightly autistic comic character of Buster Keaton, an artist with whom Chaplin had little in common beyond their mutual profession.

Keaton is an abstract artist with a strong bent toward the surreal, not to mention the depressive. His character relates more to things than people—he's focused on getting his cow back, or his locomotive. People are an afterthought.

Chaplin is a figurative artist and a romantic, and his area of interest is always people and their place in the world—*Modern Times, The Great Dictator*, and *Monsieur Verdoux* all examine societies tightly organized against the powerless, while *Limelight* focuses on the ostracizing effects of age and failure.

In her "Notes on Camp," Susan Sontag posited that "the two pioneering forces of modern sensibility are Jewish moral seriousness and homosexual aestheticism and irony." Chaplin wasn't Jewish but he might as well have been, for he was morally serious long before the Holocaust, even as his cultural and political enemies insisted on defining morality as strictly relating to sex.

This book focuses on the planned ideological strikes that banished Chaplin from his adopted country while he was engaged in making the most controversial films of his life—a story that eerily foretells the homicidal cultural and political life of the twenty-first century.

It is also about an indomitable, compulsively creative man struggling to sustain his voice in an art form evolving in ways that didn't play to his strengths. Finally, it is about how Charlie Chaplin lost his audience, then gradually found it again.

It's time to see Charlie clear.

PART ONE

"Chaplin was Chaplin and would always be Chaplin."

—Michael Powell

CHAPTER 1

Before he was the most famous man in the world, Charlie Chaplin was just Sydney Chaplin's little brother. Technically, Charlie was Syd's half-brother, but Syd paid no attention to that fine distinction, or to the fact that Charlie had genius while Syd only had talent. Syd was never jealous. Charlie needed tending, so Syd became the unheralded hero of Charlie's life, always hovering protectively over his brother.

It was Sydney who providentially rescued Charlie from a period of sleeping rough that followed their mother's incarceration for insanity. It was Syd who took his brother to Fred Karno and talked Karno into hiring the unprepossessing young man as a stage comedian. It was Syd who ordered his brother to get out of the stock market three months before the 1929 crash.

"I just made $100,000 with a phone call," protested Charlie.

"Did you hear what I said?" replied Syd. "Get out now."

For all this and more, Chaplin named one of his sons after Sydney.

In May 1903, Syd was finishing a sailing stint when he wired his brother: "Will arrive ten o clock tomorrow morning at Waterloo Station. Love, Sydney."

When Sydney got off the train, he saw his fourteen-year-old brother unwashed, in filthy clothes, shoes coming apart.

"What's happened?" Sydney asked curtly.

"Mother went insane and we had to send her to the infirmary."

"Where are you living?"

"The same place, Pownall Terrace."

This was an evasion. Since his mother's institutionalization, Charlie was afraid of being sent to the workhouse and was avoiding the landlady by sleeping on the streets.

The porters began piling up Sydney's luggage. On the top was a bunch of green bananas.

"Is that ours?" asked Charlie.

Sydney nodded and said, "They're too green. We'll have to wait a day or so before we can eat them."

In the carriage, Sydney told his brother that he was going to give up the sea and become an actor. He had saved enough money for twenty weeks of expenses, which he idealistically thought would be enough to break through in his chosen profession. The first order of affairs for Sydney was to take his brother out and buy him new clothes. That night Charlie and Sydney got dressed up in their Sunday best and went to the South London Music Hall. "Just think what tonight would have meant to Mother," Sydney repeated over and over.

Later that week they went to visit their mother at the Cane Hill Asylum. She was vague, preoccupied. The playful spirit that had endeared her to her boys was gone. "Of course," she told Charlie, "if only you had given me a cup of tea that afternoon I would have been all right."

IN THE 1881 census, Charlie Chaplin's father is eighteen years old and working as a barman at the Northcote Hotel Battersea Rise, where his brother was the manager.

Charles Chaplin Sr. married Hannah Hill in June 1885, just fourteen weeks after she gave birth to her son Sydney, whose paternal parentage was something of a mystery. Hannah would claim that she had eloped with a man to South Africa where she lived on a plantation—a luxuriously ornate saga that became a family legend. Sydney's birth certificate tells a more prosaic tale—he was born Sidney John Hill on March 16, 1885, at 57 Brandon Street in Lambeth. It should also be noted that as an adult Sydney Chaplin bore a distinct familial resemblance to Charles Chaplin Sr. In fact, he looked like his brother—same size, same coloring, roughly equivalent handsome features.

Hannah Harriet Pedlingham Hill Chaplin was from Walworth, a bootmaker's daughter born in August 1865 close by Elephant and Castle. Under her stage name Lily Harley she was getting consistent music hall bookings as early as 1885 in such major cities as Bristol, Dublin, Glasgow, and Aberdeen. Similarly, by 1887 the senior Charles was a professional entertainer getting regular bookings at provincial music halls.

Hannah Chaplin was earning as much as £25 a week, and getting occasional London dates as well. By 1888, however, the noose had begun tightening. An ad in the theatrical paper *Entr'acte* in November 1888 reads: "The original and refined Lily Harley—terrific success nightly after her indisposition. Bedford, special concerts. Open for pantomime."

Her second son's birth in April 1889 was not formally recorded at Somerset House, but his parents made sure to include it in *The Magnet* and *The Era*—the theatrical trade papers: "Birth—April 15th, the wife of Mr. Charles Chaplin, nee Lily Harley, of a beautiful boy. Mother and son both doing well." Despite the birthdate being announced as April 15, all his life Chaplin celebrated his birthday on April 16.

Charlie Chaplin was often described as a Cockney, but a Cockney is born within the sound of Bow Bells. Lambeth, where he was born, is five miles away from Bow Bells, so Chaplin doesn't qualify. He was a boy from South London, not East London.

The birthplace was said to be East Street, but nobody was ever sure of the number. At various times, it was cited as 87, 91, 191, 256, 258, and 260. All of those houses were destroyed by Luftwaffe bombing in World War II.

In August 1889, a few months after Charlie was born, the elder Chaplin made his London debut. In short order, he was playing up to four different London music halls a night as well as headlining the bill in the provinces.

In the summer of 1890, the elder Chaplin made a successful tour of America, including an engagement at the Union Square Theatre in New York City. At the same time, his marriage began to break up, although whether that was because of his drinking, his wife's promiscuity, or some combination of both is impossible to ascertain.

What is certain is that while her husband was touring America, Hannah began an affair with the music hall star Leo Dryden. By April 1891, Hannah was separated from her husband. She and her boys were sharing a house with her mother in Walworth. (Hannah's mother was also separated from her husband at the time.)

The result of Hannah's affair was a child named George Dryden Wheeler, born on August 31, 1892. In early 1893, the baby was snatched by his father and never returned until he was reunited with his half-brothers in Hollywood, by which time he had taken the name Wheeler Dryden. In due time Wheeler became the father of Spencer Dryden, the drummer for Jefferson Airplane.

The upshot of all this is that when Chaplin Sr. returned to London, he discovered he had another mouth to feed for whom he was not technically responsible. Eighteen ninety-three also saw Mary Ann Hill, Hannah's mother, transition from alcoholism into vagrancy and mental illness when she was adjudged a "pauper lunatic" in February and committed.

And so Hannah and her children began their own descent into poverty. In 1895, when she was admitted to the Lambeth Infirmary for the first time, Charlie stayed with relatives, while Sydney was sent to the Norwood Schools. From 1895 to 1898, Chaplin Sr. refused to pay child support mandated by the court—15 shillings a week. In November 1897, he was £44 in arrears.

While all this was going on, Hannah's stays in mental hospitals went on for longer and longer periods, while her children were remanded to institutions. Syd was sent to the custody of the Lambeth Workhouse and the West Norwood Schools, while Charlie was taken in by Hannah's relatives. In May 1896, both boys were placed in the Newington Workhouse. By this time, Charles Sr. was living with another woman by whom he had a child. He was willing to take care of Charlie but not Syd.

In order to keep the boys together, in June 1896 they were both sent to the Hanwell Schools for Orphan and Destitute Children, but once they were there the boys were separated. On the upside, it was at Hanwell that Charlie received his formal education. On the downside, Hanwell placed an emphasis on physical discipline. Charlie was flogged for something he didn't do, and an infestation of ringworm caused his head to be shaved, after which he was placed in isolation.

"The treatment took weeks and seemed like an eternity," he remembered. "My head was shaved and iodined and I wore a handkerchief tied around it like a cotton picker. But one thing I would not do was to look out of the window [of the isolation ward] at the boys below, for I knew in what contempt they held us." That same year his father was arrested for failure to make support payments.

When Syd was eleven, he began an apprenticeship on board the *Exmouth*, as preparation for a career at sea. Charlie was now alone. In December 1897, Charlie was reunited with his mother, but money was now harder and harder to find, and there were frequent trips back to the Lambeth workhouse, or West Norwood. In September 1898, Hannah was adjudged insane, and both boys went to live with their father. Hannah was transferred to Cane Hill Asylum, twenty miles outside of London. The abbreviation "syph," i.e., syphilis, was entered on her medical records that same year. She was thirty-three years old. Her son Charlie was nine. At the end of 1898 young Charlie began his career in vaudeville when he joined "The Eight Lancashire Lads," a clog-dancing troupe, occasionally attending schools in the towns in which the troupe played.

Hannah's admission document for Cane Hill states, "Has been very strange in manner—at one time abusive and noisy, at another using endearing terms. Has been confined in padded room repeatedly on account of sudden violence—threw a mug at another patient. Shouting, singing, and talking incoherently. Complains of her head and depressed and crying this morning—dazed and unable to give any reliable information. Asks if she is dying. States she belongs to Christ Church (Congregation) which is Church of England. She was sent here on a mission by the Lord. Says she wants to get out of this world."

Hannah could have contracted syphilis from her husband or her lover, or she could have been working as a prostitute, although neither of her boys ever referred to a procession of strange men parading through their rooms. The doctors did not specify the stage of Hannah's disease, but the lurching gait that her son observed, the terrible headaches that she began experiencing in 1895, and her spasms of dementia are all classic symptoms of tabes dorsalis, a motor disturbance common to untreated syphilis.

"Hannah had tertiary neurosyphilis," says Dr. Tracey Goessel, a film historian and medical doctor. "She could also have had mental illness—crazy behavior comes later in the disease. Mental illness is hard to diagnose retrospectively, so it's certainly possible she had bipolar schizophrenia before the syphilis."

Charlie knew the reality of his mother's condition—more than half a century after his mother's diagnosis, he revealed it to Jerry Epstein, his assistant on *Limelight*. Prostitution was originally a plot point in *Limelight* via a flashback sequence that Chaplin shot but eventually cut. It's impossible to determine the source of Hannah's infection, but two things are clear: it was the most mortifying secret of Charlie Chaplin's life, and it left him terrified of sexual diseases. He would adopt extreme—and unscientific—measures to avoid it.

This horror show of disease, instability, and madness inflicted on a powerless young child shadowed Chaplin for the rest of his life. His lost paradise consisted of the times he was with his mother before her natural personality was obliterated. He remembered her as "a *mignonne* . . . with fair complexion, violet-blue eyes and long light-brown hair that she could sit upon. . . . Those who knew her told me in later years that she was dainty and attractive and had compelling charm."

Chaplin told of her attempts to maintain shards of respectability as she and her boys downshifted from one forlorn state to another. She accepted nothing from her children but proper standards of speech and behavior, and did her best to mend their ragged clothes. Chaplin would watch his mother observing people from their apartment windows, commenting on how they dressed and moved, then imitating them, causing her son to laugh at the accuracy of her impersonations.

Chaplin remembered his childhood as a haphazard stew of equal parts humiliation and delight. Of the latter, there was "riding with

Mother on top of a horse-bus trying to touch passing lilac trees—of the many colored bus tickets, orange blue, pink and green, that bestrewed the pavement where the trams and buses stopped—of rubicund flower girls at the corner of Westminster Bridge, making gay boutonnieres, their adroit fingers manipulating tinsel and quivering fern—of the humid odor of freshly watered roses that affected me with a vague sadness—of melancholy Sundays and pale parents and their children escorting toy windmills and colored balloons over Westminster Bridge; and the maternal penny streamers that softly lowered their funnels as they glided under it. From such trivia, I believe my soul was born."

But the poverty was scalding: "I didn't feel the hurt so much as the humiliation. [My mother would] stagger from one side to the other as though she was drunk, but she was just weak. . . . All that is very vivid to me . . . . I suppose within three months we must have lived in four, five or six places. Then suddenly the pity of it—this poor woman with two children—from one room to another. One room . . ."

But all that began to recede slightly when, probably by his father's arrangement, young Charlie became a show business professional with the Eight Lancashire Lads. He stayed with them until the end of 1900.

Within five years, Charlie Chaplin's days of want would basically be over. In a deeper sense, they never ended.

THROUGHOUT THIS PERIOD, Chaplin's father was in declining health due to alcoholism. He died in 1901 at St. Thomas Hospital at the age of thirty-seven. The funeral was fairly elaborate—a satin-lined oak casket, horse-drawn carriages, wreaths—with costs split between the Variety Artists' Benevolent Fund and the deceased's brother. Charles Chaplin was buried in an unmarked grave in the Tooting cemetery. Indifference breeds indifference—when Charlie and Syd Chaplin were both rich and famous, they never bothered to place a marker on the elder Chaplin's grave.

Before show business beckoned, young Charlie subsisted on odd—very odd—jobs: glassblowing, making toy boats. With his mother in the madhouse and his brother (literally) at sea, Charlie took to working with a group of woodcutters and sleeping on the streets, to avoid having his landlady turn him in as an orphaned indigent. Clearly, he was determined to stay out of the workhouses by any means.

After Sydney returned from the sea, taking care of Charlie became a preoccupation, but the fact remains that it was a definitively grim childhood. A mother in the grip of profound mental and physical illness; an alcoholic father who drank himself to death; a child cast onto the streets, workhouses, and orphanages. Chaplin's childhood defined "high-risk," an environment calculated to breed sociopaths. The psychiatrist Stephen Weissman estimates that roughly 10 percent of such children manage to transcend environmental and emotional catastrophe and become successful adults. These are what is known as "invulnerables."

Charlie Chaplin was an invulnerable all his long life. In youth and middle age, his memories of childhood poverty were predominantly of shame and grief, but in old age he permitted himself a touch of nostalgia's amber glow. Sometimes the past came to him "like a dream. Buying lamp oil from two old ladies in a shack because it was a farthing cheaper. Falling into the Thames and being rescued by a big black retriever. Going up to Piccadilly, where every doorway seemed to lead to something charming."

More typical was his memory of his mother's friend Eva Lester, who had once been a star of the music halls. Eva Lester had descended into poverty and was a vagrant being tormented by street urchins when Hannah recognized her. Hannah drove the boys away and told her to go to the public baths to clean off and come back to the rooms in Kennington where Hannah, Charlie, and Syd were eking out their existence. Lester stayed for three days, sleeping on Syd's fold-down bed. Hannah finally gave her two shillings and some old clothes. Chaplin was mortified by Lester's degradation, not to mention her desperation, and of what could happen to even successful practitioners of his parents' profession.

On May 9, 1903, Hannah was again adjudged insane and remanded back to Cane Hill. Her commitment papers contain testimony from her son Charlie: "Charles Chaplin, son . . . states she keeps on mentioning a lot of people who are dead and fancies she can see them looking out of the window."

It was the same day that Sydney arrived at Southampton to take charge of his brother's life. "If Sydney had not returned to London I might have become a thief in the London streets," Chaplin mused. "I might have been buried in a pauper's grave."

Hannah would be released, but on March 6, 1905, she relapsed yet again, this time permanently. She would spend the rest of her life cared for by either institutions or her sons. Dr. Marcus Quarry, an attending physician at the Lambeth Infirmary, examined her and reported that she was "a lunatic and a proper person to be taken charge of and detained under care and treatment. . . . She is very strange in manner and quite incoherent. She dances, sings and cries by turns. She is indecent in conduct & conversation at times and again at times praying and saying she has been born again."

The short version of all this is that until Charlie Chaplin became a star in the theater, his environment was definitively infirm, marked by alcoholism, mental illness, and sexually transmitted disease. Between heredity and the free and easy atmosphere of the music hall in which they grew up, it's easy to see why sexual conflagration was a frequent feature of Charlie's and Sydney's lives.

The travails that Syd and Charlie went through as children formed a bond that never was broken, although Sydney would frequently complain about Charlie's lack of response to his letters. "For one reason, I could not spell very well," Charlie explained. "[But] one letter touched me deeply and drew me very close to him; he reproached me for not answering his letters and recalled the misery we had endured together which should unite us. . . . 'Since Mother's illness,' wrote Sydney, 'all we have in the world is each other. So you must write regularly and let me know that I have a brother.' His letter was so moving that I replied immediately. . . . His letter cemented a brotherly love that has lasted throughout my life."

Charlie Chaplin only had the equivalent of a haphazardly acquired fourth grade education, but his imperiled life was redeemed by a precociously natural talent for performance. A quick rise through the music halls, where he played with some of the era's greatest stars—Dan Leno, Harry Lauder, Marie Lloyd—enabled him to learn the craft of show business while simultaneously getting a sense of its possibilities as an art.

Charlie eventually latched on to a job with William Gillette in his play *Sherlock Holmes*, which lasted for more than two years until 1906. That same year, Syd got a job with Fred Karno's legendary comedy troupe.

Fred Karno was the music hall equivalent of Mack Sennett, a tough entrepreneur who mastered the business of manufacturing comedy on an industrial basis. As one theater historian has noted, "Fred Karno mass-produced comedy and sold it by the lorry load." Karno and his staff designed programs of comic sketches that toured England and, eventually, America, with an interchangeable troupe of comics who were relentlessly drilled in the proper approach and timing.

Karno's headquarters on Vaughan Road in Camberwell was as organized as a film studio. It consisted of three adjacent houses and a rehearsal room with a ceiling so high it could accommodate trapeze artists. By the time of Chaplin's arrival, Karno was supervising eight to ten traveling troupes and making a great deal of money.

In January 1908, Sydney convinced Karno to give his little brother a tryout. Fred Karno remembered the day: "Syd arrived, accompanied by a young lad, very puny, pale and sad looking. He seemed undernourished and frightened, as though he expected me to raise my hand to hit him. Even his clothes were too small for him! I must say that at the first moment he seemed much too timid to do anything good on the stage, especially in the knockabout comedy shows that were my specialty. Still, I didn't want to disappoint Sydney, so I took him on."

Charlie signed his contract with Karno a month later. The contract specifies that he is a "Comedian Pantomimist" and paid him a weekly salary of £3, 10 shillings, with a second year payable at £4 a week.

From this point, the boys' professional and personal lives began a slow but steady ascent. Charlie Chaplin was about to turn nineteen years old, and his days of financial want were over.

* * *

STAN LAUREL WORKED for several years as Chaplin's understudy in the Karno troupe, and remembered that Charlie had a bad habit of drifting in a few minutes before a performance, thereby frustrating Laurel, who was just about to go on. "He always showed up just in the nick of time," said Laurel, "smiling and unperturbed. His mind was usually a thousand miles away, dwelling in some land where the rest of us poor troupers could not follow."

Laurel recalled, "Fred Karno didn't teach Charlie and me all we know about comedy. He just taught us most of it. If I had to pick an adjective to fit Karno, it would be supple. . . . He was flexible in just about everything, and above all he taught us to be supple. Just as importantly he taught us to be precise. Out of all that endless rehearsal and performance came Charlie, the most supple and precise comedian of our time."

Chaplin was extraordinarily shy and self-conscious throughout his life. He would remember, "I would go to the saloons where members of the company gathered, and watch them play billiards, but I always felt that my presence cramped their conversation, and they were quite obvious in making me feel so."

Fred Karno was not given to sentimentality and said that, "[Chaplin] wasn't very likeable. I've known him to go whole weeks without saying a word to anyone in the company. Occasionally he would be quite chatty, but on the whole he was dour and unsociable. He lived like a monk, had a horror of drink and put most of his salary in the bank as soon as he got it."

Stan Laurel added, "To some of the company I know he appeared stand-offish and superior. He wasn't, he wasn't at all. . . . He is a very, very shy man. You could even say he was a desperately shy man."

Warming to the subject, Laurel went on. "People through the years have talked about how eccentric he became. He was a very eccentric person *then*. He was very moody and often very shabby in appearance. Then suddenly he would astonish us all by getting dressed to kill. It seemed that every once in a while he would get an urge to look very smart. At these times he would wear a derby hat (an expensive one), gloves, smart suit, fancy vest, two-tone side button shoes, and carry a cane."

The cane would disappear except when he was working, but the button shoes would remain for decades, causing no end of odd looks in casual California.

Chaplin had no illusions about the quality of Karno's shows. "All of the pieces we did, as I remember them, were cruel and boisterous, filled with acrobatic humor and low, knockabout comedy. Each man working for Karno had to have perfect timing, and to know the peculiarities of everyone else in the cast so that we could collectively achieve a tempo. . . . It took about a year for an actor to get the repertoire of a dozen shows down pat. Karno required us to know a number of parts so that the players could be interchanged. When one left the company it was like taking a screw or a pin out of a very delicate piece of machinery."

Chaplin came to America for the first time in 1910 after re-upping with Karno for three years. By this time, he was a star in a successful touring show—in the third year of his contract, his salary would rise to £15 a week.

His initial reaction to New York City was loneliness, but that changed as he walked down Broadway for the first time. "As I walked along Broadway it began to light up with myriads of colored electric bulbs and sparkled like a brilliant jewel. And in the warm night my attitude changed and the meaning of America came to me: the tall skyscrapers, the brilliant, gay lights, the thrilling display of advertisements stirred me with hope and a sense of adventure. 'This is it,' I said to myself. 'This is where I belong.' "

Over the next few years he grew familiar with all the corners of what would become his adopted country. "Such cities as Cleveland, St. Louis, Minneapolis, St. Paul, Kansas City, Denver, Butte, Billings, throbbed with the dynamism of the future, and I was imbued with it."

Chaplin's shyness made making friends difficult. For female companionship, he and four or five others would go to the red-light districts. "Sometimes we won the affection of the madam of a [bordello] and she would close up the 'joint' for the night and we would take over. Occasionally some of the girls fell for the actors and would follow them to the next town."

That was Chaplin's story in 1964. Groucho Marx, who knew Chaplin more than fifty years before that, had an alternate view of a young man quite different from the one portrayed in his memoir. Marx saw Chaplin in vaudeville and told his brothers that he was "the greatest comedian I'd ever seen" and held to that opinion for the rest of his life.

"We were in Salt Lake City," remembered Groucho, "and we [all] went to a whorehouse. Chaplin was so shy. The Madame of the whorehouse had a dog. And [Chaplin] sat on the floor and played with the dog all evening. He was too shy to take a girl to bed. . . .

"Five years later I came out to see him and he was living in a home like Mary Pickford. . . . He invited the boys up to dinner with him. And he had a girl with him. And he was always fucking. Fucked every leading lady—like Chico. Edna Purviance was her name. I tried to fuck her too. But she was with Chaplin. . . . The world went crazy about this guy."

This sounds like an old vaudevillian spinning fanciful anecdotes, but the author and documentarian Robert Bader did his due diligence. The Marx Brothers were playing in Salt Lake City from November 12 to November 18, 1913. Chaplin, along with the Karno troupe, was there the week ending November 8. Sunday was the 9th, and because of Blue Laws vaudeville theaters were dark on Sunday. Performers traditionally used Sundays to do laundry, relax for a few hours, then catch a train for their next booking.

The Marx Brothers rolled into Salt Lake City on November 9, even though they wouldn't start performing for a few days. Chaplin and Karno's "Night in a London Club" troupe didn't open their next engagement in Colorado Springs till Monday, November 10. Since everybody had some time on their hands on a slow Sunday, Chaplin went to the whorehouse with the Marxes on Sunday the 9th, then caught a train to Colorado Springs.

His lack of interest in the girls might have been due to preoccupation, not shyness. On September 25, Chaplin had signed a contract with Mack Sennett's Keystone company in Edendale, California. His last engagement with the Karno company was on November 29, 1913, in Kansas City.

After he signed the Sennett contract, Chaplin wrote his brother in an exultant mood:

"Oh." Sid I can see you!! Beaming now as you read this, those sparkling eyes of yours scanning this scribble and wondering what [is] coming next. I'll tell you how the land lies. I have had an offer from a moving picture company for quite a long time, but I did not want to tell you until the whole thing was confirmed and it practically is settled now. . . . I don't know whether you have seen any Keystone pictures but they are very funny. They also have some nice girls etc. . . . . Just think Sid, 35 pounds per week is not [to] be laugh[ed] at and I only want to work about five years at that and then we are independent for life. I shall save like a son of a gun. . . . Hoping you are in good health and Mother improving also I would love her and you to be over hear. [*sic*] Well we may someday when I get in right.

Love to Minnie
And yourself
Your loving Brother,
Charlie

The contract with Keystone ran for one calendar year, and mandated a weekly salary of $150, about twice what he was making from Karno. Interestingly, there is another surviving draft of the contract containing a provision stating that he could be released from his contract with one week's notice, but it was unsigned. Chaplin held out for the security of a full year no-cut contract and got it.

Charlie Chaplin was going into the movies.

CHAPTER 2

On December 16, 1913, Charlie Chaplin went to work at the Keystone studio. He was twenty-four years old.

As shy as he was with women, Chaplin was the antithesis when it came to his work. Almost immediately he began arguing with directors and pressed Sennett to let him direct his own pictures. "The average actor . . . is just an actor," Sennett would remember. "When it's quitting time, he's through. . . . [But] Chaplin used to fairly sweat if he thought he hadn't done a thing as well as he should have . . . and when the time came that he could see the film of the day's work, he was always there, whereas most of the others in the picture would never come around. And if anything in the run didn't please him, he'd click his tongue or snap his fingers and twist and squirm. 'Now, why did I do that, that way?' he'd say."

Within three years, Charlie Chaplin would be besieged by twin cascades of fame and money, a response motivated by his creation of the Tramp in the first month of his Keystone contract. It remains the most stunning rise of any twentieth-century performer. As Charlie's friend Max Eastman wrote, "this little modest actor of one role, his birth timed and his genius cut and trimmed to fit a new kind of entertainment, became in three short years known and loved by more men, and more races and classes of men, than anyone, even the great religious leaders, ever had been before."

Chaplin's life informed his work to a startling degree. "I didn't have to read books to know that the theme of life is conflict and pain," he wrote. "Instinctively, all my clowning was based on this." In the beginning, the Tramp, a makeup he created on the spur of the moment after Sennett told him to put on a funny costume, was a creature from the id—anarchy set loose amidst social regimentation. As the critic Dave Kehr noted, the early Chaplin films are allegorical—and probably unintentional—versions of the Progressive movement that was happening all around the young comedian. He was the little guy, living in the slums and fighting for survival against the system represented by cops and other authority figures. But Chaplin gradually added colors to the character—the Tramp's aggression was gradually muted. Violence would be replaced by indignation, lechery with courtliness.

From comedies about pursuit—women, money, work, status— Chaplin's work soon settled into a narrative groove in which his character rescues women—often deeply damaged, sometimes just desperate. This describes every Chaplin feature from *The Kid* in 1921 to *Limelight* in 1952. Chaplin coped with his inability to help a mother who was beyond help by perpetually imagining himself as a chivalrous adult saving a woman in perilous circumstances.

The central pressure point of Chaplin's life was the fact that he became rich and famous by continually reimmersing himself in his memories of poverty and deprivation. For Charlie Chaplin, there was no escape.

One day in the late 1920s Chaplin was having lunch in Venice, California, with a coworker. "You've always had all you wanted to eat, I suppose, haven't you?" Chaplin inquired.

"Yes, thank goodness. I've never gone hungry."

"It's funny, but every once in a while when I sit down for a meal I think how marvelous it is not to have to consider price. An ordinary middleclass family, I suppose, must look at the price list, don't you think?"

This set Chaplin off on a soliloquy about his diet as a child. "My memory is so clear of the days when meat once a week was a luxury.

On Sundays we had meat. And what meat! If we were lucky, it was four-penny ends, which were the odds and ends of all first-class cuts, made into stew for the family. And if we were not so lucky, it was thrup-penny ends, which were ends of the meat which were a little rancid.

"On other days we had potatoes and greens, or bread and drippings—do you know what drippings are? They're the odds and ends of fat off meat which have solidified. They're used like butter. Very good, too, with salt!"

Over time, Chaplin thought long and hard about his creation. He would muse that "[The Tramp isn't] a character. He seems to be more of a symbol . . . more Shakespearian than Dickensian. Dickens has characters, Shakespeare symbols. I sometimes bridge the two."

As the character broadened, so did the ancillary benefits. There were Chaplin dolls, books, toys, comic strips, jewelry. There were even Chaplin imitators. Above all, there were Chaplin films, turned out and greedily consumed in mutually shared bursts of enthusiasm between artist and audience.

Foremost among benefits were the financials. At the end of 1914, he signed a contract with the Essanay company for $1,250 a week. A year after that, he signed a deal with the Mutual Film Corporation for $10,000 a week, accompanied by a $150,000 signing bonus that he split with Syd, who had acted as his agent. John Freuler, the head of the Mutual Film Corporation, reported that Charlie took a look at the bonus check, undoubtedly more money than the young man had imagined existed in the entire world, and handed it to Sydney. "Take it, Sydney," he said. "Take it away from me, please. It hurts my eyes."

Less than a year and a half later, he signed a million-dollar contract with First National that also paid him 50 percent of the profits. The deal sounded rich, but Chaplin had to pay his own production costs, which meant that the deal was actually inferior to his contract with Mutual. What made the difference to Chaplin was that the deal gave him ownership of his films seven years after release. From 1918 to 1957, Chaplin would own all of his films—a patrimony he never gave up. Today, the Chaplin estate still owns those films.

Part of the First National money went into building his own studio on La Brea Avenue, just south of Sunset. It was designed to resemble a row of English cottages surrounding a large open-air stage. The studio would be his professional home until 1952.

In January 1919, Chaplin and his best friend Douglas Fairbanks combined with Mary Pickford and D. W. Griffith to form United Artists, a company designed to insure that they would never become employees of the increasingly grasping corporations typified by the perennially expanding Famous Players-Lasky, which would change its name to Paramount Pictures. As equal partners, Chaplin and the others each had autonomy with their own production units. They had to provide their own financing, but they would also receive all the profits after UA deducted 20 percent of the gross for domestic distribution and 30 percent for foreign—well below what Famous Players and the other studios were charging.

Now the unchallenged master of his domain, Chaplin's personality had expanded to include utter obstinance coexisting with his shyness. He was recessive yet curious, radiant when performing but inclined to isolation otherwise, often hiding from the public and friends alike. He was an Aries—enthusiastic, full of pride and drive, with a touch—well, more than a touch—of impetuousness. And he was uninterested in what other people thought—a trait which would cause him a great deal of trouble.

Chaplin the man was profoundly individualistic, but Chaplin's character of the Tramp swept the world as a universal figure incarnating beleaguered humanity. He was welcome everywhere—the French saw him as French, the Japanese saw him as Japanese.

Success on such a scale involves more than talent; it's a specific personality meshing with a historical moment. A case can be made for Chaplin as the single most important figure in motion picture history. For one thing he united all components of the international audience in a way nobody else had—or could have. The working class came for the slapstick, while the swells stayed for the elegance and stabs of elevated emotion.

And for ambitious filmmakers in Hollywood and elsewhere, he created the identity of a remote, autocratic law unto himself that has served as the role model for every other independent auteur right up to the time of Stanley Kubrick and Christopher Nolan.

Throughout this period, Charlie depended on Sydney for support, for his facility with gags and stories. When he was making *The Count* for Mutual, Chaplin wired his brother in New York, "Have you any suggestions for scenes? Have dining room and ballroom. I am playing a count but an imposter to win heiress but cannot get story straight. Wire me some gags if possible. Playing in Chaplin makeup in fancy dress ball."

Chaplin was still wrestling with the picture when his assistant Tom Harrington wired Sydney again. "He wishes nearly every other day you were here. Unless he pulls up within next couple of days am afraid he will miss release [date] on this picture. Think it very important for his future success for you to drop everything in New York and come here immediately spending at least three or four weeks. . . . He always wishes Syd were here. Don't let Charlie know I wired this as it might make him feel badly, but it is my honest opinion he needs you and that you should take the next train for coast."

Five days later, Charlie chimed in once again: "I need you here to help me. Drop everything and arrange to be in Los Angeles by Saturday August 12 to help me in directing next picture. Wire answer immediately."

Sydney didn't act in any of the Mutual films, but outtakes show him demonstrating everything from juggling tricks to pratfalls. For Charlie's next contract with First National, Charlie made sure that Sydney was part of the acting company, playing some delightful comedy scenes with his brother in *The Pilgrim* and *A Dog's Life*, among others.

While all this was going on, Sydney was trying to get their mother into America, which was difficult as she had been adjudged insane and American immigration laws were stacked against the indigent and the insane. Initially, Charlie was gung ho on bringing her over, but in April 1918, he sent his brother a telegram: "Second thoughts. Consider will be best mother remain in England. Some good seaside resort. Afraid presence here might depress and affect my work."

Hannah Chaplin would finally come to America in March 1921, with the Immigration Service being told she was a victim of shell shock from the war. Charlie bought a house for her and hired a married couple to care for her. He rarely visited because observing her mental condition juxtaposed with his memories of the lively, lovely young woman he had adored invariably plunged him into depression. When he did visit, she would stuff his pockets with pieces of bread or fruit. "Here," she would say, "take this; you never can tell when you may need it."

Chaplin let his friend Max Eastman meet her, and Eastman categorized her as "a little crazy, but [she] was aware of it and able to manage it some of the time. . . . She was rosy-faced, red-haired . . . a music hall singer and dancer by profession. She put on the phonograph and did us a merry little song and dance. There was a canary on the piano. He chirped in the midst of her dance and she stopped— her gay expression turned to utter pathos. 'Poor thing, he's lonely here!' she said, or sang—for it was all in time to the music—and then she was dancing merrily again, and she twirled at the end, and with the last note sat down accurately and lightly in the chair she had risen from."

On Christmas night 1927, Hannah dined at Charlie's house. After dinner, he ran *The Kid* for her. When the lights went up, she turned and looked at him. "My, you must be terribly fatigued after all those adventures!" she said. Then she studied him for a moment, as if seeing him for the first time. "Did you really write and direct the entire picture?"

Chaplin nodded.

"You have great talent. If you persevere, you are certain to make a great success of yourself and your work."

Hannah remained a live wire that compelled all around her to be on the alert. When her caretakers took her shopping at a Los Angeles department store, she asked the clerk for "shit-brown gloves." The clerk brought out several pairs for her approval, but she protested, "No, no! That's not shit-brown!" On occasions when she would do an encore of an old music hall number, she would raise her skirt high enough to leave no doubt that she was not wearing undergarments.

Chaplin would talk about Hannah, her beauty and her gifts, as well as her eccentricities. She was concerned about open manhole covers, fearing that the men working under the street would be too hot. If possible, she would get an ice cream cone and dump it on any head that emerged and say, "Cool down, cool down."

In the summer of 1928, Hannah was hospitalized. Chaplin visited her every day. Her last words as she lay dying were to ask the nurses to remove the glass of water beside her bed. "Those poor little fish," she said. "Take them out. They're going to drown." She died on August 28, with the cause of death listed as "cholecystitis." She was buried at what is now Hollywood Forever Cemetery, in a grave adjacent to the family tomb of Marion Davies. Chaplin made sure that, unlike his father, his mother's grave was marked for posterity.

THE LIFE OF Charlie Chaplin has much to do with courage, or, if you prefer, perseverance taken to the edge of obsession. All of his life he demonstrated traits closely allied to parental disruption—basically isolated while simultaneously pursuing love and affection, a need that went unfulfilled until his final marriage, when he received the acceptance he had always craved. His work was the only means by which he could control, not just others, but himself. Acting emotions meant that he could control them instead of letting them control him. Therefore the work always came first.

Because of his early experiences with his father and other alcoholic victims of the music hall lifestyle, Chaplin always drank sparingly and had little interest in artificial stimulants. "I have taken cocaine and smoked opium," he told Harry Crocker, "but I must confess I got no effect whatever from cocaine. . . . Opium, on the other hand, had terrific effect. [I was] violently ill for three days, [and that] cured me of any further desire to try narcotics."

On the other hand, the erotic and romantic stimulus represented by women would play a vital part in Chaplin's creative as well as emotional life. As a young man, Chaplin's interest in women had been hamstrung by his shyness and poverty. As Chaplin told the story, the first woman he loved was named Hetty Kelly. They met in the fall of 1908, when Chaplin was nineteen and Hetty was fifteen. Actually, there had been an earlier infatuation, when he was eighteen. The girl's name was Phoebe Field, the daughter of a woman who kept a lodging house where Chaplin lived for a time. Phoebe was twelve years old, although Chaplin increased her age to fifteen when he wrote about her in his memoirs. It was the beginning of a continued interest in young girls.

Hetty Kelly was a dancer at the Streatham Empire Theatre, where Chaplin was working with the Karno troupe. Chaplin fell completely in love, but Hetty's mother had higher ambitions for her daughter than a music hall comedian. Chaplin believed they met only five times, for perhaps twenty minutes apiece. Chaplin asked her to marry him, but she turned him down. "The episode was but a childish infatuation to her, but to me it was the beginning of a spiritual development, a reaching out for beauty."

Years went by, and Hetty married an army officer. In 1921, Chaplin and Hetty's brother Arthur were on a boat train when, as Chaplin remembered, "The question of 'How is Hetty?' burned in the back of my brain. Would nothing suggest it? I must create an opportunity.

"'How are the folks?' was a starter.

"'Fine, fine!'

"I strove to be calm, but my head swam. I found myself saying the words, 'And how is Hetty? She told me to look her up if ever—'"

Kelly looked at him strangely. "Hetty died, you know," he said. Kelly explained that the Spanish Flu had killed her in November 1918. Chaplin was devastated. "There was nothing left of my castle in the air."

In retrospect, he was abashed as he showed her picture to a friend. "It was nothing," he said. "She was a fetish. I knew nothing about girls then." If Hetty was a fetish, she was a fetish he clung to. At the end of his life, he still thought of her and spoke of her, and he employed Arthur Kelly as his representative at United Artists for decades.

As Chaplin's circumstances improved, so did his success with women. Sexually, Chaplin was a libertarian—people should be free to do as they pleased. He was handsome—five foot six, trim, with deep blue eyes and a sensual mouth. He was still shy, but renown has a way of rendering reserve irrelevant.

For some time, Chaplin kept company with Edna Purviance, the leading lady he hired to work with him at the Essanay company in 1915. Purviance was born in Nevada in 1895, had graduated from high school in June 1913, and was in San Francisco when she was hired by Chaplin. She was lovely, with a radiant smile, an eager but untrained actress with a charming sense of mischief. She adored

Chaplin. They began working together in late January 1915, and within a month they were in a relationship:

Well Honey Boy,

I really don't know why you don't send me some word. Just one little telegram so unsatisfactory. Even a night letter would be better than nothing. You know "Boodie" you promised faithfully to write. Is your time so taken up that you can't even think of me.

Every night before I go to bed I send out little love thots [sic], wishing you all the success in the world and counting the minutes until you return. How much longer do you plan to stay. Please, Hon, don't forget your "Modie" and hurry back. Have been home for over a week and believe me my feet are itching to get back.

Have you seen Mable [Mabel Normand] and the Bunch? I suppose so. Am so sorry that you couldn't have taken me. Have you been true to me. I'm afraid not. Oh, well, do whatever you think is right. I really do trust you to that extent.

Did you receive the letter that I sent to the Astor.

Lots of love and kisses.
Yours faithfully,
Edna

Lovelock, Nev.

For a time, Chaplin returned her ardor:

March 1st 1915

My Own Darling Edna,

My heart throbbed this morning when I received your sweet letter. It could be nobody else in the world that could have given me such joy. Your language, your sweet thoughts . . . of your love note only tends to make me crazed over you. I can picture your darling self setting down and looking up wondering what to say, that little

pout mouth and those bewitching eyes so thoughtful. If I only had
the power to express my sentiments I would be afraid you'd get
vain.

Well, little girl I hate to stop this outburst of divine emotion but
you are the cause of my being the happiest person in the world.

Charlie.

The way to get to Chaplin was to go through Edna, as was proved
by a letter that arrived in the fall of 1917, postmarked Bombay:

Dear Miss Purviance,

Kindly excuse the liberty I take in writing you, but I am sending
you this letter in the hope that you will assist me in my hitherto
futile attempts to obtain recognition and acknowledgement from
my half-brother Charles Chaplin, for whose Company I believe
you are Leading Lady. . . .

In September, 1915, I heard from my father, and in his letter he
mentioned that my half-brother, Charlie Chaplin, had been making
a great name for himself in Cinema work in America. Well, when
I read this you can imagine my surprise, for my father had always
kept the secret of my birth unknown to me, and had always
evaded any questions on the subject.

Wheeler Dryden, Hannah's child by Leo Dryden, explained that
he didn't want anything from Charlie and Sydney except a meeting with the brothers he had never known. Unfortunately, they had
ignored his letters. "And so, Miss Purviance, I am asking you to in-
tercede with Charlie on my behalf, and let me know what he says."
Dryden eventually made his way to Hollywood where he became a
general assistant around the Chaplin studio lot.

Edna Purviance clearly got under Chaplin's skin; in his memoir,
he writes of his dismay at what he presumed to be her affair with
the actor Thomas Meighan, which might have been her revenge for
an affair of his own.

Chaplin married his first wife, Mildred Harris, in September 1918.

She was a seventeen-year-old actress he had been seeing and who told him she was pregnant. Since the age of consent in California was eighteen, he was playing with fire . . . or imprisonment. The pregnancy mysteriously vanished as soon as they were married, but Harris became pregnant for real soon thereafter. Norman Spencer Chaplin was born on July 7, 1919, and lived for only three days. Within a few weeks of the child's burial in Inglewood Cemetery, Chaplin began work on a movie about the Tramp adopting an abandoned child and caring for him with utter devotion—*The Kid*. The marriage broke up because of a combination of what Chaplin regarded as Mildred's insipid intellect—a fairly common feature of seventeen-year-olds—and the fact that, according to Douglas Fairbanks, she was having an affair.

By the time of the marriage to Mildred Harris, the relationship with Edna had downshifted from that of ardent lovers to trusted friends, as is clear from a letter Purviance wrote after seeing *Shoulder Arms* in 1918.

Dear Charlie,

Saw this picture this afternoon at the Iris Theater in Hollywood—I cannot tell you how good it was—Everybody was thrilled, although there were not many people there.

I know you were just a wee bit discouraged, but please forget that, as it is wonderful and very pathetic when you did not receive a package—A lump came in my throat as it did with everyone else around me.

Just one thing I did not like especially—When the German shook your hand in the trenches and you accepted it—such might not be liked in foreign countries. Of course, no one else noticed it, but I being one of your most true and sincere critics tell you this.

The time spent on the picture was well worthwhile, so have a good time and catch lots of fishes.

Always, Edna.

Lita Grey, Chaplin's second wife, was hired in March 1924 as the leading lady in *The Gold Rush* shortly before she turned sixteen

years old (she was born in April 1908). In late September, she told
Chaplin she was pregnant. Chaplin was once gain flirting with disaster, so he had little choice but to marry her in November. He paid a
doctor $25,000 to falsify the birth certificate of Charles Chaplin Jr.,
who was actually born May 5, 1925, although his birth certificate
reads June 28.

The marriage ended a few years later in a legendarily rancorous
divorce. Grey's complaint accused Chaplin of things both factual
and fantastic: seduction of a minor, statutory rape, perversion, adultery, soliciting abortions, and murderous threats. It mentioned that
Chaplin had relationships with other unnamed but well-known actresses during the marriage (the women were Marion Davies, Edna
Purviance, Pola Negri, Claire Windsor, Peggy Hopkins Joyce, and
Merna Kennedy) and also specified that he had "solicited, urged and
demanded that plaintiff submit to, perform and commit such acts
and things for the gratification of defendant's said abnormal, unnatural, perverted and degenerate sexual desires, as to be too revolting,
indecent and immoral to set forth in detail in this complaint." The
complaint proceeded to specify Statute 288a of the California criminal code, i.e., fellatio.

The complaint was hawked on street corners as erotic lagniappe
for the masses or, alternately, kindling for prudes. It led Chaplin to
stop production of *The Circus* for eight months while he went to
New York and had a nervous breakdown. The divorce cost Chaplin
$950,000—$650,000 for Grey, $100,000 in trust for each of the two
sons they had together, plus court costs.

It was the largest divorce settlement in California history up to
that time, and it left Chaplin with an unyielding dislike for Grey. In
later years, if Grey came up in conversation, Chaplin would say, "I
loved all the women in my life except her." Chaplin's son Sydney, the
second child from the marriage, would remember with some amaze-
ment that his father never, under any circumstances, mentioned the
marriage, and never once inquired after his mother. "Nothing. Not
a single word."

Occasionally Chaplin would become involved with age-appro-
priate women—such as Negri, Hopkins Joyce, and Davies—but they
coexisted with his attraction to teenagers.

Amidst this revolving door of women, Chaplin remained loyal to Edna Purviance professionally if not personally. In 1923, he made *A Woman of Paris*, a beautifully directed melodrama about an innocent country girl who goes to Paris and becomes the mistress of a sophisticated boulevardier played by Adolphe Menjou. The story had obvious resonance with Purviance's own life, but despite rave reviews it failed to make her a star.

Chaplin made Purviance a partner in Regent Films, a company he formed to make the film, probably as a means of providing her with extra income. After that, he financed *The Sea Gull*, a story he had written for her that was directed by Josef von Sternberg, but he never released the film and burned the negative for a tax loss in 1933.

Purviance made one film in France, *The Education of a Prince*, which is now lost. She never appeared before a movie camera again, but the emotional bond still existed in spite of the fact that Edna gradually became, in the words of actress Virginia Cherrill, "a terrible alcoholic."

On April 1, 1932, Edna wrote Chaplin a letter asking for help. The tone is hesitant but desperate:

> Fearing I might bother and trouble you, I have hesitated writing, but finding it absolutely necessary I am doing so, hoping you will not be angry and misconstrue my real thoughts toward you, as they are constantly for you and with you on your so long and interesting travels. . . . You said many years ago (perhaps you have forgotten) what you were going to do, have been doing and are doing, and though you may not know I have been very silently and keenly watching, with great pride, your most every achievement.

She went on to tell Chaplin she had been ill with a perforated ulcer which caused a stomach hemorrhage. On top of that she had developed pneumonia and had been in the hospital for a month. Her father had died on the same night she collapsed with the ulcer. Her mother had gone to Alf Reeves, the general manager of the Chaplin studio, who had advanced her $750 for her medical bills, but she was still in desperate shape.

So all and all I am in a most difficult and needy situation.

Charlie I know it is bothersome and a damn nuisance to have to read of or listen to anyone's troubles, and I feel that you know well enough that I would not take up your time, not even for a second, unless I simply had to—please forgive me . . .

All my love
Edna

Chaplin put Edna on the studio payroll for $100 a week, and carried her there for more than twenty years. In 1938, she married John Squire, a pilot. They were happy until his death in 1945. Home movies of the couple show Edna had added pounds but retained her delightful smile.

Chaplin was similarly gracious with Georgia Hale, who replaced Lita Grey as his leading lady in *The Gold Rush*. Hale became his on-and-off companion during the late 1920s and early 1930s. She went back on the studio payroll in October 1941 for $25 a week. Her contract was for one year, but she kept drawing her salary through March 1953—six months after he had left America.

Ultimately, Edna Purviance may have been too uncomplicated for Chaplin. It would take him more than twenty-five years to find her equivalent—an intelligent, selfless woman who lived to tend his needs.

CHAPLIN HAD BECOME as rich as he was famous. In 1932, the year generally regarded as the pit of the Depression, the Los Angeles County tax assessor announced that Chaplin had "taxable stocks and bonds" worth $7.6 million. Appalled, Chaplin quickly filed an appeal asserting that his securities were worth only $1.6 million.

Alienated from England because of his childhood, politically indifferent to his newly adopted country, the outbreak of World War I caused Chaplin to flirt with antiwar sentiments. Nevertheless, in April 1918, Chaplin, Mary Pickford, and Douglas Fairbanks embarked on a tour of America to raise money for the Third Liberty Loan campaign. The first stop was the White House, where they met

President Woodrow Wilson. Chaplin remembered getting so excited at meeting political celebrities that he "slipped off the platform and landed on top of the Assistant Secretary for the Navy"—a young man named Franklin Roosevelt.

They traveled to New York City, where Fairbanks and Chaplin spoke at the intersection of Broad and Wall Streets to a crowd of more than twenty thousand people and sold $2 million worth of bonds. After that, they split up; Fairbanks and Pickford sold bonds in the Northern states, while Chaplin worked the South, starting in Petersburg, Virginia, and making his way through North Carolina, Kentucky, Tennessee, Mississippi, and Louisiana. The tour raised several million dollars, including $350,000 from Chaplin himself, but left him exhausted. He returned to Los Angeles and in six days shot a delightful propaganda short entitled *The Bond* to promote the sale of war bonds throughout the country.

Privately, Chaplin continued to regard all wars as intrinsic absurdities that had little to do with the soldiers who died in them. He told the cartoonist Milt Gross that, "I'd have gone to jail rather than have gone into" World War I. "I'd have gnawed off my fist rather than get into that sort of thing!"

CHAPTER 3

Chaplin probably met Rob Wagner in 1914, when both men were working at Keystone. Wagner was a Socialist, an entertaining character who would dabble in writing and directing silent films for Will Rogers while gearing up to start *Script*, a sort of Hollywood version of *The New Yorker* that began publishing in 1928.

Script was a good magazine, but unlike *The New Yorker* it operated on a shoestring—Wagner didn't pay his contributors and didn't accept national advertising, but his open-door policy attracted writers from all over the political spectrum: Left-wing writers (Dalton Trumbo, William Saroyan), middle-of-the-roaders (Edgar Rice Burroughs), and right-wingers (Rupert Hughes).

Wagner served as Chaplin's part-time secretary and ghostwriter as well as guide to the political avant-garde. Wagner's politics interested Chaplin, who occasionally accompanied Wagner to meetings of the Severance Club, where the conversation often centered on the morality of World War I. Eventually the pages of *Script* would contain contributions from Chaplin, as well as editorials advocating for such radical proposals as collective bargaining.

In February 1919, Wagner introduced Chaplin to Max Eastman, a handsome writer and lecturer, a Socialist who opposed World War I, supported the Russian Revolution, and narrowly managed to avoid jail. Wagner always remembered Chaplin's first words to Eastman: "You have what I consider the essence of all art—even of mine, if I may call myself an artist—restraint." The three men went out to dinner and Chaplin invited Eastman to visit his studio.

Eastman was tall, blond, and was called by one biographer "the Byron of the Left." His first magazine, *The Masses*, had been shut down by the postmaster general in 1917 and Eastman had stood trial for sedition. The result had been a hung jury, which was repeated in a retrial, after which the government dropped the charges.

Eastman was charismatic, attractive to women and knew it. When he met Chaplin he was separated from his wife because of an affair he was having with a lushly beautiful young actress named Florence Deshon. She had been born Florence Danks in 1893, but dreamed up her new last name because it sounded French, especially when the accent was put on the last syllable.

Aside from being a good writer, Eastman was also something of a salesman. He put the arm on Chaplin for a contribution for a new magazine he was planning called *The Liberator*. Chaplin seemed interested, but Rob Wagner took Eastman aside and told him that Chaplin was tight with money, and tended toward short-lived enthusiasms about everything except his movies. It would be wise, Wagner said, for Eastman to take Chaplin's commitment lightly. "Charlie liked radical ideas," wrote Eastman, "he liked to talk about transforming the world; but he didn't like to pay for the talk, much less the transformation."

Wagner was proven right when Chaplin gave Eastman a contribution of $25. On the other hand, when Eastman's bookkeeper absconded with $3,000, Chaplin covered $1,000 of the loss.

Eastman would come to believe that Chaplin's attitude toward money was not particularly complex. Chaplin "isn't stingy. . . . It is more subtle than that. He is *anxious* about money. He might just as well [have given] me the whole three thousand or a million. But he couldn't, because he lives in dread of poverty."

Eastman knew Chaplin for more than forty years and his opinion of his friend never changed: "He impressed me . . . as having no unity of character, no principles or conviction, nothing in his head that, when he laid it on the pillow, you could sensibly expect would be there in the morning.

"He was an actor so deep down and completely that, if you let his charm bewitch you into resting any hope on what he said, you would certainly sooner or later find that hope floating in the air." Eastman said that the day after Chaplin praised Eastman's speech, he heard him endorse slavery as an "immortal institution." Around the same time, Chaplin stated that, "Any perfectly free and profound intelligence would be Bolshevik today. H. L. Mencken, for instance, if he should really get down and study the problem of life. But I hope he won't, for he's more entertaining as an acrobat."

In Eastman's telling, Florence Deshon had rich chestnut hair, some acting talent, a lot of ambition, and a natural intelligence to go along with her beauty. But Deshon also had wild mood swings—depression salted with rage. When Chaplin and Eastman met, Deshon had been modeling for Arnold Genthe and Baron de Meyer, but in August 1919 she was hired by Sam Goldwyn and reported to his studio in Hollywood.

A month after that, Max Eastman moved into her apartment on De Longpre Avenue. Rapture ensued, interspersed with loud arguments. Their social circle soon included Chaplin. "We . . . were as intimate as one can be with Charlie, who carries a remoteness with him however close he comes," wrote Eastman. "We formed almost a nightly habit of coming together, Charlie and . . . some friends from the movie colony, to play charades and other dramatic games. I remember these nights' entertainments as the gayest and most enjoyable social experiences of my life."

The inevitable took place on Christmas Eve 1919, when Chaplin and Deshon had dinner together *sans* Eastman. The affair was not a secret. Deshon's letters to Eastman are full of sentiments about her emotional intimacy with her new lover despite—or because of—his deteriorating marriage to Mildred Harris: "Charlie speaks of going away, but it all depends on this picture [*The Kid*] and at the rate he is working, he will never finish it. I know I am naughty, but I become tired of Charlie's matrimonial troubles. He stays in that frightful situation at his home, and his powerlessness to move wears me out."

Through the early months of 1920, Deshon was seeing Chaplin regularly and spending time at his studio where he was beginning to edit *The Kid*, which Deshon told Eastman was "the most exciting thing" she had ever seen. Despite all of Eastman's speeches about free love and the imprisonment of monogamy, he became jealous. After another letter from Deshon full of praise for all of Charlie's enchanting qualities, Eastman responded with sarcastic reminders of Chaplin's short attention span.

For a time, it was a grudging version of *Design for Living*, except for an ending harsher than anything Noel Coward could write. "Our friendship," wrote Eastman of the ménage à trois, "became a three-cornered one in which a lot of unusual emotions were given a place in the sun."

Eastman went back to New York and started seeing someone else, while Deshon's affair with Chaplin deepened. At the same time, Chaplin began negotiating his divorce from Mildred Harris. In September 1920, Deshon accompanied Chaplin to Salt Lake City, where he continued editing *The Kid* away from Harris's lawyers, who were trying to attach the negative of the film.

Deshon fell ill, but Chaplin was focused on the film, not his mistress. Deshon contacted Eastman, who sent her a telegram telling her he would meet her at the railroad station. When she got to New York, Eastman rushed her to a Greenwich Village doctor who diagnosed blood poisoning from a botched abortion. The baby wasn't Eastman's—he had been in the East for more than four months.

Deshon recuperated in New York, attended by Eastman. Chaplin arrived with the final print of *The Kid* in hand and attempted to make amends. Deshon again volleyed back and forth between the two men—Eastman in Croton-on-Hudson, Chaplin at the Carlton Hotel in Manhattan. "We both admired her extravagantly," remembered Eastman. "There was something royal in her nature that gave her the right to have things as she pleased."

Eventually, Deshon began moving away from both of them. She returned to Hollywood in October, after telling Eastman that she would not commit to either of them. With no acting jobs on offer, she began writing stories for fan magazines.

In March 1921, Eastman was back in Los Angeles and he and Deshon once again fell into bed. Not only that, they renewed their friendship with Chaplin. "The fact that we had both loved her made us better friends, but not more confidential," wrote Eastman. In June,

Eastman headed back east, and he and Deshon had one last blowout. They couldn't live with each other, they couldn't live without each other.

As summer turned to fall, Deshon was having a bad time. Chaplin had paid off the balance on her Buick and fronted the insurance for the car. He also probably paid for her apartment at 1743 Cherokee Avenue, just off Hollywood Boulevard. In August he went to Europe—his first visit since he came to America in 1910.

In October, Deshon gave up on Hollywood and returned to New York City, hoping to find work in the theater, or, perhaps, journalism. Eastman told Deshon that he had come to the conclusion that their relationship was too destructive to continue, and in any case he was thinking of leaving for Russia, to write an eyewitness account of the aftermath of the Revolution.

On February 3, 1922, Eastman and Deshon ran into each other at the Times Square subway station. That night, Deshon turned on the gas jets in her borrowed apartment at 120 West 11th Street. In the hospital, Eastman donated blood for her, but early in the morning of February 4, Florence Deshon died of carbon monoxide poisoning.

Max Eastman seems to have blamed himself for this romantic catastrophe far more than he blamed Chaplin. In later years, Eastman believed that she meant more to Chaplin than any woman he was ever involved with, with the exception of Oona O'Neill. Contradicting Eastman is the fact that there is no trace of Florence Deshon in the voluminous Chaplin archives.

The Deshon/Chaplin/Eastman ménage underscores Chaplin's innate interest in and sympathy for bohemians, as well as his ability to drift away from people when they ceased to interest him.

For all of his cruising of Socialism, Chaplin remained more of an observer than a participant. "Chaplin never embraced radicalism," wrote Rob Wagner's great-grandson. "He was too much a freethinker and artist to get caught up in politics. He confounded the press and his friends by rarely answering questions directly about his political leanings, giving the impression that his thinking was muddled. He generally declined to give money to leftist causes when his radical friends approached him hat in hand asking for donations. . . . Wagner frequently coached him on how to respond to the press although he found that it was a job more or less like herding cats. Chaplin being Chaplin, he said what he pleased."

THE WRITER JIM Tully worked for Chaplin for eighteen months beginning in 1922. Tully's salary was $50 a week and his job was to be Chaplin's ghostwriter. He believed he knew the man well: "Like Dickens, he came from the dregs of London. His vision was greater than the novelist in that he could see futility. With the exception of his work he was generally devoid of sentimentality or self-pity.

"Volatile, turbulent and petulant, his malice died with his anger. He had often the detachment of a first-rate man. His charm, his ease of manner, his graciousness, were undeniable. He never made comment on those who had wrongfully used him. Neither did he ever speak of a kindness he had done for another. . . .

"With the exception of stage and screen, his knowledge of all subjects was superficial. . . . With love for no country, he had none of the duplicity so common in business and politics. . . . 'My moods are all I have left.' They were many and variable. Like beautiful women, they were the problems of his life. . . .

"He was fond of animals, and might, in a mood, have stopped his limousine to be kind to a stray dog. The canine that played with him in *A Dog's Life* remained a pet at the studio until the end of his decrepit days. He lived with the watchman at the front gate. Whenever the comedian appeared, the dog would follow him. This pleased Chaplin more than the plaudits of the great.

"He made peaceful the last years of his mother's life, and discussed her in lingering wonderment. . . . 'They can say what they want about her,' he said. 'She was a greater artist than I will ever be. She was a great actress. I've never seen anyone like her. She was good to me when I was a kid. She gave me all she had and asked nothing in return.'"

Tully's appraisal was accurate. Chaplin's charities were unconventional, not to mention unpublicized. There was, for instance, Granville Redmond, a talented artist who had been rendered deaf by scarlet fever when he was two and a half. He was educated at the Berkeley School for the Deaf, where he was found to have artistic talent. Redmond studied in France, where he was influenced by both the Barbizon school and the Impressionists. His time in France culminated in an exhibition at the Paris Salon. In 1898 he returned to California and married.

While working in Los Angeles he met Chaplin, who was impressed by Redmond's personality as well as his art. He invited Redmond to use space at the Chaplin studio as his own. Not content with offering Redmond a place to live and work, Chaplin learned sign language so he could converse with him. When he asked Redmond what he thought of a scene, Redmond would respond with thumbs up—approval, a little finger angled down—disapproval, or little finger and thumb wiggled side to side—mediocre.

Chaplin used Redmond as an actor in *A Dog's Life*, *The Kid*, and *A Woman of Paris*, culminating with Redmond playing the sculptor of the statue in the opening scene of *City Lights*. Redmond's landscapes mark him as an exceptional California Impressionist, and in the twenty-first century several museum retrospectives have featured his work.

When Chaplin was publicly accused of being stingy with both his money and his affections, he would invariably refuse to enumerate his charities to Redmond, Edna Purviance, and others. It was a response he would repeat when he was said to be Jewish, which he refused to deny because he felt that denial played into the hands of anti-Semites. As he once noted, "It's easy to judge. It's not so easy to understand."

Nineteen twenty-two was the year Florence Deshon committed suicide. It was also the year the Bureau of Investigation opened a file on Chaplin. The year before that, an agent had interviewed Mildred Harris, Chaplin's ex-wife. The agent reported that Harris "gladly volunteered any and all information" pertaining to Chaplin's politics, yet "was unable to provide agent with any definite information except as to her positive knowledge that *Mr. Chaplin* entertained Socialist beliefs."

A BOI informant attended an August 1922 party at the Chaplin studio that, the report states, was attended by "parlor Bolsheviki," including William deMille, Rob Wagner, and William Z. Foster, the

future head of the American Communist Party. Chaplin told Foster
that neither he nor any other stars hobnobbed with Will Hays, recently hired to run a comparatively toothless Motion Picture Association formed to stave off censorship by individual states. "We are
against any kind of censorship, and particularly against Presbyterian
censorship," Chaplin told Foster. He showed his guest a pennant with
the words "Welcome Will Hays" which he had mounted over the
door to the men's toilet.

The report was forwarded to Hays and BOI director William J.
Burns, who noted that, "This Communistic propaganda in the movie
industry should be followed very closely, in view of the effect which
such pictures will have upon the minds of the people of this country."
Hays wrote Burns that "[Chaplin] did not participate at all in the
activities when I was in California. He was the only one who did
not and word came very definitely that he is 'against everything.' . . .
I think the party mentioned is really a little odd in his mental processes, to say the least, in the direction you mention. I did not know
he had gone as far, however, as the report indicates."

The BOI's follow-up was desultory. In January 1923, an informant reported that Chaplin had made a $1,000 contribution to the
American Communist Party but "the name of the donor is held back,
and no official record will be made of it."

J. Edgar Hoover took over as interim director of the agency in
1924. At that point the BOI was a relatively obscure government
agency that spent most of its time chasing car thieves across state
lines. That would change with the kidnapping of the Lindbergh baby
in 1932, which electrified the nation. In 1933, the BOI's mission
was broadened to include kidnapping, and Hoover grew increasingly
skilled at bolstering the profile of both the agency, soon renamed
Federal Bureau of Investigation (FBI), and its director, who gradually
became synonymous.

Twenty years went by before the Bureau again turned its attention
to Charlie Chaplin, at which time attention evolved into obsession.
Over time, the Bureau's file on Chaplin would grow to 1,900 pages,
with more space devoted to Chaplin's sex life than his politics.

*   *   *

CHAPLIN'S BASIC CONTEMPT for authority had been integrated into his films as asides about society's reflexively oppressive behaviors. Chaplin the filmmaker was usually willing to give individuals the benefit of the doubt. Society in general, not so much.

Chaplin regarded himself as a pacifist, which the people around him thought was accurate. "He seemed paralyzed by any emergency," was the way one friend put it. When his assistant Harry d'Arrast's dog fell into the studio swimming pool, Chaplin yelled frantically for help, but made no move to rescue the dog himself. Similarly, when he and a friend were eating at a place called the Russian Eagle, the restaurant caught fire. Chaplin didn't panic, but he seemed powerless to move.

He would frequently claim to be an anarchist, not in the bomb-throwing sense, but in a dislike of rules and a preference for as much liberty as the law allowed, and maybe just a bit more. That said, politics were not a defining issue for Chaplin in the 1920s. Harry Crocker recalled that during the four years he worked for Chaplin, from late 1925 to late 1929, there were only a few conversations concerning politics.

"The most advanced revolutionist that visited Chaplin—and he came but once—was [the Socialist] Upton Sinclair," Crocker remembered. Chaplin described Sinclair as "a minister with his head turned wrong," which didn't stop him from supporting Sinclair's 1934 EPIC (End Poverty in California) run for governor of California.

At one point during the campaign, Sinclair wrote a one-act play entitled *Depression Island* to be enacted as a fundraiser at Grauman's Chinese Theatre. Sinclair told his campaign staff that he was going to invite Chaplin to host the evening. Everybody told him it was a ridiculous request, that Chaplin would never do such a thing. But Chaplin said he would do it and he did. "We had an uproarious time," remembered Sinclair.

After much scurrilous anti-EPIC propagandizing by the motion picture industry, specifically Irving Thalberg and MGM, Sinclair lost the race. Chaplin and his best friend Doug Fairbanks must have had some stimulating conversations about Sinclair—Fairbanks was a Republican and part of a group of producers who were threatening to move the entire movie industry to Florida if Sinclair won. Fairbanks was bluffing—air conditioning didn't become widely available until after World War II and the oppressive Florida summers could melt the emulsion on 35mm film.

His enthusiasm undiminished by Sinclair's loss, Chaplin remained a supporter of President Franklin Roosevelt and donated $500 to Roosevelt's 1936 reelection campaign.

Even in a town as full of odd characters as Hollywood, Chaplin stood out. The great Russian director Sergei Eisenstein came to America for six months early in the decade, and called Chaplin "the most interesting man in Hollywood." They met in Douglas Fairbanks's steam room at United Artists. Chaplin cried out, "*Gaida, troika, sneg pushistyi*" in an undoubtedly planned greeting. Joe Schenck, wrapped up in a huge towel, explained to Eisenstein that "Charlie and Pola Negri were close for a year, so he reckons his Russian's fluent." Negri was Polish, not Russian, but Schenck must have figured it was close enough.

As they got to know each other, Eisenstein recognized that Chaplin's compulsion to dazzle guests rather than simply be with them implied that he was "afraid of solitude . . . like a child scared of being alone in the dark." Eisenstein also noticed the deep connection between Chaplin and Marion Davies and referred to her as "Charlie's one and only real, long-lasting love."

The times with Chaplin were among the most satisfying for Eisenstein, who was otherwise beset by enemies both foreign and domestic. Moscow was angry at him for even thinking about Hollywood, while Paramount was scared of him—bringing him to America was Jesse Lasky's idea, and might have been a contributing factor to Lasky's losing his place in the company.

At the end of Eisenstein's frustrating sojourn in Hollywood, Chaplin signed a photo for him: "For my friend Sergei Eisenstein, with my sincere admiration. Charlie Chaplin. Hollywood, Nov. 18th, 1930."

THROUGHOUT THE FIRST twenty years of his movie career, Chaplin maintained a shrewd sense of his own strengths and limitations, and he meant to maximize those strengths—focus, energy, imagination—rather than risk dissipating them with outside activities.

Despite his liberal political sympathies, Chaplin studiously avoided organizations. As Fascism gradually infected Europe, he refused to join the Hollywood Anti-Nazi League, which attracted luminaries from Fritz Lang to Fredric March among its membership of more than four thousand. He also avoided the Motion Picture Democratic Committee, a reaction against the studio machinations that helped defeat Upton Sinclair.

But the Depression would politicize Chaplin just as it would an entire generation of young American artists. Beginning with 1936's *Modern Times*, Chaplin's views about capitalism and its victims would be front and center.

CHAPLIN REMEMBERED THAT the proximate inspiration for *Modern Times* was a 1925 interview he had with Paul Sifton, a young reporter for the New York *World*. "My next picture," he told Sifton, "is going to be . . . the story of the city, the noise, the rush, the demand for efficiency and success."

What moved Chaplin's feelings from theory to action was a leisurely around-the-world trip he took from February 1931 to June 1932. The ostensible motivation for the trip was publicity for *City Lights*, which Chaplin and everybody else regarded as a problematic commercial venture, if only because it was a silent picture released four years after sound movies landed.

Chaplin left for Europe on February 13, 1931, aboard the *Mauretania*. The London premiere of *City Lights* was on February 27, after which he moved on to Berlin, Vienna, Venice, Paris, Nice, Marseilles, Algiers, Marseilles again, the Riviera (Nice, Cannes, Biarritz), then San Sebastian, London, Manchester, Stratford, Blackburn, Chester, Plymouth, London, and back to St. Moritz.

Nineteen thirty-two took him to Rome, Milan, Naples, Kobe, Cairo, Ceylon, Singapore, Java, Bali for several weeks, Singapore, Kobe again, Tokyo, Vancouver, then Los Angeles, arriving home on June 16, 1932.

During his time in England he made time for nostalgia—a trip to Lambeth where he once again immersed himself in the scalding humiliation of his childhood in the workhouse. "I spent two years as a child [there] from the age of five to seven. I suppose I spent the unhappiest time of my life there. To me it was a prison and house of shame. We had gone through extreme poverty, and poverty was a crime. Even at the early age of seven I realized this. . . .

"I went in and up the stairs that used to seem so close to me as I climbed them, the walls pressing in on me, the tread of the stairs so near my face. It was the same now. These stairs, enclosed, steep, narrow, pressed in on me just as they had then. I felt those walls. I felt the steepness of the steps. I felt myself going up them with the same sensation of oppression and confinement that I had then. . . .

"I went into the dining room—a large hall—and there was my place, the third seat at the fourth table. . . . How well I remember one Christmas Day sitting on that same seat, weeping copious tears. The day before I had committed some breach of the rules. As we came into the dining room for Christmas dinner, we were to be given two oranges and a bag of sweets.

"I remember how excited I was awaiting my turn. How joyous and bright the oranges looked in contrast to the gray surroundings. We never saw oranges but once a year and that was at Christmas.

"I am speculating what I shall do with mine. I shall save the peel and the sweets I shall eat one a day. Each child is presented with his treasure as he enters the dining room. At last it is my turn. But the man puts me aside.

"'Oh no—you'll go without for what you did yesterday.' And there, on that seat at the fourth table, I wept bitterly."

The series of humiliations is recounted with a bitter detail verging on masochism.

Chaplin's stay in Vienna provided Sigmund Freud with an opportunity for some long-distance analysis. "In the last few days, Chaplin has been in Vienna," Freud wrote Yvette Guilbert, "but it was too cold for him here, and he left again quickly. He is undoubtedly a great artist; certainly he always portrays one and the same figure; only the weakly poor, helpless, clumsy youngster for whom, however, things turn out well in the end. Now do you think for this role he has to forget about his own ego? On the contrary, he always plays only himself as he was in his dismal youth. He cannot get away from those impressions and humiliations of that past period of his life. He is, so to speak, an exceptionally simple and transparent case."

There was relaxation built into the trip, as in a meeting with his brother Syd in Nice in June of 1931, after which they moved on to St. Moritz, where they went skiing with Doug Fairbanks. As Syd wrote to a friend, he "was just getting ready to hibernate . . . and figuring out how I could reduce my debts by going off the Gold Standard or the end of the pier when I received a telegram from he of the quarter to three feet, asking if I would care to join him in the solidified water sports. . . . Charlie received me with open checkbook. I found Charlie looking well and madly enthusiastic about skiing."

Syd stayed with Charlie for the rest of the trip, including stops in Java and, at Sydney's suggestion, Bali, both stops well documented by Syd's 16mm camera, with special emphasis on the giggling, bare-breasted Balinese women. Chaplin can be seen mingling with the native people without a trace of condescension. In one tantalizing shot, he slides effortlessly into a Chaplinesque version of a Javanese dance.

One of the few Western faces in the Bali footage is a tall, blond-ish man accompanying Charlie and Syd who turns out to be Walter Spies, a gifted German artist who had reputedly been one of F. W. Murnau's lovers. Spies spoke the local language and gave Chaplin and his brother a guided tour of a ceremony involving ritual flagellation among young men and priests.

Bali and its people appealed to Chaplin's inner Gauguin as well as his distrust of Western metropolises: "Silvery downy clouds encircled the green mountains, leaving their peaks looking like floating fairy islands. Majestic landscapes and smiling inlets passed until we reached our destination. How different this port looks from those of civilized countries; no chimney stacks to mar the horizon, no begrimed dry docks nursing rusty ships, no iron foundries, stockyards, or tanneries. Only a small wooden wharf, a few picturesque boats, and houses with red tiled roofs. . . .

"How nice to be away from civilization, relieved of stiff shirt-fronts, and starched collars. I had made up my mind to go around native-like with just a loose shirt, a pair of trousers, and sandals. You can imagine my disgust when I found a notice posted in the room that read that all guests must be fully dressed when entering the dining room. I was most indignant. Nevertheless, I dined deliberately without changing my clothes or shaving."

In Bali, Chaplin met the artist Al Hirschfeld and his wife, who had been there for some months in a house vacated by artist Miguel Covarrubias. They were living, Chaplin remembered, "like landed aristocrats for fifteen dollars a week." Hirschfeld found that Chaplin had "an original mind, a probing mind."

All this was in contrast to Hirschfeld's perception of Syd, who he said "was not in the same league as Charlie, really. He sort of found the natives amusing and so on, but Chaplin found them very inventive and creative—and he could do a little Balinese dance that was absolutely accurate, you know, it was so beautifully done in pantomime. It was as though he had been studying that dance for years."

One night Chaplin and his friends were sitting around when he said, "I wonder if they will laugh at the same things?"

"Why don't you try it, Charlie?" said Hirschfeld. "Do something and see if they laugh." Chaplin did the bit where he made his derby pop off his head, except he was wearing a pith helmet at the time. "The people were just startled, they thought he had some kind of demonic powers, you know, and then he showed them how he did this, and they were screaming with laughter. . . . He was known as the funny man."

When Chaplin left Bali, he took a cache of Hirschfeld's watercolors with him. The money Chaplin gave Hirschfeld enabled the artist to come home and restart his American career.

Chaplin was nothing if not romantic, so he was utterly seduced by Bali, which he termed a "paradise. Natives worked four months in the rice-fields and devoted the other eight to their art and culture. Entertainment was free all over the island, one village performing for the other. But now paradise is on the way out. Education has taught them to cover their breasts and forsake their pleasure-loving gods for Western ones."

Some years later, Al Hirschfeld was in Los Angeles and visited Chaplin at his home on Summit Drive. "He was dancing," wrote Hirschfeld, "laughing and being the greatest pantomimist I had ever seen. White hair, honest blue eyes, a laugh more eloquent than prose. Young in a way few youths have ever been. Old with a rare dignity."

Chaplin told him, "I don't know a damn thing about writing, that is, words divorced from action. When I write, I invariably think of the pantomime and translate this into words. Unsuccessfully, because the words are constantly restricting the movement.

"Lines spoken from the screen are easily forgotten. It's the action that is remembered. Movement is liberated thought."

Hirschfeld concluded that Chaplin "trusts his instincts rather than his intellect. If a thing seems right or feels right he accepts it. His art is not cerebral, it's natural."

Syd had recommended a woman named May Reeves as a likely candidate to help his brother with his mounting correspondence. "She speaks six languages perfectly," Syd announced. Reeves accompanied Chaplin on his travels and quickly became something more than a secretary until Chaplin's publicist Carlyle Robinson told him that Syd had taken a turn with her before introducing her to Charlie. It was a piece of embarrassing news that eventually resulted in Robinson leaving Chaplin's employ—a rare occurrence, as he generally kept his staff around for decades.

The incident didn't come between Charlie and Syd. As for Reeves, she provided the inspiration for a romantic comedy entitled *Stowaway* that Chaplin wrote in the 1930s that was originally intended for Paulette Goddard and Gary Cooper. Chaplin eventually made it in 1966 as *A Countess from Hong Kong*.

Aside from Chaplin's idyll in the Far East, much of the trip was given over to political and social inquiry. Lunch at Lady Astor's, a meeting with Bernard Shaw, dinner with Churchill at Chartwell, a lunch with Lloyd George, a stay with H. G. Wells, a second dinner with Churchill, this time at Biarritz.

Churchill was cooling his heels waiting for his political rebirth, and this particular period of limbo involved spending a lot of time at the typewriter. He seems to have liked Chaplin; in an article for *Collier's* a few years later, he would offer some unsolicited advice about Chaplin's creative course: "The future of Charlie Chaplin may lie mainly in the portrayal of serious roles in silent, or rather, non-talking films, and in the development of a universal cinema . . . but let him come back—at least occasionally—to the vein of comedy that has been the world's delight for twenty years."

Chaplin met both Gandhi and British prime minister Ramsay MacDonald, and again spent time with Albert Einstein, whom he had first met at the Los Angeles premiere of *City Lights*. According to Chaplin, he and Einstein spent most of their time discussing economics and the gold standard, in which Einstein was only modestly interested. Einstein's political philosophy was simple: "I think every man living should be clothed and fed, with a roof over his head, for there is enough for all." Einstein signed a photograph for Chaplin: "To Charlie, the Economist."

A more stimulating time involved several days spent with Aimee Semple McPherson, who met Chaplin in Marseilles. "Religion— organized religion," he told her, "is based on fear, fear of doing something on earth which will keep them out of heaven. My God, they miss out on all the glorious freedom of life in order to reach a mythical heaven where they can walk on golden streets and play a harp—a bait of pure boredom, if you ask me."

As for Ramsay MacDonald, after the introductions were made, Chaplin got down to business: "Do you know, I find a great difference in England since I was here ten years ago? Then there were gray-haired old ladies sleeping on the Thames embankment and shops looked poorly stocked and the children poorly clad.

"But today there is a difference. Those old ladies have gone, the shops look well-stocked, and the children well clad. And they can say what they like about the dole, but I think it's been the saving grace of England. It has kept the wheels of industry going and money in circulation is necessary, no matter where it comes from."

MacDonald felt a certain tedium seeping into the conversation, and evinced no interest whatever in the subject. "He just nodded with an 'Is that so?' expression," Chaplin noted. "To draw him into politics was quite hopeless."

Syd Chaplin noted with dismay some of the books Charlie was reading: *Behind the Scenes of International Finance, The Economic Consequences of the Peace, My Reminiscences of the Russian Revolution.*

In contrast, Syd was reading *The World's Best Humorous Anecdotes* and *A Beachcomber in the Orient.* "I'm out for a good time," Syd concluded. "Let Charlie do the worrying."

Just before Chaplin returned home, he spent time in Japan, where the liberal prime minister Inukai was assassinated. Chaplin was informed that, as a Western celebrity, his life was also in danger. It was definitely time to go home.

THE YEAR AND a half away from America solidified Chaplin's ideas about people in general and nationalism in particular. "Patriotism is the greatest insanity the world has ever suffered," he told one reporter. "I have been all over Europe. . . . Patriotism is rampant everywhere and the result is going to be another war."

Without the aid of a ghostwriter, Chaplin spent the remainder of 1932 writing a book-length series of articles about his trip for *Woman's Home Companion,* for which he was paid $50,000—probably enough to cover the cost of the trip.

The articles seem to have given Chaplin his entrée into the fragile joys of the writing process. His earlier films had been more or less written on film, with little relegated to paper. But after his trip around the world he would spend the rest of his life composing multiple drafts of scripts as well as an autobiography that would become one of the most widely read memoirs of the twentieth century.

His process never changed. First, he would write a draft in longhand, then dictate the results to a secretary. With a clean text at hand, he would labor long and hard over succeeding versions, adding and subtracting, making minute changes in words and phrases.

The text of the *Woman's Home Companion* articles ranges from the humorous to the deadly serious. The former: "Expect news from Mussolini. In the meantime, visit St. Peter's, the Roman Forum, and Museum. Back to hotel. No news from Mussolini. Out again sightseeing. Return to hotel. This time news of Mussolini. Impossible to arrange meeting on such short notice."

Then there was the unintentionally humorous, as when Chaplin mentions meeting the man who would become the foremost English Fascist: "Sir Oswald Mosley, one of the most promising young men in English politics in spite of his momentary defeat."

On balance, he thought Europe was tilting toward chaos: "Europe and the different countries I visited, embroiled in unrest, seem brewing a new epoch—theistic, sociological, and economical—unprecedented in the history of civilization."

In closing, he professed an optimism he may not have actually felt: "As I journey from Seattle to Hollywood, passing through the rich farmlands of Washington, the dense pine forests of Oregon, and on into the vineyards and orchards of California, it seems impossible to believe ten million people wanting when so much real wealth is evident.

"Nevertheless I am glad to be back in America. I'm glad to be home in Hollywood. Somehow I feel that in America lies the hope of the whole world. For whatever takes place in the transition of this epoch-making time, America will be equal to it."

Chaplin's immersion in economics resulted in an unpublished article entitled "An Idea for the Solution of War Reparations." He attacks high tariffs, and "overburdened taxation." As for war reparations, he suggests that the Allies issue the amount that Germany owed them in "an international currency" and pay themselves, "each nation to be given her share according to her agreement . . . a fiduciary currency guaranteed by the Allies to have the same par value as gold." He believed that "This is the nucleus upon which to print an international money. It is more scientific to print internationally, than nationally, because an international currency would have less fluctuations than a national one."

A little of this goes a long way—there's a reason why economics is known as the dismal science—but it confirms Chaplin's abiding hostility toward any form of nationalism, even economic nationalism. Chaplin's last words on the world economy he witnessed during his tour: "I saw food rotting, goods piled high while people wandered hungrily about them, millions of unemployed and their services going to waste."

This series of encounters and revelations aroused by the deprivation of the Depression would provide the foundations of the next three pictures he would make. The plight of the worker would form the spine of *Modern Times* and, to an extent, *Monsieur Verdoux*, while homicidal nationalism inspired *The Great Dictator*.

CHAPLIN'S DEEP DIVE into current events did not change his opinion of sound movies—he was still dodging the idea of talking. His speaking voice was excellent, but he felt that the Tramp was an archetypal silent film character—the minute the Tramp opened his mouth he would become an Englishman. In a phone conversation in January 1932 while Chaplin was still in Europe, Alf Reeves asked him, "Don't you want us to get the studio fixed up for sound? We don't want you . . . finding it unprepared. Can we get busy on it right away?

"Oh, nothing doing, eh?"

In other areas, he was ripe for something new. In July 1932, Chaplin met Paulette Goddard on a shipboard party hosted by Joe Schenck, the chief executive of United Artists. Chaplin and Goddard quickly paired off, first spending Sundays together, then spending the next ten years together. Along the way, Goddard's vivid beauty and sunny, exuberant character as showcased by Chaplin in *Modern Times* and *The Great Dictator* made her a movie star. For a time, she made him happier than any other woman ever had.

CHAPTER 4

It was time to get to work.

On March 14, 1933, Alf Reeves wrote Syd Chaplin about his brother's new project: "Charlie has a story milling around in his mind. It will probably appertain to a modern factory, in which he as a newcomer becomes involved in the machinery and gadgets of all kinds. Charlie will be touching the wrong buttons and getting entangled in devices with amusing results. There may be a foreman who is addicted to using his spare time exhorting the populace to better things, and there may be a daughter who looks through Charlie to the boss's son. Everything is done in the factory to reduce the use of labor. Even the workmen are fed by mechanical processes and there is an efficiency expert who is very hard on the hired help."

Chaplin remembered that *Modern Times* derived almost completely from the juxtaposition of his world tour with what he saw on his return to America. "I was shocked at the utter bewilderment of people here over what was happening to them. I felt the same bewilderment myself. Much that we had once believed in was proving to be foolish and unworkable, and no one had much idea what to do about it. People were in mental chaos.

"It seemed to me that here was material for treatment in pictures. But the only way to handle it for entertainment purposes was to poke fun at our whole crazy situation, to satirize modern times. Here we had gone to great lengths to attain what is called efficiency, to enable us to produce more and more, and now we could not dispose of what we produced. Our very ability to make in vast quantity everything we needed was creating poverty."

An early draft of the story called *Commonwealth* begins thusly: "A factory whistle blows, getting louder and louder, as the music gets heavier, to series of dissolves of machinery—crowds of men going to work—cattle being herded on train—crowds being belched up from subway, etc. etc., to 'Stop' and 'Go' signal.

"Street scene to business in store window—arrest and court room scene.

"Walking down street, sees truck with red flag on back. Flag business. Riot and arrest."

Clearly, Chaplin has specific scenes already in his mind. The "business in store window" refers to a bewitching sequence he cut from *City Lights* involving a stick stuck in a grate that gradually brings an entire city to a halt. (He never did find a place for the sequence, one of the few times he let a good idea go to waste; he played with a flea circus routine he finally worked into *Limelight* for more than thirty years.)

As far as the Tramp's relationship with the Gamine—his word for the character played by Paulette Goddard—he outlined it in story notes: "The only two live spirits in a world of automatons. They really live. Both have an eternal spirit of youth and are absolutely unmoral. . . . There is no romance in the relationship. Really two playmates—partners in crime, comrades, babes in the woods. We beg, borrow or steal for a living. Two joyous spirits living by their wits."

The ending he initially planned involved the Tramp in a hospital recovering from a nervous breakdown. He gets out to find that during his hospitalization the Gamine has become a nun. Instead of finding a life with her, he is once again exiled to going down the road alone.

In a later draft the title was changed to *The Masses*, and the opening is broken down into a series of specific shots that are more or less present in the finished film. Chaplin effortlessly transposes the

Tramp's traditional, basic problem—as author Dan Kamin described it, the Tramp is "the natural man being put upon by the restrictions, roles and expectations of others." This time, though, the restrictions, roles, and expectations are presented as the inevitable by-products of a mechanized, impersonal society.

Shortly after *Modern Times* began production, Sydney Chaplin wrote a letter of brotherly advice from his penthouse in Nice: "I am so glad to hear you are making rapid progress with your new picture. I hope it will be a 'Knock Out' but don't spend too much money on it. That is the reason I am writing you. Europe at the present moment is a powder barrel that is likely to go up at any moment. You have no idea of the tense political situations that exist over here. Lots of Americans & English are moving out of France. It is only a spirit of bravado that keeps me here. . . .

"The policy is to get your new picture out quickly before Europe blows up, because you can bet your life it will not be the same as 1914, with theaters in full swing behind the lines. There ain't going to be no lines, or lighting stations. Those who are left alive will be going to bed with candles, when they are not busy burying the dead."

Syd was often an alarmist, but on this occasion he has to be awarded points for prescience.

Modern Times started production on October 11, 1934, with scenes in the Boss's office in the factory. Interestingly, the shooting day ran from 5 p.m. to 8 p.m. Three days later, the company pulled an all-nighter, working from 7:30 p.m. to 4:45 a.m. on the assembly line scenes that introduced Chaplin in the picture.

Despite his misgivings about sound, Chaplin gave serious thought to shooting the film with dialogue; there are scripted scenes with dialogue. "Don't sit in that clam chowder!" Tiny Sandford was to say to Chaplin during a break from the production line.

"Huh?" was the reply.

"Give it here. Hey! Be Careful. What are you doing?"

"Quick! Quick! Quick! Take it!—Take it!"

"Tramp (continues, feeling in trousers) 'I have a clam here somewhere—seems to be traveling. Umph! There it is. It bit me.'"

When the workers go on strike, the Tramp is asked what he thinks. "I have nothing to say," he replies.

"Well, you'd better make up your mind."

"The political machinations involved in paragraph 16 are beyond my comprehension."

"What are you talking about?"

"I don't know."

"Then (emotionally)

"'Life is too complicated.'"

Chaplin didn't limit his activities on the picture to writing, acting, and directing. One production still shows Chaplin alongside an anonymous laborer, both of them pulling the camera for a tracking shot. Other shots show him dressing Paulette Goddard's hair. And when it got down to his own scenes he was relentless, taking exhaustive pains. Years later, a reporter asked him about his working methods and he replied that the only way he knew how to make movies was to "slug my guts out."

Case in point: the feeding machine sequence, the comic highlight of *Modern Times*. In his silent films, Chaplin worked on one sequence at a time, shooting and editing until he was satisfied, then moving on to the next sequence. Once several sequences were spliced together, he would often go back for retakes to sharpen a given sequence. The film grew slowly but inexorably until he judged it complete.

The feeding machine sequence was shot from October 26 to November 16, 1934. Chaplin made over two hundred takes, mostly shooting at eighteen frames per second, so that the action would be slightly sped up when projected at the standard sound speed of twenty-four frames per second. After completing a rough cut of the sequence, he shot another 133 takes in order to get the precise rhythm and effect he was after. By the time he was finished, Chaplin had done nearly four hundred takes on this sequence alone.

The factory sequence generally and the feeding machine sequence specifically are the high-water marks of Chaplin's instinctive understanding of a world in which society carries its devotion to tools beyond the edge of sanity. (What Chaplin would make of social media and smartphones can only be imagined.)

For the first several months of shooting, Chaplin hedged his bets, preparing two different versions of scenes—silent as well as dialogue. The daily production report for December 18 notes, "Expected to shoot 'Dream House' with sound, but changed plans. Did not shoot. Took sound track of [stomach] rumbles."

Ultimately, Chaplin made the decision to keep the Tramp silent except for a song in the last reel. "He felt," said friend Douglas Fairbanks Jr., "that he was an artistic law unto himself. He felt it's all right for other people, he enjoyed watching other people's [sound] films, but he said 'That's not for me.' It's like someone saying 'I'm a water-colorist, and if everybody wants to paint in oils, that's their business, but I'll stick to watercolors.' "

The Masses was eventually titled the less incendiary *Modern Times*. It was the most complicated production Chaplin had made up to that time. The factory set involved impeccably engineered foreground miniatures that made the sets look much more elaborate than they actually were. The gears that move Charlie through huge machinery like film winding through a projector were actually made of wood and rubber painted to look like steel.

There is a sense that Chaplin wanted to avoid bludgeoning the audience with a film focusing on politics. When Charlie is called back to work with Chester Conklin to get the factory going again, the workers promptly go out on strike. The Tramp and Conklin just stare at each other, stupefied at the counterproductive act. The workers may struggle beneath the iron boot, but they are fully capable of shooting themselves in the foot, not to mention other, more sensitive areas.

While *Modern Times* was shooting, Chaplin gave an interview to the syndicated columnist Karl Kitchen, who asked him if he would ever become an American citizen. "If I were to take out citizenship papers," he replied, "it would be in Andorra, the smallest and most insignificant country in the world."

Kitchen went on to write that "Years and the responsibilities of wealth . . . have made him more conservative and less enthusiastic about socialism. He has a good laugh in telling me how Upton Sinclair had planned to give him a place in his cabinet if he had been elected, the EPIC candidate forgetting that Charlie's nationality would bar him from holding any public office here."

For a fairly complicated shoot, Chaplin drove the film through with some efficiency. The film took 147 days to shoot—the shortest schedule of any film he had made since *The Gold Rush*. Toward the end of the production he actually moved into the studio to live. When he was finally satisfied, he had yet another hurdle—he had to compose and record an extremely complicated musical score.

ON AUGUST 8, 1935, David Raksin got a telegram from the orchestrator Edward Powell:

HAVE WONDERFUL OPPORTUNITY FOR YOU IF
INTERESTED IN HAVING SHOT AT HOLLYWOOD STOP
CHAPLIN COMPOSES ALMOST ALL HIS OWN SCORE
BUT CAN'T WRITE DOWN A NOTE YOUR JOB TO WORK
WITH HIM TAKE DOWN MUSIC STRAIGHTEN IT OUT
HARMONICALLY DEVELOP HERE AND THERE IN
CHARACTER OF HIS THEME PLAY IT OVER WITH PICTURE
FOR CUES WE WILL ORCHESTRATE TOGETHER NEWMAN
WILL CONDUCT STOP BEST CHANCE YOU COULD EVER
HAVE TO BREAK IN HERE CHAPLIN FASCINATING PERSON
ALTHOUGH MUSIC VERY SIMPLE AM SURE NEWMAN
WILL LIKE YOU AND KEEP YOU HERE YOU SPENCER AND
I CAN HAVE GRAND TIME WORKING TOGETHER STOP
THIS OFFER TWO HUNDRED PER WEEK MINIMUM OF SIX
TRANSPORTATION BOTH WAYS STOP YOU CAN STUDY
WITH [ARNOLD] SCHOENBERG WHILE HERE I HAVE
SOLD YOU TO NEWMAN BECAUSE FEEL HOLLYWOOD
PROVIDES BEST OPPORTUNITY FOR YOUR DEVELOPMENT
AS COMPOSER AND ORCHESTRATOR CAN ALSO GET YOU
JOB IN WITH MAX STEINER AT END OF THIS JOB IF YOU
WISH ANSWER IMMEDIATELY.

David Raksin was twenty-three years old, lately sprung from the University of Pennsylvania and desperate to get out of New York City after playing tenor sax in a dance band. He was working on arrangements for Fred Allen's radio show when the telegram from Eddie Powell arrived. He took the job.

When he arrived at the Chaplin studio, Raksin was shown to the projection room, where Chaplin was waiting for him. Raksin was struck by his new employer's abundant white hair, his anachronistic shoes with high suede tops and mother-of-pearl buttons, and his charm and graciousness.

After the introductions were out of the way, Chaplin showed him *Modern Times* in a polished but not final edit. "I loved the picture at once," Raksin remembered, "and I laughed so hard at some of the scenes (particularly the feeding machine sequence) that some time later Charlie told me he had wondered whether I was exaggerating for his benefit." With the preliminaries out of the way, the two men set to work.

Chaplin fired him a week later.

It seemed that Raksin was less than appreciative of some of Chaplin's musical ideas. In Raksin's telling, "There is a special kind of genius that traces its ancestry back to the magpie family, and Charlie was one of those. He had accumulated a veritable attic full of memories and scraps of ideas, which he converted to his own purposes with great style and individuality. . . . In the area of music, the influence of the English music hall was very strong, and since I felt that nothing but the best would do for this remarkable film, when I thought his approach was a bit vulgar, I would say, 'I think we can do better than that.' To Charlie, this was insubordination pure and simple—and the culprit had to go."

The same day Raksin was fired, Alfred Newman hunted him down at Don the Beachcomber's, where Raksin was drowning his disappointment. "I've been looking at your sketches and they're marvelous," Newman said. "He'd be crazy to fire you."

The next day, Alf Reeves called Raksin and had him come to the studio. They wanted him back. Raksin said he'd love to return but he wanted to talk to Chaplin first. They again met in the projection room and talked it out. Raksin told Chaplin that if all he wanted was a musical secretary, he certainly didn't have to pay $200 a week. If he wanted yes men, ditto. But if he needed someone who loved the picture and was prepared to risk getting fired each and every day in a quest to make it as good as it could possibly be, he had found his man. They shook hands and that was that.

For the next four and a half months, Raksin and Chaplin worked side by side on the music score. "When he appeared, Chaplin was generally armed with a couple of musical phrases; in the beginning, apparently because he thought of me as an innocent, he seemed to enjoy telling me that he got some of his best ideas 'while meditating [raising of eyebrow] on the throne, you know.'"

They would review the music for the sequence and Raksin would write down the notes. Then they would run the footage over and over, discussing how the music could be adjusted to the scene. "Sometimes we would use his tune, or we would alter it, or one of us might invent another melody. I should say that I always began by wanting to defer to him; not only was it his picture, but I was working from the common attitude that since I was ostensibly the arranger, the musical ideas were his prerogative. . . . We spent hours, days, months in that projection room, running scenes and bits of action over and over, and we had a marvelous time shaping the music until it was exactly the way we wanted it."

Chaplin always mispronounced "rubato" as "vrubato," which Raksin came to see as an improvement. The younger man was surprised by Chaplin's sophisticated music collection. Chaplin brought recordings from home for them to listen to, including Mozart conducted by Sir Thomas Beecham, Scriabin conducted by Leopold Stokowski, Stravinsky conducted by Stravinsky, not to mention some Balinese gamelan records. Chaplin would occasionally invoke other composers for a stylistic sense of what he wanted: "A bit of Gershwin might be nice here."

Most days Chaplin would invite Raksin and assistants Henry Bergman and Carter DeHaven to lunch at Musso & Frank's on Hollywood Boulevard, a few minutes from Chaplin's studio on La Brea. Chaplin would take his customary corner booth to the left of the front door. If he was in a good mood, he would order his favorite dishes while singing. One of Chaplin's frequent requests was sung to the tune of "I Want a Lassie": "I want a curry/ a ricy, spicy curry/ with a dish of chutney on the side!" Friends of Chaplin's—King Vidor, Rouben Mamoulian, Harry d'Arrast, Alexander Woollcott, Marc Connelly—would occasionally show up as well.

Raksin gauged Chaplin as calmly exuberant—a man happy with his life, happy with his film. He made a series of sketches for Raksin, including one of the Tramp's hat, shoes, and cane. Under his signature, he wrote, "Two shoes, a hat and a cane—rampant."

Raksin noted that Chaplin and Alf Reeves had a way of playfully communicating in a Cockney code, with slang substituted for words that rhymed. One day Chaplin said, "I can hardly keep my *minces* open. [Mince pies, rhymes with eyes.] Can't wait till I get home and lay the *barnet* [barnet fair equals hair] on the *tit-willow* [pillow] and go *bo-peep* [sleep]." Reeves understood this gibberish perfectly.

Although there were no further explosions, Chaplin would occasionally frustrate Raksin—"I'd stalk out of the rooms sometimes and he'd send [assistant director] Carter [DeHaven] after me. . . . But somehow we got along. It became a sort of father and son thing. He was trying to educate me away from my innocence. I loved the picture and I loved working with him. I found him the most entertaining person I've ever met in my life."

The score for *Modern Times* included the romantic melody that became the standard "Smile," which had its origin in a Chaplin suggestion: "What we need here is one of those Puccini melodies." Chaplin came in with the opening, the first couple of bars, and Raksin extended Chaplin's idea with the next couple of bars. The rest of the song was written the same way. As Raksin said, "I didn't get credit on the song but there was no point in making anything of it, because that's how things were done in those days. I was credited as arranger and orchestrator, though I did all the sketches. I didn't mind. When you were an arranger, you were sometimes asked to compose. That was what the arranger did." As Raksin noted, "Although the notes are not Puccini's, the style and feeling are."

Raksin and Chaplin's collaboration has to be considered a success, even though it ended on a chilly note. Alfred Newman liked to record at night and during a session on December 4, 1935, he and Chaplin had an argument that ended when Chaplin accused the orchestra of "dogging it." A furious Newman snapped his baton in half, stalked off the stage, and refused to come back.

It became clear that Raksin was expected to finish conducting the score, but he refused out of loyalty to Newman, who had, after all, talked Chaplin into taking him back. Instead, Edward Powell finished conducting. Raksin's loyalty to Newman bore fruit a few years later when Newman, by then the music director at 20th Century-Fox, assigned him to write the score for a movie called *Laura*. The resulting song made Raksin a very comfortable, not to mention famous, composer.

MODERN TIMES WAS completed by the end of 1935. Some measure of the respect the Hollywood industry had for Chaplin can be gleaned from the letter the Breen Office sent Chaplin after screening the film for its adherence to the all-powerful Production Code, i.e., censorship: "We had the very great pleasure this afternoon of witnessing a projection room showing of your production . . . and I am sending this to advise you that it is our judgment that the basic story is acceptable under the provisions of the Production Code. . . . We respectfully urge upon you the following eliminations:

1. The first part of the 'pansy' gag;
2. The word 'dope' in the printed title.
3. Most of the business of the stomach rumbling on the part of the minister's wife and Charlie.
4. The entire brassiere gag in the department store; and
5. The closeup shot of the udders of the cow.
6. Because of the outstanding entertainment quality of this picture, it is our judgment that you can well afford to 'lean backward' in your effort to make the finished picture completely acceptable to the untold millions of patrons who will surely view it and enjoy it thoroughly."

The brassiere shot was modified, and the close-up of udders did indeed disappear, although why that was a problem is known only to the cultural commissars who populated the Production Code office. Chaplin kept the stomach rumblings.

Just before the movie opened, Chaplin was confident that it was good, but he was not really sure—nobody is ever sure. "It's now in the lap of the gods," he said. "If the public likes it, it's a good picture.

If the public stays away, it's a failure. The public has pretty sound judgement about pictures."

"You don't think a bestselling book is the best book?" a reporter asked.

"No, not about books. Books are aimed at the intellect. But pictures appeal to the emotions, and the public knows when its emotions are stirred."

When the film opened on February 5, 1936, the reviews were good, although a number of critics mentioned that it felt like a Chaplin anthology—there was the skating bit, the waiter bit, and so forth. *Liberty* magazine was more discerning: "Charlie is a brave and wistful Don Quixote tilting with modern machinery and squirming against regimentation. All he wants is to find his modest place in the world. . . .

"The film easily overcomes its old-fashioned photography and staging. . . . The comedy is set on a story as starkly grim as any ever sent out from Hollywood. Indeed, if *Modern Times* were anything but a laughing matter, it would be too strong for popular consumption. It tells of a pieceworker in a factory whose nervous breakdown is brought on by the monotonous rigors of his job. After a spell in an asylum, the little man is sent to jail because he happens to pick up a red flag during a Communist parade. From there it is a study of a dreamer trying to adjust himself to a practical world. In and out of jail; in and out of work; always in trouble. . . .

"*Modern Times* reaches hilarious heights in those giddy scenes where Chaplin is fed by a mechanical feeder. Yet, for all its roughhouse surface, the picture really is a delicate thing, with a quality too elusive to be set down on paper."

Nineteen thirty-six was a mediocre year at the box office, and *Modern Times* returned $3.6 million compared to the $5 million that *City Lights* had earned. The shortfall was largely attributable to the fact that it wasn't shown in Fascist Germany, Italy, or Japan. Alf Reeves estimated that after United Artists deducted their distribution charges, the picture would eventually return $3 million to Chaplin on an investment of $1.2 million. Besides that, Reeves noted that Chaplin's stock portfolio was returning about 5.5 percent.

Despite its segmented construction, *Modern Times* feels all of a piece, united by its theme of rootlessness, and an almost surreptitious bleak humor, as with the sheep rushing past the camera in the first shot, with a single black sheep in the middle of the flock—Charlie.

It's also one of Chaplin's most effective physical productions; the hanging miniatures give a strong sense of gleaming, impersonal industrial might. *Modern Times* illustrates the wisdom of Howard Hawks's dictum that a good movie has to have three or four great scenes and no bad ones. *Modern Times* ups the ante by having five great scenes and a transcendent, definitive ending.

Aside from functioning as a delicious collection of Chaplin gags, *Modern Times* syncs perfectly with the period of the Popular Front, acknowledging all of the difficulties of the moment, but with a residual optimism based on the ability of socially concerned citizens to pull together and solve problems. As with all the Chaplin features, it's a comedy with something on its mind, and that something isn't really funny—the Tramp and the Gamine are continually forced to move on. Chaplin even invents Orwell's Big Brother more than ten years before *1984*, as the factory owner peers over the workers' shoulders in the men's room via large screen TV.

A subsidiary theme is society's implicit stance of viewing human beings as expendable, with death and drugs thrown into the mix. And the sequence where Charlie is gobbled up by giant gears remains eternally, brilliantly relevant. The idea derived from a printing shop Chaplin had worked in as a boy. The machinery was over twenty feet high, and the noise of the gears grinding had frightened him; he felt the printing press had the potential to devour him.

In the end, the only option for the Tramp and the Gamine is to head down the long road toward the horizon, toward the next adventure. As Chaplin says goodbye to the Tramp, he at least gives him a companion—for the first time, the Tramp is not alone. After nearly ninety years, the film still enthralls. It portrays a chaotic world of poverty, unemployment, strikes, automation, addiction, and religious bigotry, all circling around Chaplin's core theme of inhumanity.

The movie is also brightened by Paulette Goddard's beauty and spirit. Goddard and Claire Bloom were the only Chaplin discoveries to achieve genuine stardom. Goddard's vivacity and looks masked ambition and what Orson Welles referred to as "a cash register for a brain." In short, she had a sense of her own worth that could never be subsumed by Chaplin. She was adored by his sons by Lita Grey—Goddard worked hard to integrate Charlie Jr. and young Sydney into Chaplin's life.

She must have loved him—they told people they were married, but no marriage license has ever turned up. In fact they were just living together, which Chaplin believed was nobody's business but theirs. In this, as in all things, Chaplin kept his cards extremely close. A letter Alf Reeves wrote to Syd Chaplin in December 1936 makes note of the situation. "As you will have seen by the newspapers, it is generally assumed he and P.G. are married. He has never said it to me, but visitors such as young [Randolph] Churchill and others who visit up at the house seem to assume it, and accordingly write in that direction to their newspapers."

The lack of a marriage license probably cost Goddard the part of Scarlett O'Hara in Gone With the Wind—Goddard was one of the four finalists and David Selznick seems to have favored her. Things worked out for the best, at least for Gone With the Wind. Vivien Leigh gave the part more depth than Goddard could have—she would have been merely kittenish. Leigh was also living with her lover Laurence Olivier, but the general public was unaware of that arrangement, unlike the Goddard-Chaplin affair, which was common knowledge.

To assuage her grief at losing the part of Scarlett, Chaplin gave Goddard a diamond and cabochon emerald bangle bracelet from Trabert & Hoeffer. He knew his woman—Goddard loved jewelry more than she loved acting. Late in her life, Sotheby's would auction off the bracelet as well as a necklace with fifty diamonds, both given to her by the men in her life. The necklace was bulked up by what Goddard said was her engagement ring from Chaplin.

Goddard was the right woman at the right time. She convinced Chaplin to relax and enjoy what he had earned. At her urging, he bought a boat, a modest—by Hollywood standards—thirty-eight-footer called the Panacea, on which they made numerous trips to Catalina Island. "All boats should be called Panacea," he observed, "for nothing is more recuperative than a sea voyage. Your worries are adjourned, the boat adopts you, and cures you and when finally she enters port, reluctantly gives you back again to the humdrum world."

EVENTUALLY, *MODERN TIMES* made its way to Nice. Syd was unimpressed. To be specific, he was eight single-spaced pages of unimpressed, taking his brother to task for a variety of failures of imagination:

"Well Charlie I saw your new picture & although it handed me quite a number of good laughs I must confess I was disappointed, & so were a great number of my friends here on the Riviera. The general impression is that there are not enough laughs considering the costly sets, & I agree with this. You certainly had a bunch of 'Nitwits' around you for help. I saw numerous gags & laughs that you had over looked in your machinery. I will explain to you later how I think you could have done this. I want to confine myself now to a general criticism of your film.

"I think you made a mistake by trying to introduce too many [segments] instead of confining yourself to the menace of the machine age. You started your picture off with a fast tempo then faded away. You gave them the best first instead of saving it until last. You had no personal heavy running throughout your picture. Your only heavy was inanimate machinery & conditions. You introduce a father who is shot in a strike riot. A daughter who steals, & younger children who are taken away by the authorities, but the preceding home life & their characters are not established. The result is they fail to raise the slightest interest or sympathy in the audience. The situation is similar but not to be compared in its dramatic effect as you created in *The Kid*. . . .

"All these sets I think could have been hooked together & woven into your Machinery story by carrying a personal heavy throughout the film."

Syd proposed making the Gamine's father the foreman of the factory where Charlie works. He thought the factory owner should have been the heavy who fires the foreman and sends the workers out on a starvation strike rather than a bored mogul doing jigsaw puzzles to pass the time. Syd thought Charlie should have been drunk during his roller-skating sequence in the department store simply because "comedy is usually based upon the imperfect & not the perfect."

In closing Syd mentioned the failing health of his wife, Minnie—she would die of cancer in September 1936—and closed with another naked plea for attention: "I should love to hear from you sometime that is if you can ever be persuaded to dictate a little line. I hate getting your thoughts second-hand & those beautifully engraved Xmas cards that I receive from your office with the seasons greetings from Mr. Charles Spencer Chaplin—go like a knife through my heart.

"Your loving brother."

Syd's criticisms were simultaneously correct and profoundly wrong. What he wanted from Charlie was a new iteration of Eric Campbell, the massive Scottish actor who had personified the heavy in the 1916–1917 era. But the point of *Modern Times* was not an easily vanquished adversary who happened to dislike the Tramp. Rather, the film was an indictment of a world whose main characteristic was not hostility but indifference. Most of Syd's suggestions would have been funny, but they also would have firmly placed the film in the realm of a conventional silent comedy instead of a timeless film about the imprisoning nature of social conventions.

Beyond that, Syd's letter reveals a frustrated comedian yearning to be at work making people laugh, but that was not going to happen. Sydney had become a star in 1925 with a delightful performance in *Charley's Aunt*, after which he was signed by Warner Bros., where he made a series of amusing comedies that included an adaptation of Bruce Bairnsfather's *The Better 'Ole*.

Among Sydney's writers was the young Darryl Zanuck, who remembered in his old age that Sydney was "the greatest cocksman that ever lived, greater even than Errol Flynn." Zanuck said that Sydney would troll girls at Hollywood High using his real name. After finding a willing partner, he and the girl would retire to his car while Zanuck sat in the front seat or moved to the curb.

But Sydney's career came to a crashing halt in 1929 after he was sued for assault, libel, and slander by a twenty-two-year-old actress named Molly Wright, who asserted that Sydney had bitten off one of her nipples during a sexual encounter at the studio of British International Pictures in London. In July 1930, British International settled the matter out of court.

Sidney Gilliat, later a superb screenwriter (*The Lady Vanishes*, etc.) was working at the studio at the time, and with profound British understatement remembered that, "Syd was talented and efficient—a rare combination—but unfortunately . . . there was an awful scandal over a girl whom he approached too enthusiastically in his dressing room, which led to a hurried departure for sunnier climes before charges could be brought. . . . That kind of episode was far from unknown at Elstree [studio] in those days, but it generally took a milder form."

Sydney's side of the story was that the studio had failed to outfit their facility with sound equipment so that his planned film *Mumming Birds* could be produced, and the suit was trumped up to get rid of Sydney and his weighty contract. The fact that Sydney didn't sue BIP for breach of contract indicates his story was a weak dodge. "I will always maintain my innocence of these charges, even on my death bed," Sydney wrote a friend. "I have been made the goat & sacrificed & I certainly would not slink back to the studio like a whipped cur."

As Chaplin wrote with wry awareness in his memoirs, "To judge the morals of our family by commonplace standards would be as erroneous as putting a thermometer in boiling water." More specifically, it is clear that both the American and the British movie industry considered Sydney guilty, because he never worked for anybody but his brother again, despite making occasional gestures in that direction. BIP sued Sydney for breach of contract, and Sydney was declared bankrupt in March 1931. In fact, Sydney had plenty of money and after World War II lived in a series of penthouse apartments in Nice for the rest of his life.

Sydney's character was situated somewhere between raffish and unsavory. He was forever devising schemes to avoid income taxes that helped fill in the times when he wasn't pursuing women . . . or girls. The Wright matter didn't seem to faze him; he read continually, cherished his encyclopedic memory for music hall gags and songs, became an enthusiastic nudist, and maintained an active and witty correspondence with friends in England. Charlie would make good use of Syd's professional expertise in the near future.

For Christmas 1936, Syd shipped his brother a two-volume biography of Lady Hamilton inscribed by the author (Julia Frankau) to the writer Frank Harris, author of *My Life and Loves*. The books were illustrated with color reproductions of George Romney's paintings. Syd was still pining for some small token of notice. A letter, perhaps? "I read lots of articles in the press concerning your private life but knowing the press, I treat them for what they are worth. You are always in my thoughts."

CHAPTER 5

Chaplin's method of directing actors was already enshrined in legend—he acted out each moment of each shot for each actor, who were expected to replicate Chaplin's performance as closely as possible. This worked well for inexperienced actors such as Virginia Cherrill or Paulette Goddard, but professionals could have a difficult time sublimating their own instincts and rhythms.

Children required something different as well. Chaplin got a great performance out of Jackie Coogan in *The Kid*, and a very good one from Dean Riesner, the hilariously obnoxious child who slugs everybody he meets in *The Pilgrim*. (Years later Riesner became a noted screenwriter with *Dirty Harry* and *Charley Varrick* among his credits.) Riesner was only three when he worked with Chaplin, but he remembered it all perfectly.

"[Chaplin] treated me as an equal," said Riesner. "He was very kind and patient. He was very thoughtful and affectionate. . . . He was a stubborn man and if it wasn't working for him, he would become very morose and fretful and would become difficult to live with. He used to buy out second-hand stores—just buy the whole thing and put it into his prop room and he would look and there would be a funny looking little teakettle or something like that, and he would notice and he would think what if he put a nipple on the end of that spout for feeding the baby with? . . .

"I did all the things Charlie asked, except at the end I had to slap him. And I said, 'I'm not gonna hit Uncle Charlie.' And you have a three year old kid who's not gonna hit Uncle Charlie and you're in trouble. So Sydney and Charlie both sat me down—I can see them now, sitting on this prop couch that they had—and Charlie said, 'Oh, I love to be hit, don't you like to be hit?' and they were whacking themselves and hitting themselves and they finally convinced me that they really enjoyed being slapped—it was so much fun. So I finally bought who, you know, and did I buy it? Everybody got hit!"

The raucously funny scene ends with the nasty kid getting a kick in the pants from the Tramp, but it wasn't Riesner. Chaplin hired a midget who fit into Riesner's costume to be the recipient of the kick.

Socially, Chaplin usually coped with his shyness by forcing himself to be entertaining, although he seems to have felt some guilt over his habit of substituting performance for intimacy.

"That's one of the worst traits in me. I like to impress people. I do things I am afterwards ashamed of when in such a mood. When I was a child and had no other means of impressing people, I let my hair grow much longer than became me. Whenever I was in company, I was anxious to be observed. Even to this day, this trait is probably the strongest in me. And yet I am not keen, you know, to meet people. I am happiest when alone; alone with my books and my music. But once I have gone and done it, I sort of feel obliged to carry it on. I hesitate taking the center of the platform, but once there, I keep it, relying entirely upon inspiration for the means of staying there. I believe it is the result of hereditary actorship.

"Center stage. Always center of the stage."

THE FRENCH CINÉASTE Maurice Bessy visited Chaplin's studio in 1938 and was given a guided tour by Alf Reeves. "The sets were tatty, dilapidated, old painted flats," wrote Bessy. "I discovered that the swimming pool where the drowning in *City Lights* was shot was not much more than a ditch, and there was 'the street,' always the same in all his films, the shop on the corner becoming a florist's in *City Lights*, a drugstore in *Modern Times*. An air of neglect hung over it all. The wooden panels were crumbling away, the paint was flaking. The refuse bin was old and dented. The old dog that was the studio mascot could hardly stand on its four legs and lived in a battered kennel."

Chaplin reminisced with Bessy about his early days in the movies, mentioned how upset he had been over the Pickford/Fairbanks divorce. Chaplin invited Bessy into his dressing room, which was merely functional compared to Goddard's dressing room, which was outfitted in "modest luxury." By contrast, Chaplin made do with a bathroom, a small kitchen, a desk covered with tubes of theatrical makeup. The Tramp's costume hung in a cupboard, accompanied by a single bowler hat. "It's just a small studio," Chaplin explained to Bessy. "Really quite small, but it's enough for one man."

It was the dressing room that appalled Alistair Cooke. "This . . . room had peeling wallpaper, a terribly worn carpet, an upright piano about eighty years old and terribly out of tune and a trestle table with a couple of ashtrays—on those days Chaplin smoked—and bentwood chairs. There isn't a movie company, however modest, making three minute documentaries that has such a humble office. He said he wasn't at ease working in comfortable surroundings. He always suspected, not so much his success, as the monetary rewards, and it's one reason he wouldn't handle money. He was comfortable in the kind of shabby surroundings he'd known as a vaudevillian."

Maurice Bessy concurred. "Poverty fitted Charlie like a glove. You could feel it everywhere."

Chaplin's studio was only twenty years old in 1938, so Bessy and Cooke may have been exaggerating the shabbiness endemic to all soundstages, but the starkness is something else. Similarly, the crew he kept with him for decades emphasized his loyalty and feeling for the comfortable, even if it gradually transitioned to dilapidated.

There was Rollie Totheroh, Chaplin's cameraman since 1915, and Alf Reeves, the general manager of the studio. Reeves had been the general manager of the Karno company's tours of America, and was characterized by Alistair Cooke as "a wiry, courteous Cockney sparrow, impossible to place in any fantasy of the Hollywood hierarchy as anything but a gaffer, a carpenter maybe, one of those strange, self-contained Englishmen one meets in the unlikeliest places in America."

The cozy little studio, the cozy old retainers, all situated in the boomtown of Hollywood gave Chaplin the cocoon, the security the Tramp was always seeking and never finding.

Reeves, Totheroh, Edna Purviance, and a dozen others were all prominent examples of Chaplin's unflagging loyalty to people he had encountered during his earliest years in show business. They were loyal to him and he reciprocated. Alistair Cooke again: "[Chaplin] was like the sergeant who has been through years of trench warfare with a motley pack of privates and ever afterward uses them as a protective base of sanity against the fits and starts of the higher-ups."

Practically as well as psychologically Chaplin was loath to leave the past behind, in memory or in practice. At the same time, he realized that the times were changing in ways that made the continued adventures of the Tramp impossible.

"I don't think I'll ever wear my tramp costume again," he told Bessy. "Any more than I'll ever make a [movie about] Napoleon." At the end of their meeting, Chaplin handed Bessy one of the Tramp's bamboo canes. "Here you are, take my stick, Charlie the Tramp is dead and I don't need it anymore."

THE CONTRAST BETWEEN the bedraggled Tramp and Chaplin himself was now startling. With his hair starting to turn gray by the late 1920s—he dyed his hair for the screen until *Monsieur Verdoux*— and his midlife habit of custom-tailored clothes, Chaplin cut a far more elegant figure than his previous incarnation as a moody, shabby music hall performer. But it was the actor's innate shapeshifting that struck many.

The author Thomas Burke wrote a penetrating analysis of Chaplin in 1933 in which he asserted that "He is first and last an actor, possessed by this, that or the other. He lives only in a role, and without it he is lost. As he cannot find the inner Chaplin, there is nothing for him, at grievous moments, to retire into: he is compelled to merge himself, or be merged, in an imagined and super-imposed life. He can be anything you expect him to be and anything you don't expect him to be, and he can maintain the role for weeks. . . . He likes to enjoy the best of the current social system, while at heart he is the reddest of the Reds."

Alistair Cooke had much the same impression when he became friendly with Chaplin in the early 1930s. "I like to think I would have been arrested anywhere by the face," wrote Cooke. "Features evenly sculptured into a sensuous whole, strong and handsome beyond any guess you might have made by mentally stripping away the black half-moon eyebrows and the comic moustache. . . . Seeing Chaplin for the first time was a more curious pleasure than having the screen image of any other star confirmed in the flesh."

A more ambivalent opinion was that of Georgia Hale, the leading lady of *The Gold Rush* and an occasional girlfriend for some years. Hale's memoir was posthumously published in 1995, but she had been working on it for decades. In an early draft, she went into the differences between the two aspects of Chaplin: "Charlie, the genius, had a feeling of great concern for the underdog. He breathed this tender solicitude for the poor, the underprivileged, the forgotten, the ignorant . . . throughout his pictures."

On the other hand, she said, "Mr. Chaplin was cold, sometimes cruel. He was a snob. Although he went through the motions of caring, his philosophy was conservative. No one enjoyed more being at the top of the heap, looking down. He loved high society and he loved wealth, which he never shared, unless forced to do so."

Charlie and Mr. Chaplin were mostly opposing personalities, but there were some aspects in which they were united. Ivor Montagu had accompanied Sergei Eisenstein on his ill-fated trip to Hollywood and one night Chaplin exclaimed to Montagu, "I'd never exchange one foot of my place here for all of England. I love it here, I love California, its climate and I admire the American people."

Montagu understood completely. "The United States has opened its arms wide to you, loved you and enriched you," he told Chaplin. "No wonder you feel the way you do."

Whether he was in Charlie mode or Mr. Chaplin mode, *Modern Times* firmly indicated that his attention was increasingly diverted from his beautiful companions and beautiful life to the world outside his studio gates—a world he felt was increasingly threatening to people like the Tramp, not to mention his creator.

And so he began contemplating the most overtly political—not to mention risky—film of his career.

PART TWO

"Chaplin was as red as that tablecloth!"

—Clarence Brown

CHAPTER 6

For comedians of his own generation, Chaplin had long since ascended to Olympus. Buster Keaton, Stan Laurel, and W. C. Fields all regarded him with professional awe, but Chaplin rarely returned the favor. He dismissed the Marx Brothers as "nothing but anarchists." In conversation with Max Eastman he revealed his reasons for his professional dislike of Groucho, Chico, and Harpo, as well as his essentially conservative aesthetic: "They go in for being crazy. It's a soul-destroying thing. They say, 'All right, you're insane, we'll appeal to your insanity.' They make insanity the convention. . . . Acquiescence in everything disintegrating. Knocking everything down. Annihilating everything. There's no *conduct* in their humor. They haven't any attitude. It's up-to-date, of course—a part of the chaos. I think it's transitional."

He always spoke fondly of Stan Laurel, but more because of their shared youth in the Karno troupe than for professional reasons. The attitude of younger comedians was mostly characterized by Red Skelton. In a series of tapes recorded by journalist Gene Fowler, Skelton said of Chaplin, "Politically I don't like the son of a bitch, but from the standpoint of a clown . . . this man has perfect timing, but his timing is with his eyebrow, his moustache. He's a great prop handler. To me, Buster Keaton was never funny, but he was a great clown. Harold Lloyd was a manufactured comedian, wholesome and clean. . . .

"All the things that [Chaplin] does, he actually paints a picture, but I would like to see him go out on a stage."

"I have," replied Fowler. "In [vaudeville]."

Undeterred, Skelton kept going. "I would like to see him go out into a picture that he didn't produce. I'd like to see him go out and on his own, win over the audience right from the beginning and then get a big reception at the finish . . . just on the spur of the moment."

"In the English Music Hall he was very funny," said Fowler. "He was in a box. Falling out of it. Stewed. I didn't know who he was till I saw him years later in pictures. It was [at] the Empress Theater in Denver."

Skelton remained unimpressed.

FOR YEARS, CHAPLIN had been reading about Hitler, watching news-reels about him, wondering about the resemblance—they were the same size, had the same mustache, and—let's face it—a similar will to power. Besides that, they were born only four days apart.

The resemblance had been widely noted. On the occasion of their fiftieth birthdays, in April 1939, *The Spectator* published an article commenting on their surface similarities: "Each is a distorting mir-ror, the one for good, the other for untold evil. In Chaplin the little man is a clown, timid, incompetent, infinitely resourceful, yet bewil-dered . . . he is a heroic figure, but heroic only in the patience and resource with which he receives the blows that fall upon his bowler. In his actions and loves he emulates the angels. But in Herr Hitler the angel has become a devil."

Much later in the twentieth century, the critic Michael Ventura noted, "It was as though the image of Charlie had been made into a photographic negative, and then given life as the spirit of Evil."

Chaplin would remember that *The Great Dictator* sprang from a 1937 conversation with another émigré: the Hungarian producer-director Alexander Korda, who said the resemblance between the Tramp and Hitler could easily be utilized for a story of mistaken identity. Chaplin acknowledged Korda's point, although it was not an original one. But the more Chaplin thought about it, the more he liked it. He wrote in his memoir, "As Hitler I could harangue the crowds in jargon and talk all I wanted to. And as the Tramp I could remain more or less silent."

This is an open admission that the Jewish barber in the film is in fact the Tramp. The barber speaks in monosyllables, or brief sentences, as was Chaplin's plan for the abandoned talking sequences in *Modern Times*, and is costumed identically to the Tramp. But, as Dan Kamin points out, the barber doesn't really behave like the Tramp—he is far more passive, at least until the final speech, but then that's Chaplin stepping out of character and speaking as Chaplin.

Chaplin had been categorized as Jewish ever since 1927, when *The Jewish Encyclopedia*, issued by a Jewish publisher in Berlin, mistakenly categorized him as "the son of Eastern Jews who originally bore the name of Thonstein and emigrated to England in the mid-19th century." This misinformation was first picked up by the Nazis, later by the FBI. The Nazis took particular umbrage at Chaplin, whose presumptive Jewish heritage immediately categorized him as racially objectionable, as well as ideologically dangerous.

In 1933, Chaplin appeared on a list of "prominent non-Aryans" promulgated by the Nazis. He was sent a typically repellent Nazi publication entitled *Jews Are Looking at You*, which featured photographs of famous Jews with their faces retouched to make them seem animalistic. Chaplin's photo was accompanied by a caption that read, "This little Jewish tumbler, as disgusting as he is boring."

When Chaplin made a joke during an interview about shaving the Tramp's mustache so he could never be mistaken for Hitler, the Nazis responded by calling him a "repellent, yapping little Jew." As for their beloved Führer, "the creator and leader of new Germany, the war veteran and staunch friend of the new German film, stands much too high to even hear the barking of a dog from London's ghetto."

The Nazis returned to this theme several times over the years. In 1937, they published the scabrous *The Eternal Jew*, 265 photographs of presumably Semitic types. Under a picture of Chaplin and Jackie Coogan, there was this caption: "The Galician Charlie Chaplin (whose mother was born Thornstein) emigrated to America. Along with Jackie Coogan, who also came from the East (Jacob Cohen) their tear-jerking comedy makes poverty both pitiable and laughable, reaching the tear ducts of the innocent viewer. The slapstick gang of this flat-footed, clumsy, impoverished yet eternally generous man with the huge shoes was a sensation for the non-Jews. Flat-footed but noble—that is Charlie Chaplin's formula." (Jackie Coogan's name was John Coogan, not Jacob Cohen.)

Similarly, the 1940 "documentary" *The Eternal Jew* included newsreel footage of Chaplin's 1931 visit to Berlin, with accompanying narration: "It cannot be denied that at that time a portion of the German public applauded unsuspectingly the foreign Jew, the deathly enemy of their race. How was that possible? A mendacious dogma of human equality had dimmed the healthy instinct of the people."

Chaplin began writing *The Great Dictator* in September 1938. He decided that the film would be his first talking picture, which meant he had to write in far greater detail than before—the script eventually ran to more than three hundred pages—this from a man who had made great movies from cursory outlines. The film would mark a complete transformation of Chaplin's working methods—sound mandated a much larger crew, not to mention input from associates more ideological than any Chaplin had used before.

CHAPLIN MET DAN James in 1938, just south of Carmel at James's father's stone house overlooking the Pacific Ocean. (In 2022, Brad Pitt paid $40 million for the James family house and property.) It was the year when England was still negotiating with Hitler, when America was officially isolationist. It was also the year that Dan James joined the Communist Party.

James had an interesting lineage—his father was a first cousin of Frank and Jesse James, and the family house was designed by Charles Greene, the founder of the California branch of the Arts and Crafts movement. James was tall and handsome, a would-be writer whose work wasn't going anywhere, which might have been one of the reasons he had recently separated from his wife. Chaplin was having trouble with Paulette Goddard, and was at Carmel with his friend Tim Durant, whom he met through the director King Vidor.

During their first meeting, James held forth on the importance of movies in the fight against Fascism, which naturally segued into Chaplin's ideas for a Hitler movie. At the end of his vacation, Chaplin returned to Hollywood, and James wrote him a letter offering his services in any capacity whatever. A few days later he got a call from Alf Reeves, explaining that, while Chaplin was quite "changeable," he liked James and would pay him $80 a week to work on the picture. He would also put him up at the Beverly Hills Hotel until James got situated in Hollywood.

It was the offer James had been waiting for. "My first evening [Chaplin] took me to [the] Trocadero Oyster bar—then we dined and he told me the outline of the story. The next day I went up and started to make notes."

At first, James simply followed Chaplin around and wrote down everything he said, then typed up the notes, adding a few things of his own. Chaplin called James "Danny," and the two engaged in lengthy discussions about the world of art and politics. Chaplin always referred to himself as an "anarchist," had what James called "a real feeling for the underdog . . . for human dignity," and positioned himself against "wealth and stuffiness."

Why hire a young Communist without any experience in the movie industry as an assistant?

"I think," James remembered, "Charlie took me on because of my height, because my family had a castle out here, and because he knew pretty quickly I was a declared Communist so that my background and political preoccupations would keep me from selling him out for money."

James was on the payroll by January 1939—the projection log of the Chaplin studio shows him attending screenings of, among others, *Shoulder Arms, Sunnyside,* and the unreleased Chaplin fragment *The Professor.* (Watching his old movies was Chaplin's version of a pitcher warming up in the bullpen—getting the rhythm of performance and direction.)

On January 27, they screened *City Lights* for James, as well as Chaplin's sons, Charlie Jr. and Syd. A few days later, Chaplin, James, Rollie Totheroh, and Henry Bergman watched Hitler footage from *The March of Time* newsreel. Watching Nazi newsreels continued on and off for a few months, including a session at the Museum of Modern Art in New York. James remembered Chaplin shouting at Hitler's image on the screen: "Oh, you bastard, you son of a bitch, you swine. I know what's in your mind."

"I thought [Hitler] was a humorless, horrible man," Chaplin said. "Naturally a man in his position would be very fretful . . . and I'm sure he must have had that big fat man, Goering, to lean on. I'm sure there were moments when he questioned his own genius. So it's simple . . . you think of the power corrupting, at the same time defeating . . . deceit, and [false] confidence and everything else. I'm sure that there's a paradox there, where he was so effete and fearful of everything. Where he had the world in the palm of his hand."

As word of Chaplin's plans began to spread, people in Hollywood thought he had finally, irrevocably taken leave of his senses. America at the end of the 1930s was distinguished by the German American Bund dominating Yorkville in New York City, America Firsters filling Madison Square Garden, and isolationist Republicans controlling Congress. All the usual reasons the picture was a bad idea were offered—Hitler wasn't America's problem, or, conversely, Hitler was entirely too serious for humor.

"That is wrong," Chaplin snorted. "If there is one thing I know it is that power can always be made ridiculous. The bigger that fellow gets, the harder my laughter will hit him."

Dan James said that Chaplin was not impervious to worry about the project—it was going to be his first picture with dialogue, it was going to be expensive, and, as usual, he was using his own money. Chaplin remembered that he spent $500,000 before he turned on a camera.

The British Foreign Office was aware of the risk Chaplin was taking. On May 17, 1939, the British consulate in Los Angeles sent a letter to headquarters in London: "We have had some personal conversation with [Chaplin] and find that he is entering into the production *The Dictator* with fanatical enthusiasm. His racial and social sympathies are with classes and groups which have suffered most in the dictatorship countries. The directness of his attack would seem to be, to him, the picture's only motive and reason. Mr. Chaplin recognizes quite frankly that possibly only in the United States will he be able to show his film, and that even here representations will probably be made which will limit the field of distribution to him. He thinks it is possible that the Breen office will refuse to pass the film, but he is determined to distribute it, if necessary without recourse to the distribution organization [United Artists] with which he is associated . . ."

Chaplin wasn't kidding; he had personally financed the New York premiere of *City Lights* because United Artists had no faith in a silent movie in 1931. Chaplin made it clear that if UA didn't have the guts to distribute the Hitler film, he would hire venues or, if necessary, show the movie in tents.

It is hard to overstate the level of free-floating anti-Semitism permeating all levels of the American body politic in these years. Joseph P. Kennedy, FDR's ambassador to England, spoke to an audience of predominantly Jewish movie moguls in late 1940 and told them, "There [is] no reason for our ever becoming involved in any war." Kennedy believed that Charles Lindbergh and the American First crowd were "not so far off the mark when they suggest this country can reconcile itself to whomever wins the war and adjust our trade and lives accordingly." He also said that if the moguls wanted their films shown in Germany, "You're going to have to get those Jewish names off the screen." He warned the moguls that they had to "stop making anti-Nazi pictures or using the film medium to promote or show sympathy to the cause of 'democracies' versus 'the dictators.'"

Franklin Roosevelt wrote one of his sons-in-law that he believed Kennedy and his ilk thought "the future of a small capitalistic class is safer under a Hitler than under a Churchill."

David Nasaw, Kennedy's best biographer, says that "Joe Kennedy's greatest mistake was that he thought Hitler was a rational actor. He thought that if Roosevelt let him sit down with Hitler he could negotiate an end to the war and end the persecution of the Jews.

"Kennedy wasn't an anti-Semite in the sense that Henry Ford was or Charles Lindbergh was. Yet he swallowed whole thousand-year-old myths about Jews. He repeated anti-Semitic canards and myths over and over again. He'd talk about the Jewish conspiracy, Roosevelt being the captive of the Jews, and how the Jews owned the press, even though he was friends with William Randolph Hearst, who actually did own the press."

Roosevelt eventually fired Kennedy, but Chaplin had to deal with the reality of the movie industry in 1940. The craven behavior of most of the moguls combined with the anti-Semitism of much of the public accomplished what would otherwise have been a difficult task: driving most of the artistic community to the left.

Donald Ogden Stewart, a highly successful screenwriter (*The Philadelphia Story, Holiday, Love Affair, Dinner at Eight*) was typical. He remembered that "At Yale, I had taken a course in economics in which it was proven to me that Socialism wouldn't work—that seemed to me to be the answer, at least I never disputed that. And then came 1929 and the Depression began. . . . Little by little, some of us began to feel . . . partly guilt, I suppose, but we wanted to do something. We became, as they say, 'Politically conscious.' "

In time, Dorothy Parker, Fredric March, Edward G. Robinson, Oscar Hammerstein II, and others formed the Hollywood Anti-Nazi League, which Stewart joined. Just before he began shooting *Stagecoach*, John Ford spoke at a meeting of the League, saying, "May I express my whole-hearted desire to cooperate to the utmost of my ability with the Hollywood Anti-Nazi League. If this be Communism, count me in." The Anti-Nazi League vociferously protested against the pro-Nazi filmmaker Leni Riefenstahl's 1938 visit to Los Angeles, which didn't stop Walt Disney from giving her a tour of his studio.

"Most of the big stars ducked any commitment," remembered Stewart. "Freddie and Florence [March] were very brave. Most of the writers were with us, and the producers at first were very anxious to help us, especially the Warner brothers." Stewart estimated that the Anti-Nazi League had between five and six thousand members.

What Stewart neglected to mention—and what Fredric March and many of the other celebrities other than John Ford were ignorant of—was that the League was financed by the American Communist Party, and that Stewart, among others, was a member of the Party. When the Hitler-Stalin Non-Aggression Pact was announced in August 1939, the shock waves radiated throughout the American left. Sidney Lumet, at the time a young actor attached to the Group Theatre, remembered Clifford Odets standing on a porch with tears rolling down his face. "The particular atmosphere that I ran into was of tragedy, calamity, end of the world," remembered Lumet.

And so the counterrevolution began. "Then the fear of Communism began to go around," said Stewart. "That the anti-Nazi League was run by Communists. There were Communists in Hollywood and they did a lot of the work, but a premature anti-fascist was in trouble eventually because the war hadn't broken out and here you were being politically active."

Chaplin's plans were temporarily derailed when the British government under the leadership of the appeasing Neville Chamberlain announced that it would ban Chaplin's picture. Chaplin and the smattering of other antifascist filmmakers were swimming against the tide. A Gallup poll in April 1938 showed that 54 percent of Americans felt "the persecution of the Jews in Europe has been partly their own fault," with another 11 percent saying it was "entirely" their fault. In November 1939, just a year after Kristallnacht, 72 percent of Americans polled said "No" to the question "Should we allow a larger number of Jewish exiles from Germany to come to the United States to live?" Sixty-seven percent said that even Jewish children should be excluded.

In keeping with Chaplin's utter indifference to groups, he never joined the Anti-Nazi League. He was on another level from other movie stars, and not just because he owned his own studio and was part-owner of a major releasing organization. There were other antifascists in Hollywood, but only a smattering of them were producers who flexed their muscles in terms of influencing the political content of their movies. In 1939 and 1940 the only filmmakers with a political horizon and the willingness to use their films in the service of antifascism were the Warner brothers, the independent producer Walter Wanger, and Charlie Chaplin.

The response of Germany to the news out of the Chaplin studio was just what Chaplin expected. Georg Gyssling was vice-consul in Los Angeles—Hitler's man in Hollywood, in charge of muscling Hollywood whenever they contemplated making anti-Nazi pictures. Gyssling wrote Joseph Breen, head of the Production Code Administration: "My dear Mr. Breen, I see from a newspaper article . . . that Mr. Chaplin will play in this film a defenseless little Jew who is mistaken for a powerful dictator, while in the other role you will see him as the dictator himself.

"The article further states that while naturally Hitler is not mentioned, it doesn't take any Solomon or Sherlock Holmes to see it is the Fuehrer, whom Chaplin is burlesquing. As this, if it should prove true, will naturally lead to serious troubles and complications, I beg you to give this matter your consideration." Breen's response was to deny any knowledge of such a movie.

In May 1939, the British Board of Film Censors cabled Breen and Alf Reeves about the rumors that Chaplin was making a Hitler film and asked for a story outline or treatment. Breen spoke to Chaplin, who said there was neither a script nor a story.

A month later, construction began on the sets for *The Great Dictator*.

That news set off letters from citizens riled because Chaplin—a British citizen!—was making a picture that would presumably belittle neutrality: "Regardless of how much we deplore the inhuman persecution of a minority race in foreign lands," wrote one detractor, "this man should not be permitted to use the United States as a background and sounding board . . . with the avowed purpose of stirring up further strife and recrimination between Germany and the United States Government."

Gyssling's implied threats—nice little industry you got here; shame if anything happened to it—didn't deter Chaplin, nor did letters from United Artists telling him that there was no guarantee the film would be able to be shown in either America or England. He ignored them all. "I was determined to ridicule [the Nazis'] mystic bilge about a pure-blooded race. As though such a thing ever existed outside of the Australian Aborigines!"

Ultimately, Chaplin had an ace in his pocket: Franklin Delano Roosevelt. On March 23, 1939, Jack Warner wrote Chaplin a letter after a visit to the White House. "During our conversation the President brought up your picture. . . . He said he hoped you had not put it aside and would make it. . . . President Roosevelt is very keen on seeing it made. . . . I hope you do, Charlie, for if the President of our country is interested in your making the picture it certainly has merit."

In case that wasn't enough, Dan James remembered that Roosevelt sent his assistant Harry Hopkins to talk to Chaplin. "Look,

Charlie, the President is all for this," Hopkins said. "You don't have to worry about the [exhibitors] boycotting this. He'll see that this will be released. He feels that this a very important thing and that you must go ahead and not listen to any of these people who are trying to discourage you."

"This came at a low point for Chaplin and really cheered things up," James said.

So Charlie Chaplin put his head down and forged ahead.

DAN JAMES REMEMBERED that by 1939 "The whole [American] left [was] hanging on this picture." James contacted writers as varied as Donald Ogden Stewart, Nathanael West, and Sidney Buchman to see if they had any suggestions regarding the script. "None had any idea at all." James thought about contacting John Steinbeck, but Chaplin wasn't enthusiastic—according to James, Chaplin thought there was "a lot of phony stuff in Steinbeck's writing."

Chaplin was beginning to think about casting. He had James write some speeches for Fanny Brice, who Chaplin thought could be very funny playing the sex-starved, extremely Semitic wife of Adenoid Hynkel: "I'm a woman. I need affection, and all you think about is The State. THE STATE! What kind of state do you think I'm in? You know last night I dreamed about blimps. I dreamed we captured Paris in a big blimp and we went right through the Arc de Triomphe. And then I dreamed about a city full of Washington monuments. . . . Remember Hynkel, I did everything for you. I even had an operation on my nose."

The fact that the film called for technical sophistication necessitated a large transition in Chaplin's filmmaking operation. Chaplin decided to replace Rollie Totheroh as his cameraman of nearly twenty-five years. The replacement was Karl Struss, a superb artist who had won an Oscar working for F. W. Murnau on *Sunrise*, then gone over to Paramount where he shot such luminous films as *Dr. Jekyll and Mr. Hyde*, *The Sign of the Cross*, and *Belle of the Nineties*. Chaplin kept Totheroh on the payroll, but Struss remembered that Totheroh's main job was operating the second camera.

Chaplin's most important collaborator on the picture wasn't

listed in the credits. In January 1939, Charlie telephoned his brother and asked him to come to Hollywood to work with him on the Hitler project. "Needless to say, I did not have to make up my mind," Sydney wrote to a friend.

The Great Dictator would be the biggest, most expensive, and most dangerous movie Charlie Chaplin would ever make and he wanted—needed—Sydney by his side. It was mutual. In one of his perennial schemes to avoid taxes, Syd had pooled his own money with that of his wife, Minnie. When Minnie died, French probate tied up all of Syd's money along with Minnie's. Suddenly, Syd was floundering financially.

Sydney arrived in Hollywood on January 21, 1939. It was announced in the Los Angeles newspapers that he would function as codirector of the new film, as well as playing the part of Garbitsch—Chaplin's stand-in for Goebbels. Unfortunately, Sydney failed to get a work visa before his arrival and was not legally able to go on the payroll, or the film's credits, which explains why Henry Daniell eventually played the part earmarked for Sydney.

Charlie undoubtedly paid his brother privately, because Sydney essentially functioned as associate producer. Dan James remembered that Sydney was part of the gag meetings and was "immensely ingenious. . . . Very few of them had any relevance to what we were doing, but that didn't matter. It was stimulating. A bad gag is always a challenge to do better." James found that Syd was "very worried about politics . . . a very scared man." Sydney recognized that James had ascended to the status of favored collaborator, and implored him to emphasize to Charlie how much the picture was costing. "He was impatient with me for not scolding Chaplin."

Sydney was also involved in wardrobe tests, casting, and suggesting specific sequences. It was Sydney's idea to have the Jewish barber shave a man to the rhythm of Brahms' "Hungarian Dance No. 5." Sydney had done a similar scene in a 1921 film entitled *King, Queen, Joker* that also revolved around mistaken identity between a king and a barber. This led to Chaplin devising the breathtaking sequence in which Hynkel does a ballet with a globe—a scene derived from a party routine Chaplin had done since the 1920s, and which had been filmed at Pickfair in 1928.

Sydney's most valuable contribution came in the casting process. He had come back to America on the *Île de France*. Jack Oakie was also on the ship, and Sydney had spent a lot of time looking at Oakie as if he was trying to guess his weight. In due time, Charlie called in Oakie for an interview and asked if he was interested in playing the part of Napaloni, the film's Mussolini. Oakie protested that he wasn't Italian, but Scots-Irish.

"What's so funny about an Italian playing Mussolini?" retorted Chaplin.

Chaplin told the comedian that he wanted Oakie to be Oakie, that is to say broad, with a prevailing attitude of anything for a laugh. Oakie thought it only fair to tell Chaplin that there were times when he drank. "If you want to drink, go right ahead and drink," Chaplin told him. "If you get drunk, just don't come in. We're shooting the picture leisurely. We're not in any hurry." Oakie was so moved he stayed rigorously sober throughout the shooting schedule.

SYDNEY EASILY SLIPPED back into the role of older brother, worrying about his brother, worried about the picture's cost. He also took on the responsibilities of studio manager, because he felt Alf Reeves wasn't up to the job. "When I arrived, I found everything in a dilapidated, run-down condition," he wrote a friend. "There was no excuse for it, because Charlie does not limit the expenditures & the studio staff has years between pictures, when there is nothing for them to do but maintenance of the studio. I found the property room like a pig sty, filthy with dust and cobwebs. . . . You should see the difference now. . . .

"The still room where Charlie keeps all the negative stills of his early pictures was in the same neglected condition. Nothing was inventoried & dozens of plates were broken. These can never be replaced. . . . I had all this remedied. The property room cleaned from top to bottom, everything segregated and inventoried, requisition and double checking systems put in on both purchases & rentals & running inventories kept. Also graphs on labour."

At one point, Sydney was approached by a potential buyer for the studio. The price mentioned was $2 million. Sydney thought it was a great offer—more money than *The Great Dictator* was going to cost, and then there was the fact that Charlie needed a studio only every five years or so anyway. Syd went to his brother and told him about the offer, but Charlie was preoccupied with some sound effects and didn't even lift his head. "Oh, tell them to leave us alone," he said. "Just where would I play if I didn't have the studio?"

Sydney had always hovered anxiously over his brother, and now he hovered anxiously over his brother's movie. Stills show him on the set watching Charlie work with a look of smiling approval on his face, and he also documented the picture's production with his 16mm movie camera. (Sydney's color footage provided the fodder for a particularly fascinating documentary by Kevin Brownlow entitled *The Tramp and the Dictator*.)

PRODUCTION OF THE *Great Dictator* got under way in September 1939. The ghetto sequences came first and took two months. In November, Chaplin shot the scenes with Reginald Gardiner in the airplane, while in December he worked on the palace scenes. January brought Jack Oakie as Napaloni. The ballet with the globe took six days to shoot—three days in December 1939, followed by three days of retakes in January and February 1940.

Chaplin loved Oakie's bombastic burlesque of the crass Mussolini and nicknamed him "Muscles." He also made a habit of challenging him. For a scene where Napaloni is forced to sit on a tiny child's chair while Hynkel is seated on a raised dais, Oakie did a take of surprise.

"All right, comedian," said Chaplin. "What do you do now?"

Oakie milked it, doing a series of takes right into the camera.

"OK," interrupted Chaplin. "Cut! Good. You see, Muscles, I always try to get three or four laughs where most comics just get one."

Chaplin spent a lot of time complaining about the staffing demanded by the unions. Makeup men, for instance. "What's a makeup man?" he asked Oakie one day. "I've been putting [this mustache] on my face long before he was born!"

Chaplin also worried about petty economies. One day he decided he needed an apron for Paulette Goddard. He told the wardrobe man to get one for the next day's shooting. It looked right and Chaplin was pleased.

A month later, he decided to retake the scene, but the apron was gone. The wardrobe man explained that he had sent the apron back to Western Costume.

"Western Costume!" Chaplin yelled. "*Western Costume!!* You could have walked across the street and bought an apron for fifteen cents. For fifteen cents, the apron would have belonged to us, not Western Costume!"

So Western Costume once again got the call to send the apron back. Oakie estimated that the rental of the apron, and the special messengers taking it back and forth to the studio cost around $400—the sort of expense that Chaplin would reliably fixate on, even though the picture itself was costing well over a million dollars.

Watching his boss run the studio, Dan James came to the conclusion that, "He hated [that] he couldn't do everything himself. If only he could be behind the camera, as well as in front." James believed that "he didn't [want] to get the best men, he wanted people he could push around." Similarly, James thought the casting director was "indifferent. . . . The small parts [were] played badly—[a] shame. [Chaplin] was hampered by having too many things to do." Ultimately—and ironically—James said that, "Charlie Chaplin's world was not a democracy."

One night, after the crew had gone home, Chaplin told Oakie to pull up a chair. Chaplin was clearly exhausted, had a towel wrapped around his neck but was in a reminiscent mood. "You know," he told Oakie, "I miss the click, click, click of those good, old fashioned hand-cranked cameras. I could hear the beat of the camera and time every one of my movements to its rhythm." Oakie suddenly realized that the silence of the cameras used for sound made Chaplin's job more difficult, because he had to establish a rhythm internally.

Chaplin went on to talk about the Keystone Cops, how they would rush into a scene swinging their clubs in a hurly-burly fashion. "I slowed all that down. I gave it tempo. First I'd find the target, like the villain's head, then I'd take off his hat and picking a good spot, I'd aim before hitting it with my club. Then I'd turn the head a little and hit it again, then turn it again to an even better spot and hit it again. I would get four laughs with one gag, just by slowing it down with deliberate timing."

The two comedians sat quietly for a while. Oakie looked at Chaplin's face and realized that the gears in his head never stopped spinning. Many nights Chaplin would have to be helped into his car, and James and the rest of the crew would wonder if he might have to take time off, but Chaplin made it to the studio every morning. "He was pretty happy," said James. "He had a damned good life. He knew how good he was. [I] never saw him significantly depressed."

In February Chaplin turned to the outdoor battle scenes that opened the picture, shot on land in the San Fernando Valley that Syd rented. Big Bertha, the huge cannon that figures in the opening sequence of the film, was actually made out of wood, but nevertheless weighed close to three tons.

At this point, the picture was more or less on schedule.

By the end of March, Chaplin had shot most of the picture, and he turned to the writing of the final speech. And then he began to worry. In the late summer, he delegated responsibility for the musical score to Meredith Willson and began fussing over the ghetto sequences again. Dan James found Willson "very capable . . . but Chaplin only accepted . . . his work . . . unwillingly." James said that Chaplin asked David Raksin to ghostwrite the music for the ghetto sequences.

Karl Struss found Chaplin's working methods . . . *unusual*. "Charlie would get there between nine and ten in the morning, and the first thing he would do would be to go into the projection room and look at yesterday's dailies. So that would take an hour, and then he'd go on the set. One day we were out on location, six o'clock at night, with the sun going down. Three hundred people on the set and for the lack of one lousy shot, he had to call everybody back the next day. I said to him, 'Charlie, why don't you start shooting an hour earlier in the morning?' He didn't want to start shooting that early, he said. He worked on a short day.

"He never seemed to give the vocal part of the film a thought; he never seemed to worry that this was his first talkie." Struss remembered that there were stories in the papers speculating about whether or not Chaplin and Paulette Goddard were married. Struss thought they must be, if only because, "He talked to her in ways that you'd never talk to a girl you weren't married to. He would ride her until she would break down and cry, and then he'd tell her to go to her room until she behaved herself; then she could come back on the set.

"The trouble with Paulette was that she simply didn't have the voice for the type of scene he wanted her to enact. It was her voice; it was very shrill, and he wanted something soft and mellow and she couldn't do it. The more he rode her, the more she froze."

Dan James remembered that as a director Chaplin was "extremely difficult." It took what James remembered as twenty-seven takes for Goddard to capture the proper mood for the last close-up of the picture, even after multiple demonstrations by Chaplin of how he wanted her to play the scene. A complicating factor was the obvious breakdown of the relationship. "There was anger on both sides," said James.

The idea of Fanny Brice as Hynkel's Jewish wife unfortunately died, while Chaplin took a gradual dislike to Henry Daniell, who played Chaplin's version of Goebbels with his customary icy hauteur. "Daniell's timing was very hard for him [Chaplin] to work against and he began to develop a hatred of Daniell," said James. "'He's trying to sabotage me.' And at the same time, he had a curious respect for Daniell, as if Daniell was a real actor and he was just a Karno man. He was really afraid to come out and tell Daniell off."

IN SOME NOTES for the film, someone besides Chaplin wrote: "First picture in which the story is bigger than the little Tramp." The culmination of the film was the closing speech, which Chaplin had firmly decided on in preproduction.

James's notes for November 9, 1939, are more or less the close of the speech: "Hannah! Do you hear me? Come! Look up: the clouds are lifting—the sun is breaking thru. Look up, Hannah. . . . We are coming out of the darkness into the light. We are coming into a new world, a beautiful world of reason, where men will rise above hate and greed and brutality. Look up, Hannah!"

It's not always clear whether James's notes are literal transcriptions of Chaplin's ideas, or James's own thoughts, but they often match ideas in the final version. One page, noted as "Handed to W.D. [Wheeler Dryden] by Dan James, May 4, 1939," includes, "Only a fool will despise another man. . . . No man can afford to despise another. Within each man is the history of hundreds and millions of years, and a direct ancestral line to God himself. For it is written in the 17th chapter of St. Luke—the Kingdom of God is within man— not within ONE man but within all men. If Christ was the son of God, so are we!"

Another: "There is no promised land—it's a promised world awaiting you—free and open to everybody. Nobody owns it—not for long—except the six feet of earth he's buried in. A man in his life may own many acres—but in the end—a fraction of an acre is enough for him. And the wind comes and blows his dust away."

One notation says "Copy of Charlie's Speech as written by C.C. on 9 November 1939. It's in fragmentary form and he's still working on it." Another note, not in Chaplin's hand, has a list of key words for "The Final Speech, 5 June 1940." The words are Reason, Beauty, Freedom, Happiness, Imagination, Adventure, Kindness, Goodness, Love, Gentleness, Progress, Science, Humanity, Tolerance, and Democracy.

Beginning on June 23, 1940, Chaplin began writing the final draft of the speech. Chaplin shot four takes of the speech on June 28, four more on July 1. He kicked Dan James and Bob Meltzer, his other assistant, off the set, telling them, "I can feel those hostile stares. Go outside. Get out." Chaplin finished shooting the film on July 9 and began editing. As was usually the case, he went back for retakes in August and September.

It WAS AT this point that Hedda Hopper began criticizing a picture nobody had seen, simply because she didn't think Chaplin could pull it off: "With the condition of the world as it is today, it will take a generation before any of us can laugh at Mr. Hitler. I doubt if it will ever be released. Like England and France, Charlie waited too long."

This was the first strike from a woman whose animus toward Chaplin would become obsessive. Hopper's hatred of Chaplin was partially political—she would be a founder of the Motion Picture

Alliance for the Preservation of American Ideals, which helped bring about the 1947 House of Representatives investigation of Communism in the movie industry. She was on persistent lookout for the termites she believed to be eating the foundations of the Republic, as in a note passed to Richard Nixon: "A survey [Hopper] has made in Hollywood indicates to her that Jews and negroes are spreading rumors that RN is anti-labor."

And part of her dislike was intensely personal and derived from rage about Chaplin's penchant for young girls. When Hopper had been a young actress, she became the fifth wife of DeWolf Hopper. He was a noted roué nearly thirty years older than his new wife, famous for his recitation of "Casey at the Bat." They eventually divorced, leaving her with a son—William Hopper earned some notice as Natalie Wood's father in *Rebel Without a Cause* and as Paul Drake in the *Perry Mason* TV series. After the divorce, financial support from her ex was lacking, so Hopper was forced into a catch-as-catch-can career as a character actress, but the *Los Angeles Times* providentially came to her rescue when she began writing her gossip column in 1938.

If Chaplin read Hopper's column, he pretended not to notice it. Nor did he worry overmuch about the Communism of Dan James and Bob Meltzer—yet another example of Chaplin utilizing people like someone impatiently flipping through magazines. "He picked them up one by one," said his friend Harry Crocker, "scanned . . . them, dropped them." Crocker also remarked on "Charlie's desire to please the individual to whom he was talking by being as close as possible an approximation of the idea which that person held of him."

Dan James's memories of Chaplin were almost entirely positive. "He did not read deeply, but he felt deeply everything that happened. The end of *Modern Times*, for instance, reflected perfectly the optimism of the New Deal period; already by 1934 and 1935 he had a sense of that. He had probably never read Marx . . . but he got it. He had a sixth sense about a lot of things."

In James's view, Chaplin was far too self-centered and independent to be prey to any dogmas but his own. "Chaplin called himself an anarchist. . . . He was certainly a libertarian. He saw Stalin as a dangerous dictator very early and Bob [Meltzer] and I had difficulty getting him to leave Stalin out of the last speech in *The Great Dictator*. . . . He was right and we were wrong. He was horrified by the Soviet/German pact.

"His description of himself as an anarchist is as good as any. He believed in human freedom and human dignity. He hated and suspected the machine, even though it was the motion picture machine that gave him his life. I would say that he was anti-capitalist, anti-organizational.

"He was always fascinated with people of the left. One of the people he wanted to meet was Harry Bridges, of the Longshoreman's Union. I fixed up a meeting and they took to each other immediately. Chaplin talked about the beauty of labor and described how in [Bali] he had heard the fishermen sing as they went out in their boats. Harry said, 'I think you would have found that it was the old men on the shore, the ones who had given up going to sea, who did the singing.'"

Chaplin's employment of two avowed Communists raised eyebrows, but it should be pointed out that he also hired Karl Struss. The great cameraman was a political conservative who had been interned for a time during World War I for suspicions of untoward sympathies for the Kaiser. Chaplin also hired the anticommunist Adolphe Menjou to star in *A Woman of Paris* in 1923. Chaplin would hire anybody he thought could make his pictures better, regardless of politics.

The professional trajectory of Dan James proved typical: joining the Party in the 1930s; leaving it in the 1940s; being punished in the 1950s.

Dan James avoided combat in World War II because of a history of tuberculosis. He and his wife cowrote the hit Broadway musical *Bloomer Girl*. They resigned from the Communist Party in 1948, were subpoenaed by the House Un-American Activities Committee in 1951, and refused to name names. After that they were blacklisted. James worked as a pseudonymous screenwriter on such films as *The Beast from 20,000 Fathoms*, *Revolt in the Big House*, and *The Giant Behemoth*. He spent years working in Los Angeles with Latino writers, and put that experience to use writing the novel *Famous All Over*

Town under the name Danny Santiago. James's friend John Gregory Dunne revealed that Danny Santiago was a seventy-three-year-old Caucasian, resulting in an early convulsion regarding cultural appropriation, or, as it used to be called, imagination. Dan James died in Monterey at the age of seventy-seven.

Chaplin finally wrapped *The Great Dictator* after 168 days of shooting and nearly a half million feet of exposed film on the way to a final cut of 11,625 feet. The cost was $1.4 million, a very high figure considering that the film couldn't be shown in Germany, Italy, or Occupied Europe, which included France, Belgium, and the Netherlands, not to mention parts of South America.

On September 4, 1940, Chaplin had dinner with Groucho Marx at Chasen's restaurant. He was obviously happy with his film. "He was in high humor—unusual for him," Marx wrote his friend Arthur Sheekman. "He told me among other things that he's not Jewish, but wishes he were. He said he is part Scotch, English and Gypsy, but I think he is not quite sure what he is."

As with *Modern Times*, the censors at the Production Code office approached the film and its creator on bended knee. Joe Breen's letter to the Chaplin studio asked only that the word "lousy" be cut. Breen went on to say that he was "considerably embarrassed" by the request, but the word was expressly forbidden by the Production Code and that was that. Breen wrote Alf Reeves "how very, very much we enjoyed *The Great Dictator*. It is superb screen entertainment and marks Mr. Chaplin, I think, as our greatest artist."

As CHAPLIN'S FIRST fully talking picture, not to mention a satire of Hitler, *The Great Dictator* was a full-fledged Event. When *Life* magazine printed a portrait of Chaplin as Hynkel without his permission, he sued. They didn't take it personally; a month before release, *Life* went ahead and printed an entire feature on the picture with nearly thirty stills—probably a way of defusing the lawsuit.

Just before *The Great Dictator* was released, Chaplin gave an interview to *Look* magazine in which he said that, "To me, the funniest thing in the world can be the ridicule of phonies and stuffed shirts in high places. The bigger the phony you have to work on, the better chance you have for a funny picture—and it would be difficult to find another phony as big as Hitler. . . . Hitler, to me, beneath that stern and foreboding appearance he gives in newsreels and news photos, actually is a small, mean and petty neuresthenic. Mussolini suggests an entirely different character—loud, noisy, boastful, a peasant at heart." He went on to offer to supply prints of the picture free of charge to any totalitarian country.

Paulette Goddard believed the film would be a big hit. "It's the best part I'll ever have," she burbled to a reporter. That assertion soon segued to a decision about what she would wear to the premiere at the Carthay Circle Theatre in Los Angeles. "I'm going to buy a long ermine coat with an ermine hood and a tie-up round the middle—rather like a bath robe."

Four days before *The Great Dictator* premiered, Syd wrote his brother from Havana, where he was cooling his heels after Congress strengthened immigration laws to forestall a flood of refugees (read: Jews) arriving from Fascist Europe. "I just want to wish you the best of luck & hope with all my heart it will prove your masterpiece, it deserves to be because you have worked hard & put a great deal of money into it & I am sure your efforts will be appreciated by the public."

Syd was obviously still betwixt and between and proceeded to float a trial balloon wherein he could become Charlie's supervisor of foreign contracts "*without* interfering with your present system of distribution."

Lisa Stein Haven, Syd's biographer, believes that between the sexual assault of 1929, and Syd's incessant oversight of his work, Charlie might have grown a trifle weary of his brother. In any case, he didn't take Syd up on his offer. One way or another Syd returned to America and managed to get his money out of France. From 1942 to 1948 Syd was more or less consistently in Palm Springs, enjoying a life of leisure and parties while living in a newly purchased trailer which he parked in a succession of the popular trailer parks that dotted the Springs. In 1948 Syd returned to his lush life in the South of France.

CHAPLIN'S OPTIMISM ABOUT *The Great Dictator* was confirmed by the critics. *Variety* said that "the picture has had much advance publicity, and the curiosity aroused in its connection no doubt is second only to that which was built up for *Gone With the Wind*."

President Roosevelt was invited to the opening in New York on October 15, 1940, but couldn't attend and sent FDR Jr. The opening night, *Variety* said, had some rocky moments, because the audience had been misled by "some of the very amusing still photographs." The crowd, said the paper, was "cool to the Chaplin effort and hesitant to respond to its theme, except in the hilarious farcical scenes. . . . The first audience reaction was that Chaplin should stick to his funny hat, cane and shoes and leave world politics to the politicians."

But *Variety* ultimately realized that Chaplin had, against all odds, accomplished something remarkable: "*The Great Dictator* is one of those milestones by which films since their early, faltering days have been led to renewed inspiration and realization of hidden opportunities. . . . In *The Great Dictator*, Chaplin has employed the full force of the screen's expressive power to crystalize the timely and encouraging idea that the world is only half-crazy and that sanity has not completely fled from human experience."

Chaplin's silent features have a blithe momentum, with most sequences carefully building toward the climax. No matter the difficulties encountered in production, in the cutting room Chaplin was ruthless about narrative. He understood that flow was crucial, and the silent features mostly feel seamless.

Chaplin's sound pictures are a different matter. Their rhythm is baggier, the running times are extended, the characters less firm. Mostly, this is because he saw sound as lending itself to political and social comment alternating with the expected amounts of comedy, which meant he had more to pack in. *The Great Dictator* is a particularly audacious mixture of satire, slapstick, tragedy, propaganda, and music hall jokes out of the Karno days:

"How's the gas?" asks the pilot of a falling plane.

"Terrible, kept me awake all night," replies Charlie.

The film also provided yet more evidence of Chaplin's psychological grasp of character that coexisted with his protean acting skills. His Adenoid Hynkel is a comic X-ray of the authoritarian personality: endless vanity fueled by pathetic insecurity that can only be quelled by absolute obedience. As Hynkel, Chaplin captures both howling fury and an almost coquettish wheedling, all communicated through a soft English diction that indicated Chaplin had done a lot of work ridding himself of his working-class accent.

"He didn't just scream and bawl," said Alistair Cooke of Hitler's speeches. "And he also had this slightly fancy toss of the hand, you know. He didn't always give the full rigid salute. I remember Chaplin telling me about the dance that he was going to do with the globe . . . which did seem like a poetic extension of Hitler. But Hitler also made very delicate gestures with his hands. Chaplin had the most beautiful, very small hands, you know, like ivory knick-knacks. . . . It's the only film I know that gives this side of Hitler."

Many critics have objected to the final speech, in which Chaplin steps out of character and addresses the audience as Charlie Chaplin—the twentieth century's emblematic comic personality using his skills to delegitimize the century's greatest threat to freedom, to art, to civilization: an apostle of compassion engaging in mortal combat with a promulgator of hate. Many people then and now consider the speech little more than sentimental utopianism, but Chaplin's passion is overwhelming:

"Greed has poisoned men's souls—has barricaded the world with hate—has goose-stepped us into misery and bloodshed. . . . Machinery that gives abundance has left us in want. Our knowledge has made us cynical; our cleverness hard and unkind. We think too much and feel too little. More than machinery we need humanity. More than cleverness we need kindness and gentleness. Without these qualities, life will be violent and all will be lost."

True then, true today.

Variety reprinted the speech in full, and did an extensive interview with Chaplin in which he tried to deny that he was speaking as himself rather than his character. "There have been objections," Chaplin said, "that the speech was not in keeping with the general practice of 'good motion picture making.' I don't agree. Others have complained that it is out of character. I don't agree on that either.

"It is not as unbelievable as they think to have the meek barber make such a speech. I could have finished it with a cliché, but that would have been still harder to believe. I could have had him triumphant, but that wouldn't have been true to life. I could have had him kick the storm troopers out of his way and escape, then showed him with Paulette Goddard in the setting sun, approaching America, the land of freedom and hope. But if you want to get on the subject of credulity, then they'd have the immigration authorities to deal with before they got into America.

"It seems entirely conceivable to me that the little barber, pushed into the position he was, could have made the speech he did. It was all the pent-up emotion resulting from the persecution he and those he loved had been subjected to. He was in a stage where he was semi-hypnotized by the situation. He was no longer the barber, nor was he the dictator, nor was he me. He was a combination of all three."

Chaplin's own take on the reviewers who objected to the final speech was that they had "a perceived notion of what I was going to do, based on what they had seen in the past. They had a groove all planned for me and I didn't fall into it. I felt I had to do something different, because times are different. There are grave things happening in the world and I wanted, in my way, to reflect them. I don't pretend to be a propagandist, but I felt I must cry out against persecution. . . .

"The world isn't a pleasant place in all its aspects, and there's no reason to make it appear that way in a picture. Furthermore, what critics forget is that I try to create enjoyment by creating emotions. I have never limited myself to the single emotion of laughter. I have attempted to stir up all sorts of emotions. The more varied the ones I create, the more enjoyable the picture."

Geraldine Chaplin believed the final speech to be one of her father's finest moments: "He steps up to the microphone, he's a little barber and then he's pretending to be the dictator. Then the camera comes in close and he starts speaking and the transformation—suddenly he's no longer the Jewish barber, he's no longer the dictator, he becomes Charles Chaplin speaking to the world. The way his face changes—I've watched that a million times. He becomes Charles Chaplin, without taking the makeup off, without anything; suddenly his face, it becomes older, you see the lines on it, and you see the man come out."

The film opened in London in December 1940—the height of the

Blitz. The critic C. A. Lejeune opined that the film was "uneven . . . harsh at some moments, sentimental at others, brilliant, even noble in many parts. . . . The ghost of every trick that Chaplin has ever played is in the film somewhere. Watching it, your memory ranges back to *The Pilgrim, The Kid, Shoulder Arms,* even further to the plain, downright days of custard-pie and mallet."

There were criticisms that Chaplin had singled out dictators of the right, while leaving out dictators of the left. "I'm not working in the political arena," he said with a straight face. "I'm working in the human arena. . . . Had I included Stalin, I would surely been getting into politics because there was no reason to include him from the standpoint I was taking. He may be a dictator, but he's not persecuting helpless people because they are Jews, or Chinese, or Mohammedan, or because he doesn't like the shape of their eyebrows." (History has since proven that Stalin was, among other things, a vicious anti-Semite and homophobe. Chaplin was completely wrong.)

Variety noted that Chaplin spoke with "a curious mixture of humbleness and the blazing conviction that he is right, his critics wrong, on all but one point—the picture's length. He said he thinks he has culled from it every possible bit of footage without removing whole sequences. He's anxious, he averred, to cut more if he can be shown how it can be done."

In retrospect, it can be seen that *The Great Dictator* was the high-water mark of Chaplin's political and social relevance. Everybody in Hollywood thought Chaplin was insane to make an antifascist film at a time of rampant isolationism. It was an opinion shared by Sydney, who believed the film was commercially dubious as well as politically dangerous. But Chaplin's indifference about what other people thought tended to make his films better, while considerably complicating his life.

Released a year before Pearl Harbor, *The Great Dictator* portrayed Jews as an oppressed minority, served as a passionate clarion call for intervention, and, in Chaplin's inspired burlesque of Hitler, was often uproariously funny in the bargain.

The Great Dictator ran for fifteen weeks in New York—a huge commercial achievement. Produced for $1.4 million, it returned rentals of $5 million to United Artists, producing a clear profit to Chaplin of about $3 million, despite the fact that most of Europe never saw the picture until after the war. The film nobody in Hollywood wanted proved to be a great hit.

As Arthur Schlesinger Jr. said, "Historically, it was one of the earliest movies to express any kind of repugnance against Hitler and Nazism, and it did so, it seems to me, with sublime artistry. It may be in some ways Chaplin's most memorable movie, and the part of the film that was most widely criticized at the time—that is, the concluding speech, might have seemed mawkish at the time, but in the context of the nuclear age, I think it has great resonance and great power."

Despite the cavils of critics in 1940 and since, *The Great Dictator* has retained its hold on audiences, and remains a popular picture, perhaps because its subject is perennially relevant—the authoritarian mindset is always with us. While there are certainly more perfect films, there are very few as courageous. Chaplin was never more confident of his physical virtuosity—the scene of Hynkel dancing with the globe is immediately followed by the Jewish barber shaving a client to Brahms' Hungarian Rhapsody. First he shows you the dictator's megalomania, then the barber's unassuming expertise, both characters defined by movement set to music.

As for theoretical pro-Communist leanings, *The Great Dictator* didn't receive a showing in Russia until March of 1989, when Raisa Gorbachev hosted a screening. By that time, Charlie Chaplin had been in his grave for twelve years.

CHAPTER 7

The evening before Franklin Roosevelt's third inauguration, Chaplin read the final speech from *The Great Dictator* in Washington, D.C. The next day he attended the inauguration and repeated the speech for the Daughters of the American Revolution and a national radio audience. And then he left the speech from *The Great Dictator* behind and began making other speeches that would change his life.

In Hollywood, things were changing. The Third Reich had forced dozens of German artists out of the country, which brought about the unintended consequence of enriching the creative life of America. Fritz Lang, Billy Wilder, and Thomas Mann all arrived and maintained—or in Wilder's case, began—stellar careers. Among the émigrés, Chaplin was close to Lion Feuchtwanger, the author of *Jew Süss*, his wife, Marta, and the composer Hanns Eisler

Marta Feuchtwanger would assert that "The whole Hollywood film population gave help to the European immigration. It should never be forgotten how many lives and existences were saved by their great generosity." There were organizations such as the European Film Fund, organized by the agent Paul Kohner and director Ernst Lubitsch, where successful émigrés tithed 1 percent of their salaries to a fund managed by Kohner, who disbursed stipends to newly arrived immigrants. It could be as little as $50 a week, but that was enough to stave off starvation until jobs came through. Kohner also put the arm on the studios to hire German actors, writers, and directors on minimum contracts, even if there was no work for them. Most of the studios complied.

As always, Chaplin avoided joining any antifascist organizations, but he made contributions nonetheless. Marta Feuchtwanger would remember that, "Chaplin was not part of the general effort. He gave privately and unstingily. I remember also that he chose to receive [the émigrés] at his parties with the greatest attention, interrupting the conversation with the Rockefellers and Huntington Hartfords to meet them at the door, and to introduce the newly arrived with almost old-fashioned chivalry."

OUTSIDE HOLLYWOOD, THINGS were changing in ways that would greatly complicate Chaplin's life. In the 1942 midterms, the Democrats took a beating, losing forty-five seats in the House and eight in the Senate. Nineteen forty-six would be worse; the Republicans took both houses of Congress for the first time since 1928. By that time, FDR was dead and Harry Truman was president. As one journalist pointed out, "between April, 1945, when Franklin D. Roosevelt's death thrust Harry S. Truman into office and January, 1953, when Truman handed the Presidency to Dwight D. Eisenhower, the war in Europe ended, Hitler killed himself, the United States dropped two atomic bombs on Japan, the Cold War began, the state of Israel came into being, the Soviet Union developed its own nuclear weapons, China underwent a Communist revolution, the West created NATO, the world created the United Nations, and the Korean War began. One could go on."

As the political climate shifted, *The Great Dictator* became a (literal) red flag for isolationists. In September 1941, a congressional subcommittee opened a hearing into pro-war propaganda. North Dakota senator Gerald Nye, a committed isolationist with ties to the America First movement, charged that "dangerous propaganda is . . . unloosed upon all the way from sixty to eighty million people a week who go into moving picture theaters of this country to be entertained."

Nye spent a good deal of time denying that he was anti-Semitic, while simultaneously emphasizing the prominence of Jews in the movie industry, which resulted, he believed, in "the most vicious propaganda that has ever been unloosed upon a civilized people." He specifically cited *The Great Dictator*, as well as *Escape, That Hamilton Woman*, and *Man Hunt*, among others.

In September 1941, Chaplin received a congressional subpoena to testify about *The Great Dictator.* His lawyers prepared material regarding the film, but he was never called to testify, as the December attack on Pearl Harbor forced the Senate Subcommittee on War Propaganda to disband.

Nye was correct in at least one respect. The films he cited were indeed interventionist propaganda. *The Great Dictator*, he said, "was a portrayal by a great artist, not a citizen of our country, though he has resided here a long, long while, that could not do other than build within the mind and heart of those who watched it something of hatred, detestation of conditions and of leadership that existed abroad."

In other words, Chaplin's film succeeded in its purpose.

IN JUNE 1942, Chaplin and Paulette Goddard finalized the split that had been obvious to everybody during the making of *The Great Dictator*. Loyd Wright, Chaplin's attorney, deputized an El Paso lawyer named Harris Walthall to handle Chaplin's end of the divorce. Walthall forwarded a certified copy of the divorce decree, and pointed out to Wright that the only evidence of the marriage was "the affidavits of Miss Goddard and another party, probably her mother, to the effect that the marriage was entered into in Canton, China." The attorney went on to say that, "all the publicity which I have seen in the press is to the effect that Mr. Chaplin denied existence of the marriage and certainly there is no such acknowledgement in the official records."

Chaplin obviously still felt they could work together. In April 1944, Goddard signed a new contract with Paramount for twelve pictures at the rate of two per year. The Paramount contract gave her the right to make one picture a year for someone besides Paramount, and in May she signed a deal with Chaplin for first call on her services for that outside picture. In return, Chaplin agreed to pay her 50 percent of the net profits from the picture against a guarantee of $100,000.

THE PREVAILING ATTITUDE toward Chaplin in Hollywood was that he was a brilliant cheapskate. Actually, if his own salary is concerned, he had a bifurcated attitude; most of his money was invested in either the stock market or the studio. According to the Internal Revenue Service, in 1939 Chaplin's salary from the studio was $152,000— more than a lot of studio heads paid themselves—Walt Disney's salary was $85,000, Sam Goldwyn's was $107,000. On the other hand, there were many who paid themselves more than Chaplin. David Selznick paid himself $185,500 and William LeBaron, executive producer at Paramount, earned $182,000.

If you take star salaries into account, Chaplin was severely underpaying himself. That same year, Gary Cooper earned $482,820, while Bing Crosby made $250,000. Even Fred MacMurray made more than Chaplin: $240,333. As for the women, it seems that a great star got great money. Ginger Rogers made $219,500, while Claudette Colbert earned $150,079. On the other hand, Barbara Stanwyck seems to have been severely underpaid at $92,500.

While Chaplin's money was of some interest, as far as the FBI was concerned there had been nothing of interest in Chaplin's politics or sex life since 1923. The scandalous divorce from Lita Grey in 1927, the Popular Front politics of *Modern Times*, and the intensely political *The Great Dictator* all mostly passed without notice as far as the Bureau was concerned.

But in 1942 the Bureau sailed into the Chaplin business full-time. The proximate cause consisted of a series of speeches Chaplin made supporting the efforts of America's Soviet allies in the war against Hitler. Specifically, it involved the idea of America opening a second front against Germany in order to lessen the burden on the Russians.

It began with a speech for the American Committee for Russian War Relief in San Francisco on May 18, 1942. The invitation came just a day before the speech—Ambassador Joseph Davies, the original speaker, came down with laryngitis, and Chaplin was asked to stand in for him. Because he had so little time to prepare, Chaplin decided to wing it. After listening to some preliminary speeches that he felt were unnecessarily temporizing, he stepped to the podium and let it rip.

Chaplin began with a ringing cry of "Comrades!" which certainly got everybody's attention. The speech didn't have a specific political viewpoint; his central point was that Russia was now American's ally, and deserved America's full support. Scheduled for four minutes, Chaplin got carried away and ended up speaking for forty minutes.

Dan James would come to believe that the final speech of *The Great Dictator* "started [Chaplin] off [with a] Messiah complex," which inevitably led to the speech in San Francisco and its successors. Another way of putting it was that it was a new venue for expressing Chaplin's social consciousness, which James believed to be entirely sincere and deeply felt.

An actor working overtime to please an audience can be a dangerous thing.

"I am not a Communist, I am a human being, and I think I know the reactions of human beings. The Communists are no different from anyone else; whether they lose an arm or leg, they suffer as all of us do, and die as all of us die. And the Communist mother is the same as any other mother. When she receives the tragic news that her sons will not return, she weeps as other mothers weep. I don't have to be a Communist to know that, at this moment, Russian mothers are doing a lot of weeping and their sons are doing a lot of dying."

Winding up, Chaplin roared, "Stalin wants it, Roosevelt has called for it, so let's all call for it—let's open a Second Front now!"

Chaplin's speech was greeted with tumultuous applause. Afterward, John Garfield told Chaplin, "You have a lot of courage." Chaplin found this disturbing, because he didn't think his stance was particularly controversial. As he would write years later, "I dislike being told whom to kill and what to die for—and all in the name of patriotism. . . . The fact is I am no patriot—not for moral or intellectual reasons alone, but because I have no feeling for it. How can one tolerate patriotism when six million Jews were murdered in its name? Some might say that was in Germany; nevertheless, those murderous cells lie dormant in every nation."

What Chaplin failed to understand was that many Americans distrusted the alliance with Russia and thought Germany fighting Russia was a case of enemy fighting enemy—ultimately good for America.

The San Francisco speech led to several more in the same vein in Chicago and New York, all of which were carefully monitored by the FBI. James Kevin McGuinness, a writer and producer at MGM, would write that the conservative Motion Picture Alliance, the primary instigator of the 1947 hearings of the House Un-American Activities Committee, was formed because its members "were tired of having their industry represented by Charlie Chaplin demanding a Second Front at Carnegie Hall."

The Carnegie Hall speech took place on October 16, 1942. Among the other speakers were I. F. Stone, Carl Van Vechten, and Lillian Hellman. Orson Welles introduced Chaplin, who began his half hour speech by once again getting everyone's attention: "Dear Comrades. Yes, I mean Comrades. When one sees the magnificent fight the Russian people are putting up, it is a pleasure and a privilege to use the word 'comrade.' "

He compared FDR to Washington, Jefferson, and Lincoln, and praised the president for releasing Earl Browder—the former general secretary of the Communist Party of the USA—from jail. Chaplin made an encore appearance at the end of the evening by raising his fingers in the V sign and telling the crowd that it stood for "victory and for '2'—a second front."

There were several more of these speeches, including one at the Hotel Pennsylvania in New York on December 3. As one FBI informant reported, "The speeches enumerated therein were the usual pro-Soviet 'cultural' propaganda . . . typical fellow-traveler speeches: snide and would-be subtle cracks at our 'capitalist' system without, however, any outright subversive statements, plus the usual bleeding-heart stuff about the valiant Soviet people and our own ill-housed, ill-clad and ill-nourished."

The informant reported that Chaplin said, "We are fighting this war to preserve art and culture. In Hollywood that will be a difficult task. The moment we try to inject life into the movie art we have trouble with the Hays office—the moment you try to tell the people the truth about life we run up against censorship.

"We must be more tolerant of the Russian system. Let's stop all this nonsense and evasion and call it what it is: the Communist system. And that Communist system is a very convenient ally. They have been very convenient for us up to now. They did the real fighting for us. Why should anyone object to the Communist system. . . . I am getting fed up with hearing people say: But the Russians are not fighting for us—they are fighting for themselves. Well, what nation isn't?

"I am not a Communist, but I . . . feel proud to say that I feel pretty pro-Communist. I don't want any radical change. I want an evolutionary change. I don't want to go back to the days of rugged individualism. I don't want to go back to the days of frustration. I don't want to go back to the days of 1929. . . . I don't want to go back to a sick and crazy world like the one we had and which produced Hitler and Hitlerism. No, we must do better than that."

Less than two weeks later, Chaplin made an appearance on a radio show called *America Looks Abroad*, a roundtable show about politics that was a weekly feature on KFWB, owned and operated by Warner Bros. The host was a friend of Chaplin's named Robert Arden, while the other guests included Nigel Bruce, Sir Cedric Hardwicke, the director Frank Lloyd, and the biographer Emil Ludwig. The topic was "How much unity do we have to have to bring the war to a successful conclusion?"

"Do we have unity?" Arden asked Chaplin.

"By no means," he replied. "We have a great deal of prejudice, which I think we know if we're very clear-minded. We know that this prejudice comes from a bugaboo about Communism. You find all your 'scare sisters' and the columnists, accusing and laying everything and all the fear of disunity to Communism. . . . The public are getting confused on this issue."

Chaplin went on to say, "Every Communist in this country has subordinated his interests for the one purpose and for the sole purpose of victory. . . . We must have a unity and only by the strength of unity can we win this war. We must have the full strength of . . . the capitalists to the Communists. And they must subordinate their interests for at least the duration of the war in order that we shall achieve victory. And it's not going to be an easy task."

The subject turned to Fascism, and Chaplin jumped in. "Well, un-doubtedly, I think there is a certain amount of fascism in the United States. I think it's easily recognized if we're honest about it. I've seen it in some of the press. I've seen it as I've said before in the columnists, most certainly in the columnists. Undoubtedly there are certain factions in this country who think they can make a good deal with Hitler. And there are certain factions in this country who fear democracy and who fear the people, and fear the people's desire to make a better world after the war."

Chaplin went on to breezily ignore the 1939 Hitler-Stalin Non-Aggression Pact by saying that "All nations are opportunists. I'm speaking personally. This is perhaps off the record and on the air, but nevertheless it's very personal. Of all those nations, I think Russia has carried out her obligations and the pacts and has kept to them more than perhaps any other nation."

Chaplin's enthusiasm for a second front would be Exhibit A in the political case against him in the postwar years. Alistair Cooke pointed out that "He was anxious to tell strangers what he was not taken in by rather than to say where he stood politically. All his life his much-abused 'radical philosophy' was no more than an auto-matic theme song in favor of peace, humanity, 'the little man' and other desirable abstractions—as hum-drum politicians come out for mother love and lower taxes."

The result of all these rallies for a second front was a growing assumption that Chaplin was more pro-Communist than he was anti-Fascist.

These speeches provoked vociferously hostile pushback from the right in Hollywood and elsewhere. Westbrook Pegler wrote a column in December 1942 that said Chaplin "after years of sly pretending, when an open profession of his political faith would have hurt his business, now that he has all the money he needs and has lost his way with the public, has frankly allied himself with the pro-communist actors and writers of the theater and the movie, who call themselves artists, but who are mostly hams and hacks. . . . I would like to know why Charlie Chaplin has been allowed to stay in the United States about 40 years without becoming a citizen."

Pegler's column was a preview of coming attractions—one of the early examples of the right's continual assertion of an alternate reality, as with Pegler's claim that the public had deserted Chaplin, despite *The Great Dictator*'s huge commercial success.

A few months before Pegler's column, Billy Wilkerson's *Hollywood Reporter* ran a nasty column along the lines of "America—Love It or Leave It," which suggested that Chaplin return to England, where he and his wallet would be welcomed with open arms.

Dalton Trumbo, then laboring in the MGM vineyard, wrote a letter in response to the *Reporter*: "Germany for Germans! Send the Jews back to Palestine! If you dare raise your voice, if you don't like it here Thomas Mann, Albert Einstein, Lion Feuchtwanger . . . Alexander Seversky, Charles Chaplin, then go back where you came from!

"Such dangerous slogans, acceptable in Nazi Germany, become tragically dangerous in a democracy based upon the free commingling of all races, creeds and nationalities. Mr. Chaplin honors us by living among us. . . . As the most creative mind and the greatest artist motion pictures have produced, they'll be glad to see Charles Chaplin in any anti-fascist country. . . .

"The loudest shouter of 'go back where you came from,' the deadliest enemy of the individual's right to express himself to his government, the arch-opponent of public support for a second front, is a man named Adolf Hitler, who, if he wins the war, will make exceedingly short shrift of [both] the Rambling Reporter and your correspondent."

The Hollywood Reporter did not print Trumbo's letter.

It was around this time that an informant told the FBI that Chaplin was being supplied with black market beef, which resulted in days of surveillance by agents who waited for a car loaded with meat to show up on Summit Drive. No such deliveries were made. At another point, the agents were informed that Chaplin was moving money in order to facilitate a relocation to Mexico, but after investigation it was found that Chaplin was making no efforts to leave the country.

In a private conversation, Chaplin told the journalist Thomas Pryor of *The New York Times* that the reason he so ardently supported a second front was his genuine belief that it would end the war quickly, thus increasing the chances that his sons Charles Jr. and Sydney, both of whom enlisted and saw combat, would survive the war. They did survive, but it was a near thing. Charles Jr. enlisted on October 7, 1943, and Sydney followed on August 21, 1944. Charles Jr. was in the 89th Infantry, while Sydney was in the 65th Infantry. Sydney told his father of his experiences, which horrified Chaplin. Sydney's unit captured a house when a wounded German made a break for it. Sydney was ordered to shoot him.

"You mean kill him?"

"Yes!"

"But he hasn't got his gun . . ."

Sydney shot him—the first and last man he killed in the war. There was a man in Sydney's unit, a Southerner who Sydney believed to be a sadist. The Southerner was ordered to take prisoners back behind the lines, but would instead kill them. Sydney's stories only strengthened Chaplin's innate hatred of war.

Chaplin had always regarded public appearances with a jaundiced eye, as something of a necessary evil, if only because of his core belief that the adulation he received "is given after all, to the little fellow, not me." He understood, as his public did not, that the Tramp was not a comprehensive projection of his personality, but rather an artful, edited distillation of Chaplin's best qualities.

Chaplin's speeches are best understood as a logical extension of the social impulses that animated *Modern Times* and *The Great Dictator*. Besides that, there was his intrinsically against-the-prevailing-winds personality. Idealizing Russia was part and parcel with his pacifism, his attitude toward sex, his refusal to be a part of anything that might be construed as conventional.

His oppositional instincts would prove politically and socially disastrous, as columnists continued to descend. Westbrook Pegler launched an ongoing fusillade of scathing columns castigating Chaplin for everything except the way he combed his hair. At one point he suggested that Chaplin's three divorces were all by themselves sufficient proof of his contempt "for the standard American relationship of marriage, family and home." The process of characterizing Chaplin as a moral leper was under way.

Late in 1942, Richard Hood, the agent in charge of the FBI's Los Angeles office, went to the trouble of checking out Chaplin with a "Special Informant" in the motion picture industry. The informant stated that Chaplin was not particularly popular in the industry because "he is regarded as stingy and unfriendly; however, in view of Pegler's attack against the actor's artistic ability, the tendency is for the motion picture people to defend him."

The informant "stated that regardless of Pegler's opinion, Chaplin very definitely is an artist and has been recognized as such all over the world, and undoubtedly because of their own artistic interests and for the protection of their own industry, [the movie industry had] rallied somewhat to Chaplin's defense against these recent attacks."

The "Special Informant" was almost certainly Cecil B. DeMille, with whom Hood had a close relationship, and whose office at Paramount was regularly involved in intelligence activities within Hollywood on behalf of the Bureau. What is interesting is that DeMille didn't tell Hood that he and Chaplin were friendly, if not exactly friends. DeMille lent his Paradise ranch to Chaplin several times, and the two occasionally talked on the phone.

DeMille was quite conservative, and Chaplin was quite liberal, but they had both been present at the creation of the Hollywood film industry in 1913–1914. But if politics was the actual cause, a woman would serve as the stated reason that Chaplin would be driven from the country. One woman in particular.

CHAPTER 8

Chaplin met Joan Berry in May or June of 1941. She was twenty-two, Chaplin was fifty-three and had just split up with Paulette Goddard.

Berry's real name was Mary Louise Gribble. Her father had killed himself before she was born, after which her mother married a man named Barry. She moved to California in 1938 to become an actress. Instead, she was arrested twice for shoplifting. She would tell the FBI that she had used various aliases over the years, looking for a name that would look good on theater marquees: Mary Louise Berry, Joan Barratt, Mary L. Barratt, Joanne Barry, and Joan Barry were some of the variations, which helps explain why her name is sometimes rendered as "Barry."

For several years she was kept by a local Los Angeles businessman, then became acquainted with J. Paul Getty, with whom she lived for several months. Getty put Berry on his payroll for $150 a month because, he said with a straight face, he was "impressed at the enthusiasm and energy she put into her work."

It was another wealthy man, A. C. Blumenthal, who wrote a letter of introduction so Berry could meet people in the movie industry. She evidently believed a career in the movies, or a career with someone who made movies, would be appropriate.

Chaplin and Berry met at Perino's restaurant, with Chaplin's friend Tim Durant as the go-between. The relationship developed every bit as quickly as Chaplin's other flings, owing to a peculiarity of his character. As Chaplin would note in his memoir, he was only interested in recreational sex when not in his obsessive-compulsive work mode. In mid-1941, he was still basking in the success of *The Great Dictator*, and composing a new musical score for a future reissue of *The Gold Rush*. Berry's timing was excellent.

Alistair Cooke noted, "When Chaplin took to anyone, he was wide open from the start, spontaneous, generous, gabby, confidential, as if taking up again where he had left off with a favorite, long-lost brother. I could see how, if it were a woman who attracted him, he would soon be as deep in intimacy as Macbeth was in blood. . . . Neither in love nor in friendship did he ever tread water. He regularly took a header into deep water."

The relationship didn't take long to develop. Chaplin thought Berry had screen possibilities and signed her to a contract that paid her $75 a week. He also enrolled her in Max Reinhardt's acting school and began writing a script for her, an adaptation of Paul Vincent Carroll's play *Shadow and Substance*, about a maid named Bridget who communes with the Virgin Mary. Chaplin paid $20,000 for the rights to the play and slotted it as Berry's introductory vehicle.

Portrait stills of Berry in costume reveal an attractive, russet-haired woman with sensual features. Robert Arden would tell the FBI that if "[Berry] had played her cards right instead of being so stupid, she would have been Mrs. Chaplin, the star of pictures. . . . Chaplin was definitely in love with her . . . and that if she had acted decent about it, he would have married her."

The affair continued into 1942, although Berry later told the FBI that she continued seeing other men, including Getty. The focus of the FBI's investigation, which in documents was headed "WHITE SLAVE TRAFFIC VIOLATION AND CIVIL RIGHTS AND DO-MESTIC VIOLENCE VIOLATIONS BY CHAPLIN" was a trip Chaplin and Berry took to New York for his speech for the Artists Front to Win the War. On October 2, 1942, Chaplin authorized his studio to buy tickets for Berry and her mother to travel to New York on the Santa Fe railroad.

They left for New York that day. Chaplin followed on October 12. Chaplin's speech wasn't until October 16, and in the interim he and Berry went to dinner several times.

At one point in New York, Chaplin and Berry argued about her relationship with Getty. Chaplin evidently thought Berry might be two-timing him—he knew that both Getty and Berry liked to stay at the Pierre when in New York, and he told Berry "I'll be goddamned if I'll pay the bills for Getty." Berry would tell the FBI that Getty gave her money and liked actresses; she also insisted that she had never slept with him.

After Chaplin's speech, Berry returned with him to the Waldorf Astoria where, the FBI asserted, "the alleged immoral acts took place. The following day Chaplin gave Berry $300 to return to Los Angeles, California. She left on October 28th. Between the time she returned to Los Angeles and January, 1943, she had numerous trysts with Chaplin."

Berry's account of the affair stretches over dozens of single-spaced pages in the FBI interviews. What follows is her version of the relationship:

According to Berry, the sexual relationship did not begin until after the signing of her contract with Chaplin. "I might add here that Chaplin's success in this regard was due to his verbal persuasiveness. I have been told, and from my personal experiences with him I know it to be true, that he is very proud of his success with women along these lines. This verbal persuasiveness of Chaplin's was his violent insistence that he was madly in love with me."

After the deed was done, she spent several days in Chaplin's house, then went to New York via a car that she had been given by Getty. "This was somewhat of a bone of contention between Chaplin and myself, he insisted he was not going to pay any money on a car which somebody else had helped to get [sic]."

Berry said that she quickly became pregnant by Chaplin, and had an abortion arranged by Tim Durant. She liked to accompany Chaplin to the studio, where he was working on *The Gold Rush*. After work, they would dine at Romanoff's. At Christmas 1941, she received a bonus of $1,000. She had been outfitted with a diaphragm, but Chaplin asked her not to use it, and by the end of the year she was again pregnant.

"We were both very much enamored of each other," she said. (Berry often spoke in the self-dramatizing style of bad fiction.) But she was restless, because Chaplin hadn't started production on *Shadow and Substance*, and she was getting bored with training from both Chaplin and Max Reinhardt, whose acting school she attended from January to May of 1942. "In the meantime I was going out with friends and I did not go out with [Chaplin] during this time. I was seeing [MGM producer] Sam Marx and occasionally Paul Getty, when he was in town."

In May of 1942, Berry asked to be released from her contract with Chaplin because she wanted to make a screen test at MGM. That same month she went to Tulsa, where she visited Getty. After that, she came back to Hollywood, and resumed seeing Chaplin. In October Berry and her mother went to New York for Chaplin's speech for the Artists Front, as mentioned earlier.

According to Berry's account, Chaplin told her that Russia had offered him a commissar's position, and he told her he was giving some thought to "going back to Russia," although Chaplin had never visited Russia. She said they had sex in his suite at the Waldorf, after which Chaplin took her to the Pierre Hotel in a cab.

Back in Beverly Hills, Berry resumed seeing Sam Marx. She and Chaplin had a fight over the turmoil she had brought to his life. "Charles told me he was an old man and he could not go through this anymore, that he wanted peace and quiet. (When I gave him peace and quiet, he got bored.)"

They broke up, after which she took an overdose of sleeping pills.

Berry went to stay with Elaine Barrie, the wife of John Barrymore, then in his final stage of alcoholic dissolution. Berry called Chaplin several times, but he refused to speak to her, as did Sam Marx when she called him. She took a bus to Tulsa where she saw J. Paul Getty a few times before returning to Los Angeles in December 1942.

The third week of December, Berry bought a gun. She was continuing to call Chaplin, but he would neither speak to her nor return her calls.

On the night of December 23, she showed up at Chaplin's house with the gun, intending, she said, to kill herself. She broke the glass on a back door and let herself in. "[Chaplin] asked me why I was going to kill myself and I told him that I had been in love with him and we weren't getting anyplace."

Chaplin spent some time getting her to put the gun down. His two sons were in the house, and Berry heard them in the hallway outside Chaplin's bedroom. He left the room to talk to them, at which point the butler asked Chaplin if everything was all right, and he replied that he "could handle the situation." According to Berry, at that point he came back into the room and "we then had an affair"—Berry's way of saying they had sex. "The gun was in the night stand between the two [twin] beds where I could reach it with my right hand. Charles made some remark to the effect that having an affair with a gun nearby was a 'new twist.'"

Berry said Chaplin told her during this last, torturous night that "I've got to have peace. I would rather go to jail for twenty years and have peace. Joan, if you bring this into court, you know what it will be. The newspapers will be after you, your picture will be taken—oh, it will be grand for a couple of months. Then people will forget it."

At some point, Berry went up to "Paulette's" room and saw clothes belonging to another woman, which further inflamed the situation.

For his part, Chaplin resolutely denied they had sex that night, asserting he would never have done such a thing with his sons down the hall and a clearly unbalanced woman wielding a gun.

Soon after this manifestly insane series of events, Berry was taken to the Beverly Hills Police Department on New Year's Day 1943. Chief Anderson said that Berry told them she had no place to sleep and wanted to spend the night in jail. "We thought she was a tramp. She told us all about the guys that she'd been sleeping with: Paul Getty, Hans Ruesch, Chaplin, Durant, Arden, A.C. Blumenthal and Sam Marx."

Berry was tried for vagrancy, sentence to be suspended if she left Beverly Hills and paid her hotel bills. Chaplin gave Arden $705 for Berry's debts, her train ticket, and some spending money. She went to Omaha, where she proceeded to get arrested for bouncing checks.

In May 1943, the now pregnant Berry again showed up at Chaplin's house and was arrested for violation of probation. The next day she went to see Hedda Hopper, informed Hopper of her condition and told the columnist that Chaplin was the father. Hopper sent Berry to her own doctor, where the pregnancy was confirmed.

LET US PAUSE in this episode of extensive emotional and sexual insanity centering on a woman whose primary attribute was availability, and examine just what made Charlie Chaplin tick. Thousands of pages and trillions of brain cells of those who knew him and those who wish they had known him have spun and spun and produced nothing as penetrating as this analysis from his old friend Max Eastman:

Chaplin "remained a mystery no matter how real and familiar he grew—a baffling combination of cool and high judgment with total submersion in blind emotional drives. . . . There seemed to be some almost weird disconnection between his earnest judgments and his acts of will. He is no more neurotic, I think, than most creative artists. They do have to be easy of access to all currents of emotion. . . . But Charlie makes less effort to swim, less effort to keep his head above these currents, than most thinking people. He not only never acquired in childhood the habit of self-discipline, but never apparently even caught on to the idea. It just doesn't occur to him that he might stand up to a strong flow of feeling, or even move against it for a time. . . .

"But all of this applied only to his relations with people. Toward his art he had . . . . conscience, integrity, discipline, patience, persistence, every good and great quality. Here again he had to be understood as an untrained waif . . . a leaf of paper with sacred writings on it blown through the streets of a London slum. . . .

"His life, when I knew him, was filled to the brim with what most lives consist of yearning after—wealth and fame and creative play and beautiful women—but he never knew how to enjoy any one of the four. . . . Charlie's failure to get any fun out of his money was not so healthy. It was more purely due to his deprived childhood.

"He was so much more keenly aware of the enormous expense of running a studio than of the infinitely more enormous income from his pictures and securities that he felt poor all the time. The whole fable of his sudden fortune was beyond the grasp of this unhappy infant, and his imagination got hold of the size of it only on the debit side. Hence he took no pleasure in giving, no pleasure in having, no pleasure in spending the money—a misfortune that kept him in touch, at least, with the common man!"

Eastman then got down to cases about the women. As something of a voluptuary himself, Eastman understood Chaplin's tormented romantic relationships on the cellular level:

"Girls occupied almost as important a place in his life as dollars, and they caused him even more anxiety. It was not because there were more of them. There honestly weren't so many. But girls unfortunately are not, like dollars, all just alike. They differ fantastically. . . . It required, as I have shown, a large initial act of understanding to be, or continue to be, his friend. Some of his girl friends had this understanding, and some hadn't. Some hadn't any understanding at all. But they all went in with their eyes open, and the opinion that there was something abnormal or monstrously heartless in his behavior toward women was an invention of the public, not a private fact. . . .

"I once asked Charlie about one of his celebrated loves whom I had never met, and he answered, 'I thought she was divinely natural and real—I found she was only gawky and crude.'" (Eastman was almost certainly talking about Lita Grey, Chaplin's second wife.)

"It was said in the manner of a person who has bought a fountain pen at the five and ten cent store, and thrown it away when he looked it over. But that is the ruthlessness of a mind with a taste for knowing, however late, the essential truth. . . .

"He was, to express it very simply, incurably romantic . . . he had a veritable genius for lyrical raptures about girls. At the same time, and deeper, he had the need for a woman friend and companion, a companion not of his sense only, but his mind. This classical approach, the approach of George to Martha Washington, to take a remote example, itemizing her qualities and status and choosing her for a life companion on the grounds of her fitness for the job, could never occur to Charlie. He belongs to a different age and cult of living.

"*He could not mold his personal life as he molds a picture.*" (italics added.)

This analysis was written after the Joan Berry episode, at a time when she had helped make the name of Chaplin anathema to the majority of the American public.

AFTER BERRY WENT to Hedda Hopper, the gears of retribution began to grind. To bulk up the onslaught, Hopper enlisted Florabel Muir, a columnist based in Hollywood for the New York *Daily News*. Muir was having her hair done at Westmore's beauty salon when she got the phone call.

"Go out and call me on a public phone," Hopper ordered. "I cannot talk to you over that switchboard with all those eager ears listening in." Muir wrapped her head in a towel and rushed out to the corner drugstore. Hopper gave her the lay of the land and told her to go down to County Jail where she would get the story of her life. "That old devil has got that kid locked up for ninety days," Hopper said. "And there's much more than meets the eye in this."

Berry told Muir she was pregnant with Chaplin's child. Muir listened attentively, while the back of her mind was already forming an opinion, not to mention the lead of her story: "Thinking anything over was as abhorrent to Joan as cold water is to a cat. She was a creature of emotion, and . . . let it have full sway."

All this was confirmation of Hopper's worst intuitions about Chaplin. For Muir, a tough newswoman whose primary claim to fame would be taking a bullet in the ass during a botched murder attempt on L.A. mob kingpin Mickey Cohen, it was just a great story. "It turned out to be good, unclean fun with some indecent buffoonery lightening the more solemn moments," Muir recalled.

On August 20, 1943, J. Edgar Hoover sent a teletype to Richard Hood: "Charles Chaplin; Joan Barry, Victim, White Slave Traffic Act, SUTEL [Submit Teletype Summary] developments to date. Expedite investigation."

And so a federal investigation began.

IN ONE SENSE, this is an ordinary tale—a sexually vibrant, emotionally unstable woman who thinks it would be fun to be in show business attaches herself to a wealthy man possessed of a firm belief in his own invulnerability and who slowly comes to the alarming realization that he is in far over his head.

Rollie Totheroh, Chaplin's cameraman, thought Berry "was nuts" and described her attitude about him and the studio. "When I went to cash my check up at the bank, she was right in front of me cashing her check. . . . She turned around to me and she said, 'Rollie, money, money, money, money!' She had all this money in her hand. I said, 'Look out, somebody will take it away from you.'

"One day I was sitting on the bench [at the studio] and Charlie had gone . . . out of town. She sat on the bench and said, 'You know, Rollie, I'm fed up with this. All he does is rehearse me, rehearse me, make tests, rehearse me, rehearse me. I'm going back to my boy-friend.' And she mentioned him, Getty. . . . And I said, 'The chance that you have and you're going to throw that away?' She said, 'I don't care. . . . I'm not getting anyplace.' And I said, 'Where were you before you got in contact with Mr. Chaplin.' 'Yeah, but I have this rich boyfriend, too.'"

All the flashing red warning lights were ignored. What followed was the most catastrophic episode of Charlie Chaplin's adult life.

CHAPTER 9

In the first week of June, Joan Berry's mother filed a paternity suit on her daughter's behalf, asking $10,000 for prenatal care and $2,500 a month for child support. Chaplin refused to settle. Since California law favored the mother, Chaplin was forced to pay while the case moved toward trial.

At the same time, FBI agents flooded the zones in both New York and Los Angeles. In the former, they interviewed Pullman ticket agents and porters, bellboys, elevator operators, and front desk employees at the Waldorf Astoria and the Pierre. In the latter, they interviewed employees of the Chaplin studio—including secretaries on the low end and Alf Reeves on the high end—about the specific extent of services Joan Berry had supplied in return for her $75 a week.

Alf Reeves told the agents that Berry "was erratic, emotional, hard to talk to, and could easily effect a vacant stare in her eyes." He said that this last mannerism of hers was ideally suited for the part in [Shadow and Substance]." Reeves said that she came into his office one day in May 1942, said she was going to make a test at MGM and wanted out of her contract with Chaplin. Reeves told her she should reconsider because he believed that Chaplin really wanted to make Shadow and Substance, and she was definitely the girl for the part. Reeves even called Berry's mother and asked her to use whatever leverage she might have to convince her daughter not to quit. Mrs. Berry told Reeves that she couldn't handle Joan; that if Joan wanted to do something, she couldn't be swayed. Reeves then drew up the separation agreement.

Chaplin studio records revealed that the studio had put Berry under contract on June 23, 1941, for $75 a week, and had renewed the contract on December 22 for an additional six months. Chaplin had paid Berry a total of $10,225 in 1941 and 1942, including bills for dentists and charges from the May Company.

Reeves had a wide-ranging conversation with the agents. He told them that he believed that Berry was "nothing but a bum, and that a lot of people had been intimate with her." He was asked if Chaplin had been one of those people, and Reeves replied that of course he was, but he asserted that Chaplin was not the father of her child.

Reeves asked the agents who was behind the investigation. They told him a complaint had been made and that the agents were only engaged in a fact-finding investigation. Reeves clearly didn't believe them, because a bit later in the conversation he told the agents that Chaplin "should get out of the United States and not wait for them to kick him out. It was explained that that was not at all the purpose of this investigation—that no one was trying to kick him out of the United States."

The FBI got copies of income tax returns for several years for both Chaplin individually as well as the Chaplin Studio. They also interviewed Edward Chaney, Chaplin's butler, then moved on to Tim Durant, who had introduced Berry to Chaplin and who Berry said arranged for her abortions. At some point they also installed a wiretap on Durant's phone. (A November 1943 report to E. A. Tamm of the FBI makes prominent mention of Durant's relationship with the African-American dancer Katherine Dunham, presumably to pique Hoover's interest, for the witch hunt was already expanding from a political crusade to include perceived sexual nonconformity: "Tim Durant is known to have been extremely friendly and intimate with Katherine Dunham, negro danseuse, presently featured at the Martin Beck theater in New York . . . on Wednesday evening, November 3, 1943, Durant phoned Dunham in New York. During the conversation he [implied] that due to the developments in the matters surrounding Chaplin he was becoming apprehensive himself and was getting his affairs in such order that he could get out of the country.")

The FBI interviewed Durant, whose version of the affair began with the letter from A. C. Blumenthal of Mexico City to the effect that a young woman named Joan Berry was soon to arrive in Hollywood and was interested in getting into the movie business.

Durant resolutely denied arranging any abortions, although he did say that Chaplin told him Berry said she had had an abortion. "On several occasions also Miss Berry told me too that she had had one or two abortions. I personally had no part in arranging for these two alleged abortions."

Edward Chaney, Chaplin's butler, told the agents that he had driven Berry to the Beverly Hills Hotel when she was either drunk or sick and she had told him that Durant "had some connection with those abortions." On his return to Chaplin's house, Chaney said Durant was present and he told him, "By the way, Mr. Durant, she is opening her mouth about the abortions." Durant replied "The son of a bitch, she can't prove anything." Durant then added to the butler, "That was paid in cash."

To a great extent, Durant's estimation of Chaplin in his FBI interrogation dovetails with Max Eastman's. Durant went out of his way to tell the agents how his friend had managed to get himself into such a comprehensively catastrophic mess.

"There's nobody that knows Charlie any better than I do. I don't know whether I can express it, but I know him inside and out. I have no illusions about him. He has a great many faults and I know them damn well. He's a great artist. He's a genius for comic sense, there's no doubt about it. He's superior, I think to everyone. Like all artists, he has very little good judgment, very little ordinary discrimination, very little self-control. . . .

"Charlie is a combination of being a very warm-hearted, very demonstrative, very emotional person, and rather cold and frugal and disinterested. He's a very funny combination—a very queer paradox. His judgment in women is very bad. His taste in women is not good. . . . He has what you might call a sex inferiority complex—this is off the record. Charlie has this inferiority complex. He's a little man. He's had a terribly bitter bringing up. He was in an orphan asylum at one time. He was a struggling hoofer in England for years . . . and he can't ever forget that background.

"He's very small, he's very bourgeois, he's very narrow about a lot of things, and yet he's got a lot of spirit and it's usually used in the wrong direction. He's a parlor economist. He's a political amateur, a very absurd one. He's no more of a Communist than I am. He has these ideas that are simply a question of trying to express himself.

"He's a ham at heart—he admits that. He wants to startle people and interest people. He goes somewhere—he'll go to a dinner and he'll say these absurd things about the present government, and come out and say, 'Well, what do you think of what I said?' it's a question of declamation. It's not a real truth, or a real belief, but he has no judgment about these things.

"He just wants—he wants to give a performance. . . . He wants to always impress people. He's got great charm. He's got one of the most attractive personalities in the world [but] . . . he's not a person you could expect anything from. He's very unreliable. I've given him much more than he'll ever be able to give me, and still I'm very devoted to him and still I want to help him whenever I can; I really in a way feel very sorry for him. He has very few friends—he has categorized everybody, especially the press, when there is no particular reason to do that. . . .

"He attracts women, but he doesn't hold them . . . because he's selfish, he's very self-centered. He's very egocentric. He's like Hitler—he wants to dominate and possess, and people can't take it—especially women. He's too absorbing. He expects too much, and he always wants to express himself, not particularly sexually, but he always wants to have people like him and, you know, be involved with him to a certain extent. It's his ego. Actors are that way." (Paulette Goddard had a more succinct way of putting it: "It's laughable to think of [Charlie] as a Communist because he was a number one capitalist, as everybody who was involved with him knew.")

Durant was convinced that Chaplin's belief in Berry as an actress "was a mistake. She wasn't capable of standing and sustaining anything. She really hasn't the emotional discipline. She couldn't handle a thing like that. I think he overdid it and I think that was his crime. I think he really tried to make good on it, and was a sincere booster of hers as an actress. She's a hell of an actress. She can talk to any-body and make them believe. She really has a great quality. There's no doubt about it. I think he was sincerely trying to do something with her, but I think he got too involved with her and she just isn't constituted, isn't strong enough to handle it, and that was all. I think he really was very fond of her. . . .

"He's not a wolf, or really a cad—he's just a guy who goes over-board and the wrong kind of girl gets involved and you can't blame her. She just can't handle it and that's what happened in that partic-ular case."

Durant went on to say that he believed that along with her innate but unpolished skills as an actress, Berry was a "psychopathic liar . . . almost a borderline case of insanity. . . . I warned him, you know, I kept warning him. I said, 'You're just getting yourself into hot water having anything to do with this girl.' I mean to the point of getting him sore at me. . . . King Vidor, all his friends, warned him. . . .

"His Red activities. He hasn't got guts enough to be a Red. Any-thing to be sensational, and hold an audience—typical exhibitionist."

The FBI also interviewed J. Paul Getty, who told them he met Berry in October of 1940 and saw her "rather frequently" during that year and in 1941. Getty denied ever having sex with Berry, although he said that he had loaned her over $3,000, all secured by notes. He didn't mention whether he had been paid back, nor did the FBI press him.

Precisely two weeks after the paternity suit became public, Chap-lin married Oona O'Neill in the coastal town of Carpinteria, north of Los Angeles. He was fifty-four years old. She was eighteen.

The tumult became even louder.

CHAPTER 10

Oona O'Neill was born in May 1925 to the playwright Eugene O'Neill and Agnes Boulton, his second wife. Oona's parents divorced when she was four, and she had sparse contact with her father thereafter, which, all things considered, was probably a good thing. Eugene O'Neill was a great playwright but a rotten husband and a worse father.

No matter what Oona did, her father disapproved. Oona attended the Brearley School, an exclusive (occasional Jews, no Blacks) all-girls school on East 83rd in New York, where her classmates included Barbara Bel Geddes and Mary Rodgers, the daughter of Richard Rodgers. After that, she became a debutante around New York along with her lifelong friends Gloria Vanderbilt and Carol Marcus Saroyan Matthau.

Oona dated J. D. Salinger, who became obsessed by her although the relationship seems to have been casual, because that's the way Oona wanted it—one night she slugged Salinger on the jaw when he got too handsy. She had more serious relationships with the cartoonist Peter Arno and Orson Welles, and it's possible the latter was the basis for the lifelong uneasiness between Welles and Chaplin. It's also possible that neither Welles nor Chaplin ever encountered another human being with an equivalent ego. Dan James said that

Chaplin "was not terribly enthusiastic about *Citizen Kane*," a reaction James ascribed to the fact that Chaplin might have been "a bit jealous."

Oona was extremely beautiful, which only seemed to irritate her father. A sample of O'Neill's fatherly wisdom is a letter written after Oona had attempted to talk to him on the phone, only to be curtly told by O'Neill's wife, Carlotta Monterey, that he preferred not to see or talk to her. He was particularly appalled by her vague ambition to act, feeling that she was trading on his name: "Oona is no genius," he wrote a friend, "but merely a spoiled, lazy, vain little brat who has, so far by her actions only proven that she can be a much sillier and bad-mannered fool than most girls of her age."

Not content with venting privately, he told Oona what he thought of her in a letter: "All I know of what you have become since you blossomed into the night club racket is derived from newspaper clippings of your interviews. . . . All the publicity you have had is the wrong kind, unless your ambition is to be a second-rate movie actress of the floozie variety—the sort who have their pictures in the papers for a couple of years and then sink back into the obscurity of their naturally silly, talentless lives."

He neglected to sign off with "Love, Dad."

O'Neill's letters were buttressed by Carlotta's curt missives to her stepdaughter, which read as unintentionally pathetic: "Your father gives extravagantly and generously for your education and upbringing. Forget the cheap talk of movies, dress designing and tap dancing. Be simple, sweet, and charming, keeping yourself busy at school. If you grow up endowed with great beauty or great talent you might consider the theater.

"But if you have neither of the above qualities train yourself to be a good wife and try and marry some decent man of good family and give yourself some standing on *your own feet*."

Contrary to the beliefs of her father and stepmother, Oona was exceedingly intelligent, a compulsive reader with pithy opinions. When Carol Marcus wrote a paper on T. S. Eliot, Oona told her not to waste her time on an anti-Semite, and she referred to Ernest Hemingway as a man with fake hair on his chest. But beneath her sunny, unaffected demeanor, Oona carried a full measure of Celtic sadness about her status as an abandoned child.

She was considering a career as an actress when the agent Minna Wallis—the sister of the producer Hal Wallis—introduced her to Chaplin at a dinner party. "I arrived early," remembered Chaplin, "and on entering the sitting room discovered a young lady seated alone by the fire. While waiting for Miss Wallis, I introduced myself, saying I presumed she was Miss O'Neill. She smiled. Contrary to my preconceived impression, I became aware of a luminous beauty with a sequestered charm and a gentleness that was most appealing." On Oona's part, the attraction was instantaneous; she told Carol Marcus that it was like meeting the handsomest, sexiest man in the world.

Chaplin began thinking of Oona for *Shadow and Substance*—the same part Joan Berry had been slotted for. Oona's looks would situate her somewhere between Audrey Hepburn and a forest sprite, but she was also grounded, intelligent, and funny. A screen test she made for the producer Eugene Frenke shows that she photographed well, was extremely shy, and had a propensity for dissolving into girlish giggles.

On May 14, 1943, Oona turned eighteen. She had no doubts, Chaplin had many. For one thing, he was thirty-six years older than she was. Things would be fine for the time being, but what would happen when he became elderly? For another, he realized that the impending court case was not the sort of preliminary that foretold a happy marriage. Yet Oona was absolutely sure of her man and of her own mind. She was, Chaplin remembered, "resolute, as though she had come upon a truth."

For Eugene O'Neill, just wrapping up work on *A Touch of the Poet*, the marriage confirmed his doubts about his daughter. He wrote a letter to a friend accusing his daughter of pursuing "any kind of display no matter how vulgar and stupid—and finally ending up in this typical Hollywood scandal and marriage with a man as old as I am (probably older, for what actor gives out his real age). Of course, he's rich and that is the answer, or one of the answers. I need not tell you, I know, that you are never going to hear of our entertaining Mr. and Mrs. Chaplin, or of their entertaining us. Enough is enough!"

O'Neill peremptorily disinherited his daughter. He never saw her again.

For Joan Berry, Chaplin's marriage provoked unrestrained hysteria. "Her misery was as abject and abandoned as any I've ever looked upon in a life passed largely in viewing human unhappiness," wrote Florabel Muir. "Watching her roll and toss, listening to her . . . sobbing, realizing finally that nature had mercifully blacked out consciousness, I had to conclude that no matter what a misguided and self-centered little indolent nitwit she had been, she hadn't quite earned this kind of torment."

Shortly after the marriage, it was announced that Oona wouldn't be pursuing an acting career after all. Chaplin told Louella Parsons, "I even told Oona it might be a good idea for her to have a career, since her tests were so good. But she wants to be housewife and, of course, that made me happy."

Chaplin and Oona quickly settled into a peaceful emotional hammock. Oona had a maturity, a constancy that belied her years. Carol Matthau would write of the couple that "They clung to each other through all that went against them in the outside world. It did not put a strain on their love because they had fallen so deeply in love they had already exiled themselves in an odd way. . . . She woke up every morning to spend the whole day and night with him. He did the same, with the exception of his work. He wanted to be with her all the time."

THE PATERNITY SUIT followed closely by the marriage brought Chaplin reams of bad publicity spearheaded by Hedda Hopper and Florabel Muir, who were feeding information both correct and flagrantly incorrect to the FBI, and getting the equivalent in return.

Richard Hood, the head of the FBI's Los Angeles office, noted that Muir "in accordance with the policy of the [Robert] McCormick papers, is apparently interested in getting something on leading Hollywood figures." Both women pretended to befriend Joan Berry and, week after week, month after month, they flooded the newspapers with Berry's charges.

A headline in the *New York Herald Tribune* nicely captured the typical sentiments about Chaplin's marriage: "Chaplin and Oona O'Neill Wed; He is 54, His Fourth Wife is 18. Eugene O'Neill's daughter is Bride of Comedian; Joan Berry in Hysterics." The story itself quoted Berry as saying, "Oh, I can't believe it; I can't believe it. To think he once said we would be married and have a glorious future together as husband and wife."

Since prestigious columnists were nearly unanimous in their condemnations, the low-end equivalents were as well. Adela Rogers St. Johns, Hearst's favorite sob sister since World War I, weighed in with a long editorial in *Photoplay*: "With every front-page record, [Chaplin] has helped to destroy our sense of decency, the way every man and woman does who fails in these days to exhibit self-control and self-discipline in order to uphold that of our men at the front. . . . At exactly the psychological moment when his friends expected him to act with the dignity and honesty that went with the reputation of genius, Chaplin instead flaunted decency and good taste and made new headlines with his runaway marriage to Oona O'Neill, debutante of the Stork Club set."

Owing to the particulars of his character, Chaplin's attitude toward the uproar about his sex life, as well as his recent marriage, seems to have alternated between dismissal and disbelief. "He knew that he had had affairs," asserted Harry Crocker, "and that many of them had been with young and beautiful women, but he steadfastly held that an affair was not a crime and that when it became a crime he would be willing to brave the world." More to the point, Jerry Epstein would remember that "Charlie never gossiped, never talked about people's private lives. It never came up. He put a deaf ear to gossip. He just wasn't interested."

But Chaplin was an outlier. Most people are very interested in other people's lives, especially if they happen to be celebrities. And here was a world-famous celebrity whose dirty laundry was being aired—again. It would not be his politics that would bring Charlie Chaplin down. Rather, it was the moral ecology of postwar America.

Chaplin intended to carry on with his life. On Christmas Day 1943, Chaplin and Oona celebrated with a tree and a family breakfast. Wheeler Dryden and his son Spencer came over, as did King

Vidor and his wife. Alf Reeves was there, and Florence Wagner—the widow of Chaplin's old friend Rob Wagner—as well as Minna Wallis, and young Syd.

Spencer Dryden read "The Night Before Christmas." Chaplin gave Oona a topaz finger ring; Oona gave her husband Edward Stirling's book *Old Drury Lane* in two volumes. After the presents were opened, Chaplin played requests on the accordion and read some scenes from the script he was working on. It was tentatively entitled *Bluebeard*.

By this time, the FBI was feeling secure about their case, as well as with their surveillance of Chaplin. Richard Hood stated that he felt the Bureau had "fairly good coverage inasmuch as Edward Chaney, the butler who is still working for Chaplin, has stated he will inform us if information comes to his attention that Chaplin may be leaving [the country]." Hood also stated they had a confidential informant working with Tim Durant "who would advise of any similar information."

The FBI continued leaking information to favored columnists. On February 26, 1944, the Bureau sent "EXCLUSIVE TO WALTER WINCHELL," an item about Chaplin's friend Robert Arden, born Rudolf Kleiber in Austria, "who came to this country in the late '20s and from then on has left a trail of bad debts and shady deals everywhere he has ever been. He was deported as an undesirable from the Canal Zone and in 1936 turned up on the West Coast as Robert Arden."

Similar items were sent to Hedda Hopper. In the meantime, the Bureau was having the same difficulties with Berry that Chaplin had encountered, situations that would make it very difficult to present Berry as a victimized innocent. On January 27, 1944, Special Agent Hood advised that since Berry had appeared before a grand jury, she had hit the bottle "very heavily," had a fight with her mother, and wanted to "go away for a couple of weeks to rest up." There was some discussion about having Berry's attorney's secretary go away with her for a few weeks to "keep her out of jail. Mr. Hood wondered . . . whether we could have the secretary accompany Joan Berry and give her a couple hundred dollars or at least her expenses for the trip."

Hood's superior didn't think the Bureau would approve such a request. "That our first interest was to make a case and then we had to be very careful about being the subject of any criticism at a later date." Hood pointed out that if Berry landed in jail, "our case would be ruined."

Burdened by an unreliable plaintiff in constant danger of going off the rails, the Bureau showed signs of desperation. In January 1944, the Bureau office in Los Angeles forwarded a bluish green capsule for analysis in Washington. The capsule had been taken by a friend of Berry's while she was "incarcerated in a sanitarium near Los Angeles in May, 1943. At this time, the victim, a 23 year old girl, was in a pregnant condition and it is possible that someone might have given her pills or medicine to induce a miscarriage." Upon analysis, it was found that the pill contained liver extract commonly used in the treatment of anemia, and "would not have any adverse effect on a pregnant woman."

That same month, Hood sent J. Edgar Hoover a telegram stating that they had received information that Chaplin was contemplating "leaving this country possibly for Russia or Mexico." On the bottom of the communication someone wrote, "Give immediate attention. Don't let this fellow do a run out." Some thought was given to stationing officers at border stations just in case, but Hoover personally sent a telegram ordering everyone to stand down: "Bureau does not desire stops at Border Stations. Cancel instructions to offices."

The FBI and the media colluded far and wide. A telegram sent to J. Edgar Hoover informed him that Florabel Muir "advised agent that she talked with Berry over weekend at behest of John J. Irwin, Berry's attorney. Pointed out Berry's erring ways in becoming intoxicated in public, etc. and Berry has promised to behave herself. Muir continued that she has talked Berry out of desire to go to Mexico and now plans are to get Berry's mother away on a vacation which may alleviate Berry's troubles at home."

The overall intent of all this backstage maneuvering was clearly not the prosecution of such minor characters as Robert Arden or Tim Durant, but to gin up an aura of disreputable guilt around Chaplin. In line with that, pressure had to be applied on Chaplin's circle of friends. Hood wrote Hoover, "[United States attorney] Carr is considering subpoenaing Minna Wallis as a witness and later indicting her for perjury if she does not tell the truth. Carr indicates that this leaves as eventual subjects Chaplin, Arden, . . . and Durant."

On February 1, 1944, Hood wired Hoover that Durant told agents that on the New York trip Joan Berry had gone to Chaplin's suite with Durant and Chaplin, and that Durant had left them alone in the living room. As far as the FBI was concerned, this confirmed prosecution "on the Mann Act violation as well as Civil Liberties." (The 1910 Mann Act made it illegal for a man to transport a woman across state lines "for immoral purposes.")

As the pressure mounted, so did the hysteria. On February 10, a *Washington Post* reporter was riding home on the bus when he informed an FBI supervisor that Chaplin had died. The supervisor called Richard Hood in Los Angeles who made some calls and reported back that an informant had seen Chaplin "not more than one hour and twenty minutes previously . . . and he was very much alive."

The charges regarding arranged abortions ultimately went nowhere, probably because they would have opened up Berry's sexual history in court, but on February 10, 1944, the federal grand jury in Los Angeles indicted Chaplin, charging him with violation of the Mann Act on two counts—one count for transporting Berry to New York, the other for transporting her back to Los Angeles.

In addition, Chaplin, Robert Arden, and an Officer White of the Beverly Hills police department were indicted for conspiring to deprive Berry of her civil rights by hustling her out of town, while Chaplin and several others were also indicted on general conspiracy charges. If found guilty, Chaplin faced up to twenty-three years in prison and fines of up to $26,000. Just to be comprehensive, the same grand jury charged Chaplin, Robert Arden, Tim Durant, the police chief of Beverly Hills, and a judge for violation of Joan Berry's civil liberties.

The media response was more or less as expected. Oddly, one of the few naysayers was Westbrook Pegler, who cleared his throat by writing that Chaplin was "a little ingrate, not nice, stingy, and . . . has had the impudence to associate himself with the Communist enemies of the country in which he took refuge from the two wars while his native England sat right under the guns of the Germans."

With that out of the way, Pegler said that the government "could better use its manpower and money than to flog a man, however mean, for taking a guest on a trip. . . . This is strictly police court business and beneath the notice of the U.S. Department of Justice."

A week after Chaplin was charged, he submitted to a blood test overseen by three physicians, one representing Chaplin, one representing Berry, and another agreed upon by the first two doctors. Berry agreed to drop the paternity suit if the blood tests exonerated Chaplin. In order to get her to agree to that, Chaplin paid her $2,500 plus $100 a week, $1,000 when the child was born, $500 monthly afterward for four months, $1,000 when the blood tests took place, and $5,500 for attorney's fees and court costs.

Since Berry specified the date of conception as December 23, 1942, Chaplin must have known the events as she described them were false, or he would never have agreed to blood tests that could prove he was the father of Berry's child. A further note regarding Berry's version came from Max Eastman, who wrote that he knew Berry was lying because "a friend of mine spent with the girl involved the night on which she is supposed to have slept with Charlie and become the mother of his baby. At the first hint of a trial, my friend left town in a hurry to avoid having to state the fact in court."

The blood test results showed that Chaplin's blood type was Group O, Type MN. Berry had Group A, Type N, and the child she named Carol Ann had Group B, Type N. All three physicians agreed that Chaplin could not be Carol Ann's father.

But the case continued. As the FBI noted in one report, "The following morning, and for days afterward, stories circulated in Los Angeles [newspapers] that the test was not accurate, that Chaplin had taken some chemical to change his blood type. . . . None of these stories has the appearance of any truth."

The Mann Act trial commenced on March 21, 1944, with Jerry Giesler defending Chaplin. Giesler was an unprepossessing, pear-shaped legal magician. Among his many acquittals were the rape trials of Errol Flynn and Alexander Pantages, and, years later, the murder charge against Lana Turner's daughter Cheryl Crane. He also handled divorces for Rudolph Valentino, and, much later, Barbara Hutton and Marilyn Monroe.

Giesler plotted Chaplin's defense on the basis of common sense: "Would my client transport this woman 3,000 miles for a single alleged intimacy when she would have given her body to him at any time and place? There is no more evidence of Mann Act violation here than there is evidence of murder."

Giesler understood all too well the process that had ensnared Chaplin, a show business charade that went back to the ancient Greeks: "She had begun the routine known . . . as 'being a protege.' First a protege is signed to a contract; after that there is talk of giving her dramatic lessons or singing lessons or dancing lessons to help her with her 'career.' Somewhere along the path the protege may become the patron's mistress."

Giesler also understood that Chaplin's image was transitioning from being one of the world's foremost defenders of democracy to a louche degenerate with a propensity for young girls and Communism. In short, Giesler was defending a profoundly unpopular client.

Giesler argued the facts. The Mann Act had been enacted to stamp out commercialized prostitution; it had never been aimed at abolishing private affairs. Giesler believed that it was currently being used to prosecute people who paid for a taxi ride across a bridge. "It is an enticement to blackmail or to help women 'get back' at a man for wrongs imagined or actual. . . .

"I still don't believe that Chaplin, who could have enjoyed Miss Berry's favors for as little as 25 cents carfare, would pay her expenses as a guest at the Waldorf-Astoria, so she would be there for improper purposes."

Giesler remembered that "Chaplin was the best witness I've ever seen in a law court. He was effective even when he wasn't being examined or cross-examined, but was merely sitting, lonely and forlorn, at a far end of the counsel table. He is so small that only the toes of his shoes touched the floor. He looked helpless, friendless and wistful as he sat there with the weight of the whole United States government against him."

Chaplin wasn't acting. "There lurked in the back of my mind the possibility that I might be railroaded," he wrote in his memoirs, "but I could never quite believe it. And occasionally I had a thought about the future of my career, but now that was chaotic, remote. I put it out of my mind—I could think of only one thing at a time. . . . But the moment I left the courtroom all was forgotten and after a quiet dinner with Oona I would fall into bed exhausted."

Giesler believed that "Chaplin's greatest quality on the stand was his outward humility—whether he was inwardly humble or not. He wept as he described his relations with Joan Berry and said, 'Yes, I was intimate with her. I liked the girl.'. . . He gave the appearance of utter sincerity. He wasn't arrogant, nor did he duck the verbal blows flung in his direction."

The trial was not without moments of unintentional humor—at one point, Chaplin averred that sex wasn't important in his life.

Since the purported Mann Act violation was a federal offense, Giesler had less leeway in jury selection and questioning. He went so far as to write forty or fifty questions down and asked the judge to decide in advance which ones were permissible. The judge struck out all but about twelve, but the questions the judge allowed made it possible for Giesler to prove that Berry was not an ingénue fresh from the farm.

Giesler also worked the jury, using the same legal sheets he had submitted to the judge. He would ask a question of a witness, the question would be answered, then Giesler would say, "That was question number one. Now, your Honor, in accordance with your ruling I will skip the other questions you have ruled that I am not permitted to ask and I will go to question number nine."

"Instinctively the jurors wondered what they'd missed by not hearing the missing questions . . . the effect of this procedure was to make the jury wonder why anyone could have been afraid of my unasked questions. There was nothing improper in this, and strategically I think it had some effect."

Cumulatively, Giesler felt the hostility toward Chaplin that had been palpable at the beginning of the trial begin to lessen. "At the end of the trial, the audience was more pro-Chaplin than anti-Chaplin."

In his summation, Giesler said that he was not excusing any mistakes his client had made, nor was he there to condemn Joan Berry. The sole issue was this: was the defendant guilty of a violation of the Mann Act within the restrictions of the indictment?

"I am no longer defending Chaplin," Giesler remembered, "but it is only fair to say that he went through that experience like a man. Prejudice hounded him most of the way through his lawsuit, and it was only after we had had an opportunity to cross-examine the chief prosecuting witness . . . that the prejudice began to change. I could not only feel it change, I could hear it. Each noon, as we walked down the Federal Building hallway going to lunch, a few, then more of those who watched us pass, had kind words for Chaplin."

On April 8, the jury deliberated for six hours and fifty-eight minutes and went through four ballots before returning a verdict of not guilty.

Giesler had expected an acquittal. He also seems to have expected what followed when he submitted his bill for services rendered. "I don't suppose that anyone who knows Chaplin will be surprised to hear that he paid me my fee only after months and months had passed. In fact, there are those who have told me, 'I'm surprised you ever got it.' "

In point of fact, the amount of time it took for Chaplin to pay Giesler was eight months, probably because the amount of the fee was $60,000. In twenty-first-century terms, that amounts to slightly less than $900,000 and it undoubtedly propelled Chaplin into something approaching cardiac arrest. The check was finally forwarded to Giesler on December 5, 1944, by Loyd Wright, accompanied by this hilarious note: "I think as time goes by [Chaplin] will be more fully appreciative of the efforts made to maintain his status to the end that he could continue to be active in the motion picture business." (Twenty-first-century attorneys say that an equivalent fee is "uncommon, but not necessarily rare for top lawyers," especially one engaged in a difficult case. As one Los Angeles lawyer explained, "A lawyer of Giesler's standing today would earn 800K to one million. An entertainment lawyer would waive a fee but ask for a piece of a deal.")

The Mann Act acquittal didn't change any minds, and Chaplin's prosecutors in the press only amplified their attacks, often with flagrant lies. Ed Sullivan: "Had Chaplin lost his case, and had he been ordered deported, the Russian consul was authorized to turn over a Soviet plane to take the Chaplins to Moscow. . . . He doesn't plan to visit Russia until after the war. . . . He and Oona are studying Russian, as I reported sometime ago."

While Chaplin was fighting for his life, the government was beginning to coalesce around a long-term plan. Shortly before the Mann Act trial got under way, in a memo of January 8, 1944, that seemed to anticipate an acquittal, Hoover's aide Alex Rosen noted a phone call with Richard Hood in Los Angeles: "We discussed the possibility of [Chaplin] being deported after the war and Mr. Hood advised he thought there was an excellent chance for this."

THE PATERNITY CASE got under way on December 13, 1944. Chaplin was no longer represented by Jerry Giesler—a crucial mistake. Instead he turned to Charles Millikan, who mounted a competent defense, but who was slowly overwhelmed by the circus that Berry's attorney brought to town.

The blood tests had established that Chaplin could not be the father, so Millikan moved to dismiss the case. But Judge Stanley Mosk denied the motion. "There is no sound reason to deny, and every sound reason to accept, blood tests as a scientific advance of importance," he wrote. But, until the legislature so ordained, "courts must decline to accept any specific paternity test as conclusive, to the exclusion of other evidence. . . .

"To the adult parties to the action, this or any court owes only the obligation of impartiality and objectivity. But to the infant, unable to maintain its own rights under the law, the court owes the additional duty of protection." In conclusion, Mosk was convinced "that the ends of justice will best be served by a full and fair trial of the issues."

Berry's attorney in the paternity suit was a seventy-seven-year-old barnstormer named Joseph Scott, an English native who had come to America with $100 in his pocket. Scott regarded his American citizenship as a gift from God, and decried what he termed a "cynical disregard for religion, and a strange hankering for this un-American activity among the top flight people in the field of education and journalism and other . . . meanderings."

Father George Dunne, a Jesuit priest in Southern California, knew Scott well and respected him. Dunne characterized him as "Mr. Catholic of Southern California. High pitched, raspy-voiced, loud and eloquent orator of the old school, he was a man of strong, undiluted and simple loyalties: to the Catholic church, to Irish Independence, to the Red, White and Blue, to the Republican party—he was one of the nominators of Herbert Hoover at the 1928 [presidential] convention—and to the principles of old-fashioned morality."

Dunne had listened as Scott had honored Irish revolutionary Eamon de Valera and called down the wrath of God on the British Empire and the *Los Angeles Times*—in Scott's eyes, England's henchmen. Charlie Chaplin was about to join England and journalism as a target of Scott's moral fury.

Scott found Chaplin offensive not only for his treatment of Joan Berry, but because of his refusal to become an American citizen. As Father Dunne put it, "not to become an American was to be anti-American. There was no middle ground. . . . All of Scott's basic loyalties felt challenged and they combined to trap him into what must be accounted the most discreditable episode in a career otherwise distinguished by many virtues, laudable deeds and by the defense of many worthy causes. He was determined to pillory Chaplin by any means, fair or foul. The means chosen were foul."

CHAPLIN HAD NOT really changed since 1940, or, for that matter, since 1915. But the culture had. Suburbia was just around the corner, not to mention prosperity, and America was minimizing pluralism in favor of what would become a narrowed postwar consensus. In numbers was safety. The Tramp was a free spirit, and in many ways so was his creator. Chaplin's values were falling out of step with his environment.

Joseph Scott would write an unpublished memoir that gives chapter and verse, not only of his thinking and tactics, but his feelings about Chaplin, whom he had met in 1914. "I knew Charlie Chaplin when he came to Los Angeles first—a quiet, insignificant youngster. . . . We used to sit down together in the men's room at the Los Angeles Athletic Club, where I occasionally took lunch or dinner."

That was not Scott's only contact with the movie industry. He was close with Bishop John Cantwell, one of the Catholic prelates who had formed the Legion of Decency. In the summer of 1933, Cantwell had asked Scott to tell Hollywood producers that Catholic bishops were out of patience with a "vile industry" that was doing "untold harm" to the children of America.

Joseph Breen, at the time working in the Hays Office, arranged a meeting with the moguls that included Jack Warner, Louis B. Mayer, Adolph Zukor, and others. Scott launched into a furious castigation of the Jewish moguls, calling them "disloyal" Americans and of engaging in "a conspiracy to debauch the . . . youth of the land." He warned the producers of a connection between "dirty motion pictures" and radical Jews who held the morals of the nation in contempt. This, Scott said, was "serving to build up an enormous case against the Jews in the eyes of the American people." Scott concluded by telling the moguls that their "damnable" practices had brought "disgrace upon the Jews and upon America."

Of all the moguls, only Joe Schenck fought back, telling Scott that religious critics of the movie business were "narrow-minded and bigoted." Schenck thought the other moguls were cowards who had been intimidated by Scott's anti-Semitic implications. Later that year, the Production Code Administration was created, headed by Joe Breen. If a film failed to get a PCA seal of approval, no mainstream theater in America would show it.

Charles Millikan, Chaplin's attorney, had earlier arranged with Berry's attorney that, if the results of the blood test proved that Chaplin was not the father, the case would be dropped. (Florabel Muir got her exclusive on the blood test results by bribing a nurse in the lab where the test was conducted.) After Judge Mosk refused to dismiss the case, Berry's lawyer resigned, which left the matter of her counsel up in the air.

At that point, as Joseph Scott remembered, "Different people advised [Berry] that she hadn't gotten complete satisfaction under the law for her baby, and persuaded her to come and see me." (The "different people" almost certainly included Hedda Hopper.)

Scott said that he sympathized with Berry, and particularly with the baby, but he didn't see how he could get around the contractual stipulations. After several hours of discussion with Berry, he told her he couldn't help her, at which point, "she broke down and got somewhat hysterical."

Scott went home and had a dark night of the soul. "I suddenly hit upon the idea that the person involved here is the baby, and the only person involved is the child, *the only one who has any rights is this innocent youngster.*" (Italics added.)

The next morning, Scott told his associates that he was taking the case. The other lawyers were appalled. Scott explained that, "This is a baby who can't make stipulations and can't employ lawyers, and she has not had her day in court, and this man is her father, and he is a multi-millionaire, and I want to see what we can do."

"This man is her father . . ."

Scott managed to transfer the child's guardianship from the mother to the court, technically voiding the previous legal agreement. As guardian of the child, it was the court that was suing Chaplin for the child's support. Charles Millikan was astonished; more than that—he was indignant. He told Scott that his actions were "inexplicable" and utterly lacking in any legal justification. Scott's answer was a smug, "Wherever there was a wrong there was remedy."

The judge allowed the earlier contract to be put aside. Millikan appealed to both the district court of appeals and the California Supreme Court. Both courts allowed the suit to go forward.

The trial got under way on December 13, 1944, in the Superior Court. Scott assigned all seven attorneys in his office to the case, as well as Joseph Dunn, a former Secret Service agent who was delegated to turn up witnesses.

Scott knew that he had to bring the fight to Chaplin and rattle him, and rattle him he did. "I asked him blunt questions about his meetings with Joan; about their conversations, about their actions. I roared when I was angry; I described him as I saw him. He tried to make long speeches; I accused him of acting before the court. Chaplin forgot the answers—I reminded the jury that he had a good memory for what he said, little memory for what she said and less memory of what they did."

Watching Scott orate, haggle, and insult, Florabel Muir was impressed, as well as appalled. "Scott tore the principles of formal logic to shreds. . . . He was guilty day after day of *argumentum ad hominem*, but this was a lawsuit in which the factor of sentiment simply could not be ignored." When it came to Berry's testimony, Scott realized she was still carrying a torch for Chaplin—"that she abjectly looked up to him, was putty in his hands from the moment he began to train her, even through the days when she agreed to a prenatal settlement."

Scott slowed his case down when it came to the night Berry broke into Chaplin's house. Chaplin resolutely denied that he had sex with her that night, while Berry insisted they had. If they didn't have sex that night, he couldn't have been the father of the child. Under Scott's examination, Edward Chaney, Chaplin's butler, testified that the sheets on the bed were rumpled in a manner consistent with sex.

Scott asked Chaplin what he told her when Berry said she was destitute and threatened to kill herself.

Chaplin: "I said, well, whatever you are, or whatever your condition is, you have brought it on yourself."

Scott: "You made her feel that, did you?"

Chaplin: "Oh, yes."

Scott: "She was responsible and you were not, is that it?"

Chaplin: "Yes."

Scott: "I see."

Chaplin: "I had been trying—I said—I told her . . ."

Scott: "That is all."

Chaplin: "Just a moment, please, let me finish, will you please? I told her that I had tried—I have committed no crime."

Scott: "Just a minute, if your honor please, we want no dramatics."

Chaplin: "Your honor, I am human, and this man is trying to make inferences as though I am a monster."

Judge Willis: "I don't want any dramatics or exuberance or vehemence on either side. We will go at this calmly. He has a right to ask you the questions he is putting to you . . . now go ahead and answer."

Scott still had the blood tests to contend with. Charles Millikan put all three doctors on the stand, who testified to their conviction that Chaplin could not be the father. They explained that they had administered two different tests. The primary test produced the proof they had asserted; the other—called an M and N test—left a modicum of doubt. Scott pounced.

Scott: "Doctors don't agree on these questions of scientific proof sometimes, do they, Doctor?"

Doctor: "They frequently disagree."

Scott: "Could Chaplin have been the father under the M and N test?"

Doctor: "We could not rule him out."

Scott: "Doesn't that mean he might have been the father under the M and N test?"

Doctor: "He might have been."

Scott: "Doctor, we have no money to employ another doctor. But don't you think, if we had the money, we could find a physician with an opinion different from yours?"

Doctor: "Yes, doctors are like lawyers. They make mistakes."

Scott: "I agree, Doctor, but the difference between lawyers and doctors is this: the lawyers' mistakes are embalmed in the law books in libraries. When you fellows make a mistake, they're buried in the ground."

Scott had just slid reasonable doubt through a narrow opening at the bottom of the legal door.

As the trial neared its finish, Scott brought Berry's daughter, Carol Ann, to the courtroom. She was fourteen months old, cherubic, curly-haired. Agness Underwood, the legendary city editor of the *Los Angeles Herald-Express*, had made a 6:30 a.m. call to Scott to find out what was going to happen. He told her Carol Ann would be making an appearance in court. Underwood asked him to bring the child to his office first so the papers could get photographs of her. The child appeared, the pictures were taken, and Scott and his team set off for court.

During a recess, Underwood left her seat, picked up the child, and placed her on the defense table. Chaplin sat there ignoring the child, while the photographers went berserk. When court resumed, Scott asked Chaplin if he had curly hair when he was young. "Yes," he replied. Then Scott asked the court's permission to place Chaplin and the baby beside each other in front of the jury. Millikan objected, but the court overruled him.

Scott was beginning to realize his tactics were working. "I thought my case had been uphill all the way. Yet now I realized [Millikan's] was the greater task. I had a dimpled, cherubic baby, facing a nameless, penniless future, for my client. What attorney, I repeat, could ask for more?"

Scott: "Isn't it a fact that you had sexual relations with her?"

Chaplin: "No, it is not a fact."

Scott: "When did you last have sexual relations with her?"

Chaplin: "Around the Max Reinhardt period, when she was studying drama."

The discussion moved on to the events of December 23.

Chaplin: "She said, 'I'm going to kill you.' I said, 'There is no justification for this. From the very beginning of our association I've only tried to build you up. You had led your own life, have your own men friends. I've bought a play for you for which I paid $20,000. I've worked a whole year on that play and spent thousands of dollars on your training. All you do in return is smash my windows and harass me. I'm sick of it all."

Joseph Scott objected. The witness wasn't testifying, Scott said, "he's making a speech." Scott was overruled and Chaplin continued. He denied that he had sex with Barry the night she broke into his house, or the following morning, when he gave her $60, promised her more, then sent her away.

She told him she was pregnant in May of 1943, Chaplin said. "What do you want?" he asked her.

She told him she wanted $150,000—half for her mother, half for the child. She told him that all the newspapers were against him and that they would ruin him if he took her to court and fought the case. Chaplin said he responded by saying, "I admit the press is 95% against me. They have been ever since I dared to demand a second front on behalf of Russia—that was a mistake I made. I'll fight you even though they believe your villainous lies—your filthy scandal—your blackmail!"

Scott again objected, was again overruled and Chaplin continued. "Yes, they'll believe all your lies, but you know all this time you have been keeping up relations with Paul Getty and several other men, who I'll name . . ."

Scott bore in—pictures of the court proceedings show Scott with his hand on the witness box, just a few inches from Chaplin's own hand.

Scott: "Isn't it a fact that you had intimate relations again that morning?"

Chaplin: "That is a lie! That is not a fact!"

Millikan was not allowed to present evidence regarding Berry's other lovers during the time she was involved with Chaplin. Scott went to town in his summation, referring to Chaplin as "this pestiferous, lecherous hound. . . . Did you ever hear the story of Svengali and Trilby? This fellow is just a little runt of a Svengali. He's not even a monster . . . just a little runt. . . . This fellow doesn't lie like a gentleman. He lies like a cheap Cockney cad. . . .

"That man goes around fornicating . . . with the same aplomb that the average man orders bacon and eggs for breakfast. He is a hoary-headed old buzzard . . . with the instincts of a young bull . . . a master mechanic in the art of seduction."

The jury began deliberating and deadlocked 7 to 5 in favor of Chaplin. Under California law, a verdict of at least 9 to 3 was necessary to find the defendant not guilty. The judge offered to arbitrate a verdict, which was refused by Chaplin, who wanted complete vindication. The retrial took place three months later, beginning on April 7, 1945. This time the judge was Clarence Kincaid.

"It was," asserted Joseph Scott, "the first time in more than a half century practice . . . that I stood close to, leaned into the face of the defendant as I questioned him. Most of the time we were face to face—a foot or so apart. I . . . asked, demanded that he tell the true story. I again referred to evidence given at his Mann Act trial. . . . I didn't pull any punches."

In his relentlessly sanctimonious summation, Scott told the jury they had to judge who was telling the truth—Chaplin, or Joan Berry and Chaney, the butler. And, of course, the baby. "What is your duty as jurors to her? . . . For a man like Chaplin, with his brazen attitude, with his admission that he had something to do with the girl before, it doesn't make any sense."

He pointed to the doctor's admission that results of the second blood test could be haggled over, then said, "If you find that Joan lied, and Chaney lied, you have got to say that on the evidence, will you give Mr. Chaplin a clean bill of health? He goes out of the courtroom immaculate, just like a sunflower on a sunny day; not a thing to apologize for.

"'The jury likes me,' he can say, 'they like my manhood, my conduct. I am a gentleman, not only a genius, but a gentleman, and I am going out of this courtroom and I will do as I please, because I have gotten a mandate from the jury to go now and do likewise.'

"That's what it means, and that's why I am concerned. If you turn this man free, you invite that little youngster to be an object of charity the rest of her life. The woman has nothing . . . who would employ her in Hollywood now, but on the other hand . . . Charlie Chaplin will be larger than ever. . . .

"If you give Chaplin a clean bill of health, it is like saying, 'Go on boys, and do what you want.' It is always the woman who suffers, economically, physically, morally. There [is] no one to stop Chaplin— no one but you, ladies and gentlemen."

Scott had maneuvered Charles Millikan into a lose-lose situation— If Millikan didn't reply to Scott's theatrical outrage, he was accepting Scott's characterizations. To launch an aggressive counteroffense would mean that they were fighting Scott's implications rather than the facts of the case, which were overwhelmingly on Chaplin's side. Millikan focused on the weak case of the prosecution and essentially asserted that what the jury thought of Chaplin was irrelevant in the face of the facts.

On April 17, after three hours of deliberation, the Jury voted 11 to 1 to uphold Joan Berry's claim about the child's paternity. The *Los Angeles Times* published two pictures to accompany their story about the verdict. The first showed Chaplin on the witness stand, hand rubbing his face, looking pained and confused. The second showed Joan Berry with a radiant smile while receiving the news of the verdict via telephone, with her daughter glaring at the camera.

"Scott," wrote Florabel Muir, "gloated happily that it was a clear-cut victory for old-fashioned Americanism, the right of helpless females to redress the sanctity of the home. I doubt it. I do believe, however that our famous American spirit of fair play was a potent factor in bringing Charlie his comeuppance."

Joseph Scott couldn't argue the facts, but he could argue conduct and he could argue morality. It was on that basis that Chaplin lost the case. The issue was never really about whether or not Chaplin was the father of the child; the issue was whether or not he would be punished for sexual license over a span of decades.

Chaplin appealed the verdict; the appeal was denied. Loyd Wright wrote his client that "We feel that there has been a law established in the case that is ill-founded and destructive to the fundamental rights of citizens. . . .We have not any further appeal that can be taken."

Adding financial insult to what already amounted to personal injury, the court directed that Chaplin pay Joseph Scott's fee. Scott told Wright that he wanted to discuss the amount. Wright wrote Chaplin that "if we did not wish to discuss it he would file a petition in court. I am reluctant to see you go through the court proceeding and suggest that you authorize us to negotiate with Scott as to what his fees shall be."

There was much back-and-forth. Millikan wrote Chaplin that Scott was definitely going to petition the court for his fee, at which time "he will undoubtedly serve subpoena requiring the production of your income tax records, evidence as to the amount which you have in various banks, your stocks and other securities and all other items of property and he will, of course, require your personal presence in court by subpoena."

Millikan went on to say that he thought the court would certainly award Scott $25,000 but it might go as high as $75,000. "I should say that it is quite likely that the court may award around $50,000. It is a gamble one way or the other."

In January 1947, Chaplin sent a check for $39,706 as payment for Joseph Scott. Later that same year, Scott got the court to increase the money paid to Carol Ann to $100 a week, and then asked Chaplin to reimburse him for his work in that specific matter. The figure Scott mentioned was $500. Charles Millikan told Scott that he was "somewhat disappointed that you would think the amount suggested in your letter is a reasonable amount." Scott wouldn't budge. Millikan wrote Chaplin that both he and Loyd Wright thought the figure was high, but that if Scott followed through with his threat of going to court with an attendant hearing, he would get what he asked for. They recommended that Chaplin pay the $500 and be done with Scott once and for all. Scott received his $500 in January 1948.

For Chaplin, all this constituted blood-curdling injustice. For Joseph Scott, it was retrospective retribution for a man he believed had it coming, law or no law—rough justice.

"[Scott's] was a sordid performance," noted Father George Dunne. "And it won the case. Chaplin was defeated. So were truth and justice."

Chaplin's response was steadfast: outrage. "Did I seek her out?" he asked Harry Crocker. "No, she sought me out. Wasn't she, before she met me, the mistress of several other men? Wasn't she arrested prior to meeting me as a shop-lifter? Why do they take the word of such a woman instead of mine?"

In October 1946, Joan Berry tried a nightclub career, appearing in West Virginia's Sky Club. She was billed as "Joan Barry, Lovely—Vivacious—Captivating Ex-Protégé of Charlie Chaplin." While playing in the town of Fairmont, she was found badly bruised, and was later released. Later that year, she married Russell Seck, a thirty-six-year-old man who worked for a railroad in Pittsburgh.

In late 1952, Berry was subpoened to give testimony in the government's planned immigration proceedings against Chaplin. She replied, "I do not feel any disloyalty repeating the remarks of the gentleman from the Immigration Service: 'Come on, Miss Berry. You owe it to your government to keep this man out of the country. After all, if it hadn't been for the government being behind you, you might not have won your paternity suit.'

"I do not consider the method of eliciting information by appealing to the immaturity and weakness in one's nature is representative of the United States."

It was the beginning of Berry shifting her narrative 180 degrees, although whether that shift derived from guilt, political sympathy, or a bipolar episode is impossible to determine.

Beginning in the last week of May 1953, Berry wrote several rambling letters to Chaplin's attorney Loyd Wright. Initially they involve Carol Ann's court-appointed guardian refusing to forward the child's support stipend as long as Berry and her daughter were living in Mexico. It was a matter in which Wright had no involvement, so he ignored the letters.

But on June 11, she wrote Wright again, reporting on a conversation she had with the FBI and "my cowardice nine years ago. I refer specifically to the events leading up the Dept. of Justice instigated 'Mann Act Trial.'"

She said the Bureau insisted at the time of the trial that she remain in Los Angeles or go to jail as a material witness. "Sometimes, when I was being questioned, I would find myself unable to give an adequate explanation of certain events. Then Mr. Carr would helpfully suggest—'Could this have been the way it was—'

"Yes, many times Mr. Carr was kindness itself.

"And yet they must have recognized the weakness of the charge. Could it have been that regardless of innocence or guilt, someone was out to malign Charles Chaplin—the Chaplin who asked for a 'Second front'?

"The paternity trials were something else again. . . . 'My champions' weren't interested in my baby. They were just anti-progressive pro-reaction and anti-Chaplin.

"I ask you, Mr. Wright, who really won this paternity trial? Has this money, so dearly won, brought security for my child, happiness for my mother or peace of mind to me? Am I guilty of tale-bearing or ingratitude if I say that this unfortunate situation is still being exploited. . . .

"And their methods—spare me please . . .

"'Do you think, Miss Barry, that you were the only girl?' . . .

"'Did you meet any communists?'. . .

"Can no one speak out against McCarthyism without being called crazy? (I do not ask this facetiously.)"

On June 16, 1953, on stationery from the Motel El Patio in Ensenada, Mexico, Berry wrote a final letter to Wright in which she stated that the

scientific blood tests . . . proved, conclusively, that Mr. Charles Spencer Chaplin could not have been the parent of my child.

This is to inform you that I hereby recognize the authority of the conclusions of these medical reports.

It is my intention to ask the court to reverse its decision in the "paternity suit" and to request a discontinuence of support and maintenance.

Difficult, as it may be to understand, I take this action in the best interest of my daughter, so that she may have the opportunity to develop as a normal child.

Joan Berry Seck

Wright cautiously responded to this flurry of correspondence on June 23, telling Seck:

I am interested in the facts which you have written and would be most happy were I extended the privilege of discussing with you what you say in your communications, if you are ever in Los Angeles.

Very truly yours

On June 28, Joan Berry Seck, accompanied by a lawyer from Joseph Scott's office, was admitted to the General Hospital in Los Angeles at her own request. The *Los Angeles Times* reported, "The fact that Miss Berry has been unable to obtain employment as an entertainer and has lost an alarming amount of weight recently indicated mental depression may be a factor in her entering the hospital, attendants said." Besides Carol Ann, Berry was now the mother of two other children. She gave her address as 1725 Stanford Street, Redondo Beach—the home of Loyd Wright.

Berry was committed to the Patton State Mental Hospital in San Bernardino after being diagnosed as "schizophrenic, or person with dual personality." She was there for eleven years, after which she was released. She lived a quiet life until her death in 2007.

The same year Joan Berry was committed, California passed a law making blood tests definitive evidence in paternity cases.

Joseph Scott died in March 1958 at the age of ninety. His body

lay in state in Los Angeles City Hall for three days. Vice President
Richard Nixon sent condolences and Governor Goodwin Knight
attended the funeral, along with several Catholic bishops.

Today, a statue of Joseph Scott stands on Grand Avenue in down-
town Los Angeles, outside the court building named after Stanley
Mosk—the judge who ordered the case against Chaplin to proceed
despite the results of the blood tests.

Several years after the paternity trial, Father George Dunne spent
an evening in conversation with Chaplin. Dunne noted that "In his
brief reference to the paternity case he had nothing to say in criticism
of Joe Scott. It seemed remarkable restraint on the part of a man who
had been publicly held up to scorn and scathingly judged."

Chaplin did go into detail regarding his feelings about nationalism and his refusal to become a citizen. He told Dunne, "I have been
in nearly every country, and I have found people everywhere, regardless of color, race or nationality, to be pretty much the same—all
human beings with the same desires, the same impulses. I feel a bond
with all of them. If I were to take citizenship anywhere it would be
here. This is where I have made my home. This is where I have made
my career and my money. I am grateful to America.

"But the swearing of allegiance to any country seems to me a rejection of all the other people in the world. And this I cannot bring
myself to do."

Chaplin told Dunne that he badly wanted to visit Europe, to show
his wife and children where he had come from, but he was afraid
that once out of the country his reentry permit might be revoked. He
had made some cautious inquiries with the State Department, and
they had assured him that there was no danger of anything like that
happening. He would not be denied readmission.

Chaplin's openness to a serious discussion with a priest is interesting. Chaplin didn't broadcast it, but he was an atheist. "I was full
of religion until about the age of twelve," he told the writer Richard
Meryman in 1966. "My brother got rid of all that for me. He said,
'There's no God. If there was a God, why would he let your father
die like an animal?' He convinced me."

The court experience clearly hardened Chaplin. His next film, the most audacious of his career, would firmly position his new screen character as the antithesis of the Tramp. This time, he would portray a moral renegade—a misanthrope, a killer. In so doing, he would convince many people of the correctness of Joseph Scott's characterizations.

While he was being pilloried in the press, while he was being prosecuted by the federal government, Chaplin threw himself into two projects: preparing the film he would call *Monsieur Verdoux* and tending his growing family.

Socially, he was invigorated by his friendship with Salka Viertel, whose weekend salons at her Santa Monica house introduced him to a variety of artists both young and old who had exiled themselves from Nazi Germany.

Thomas Mann and Hanns Eisler were living on the west side of Los Angeles. Bertolt Brecht resided in a two-story clapboard house on 26th Street in Santa Monica; Heinrich Mann was a few blocks away on Montana Avenue. Salka Viertel's beloved house was on Mabery, a few blocks from Santa Monica Beach, while Lion Feuchtwanger had a Spanish mansion called Villa Aurora that overlooked the ocean. (One of Feuchtwanger's interior decorations was a dartboard featuring a picture of Adolf Hitler.) Vicki Baum, author of *Grand Hotel*, lived on Amalfi Drive, near Eisler, while Alma Mahler-Werfel, the widow of both Gustav Mahler and Franz Werfel, the author of *Song of Bernadette*, lived on North Bedford Drive, next door to conductor Bruno Walter.

Of this group, Chaplin grew especially close to Viertel and Eisler.

He helped out Viertel financially from time to time when the lack of screenwriting assignments imperiled her ability to hold on to her beloved house. As for Eisler, he was the brother of Gerhard Eisler, a Communist agent who in 1918 had established in Vienna the first Communist Party outside of Russia.

Eisler had studied with Arnold Schoenberg, and composed in the twelve-tone style, although without the dislocation usually present in Schoenberg and his adherents. In Berlin Eisler had collaborated with Brecht and done movie scores. In America, he wrote scores for the documentarian Joris Ivens and for Fritz Lang—his score for Lang's *Hangmen Also Die* got an Oscar nomination.

Eisler would remember that he helped Chaplin with arrangements for his score for *Monsieur Verdoux*. "That was just a matter of friendship," Eisler said. The relationship must have been smooth, because Eisler wrote Chaplin in 1947 regarding an Eisler score for a proposed reissue of *The Circus:* "My usual salary for a motion picture is $7,500 (this includes all orchestral arrangements).

"Of course, 'The Circus' needs much more music than any other film.

"But it is up to Mr. Chaplin to decide what salary he wants to pay me. I also want to mention the fact that my scoring of the picture will be done with the greatest economy. I use mostly 10 or 12 instruments. . . . Please let me know in a letter what Mr. Chaplin has decided."

Eisler began work, but, as he remembered, "Straight after that, as I was in difficulties with the 'Unamerican Committee,' was also arrested and that put an end to it. That was a difficult fight and I couldn't do any more film music." Eisler, however, arranged six cues he wrote for *The Circus* into a composition he entitled "Septet No. 2," a jaunty but astringently unmelodic composition that would have worked for the film after a fashion but would probably not have pleased Chaplin. In any case, Chaplin didn't reissue *The Circus* until 1970, and with his own musical score.

Eisler's situation was actually more complicated than he said. His sister Ruth Fischer had been near the top of the German Communist Party until she was expelled by Stalin for being excessively radical. She promptly became a committed anti-Stalinist. When she wasn't writing anti-Stalinist screeds, she was denouncing both her brothers as Soviet spies. Ultimately, this led to their arrest. After his sister denounced him as the "Karl Marx of music," Hanns Eisler would be deported in March 1948.

Despite her resolutely anti-Stalinist activities, Ruth Fischer aroused the interest of Senator Joseph McCarthy and managed to avoid arrest only by escaping to Paris.

Chaplin, brought up in a family environment characterized by alternating waves of indifference and incompetence, was stunned at the homicidal infighting of the Eislers, and compared them to something out of Shakespeare's history plays.

THE JOAN BERRY business took up years of Chaplin's life, but what he couldn't have known was that it was more than a storm that had to be ridden out. The tide had turned definitively against him.

In 1945, Congressman John Rankin of Mississippi deviated from a diatribe about a left-wing publication to add that he was sure it "got into the home of Charles Chaplin, the perverted subject of Great Britain who has become famous for his forcible seduction of white girls." (Rankin was a racist of legendary proportions, obsessed by what used to be called miscegenation.)

That same year, Senator William Langer (R-ND) introduced a bill directing the attorney general to investigate Chaplin for the purposes of deportation.

The bill didn't pass, but the senator didn't let up; in 1947 Langer wondered in a Senate hearing how "a man like Charlie Chaplin, with his communistic leanings, with his unsavory record of lawbreaking, of rape, of the debauching of American girls 16 and 17 years of age remains [in the country]." That same year, the notorious anti-Semite Gerald L. K. Smith falsely announced that Chaplin had set up a special fund to bring aliens into America.

Rankin put himself back in the picture in 1947 when he went a step further: "I am today demanding that Attorney General Tom Clark institute proceedings to deport Charlie Chaplin. He has refused to become an American citizen, his very life in Hollywood is detrimental to the moral fabric of America. In that way he can be kept off the American screen, and his loathsome pictures can be kept from the eyes of the American youth. He should be deported and got rid of at once."

It was only going to get worse.

THE GENESIS OF *Monsieur Verdoux* derived from Orson Welles, who approached Chaplin in 1941 with the idea of starring in a Welles film based on the wife-killer Henri Landru.

Welles was always a flamboyant pinwheel of ambitious plans, some of which actually came to fruition. Chaplin wasn't interested in acting for anybody else, but the idea stayed with him. He and Welles came to an agreement that was signed July 24, 1941, just a few months after the release of *Citizen Kane*:

"I hereby sell, assign and transfer to you my original idea of the story of Henri Desire Landru, conceived by me originally for you, and also my original title for the subject, which is THE LADY KILLER, for the sum of five thousand dollars, which you agree to pay me concurrently with the signing of this agreement. You shall have full and complete rights in and to the idea and may use the same without restriction or limitation."

Welles agreed to be available to consult on Chaplin's script "provided I am able to do so without serious interference with my own work, and I shall offer suggestions to you with reference to such scripts, which said suggestions and all ideas that may be embodied therein shall, of course, be included in the grant hereinafter provided for, without additional compensation."

For his part, Chaplin agreed to give Welles screen credit. "I agree that such screen credit shall be as determined by you." The provisional wording was specified as "Suggested by Orson Welles," but that was crossed out and replaced by the handwritten "Based on an idea by Orson Welles."

For the rest of his life, Welles claimed that Chaplin tried to wriggle out of giving him screen credit. He also asserted that he had given Chaplin a complete Welles script for the project, and that some of the film's best scenes derived from that script. "I wrote it," Welles declared to Henry Jaglom. "I have real contempt for him because I worked very hard. Offered him something out of my love for him. It was not a suggestion, it was a *screenplay*."

Chaplin stoutly denied any such thing, saying, "He never wrote anything. Nothing was ever written by him. I wrote every word of that picture."

The agreement includes only "my original idea," without mentioning any script, which surely would have been included in any legal agreement, not to mention the fact that it would have been worth a lot more than $5,000. No such script has turned up in any of Welles's papers, nor does one exist in Chaplin's papers. The story is almost certainly another one of Welles's self-aggrandizing fabrications.

On the other hand, when *Monsieur Verdoux* was ultimately previewed at the Academy Award Theater in Los Angeles on April 11, 1947, the program announced that it was "An Original Story written by Charles Chaplin," with no mention of Welles's contribution. It wasn't until ten days after the film opened in New York that Chaplin telephoned the studio from New York to add Welles's credit to the main title. Two days later, replacement reels were shipped to New York.

Chaplin began work on the script for *Verdoux* in November 1942, but the story seems to have been firmly outlined in his mind before that, if a letter Alexander Woollcott wrote to Thornton Wilder in October 1942 is any indication. Woollcott and Chaplin had just had dinner in New York, and the comedian had "lavishly acted out every scene of his coming Landru picture which, as you may know, is going to be called *Lady Killer*. . . . I suppose the picture, when released, will inspire a few throat-cuttings here and there, but, on the whole, its effect should be beneficial and will improve the home life of several million Americans."

With time out for trials both legal and emotional, Chaplin labored over the script for several years. The final script is close to the finished film, but some scenes are more elaborate: among others, the garden party scene where Verdoux once again encounters the blunderbuss Annabella is more extensive in the script than in the film, as is the sequence involving Annabella's maid accidentally mistaking poison for peroxide.

Chaplin's script opens with narration by a dead man, an audacious gambit which was stolen three years later by Billy Wilder for *Sunset Boulevard*. Some of Chaplin's stage directions are interesting in that they show how carefully he worked out character attitudes:

"After establishing shot, CAMERA DOLLIES to CLOSE UP of Mons. Verdoux. With the finesse of a tonsorial artist, he is trimming his rose bushes. PAN with him as he goes from one bush to another, showing a medium-sized incinerator in the background. . . . After reading letter, he counts the money, his nimble fingers racing through the bills with the professional air of a bank clerk. He counts it twice, then exits into hall."

Martha Raye's character of Annabella is described as "an ex-waitress of the 'Stella Dallas' type—a ridiculous, stupid woman of forty." Occasionally he slips into the terminology of the working comedian:

"CLOSEUP OF MME. GROSNAY
as she 'gives it to him' right back."

Or this: " 'He takes it big.' "

Chaplin carefully delineates the attitude of each of the characters, as in his description of Verdoux showing off his property: "Then with the air of a floor-walker showing a customer through a department store, he delivers his lines. One has the feeling he has sold many houses before."

There are occasional suggestive lines that were bound to run afoul of the Breen Office, which engaged in a long point-counterpoint with Chaplin over the script. Compared to the deferential attitude Breen had taken with *Modern Times* and *The Great Dictator*, the response toward *Monsieur Verdoux* was openly confrontational.

On February 20, 1946, Joe Breen sent his reaction to the script, which he termed "UNACCEPTABLE under the provisions of the Production Code . . . the story contains a false enunciation of moral values, which seems to be in fundamental conflict with the theory of sound ethics as set forth in the Industry's Production Code. . . . Specifically, it seems to us that the closing pages of the script attempt to present an evaluation of the moral heinousness or lack of heinousness . . . of Verdoux's Bluebeard career. As we read . . . it seems to us that the burden of the argument comes inevitably down to this conclusion . . . that Verdoux's 'comedy of murders' is not such an outrageous transgression against the moral order as the court [of law] would make it seem.

"We pass over those elements which seem to be anti-social in their concept and significance. These are the sections of the story in which Verdoux indicts the 'System' and impugns the present-day social structure. . . . Without at all entering into any dialectics on the question of whether wars are mass murder or justifiable killings, the fact still remains that Verdoux, during the course of his speeches, makes a serious attempt to evaluate the moral quality of his crimes.

"The second basic reason for the unacceptability of this story . . . lies in the fact that this is very largely a story of a type of confidence man who induces a number of women to turn over their finances to him by beguiling them into a series of mock marriages. This phase of the story has about it a distasteful flavor of illicit sex, which in our judgement is not good."

The characterization of The Girl as an obvious prostitute would have to be "substantially revised and qualified." Finally, there was the climactic exchange with the priest, which Breen found "blasphemous in flavor, if not in fact." Breen closed by saying that because of the "serious character" of his objections, "we will place ourselves at your disposal to discuss [them] should you desire."

Five days later Chaplin replied that the Production Code was perilously close to "encroaching on Constitutional rights of free speech." He was, he wrote, confused because Breen's letter had been full of "generalities, suppositions and misnomers." He asked Breen to be more specific so that "I shall be more competent to discuss [your] imputations." Breen responded by writing that "This story violates the provisions of the Production Code, in that it sets forth a false evaluation of the evil of Verdoux's crimes. The final pages of this story, in effect, enunciate the thesis that individual crimes are of little import, when one considers the crimes committed by nations on a wholesale scale."

Chaplin wrote back on March 3, arguing that Verdoux was a work of art, not a political editorial, and that Verdoux's exchanges at the end of the script "do not connote the message of the story, but are an adjunct of the plot." It was, he wrote, "the story of a man—a weak character with latent criminal tendencies" that had been "aggravated by conditions of the time. Depressions, wars, economic insecurity and frustration . . . set him on a path of crime."

He closed by saying that the censors hadn't read the script with enough care, and that if they gave it another go they would "not see any 'indictment' or 'impugning of a system' but they WILL see, in part, a criticism of it, and surely no system is above criticism."

It was a lot of saber-rattling. Chaplin came to Breen's office on March 12. Breen's opening salvo was, "What have you against the Catholic church?" Breen objected to Verdoux calling a priest "My good man." Chaplin agreed to call him "Father." Breen objected to Verdoux's "continually scoring off the priest." Chaplin said, "The criminal is going to his death and attempts to go with bravado. The priest is dignified throughout and his lines are appropriate. . . ."

"You impugn society and the whole state," Breen said.

"Well, after all, the state and society are not Simon pure, and criticism of them is not inadmissable, surely?"

It was a tiresome and intrinsically ridiculous process, but Chaplin managed to get the script approved. Breen followed the meeting with a letter summarizing the agreement they had reached. There followed more weeks of back-and-forth that resulted in minor changes in dialogue and characterization: Lydia, one of Verdoux's wives, a particularly ill-tempered termagant, had the line "Come to bed." Chaplin changed the line to "Go to bed," thereby removing the implication that both of them would be in the same bed at the same time. Other specific requests included, "Please change the word 'voluptuous' in Verdoux's speech. . . . There should be no showing of, or suggestion of, toilets in the bathroom. . . . The joke about 'Scraping her bottom' is unacceptable."

The penultimate moment of the film, when Verdoux tastes rum for the first time, is slightly different in the script. The stage directions say that "Verdoux drinks it and grimaces," but in the finished film Verdoux's expression is one of guarded appreciation.

It's a long script—215 pages—and although Chaplin didn't really cut much, the film ran only 124 minutes, because for the most part Chaplin paced it briskly, like a boulevard comedy.

Once again, he needed to cast an ingénue, an innocent reduced to prostitution. Chaplin met Marilyn Nash because of her forehand. She was a pre-med student at the University of Arizona when she came to Los Angeles for Christmas and registered at the Beverly Hills Hotel. She played tennis with a man named Karl Kramer who thought she was surprisingly good and invited her to Chaplin's house on Sunday to play. She was partnered with Tim Durant, while Chaplin played with Kramer. "They beat us because Charlie always liked to win," remembered Nash.

"The only thing I had read about Charlie was the Joan Berry case. I had never seen one of his films, I didn't know who he was." Chaplin liked Nash because of her physical grace and because she was "natural and untrained." Chaplin directed her in a silent screen test, and a few days later put her under contract for $50 a week, gradually ascending to $250 a week.

It was all a strange experience for a pre-med student. Nash thought the Chaplin studio was old-fashioned, right down to the gas jets on the walls of the dressing rooms—"when you walked in you could smell gas. This bothered me terribly. I thought the studio was gonna catch fire. But I figured, well, I guess they've been burning it here for a long time, so it must be all right."

Nash met Charlie's old assistant Henry Bergman as well as Edna Purviance. Bergman was in failing health and would die during the production of *Monsieur Verdoux*, which sent Chaplin into a tirade. It seemed that Chaplin had lent Bergman a considerable amount of money, and Bergman hadn't spent any of it. Rather, he had hidden it in his mattress, and the police had found it. "All that money was in his mattress," Chaplin snapped. "IN HIS MATTRESS! Never spent a penny, it was all there in the mattress!"

Chaplin began working with Nash on her scenes, and she found that no detail was too small, right down to the position of her fingers. "I don't want you to do your finger that way, I want it crooked just like that," he told her. "In other words, my finger was out like that, but no, it's not that way, it's this way. Every little teeny, tiny thing he wanted perfection. And maybe that's why he wanted someone green, so he could mold them without having somebody that's a pro try to mold it his way and then throw in his own personality."

Chaplin hired Robert Lewis to play the small part of a pharmacist. Lewis had been a member of the Group Theatre, cofounded the Actors Studio with Elia Kazan and Cheryl Crawford, and was the director of the original Broadway production of *Brigadoon*. He found Chaplin fascinating to watch. "He'd entertain the troops between shots with hilarious imitations, such as William Gillette's inanimate underplaying in Sherlock Holmes, a Kabuki actor pounding his feet into the floor and crossing his eyes in pain, or Maurice Schwartz, the Yiddish actor, intoning a speech while twirling an imaginary beard that went clear to the floor."

Lewis was with Chaplin the day he tested Edna Purviance for the part of Madame Grosnay. Purviance had memorized the scene, and did well, speaking simply and intelligently. But Chaplin wanted to have her serve tea during the scene to avoid it being static, and she couldn't talk and move at the same time. "What do you want me to do, Charlie?" Edna asked. "Act or talk?" The part was played by Isobel Elsom.

As far as Lewis's character was concerned, Chaplin gave him only one direction: "He's the kind of bore who doesn't talk. He lectures." Lewis noticed the pure pleasure Chaplin took in the daily act of work, and one day Chaplin explained why.

It seemed that Chaplin's grandmother had a tendency to spread her favors around. When his shoemaker grandfather grew depressed about his compromised marriage, he would sit down at his bench, pick up his knife, and start to cut leather. As the process continued, the worry on his face would dissipate and was replaced by a satisfied, peaceful expression. Practicing his craft caused everything else to recede into the distance. "Chaplin believed that an allegiance to craft, whatever it might be, was an indispensable source of strength."

Dan James, Chaplin's assistant on *The Great Dictator*, was hoping to be hired for the new picture but it didn't happen. Chaplin hadn't seen James's Broadway musical *Bloomer Girl* and, as many of Chaplin's assistants found, once he was done with the picture he was done with them. As James put it, "He drained me. . . . It took me a year to get over Charlie."

Instead, Chaplin hired Robert Florey for $900 a week to be what Florey's contract specified as "director and/or associate director," his duties to include "assistance in the preparation of the story and in cutting and editing, if so required, and such other services as may be required of directors and/or associate directors according to the custom of the industry."

Curt Courant, an eminent European cameraman who had worked for Lang, Hitchcock, and Renoir, was getting $700 a week to back up Rollie Totheroh as "production supervisor and/or production assistant and/or technical advisor," while Martha Raye was paid $2,500 a week for ten weeks of work as Chaplin's costar—good money for a comedienne who hadn't made a movie in several years. Chaplin's first choice for the part had been Fanny Brice, but she was satisfied with the comparatively easy job of playing Baby Snooks on the radio and didn't want to make movies. In any case, Raye proved to be perfect casting, and Chaplin knew it.

Robert Florey had known Chaplin for more than twenty years, and was unpleasantly surprised by his explosions of temperament on the set. "Often, Charlie gets into great rages which last only a few moments. . . . His film is ruined, destroyed, it's a real conspiracy. He has to do it all over, that's going to cost him an arm and a leg—all because a corner of the set seemed a little dark. And then the storm passes, he films a scene that pleases him, everything is better, he smiles, he is content, he is gracious, charming, enchanting and what an enchanter. Probably to obtain complete forgiveness, he begins to play for us one of his pantomimes, and everybody splits their sides laughing. . . . Everyone is pleased, at least until the next thunderbolt, which will strike in five minutes or three days, depending on the will of the master."

Chaplin's designated target seems to have been Wheeler Dryden, who was working as a general assistant. Florey transcribed a Chaplin monologue regarding Dryden during the shooting of the greenhouse scene: "No, no, no, shut up, you silly bastard, for Christ's sake, we cut to Annabella, you don't understand anything about motion pictures, I know what I am doing, yeah, that's what I cut to, I have been in this business for 20—for 30 years, you don't think I'm gaga? Oh, shut up. . . . Syphilitic Christ. . . . We cut to Annabella, I know goddamn well what I am doing. . . . For Christ's sake, I have been cutting this scene in my mind for the past three years."

Chaplin was completely focused on performance, and any technician getting in the way of his priority was quickly set straight. Curt Courant wanted to adjust a light in order to avoid a shadow on Chaplin's face, and was met with, "I laugh at your shadow. It's natural to have some shadows after all. Let's go, let's start. Hurry! Hurry!" A microphone shadow showed up on the wall and Courant pointed it out. "It doesn't matter to me. They will think it's a bird; let's go, hurry up, film!" Courant shifted the light anyway and Chaplin didn't understand. "Why are you changing again? You annoy me with all your technical tricks. Come on, hurry up!"

The film was shot more or less efficiently from May 21 to September 5, 1946, but Chaplin missed Karl Struss's sculptured lighting and the myriad of gray tones he had given *The Great Dictator*. Totheroh and Courant's lighting was flat and uninteresting by comparison.

Chaplin immediately accepted Raye as a high-end pro on his own level. Outtakes show Chaplin breaking up with and at Raye. "With Martha Raye he gave no direction," remembered Marilyn Nash. "They would get together after she got her make-up on—he's all ready, and they're ready to shoot—and all of a sudden she'd tell a joke, or he'd tell a joke, and everybody'd crack up laughing. And this would go on and on, and then finally he'd say, 'OK, let's settle down.' Then she'd crack another joke and then everybody'd crack up laughing. I mean, if you got two hours work out of a whole day, that was a lot with Martha. And she was funny. I mean, she was hilarious. But so was he. They were like two peas in a pod. When two people click, it's wonderful. And they clicked."

Raye was essentially playing the same part Jack Oakie played in *The Great Dictator*—a crass, unkillable force of nature who reduces Chaplin's character to a state of flustered impotence. Chaplin's generosity in throwing scenes to his costar is one of the most charming things about the picture, and about him.

"You can do anything if you don't have a vulgar mind, Maggie," Chaplin told her. "Have a little pixyishness. Let them have fun, it won't be vulgar. Some can swear, others can't. It's like another gift, a talent. It's there or it isn't. You have to be what you are naturally." That advice gave her the key to the character.

Chaplin only offered suggestions on the margins of Raye's performance—telling her not to wear large earrings, which would distract the audience from her face. "Dress well and be sure your makeup and hair are perfect. That way you can be funnier just tripping than you would be doing a complete pratfall in plainer clothes."

When the company went on location to Lake Arrowhead to shoot Verdoux's unsuccessful attempt to murder Annabella, things slowed down even more. "I thought that scene would never get done," said Marilyn Nash. "As soon as they would start rocking, they'd start laughing so hard they'd both plop down. And Rollie would just sit and wait and everybody'd wait until they got themselves together again."

If Martha Raye could do no wrong, Robert Florey could do no right. Chaplin's intention in hiring Florey was to have him help with French atmosphere. Florey had enthusiasm, a good camera eye, and adored Chaplin. Florey remembered that "Long before he immortalized his 'dance of the rolls' [in *The Gold Rush*] on many occasions when we lunched at Musso-Frank's restaurant, Chaplin provided us with endless fun by draping a napkin around his neck like a curtain, spearing two rolls with forks and making them dance to the accompaniment of songs in the style of the Lancashire Lads."

But if Chaplin's history proved anything, it was that he didn't—couldn't—delegate. Florey worked with Chaplin on the script's final draft and was uncomfortable with the sermonizing. "The mood of the text sometimes seemed to me much too macabre; besides, there was much repetition, and the exposé of the theories was rather confused. Many little things which could have been shown on the screen were explained at length in sometimes awkward dialogue."

Chaplin accepted some of Florey's ideas—Florey claimed the last glass of rum was his idea. But once the picture went into production, Chaplin had no patience for Florey's suggestions, and he was gradually relegated to the status of a quietly fuming onlooker, credit or no credit. "He was very unhappy—you could tell that," said Marilyn Nash, "but he never said a word. . . . He thought he was going to be an associate director—he was not. He was what we called the 'runner,' the 'go-fer.' Florey didn't have any involvement in direction, blocking, camera set-ups, nothing, nothing."

Florey saved some of Chaplin's rough storyboard sketches, proving that his setups were basic but planned, and, for his purposes, generally effective. After the film wrapped in September 1946, the two men never spoke again.

Marilyn Nash noticed that Oona never came to the studio, and didn't play tennis. "Charlie . . . respected her, her opinion. He always asked her opinion. She was a very classy woman. She had a lot of introspection, and could carry on a conversation without being silly. A lot of the women I had met in Hollywood thought only about themselves, but Oona was very deep and she loved Charlie dearly. She wasn't insecure; she was very sure of him."

CHAPLIN SHOT MONSIEUR *Verdoux* under a total news blackout. All Hollywood knew was the title and that the story didn't involve the Tramp. Chaplin's intentions were to release the film with little fanfare—*Variety* wrote that all he thought necessary was "a series of simple ads announcing the picture, the theater and the date." Both *City Lights* and *Modern Times* had been released that way, and both films had been hits. But both of those films had involved a familiar character and approach. *Verdoux* was something entirely new. United Artists, a company that was about $1 million in the red, had only about two weeks to prepare the public for a film unlike anything Chaplin had made, unlike any movie anybody had made. Its originality, not to mention its problems, would make it the most torturous professional experience of Chaplin's life.

Chaplin did give an interview to the *Los Angeles Times* in which he intoned his intentions for the title character: "Verdoux is a very complex character who, under certain social conditions, breaks down. . . . His tragedy is that of the *petit bourgeois* during the depression—any depression. Not that he personifies the rank and file; he is an exceptional character, a madman who verges on genius. . . . *Verdoux* is the only one of my films with which I have been satisfied."

Chaplin attempted to minimize the pushback he was obviously expecting. He responded to a question about the fact that the public might see some awkwardly autobiographical elements in the character's attitude toward difficult women. "One's work is one's work. One's private life is one's own. I believe the two should be kept separate. I have been given a great deal of unfavorable publicity—and, like everything else in this industry, it has been amplified out of all proportion to the truth. . . .

"Funny as [*Verdoux*] is, it has a great morality. It shows that crime is unprofitable; this man is frustrated by it. It contains no sex, and less violence than a western."

Shortly before the film was released in April 1947, the publicity office at United Artists received a cautionary notice from the Chaplin studio stating UA was not to use any of the following words in their advertising: "Wives, Lover, Passionate, Bigamy, Sex."

HEDDA HOPPER WAS furious at Chaplin's temerity in releasing a new movie. She wrote J. Edgar Hoover, "I'd like to run every one of those rats out of the country and start with Charlie Chaplin. In no other country in the world would he be allowed to do what he's doing. And now he's finished another picture. . . . It's about time we stood up to be counted."

And there was this sentence she wrote but crossed out: "You give me the material and I'll blast." Later in 1947, she wrote Hoover another letter, telling him, "If you had your way, I feel sure you'd name names, which is the only way we'll ever get rid of them. Some day they've got to stand up and be counted." She closed by telling Hoover he was her choice for president.

While *Monsieur Verdoux* was being shot, Hoover requested that the Los Angeles office update him on current Communist activities in Hollywood. There was no reply for three months, at which point Hoover snapped the leash and demanded that Richard Hood's office "immediately comply with the Bureau's request." The Los Angeles office responded with a roster of films that included *The Strange Love of Martha Ivers* and *Cloak and Dagger*, specified mainly because of the suspected political sympathies involving the cast or crew.

A few months later, the Los Angeles office began emphasizing that the root problem rested with producers. Specifically, Walter Wanger, David Selznick, Sam Goldwyn, the Warner brothers, and Chaplin were regarded as employers and protectors of Communists.

* * *

CHAPLIN PREVIEWED HIS new film for friends. Not surprisingly, the response was overwhelmingly positive. Lion Feuchtwanger wrote him, "The picture wins in recollection and the more one thinks over it. There is no slack spot, and everything imprints itself lastingly on one's mind, since everything has meaning and significance. It is a great achievement made so no less by your courage than by your artistic perfection. Your work will cause hundreds of thousands to think, it will improve many people and will make them more intelligent and better aware of what is going on. Your film is a great ethical lecture."

Chaplin responded with a telegram thanking Feuchtwanger for his "wonderful letter" and informing him that the Hays Office and the New York censors had passed the picture without a cut. If Feuchtwanger's categorization of the film as an "ethical lecture" didn't alarm Chaplin, the bulk of the reviews soon would.

The newspaper ads on opening day in New York featured a still of Chaplin in costume as Verdoux looking every inch the successful bourgeois. "Full of Comedy!" "Full of Drama!" were the taglines. There was nothing about the actual content of the film.

Chaplin was obviously under the comforting illusion that his audience would follow wherever he led them, if only because they always had. He failed to take into account the drip-drip-drip of comprehensively negative publicity that had been his norm for the previous five years.

The audience on opening night in New York let him know that his confidence was irrelevant. They were not enthralled. "There was an uneasy atmosphere in the theater that night," Chaplin remembered, "a feeling that the audience had come to prove something. The moment the film started, instead of the eager anticipation and the happy stir of the past that had greeted my films, there was nervous applause with a few hisses. I [am] loath to admit it, but those few hisses hurt more than all the antagonism of the press. . . . I whispered to Oona, 'I'm going out in the lobby, I can't take it.'"

Ruth Conte, the wife of the actor Richard Conte, was leaning against the lobby doors when they were pushed out from the inside of the auditorium. It was Chaplin, who muttered as he stormed past her, "I should never have made this film. It was a terrible mistake."

Robert Lewis attended the New York premiere and noted with astonishment the audience's low rumblings of displeasure. The movie wasn't merely provocative, as *Modern Times* and *The Great Dictator* had been. It was defiant, with a harshness unalleviated by Chaplin's innate charm.

The party after the premiere was at 21, where Chaplin quickly downed a couple of drinks—highly unusual for him. Only a few people complimented him on the picture, and the other celebrities didn't comment on it. "I watched Louella Parsons, dressed in black, sitting in a corner, her disapproving eyes glued on Chaplin," recalled Lewis. "She looked like some predator waiting for him to do or say something that might be used against him in her column."

Hoping to lighten the oppressive mood, Chaplin took center stage with his bullfight routine in which he played both bull and matador. Watching his friend, Lewis remembered Chaplin telling him of a recurring nightmare. He was playing in front of a large audience and nobody was laughing. He would wake up in a cold sweat. It was the classic comedian's anxiety dream, and now it was actually happening.

Lewis and Donald Ogden Stewart got Chaplin back to his hotel. He was slightly drunk and let his friends undress him as he sat on the edge of the bed. "They couldn't take it, could they?" he kept saying. "I kicked them in the balls, didn't I? I hit them where it hurt."

The reviews were dire: "I am one of the old Chaplin idolators who expects a miracle every time he steps before a camera. For the first time, the miracle failed to occur."—*New York Telegram*

"The mood shifts from broad comedy to sinister melodrama, brings in long, sentimental scenes, prolonged philosophical conversations and finally dribbles away to a dull finish."—New York *Sun*

"*Monsieur Verdoux* has some funny spots but they are too few and far between."—*Newsweek*

"A woeful lack of humor, melodrama or dramatic taste. . . . Chaplin is enmeshed in a world of his own personal confusion."—*New York Herald Tribune*

"Chaplin's first new picture in more than six years will be a bitter disappointment to more people than it will please."—*Hollywood Reporter*

"A moderate success leaning upon nostalgia and affection for the

Chaplin legend. . . . Only he—a supreme and unfettered egotist—would proudly present it as a masterpiece."—*PM*

Bosley Crowther of *The New York Times*, usually a Chaplin partisan, issued an on-the-one-hand-on-the-other-hand equivocating notice: "Although it is labeled a 'comedy of murders,' and is screamingly funny in spots—funny as only the old Chaplin is able to make a comic scene—it is basically serious and bitter at the ironies of life. And those who go expecting to laugh at it may find themselves remaining to weep. . . . Unfortunately, Mr. Chaplin has not managed his film with great success. It is slow—tediously slow—in many stretches and thus monotonous. The bursts of comic invention fit uncomfortably into the grim fabric and the clarity of the philosophy does not begin to emerge till near the end. By that time. . . . Mr. Chaplin has repeated much and has possibly left his audience in an almost exhausted state."

Richard Coe, the longtime drama critic at *The Washington Post*, chimed in with a more balanced view. "There's no use saying that Chaplin hasn't brought all this on himself. He has. Nor can you feel sorry for the guy. He has pointedly set out to be an individual. He turned 58 the other day, and at that age a man certainly knows himself and whether or not he chooses to conform to society.

"All this aside, *Monsieur Verdoux* is a wise and witty picture, frequently very funny in its horseplay. It is far more stimulating than any of the current films and has emphatically been made by a man who knew exactly what he wanted to do. Which, also, is far more than you can say for most movies, which betray chaos confounding confusion."

The most enthusiastic reviews came from *Partisan Review* and *The Daily Worker*—publications that weren't going to do Chaplin any good with either the general public or the FBI. The only full-throated defense of *Monsier Verdoux* came from James Agee in *The Nation*, who wrote three defiant pieces extolling the picture as a masterpiece that had more to do with the movie in Agee's head than the movie on the screen.

The response in England was far more favorable. The composer and actor Ivor Novello compared *Monsieur Verdoux* to *Arsenic and Old Lace*, and thought it would have an equivalent success. Richard

Winnington thought *Verdoux* to be "the most exciting thing that has happened to the screen for years; very probably it is his greatest film." C. A. Lejeune didn't think the film was particularly funny, but loved Chaplin's performance.

Chaplin was stunned by the tidal wave of disapproval. Oona Chaplin wrote a letter to Lou Eisler, the wife of Hanns Eisler, that captured their hurt and confusion. Before the film opened, Oona's mood was bouncy. Hollywood seemed to have moved to New York for the premiere, as she reported that they had seen Garbo and Gene Tierney, Gary Cooper, Joe Cotten, David Selznick, and a host of others. On the other hand, Mary Pickford was coming in for the opening night, which Oona thought would almost certainly "make our life HELL."

A week later, the writing was on the wall in large letters. Oona told Eisler that the film had gotten very bad reviews and that business was not what it should be. Chaplin, she reported, was depressed about the response.

The hits kept coming. A few days after the premiere, Chaplin and Oona were at a restaurant when she spotted the theater critic George Jean Nathan, whom she had known in her debutante days. As the Chaplins were leaving, Oona stopped at Nathan's table and extended her hand. Nathan cut her dead.

It was a perfect storm. First there had been a scandal used against Chaplin by the press, the FBI, and their handmaidens—various political groups who lumped his sex life in with his reflexive sympathy for the victimized. Presto! Charlie Chaplin was transformed into a danger to the American Way of Life, which, while difficult to define, seemed similar to pornography in that everybody knew it when they saw it. And now Chaplin had provided them with a film that raised disturbing questions about Chaplin—certainly his judgment, and perhaps Chaplin himself.

In an attempt to right the listing ship, Chaplin pushed for a press conference. United Artists thought it was a bad idea, but they capitulated, and the event took place on April 12 in the ballroom of the Gotham Hotel, on 55th Street.

Chaplin seems to have known what he was letting himself in for. "Proceed with the butchery," he announced in his opening statement.

"If there's any questions anybody wants to ask, I'm here, fire ahead at this old grey head."

There were questions about his political belief system, to which he responded, "If you step off the curb with your left foot, they accuse you of being a Communist. But I have no political persuasions whatsoever. I've never belonged to any political party in my life, and I have never voted in my life. Does that answer your question?"

James Fay, representing the Catholic War Veterans, asked a series of questions in which he asserted that "the men who secured the beachheads, the men who advanced in the face of enemy fire, and the poor fellows who were drafted like myself, and their families and buddies" resented Chaplin's statement that he considered himself a citizen of the world.

"I don't know why you resent that," responded Chaplin. "That is a personal opinion. . . . Four-fifths of my family are Americans. I have four children, two of them were on those beachheads. They were with Patton's Third Army. I am the one-fifth that isn't a citizen. Nevertheless, I-I-I've done my share, and whatever I said, it is not by any means [meant] to be derogatory to your Catholic uh-uh-uh GI's."

Fay expanded his portfolio by asserting that he was not just speaking for Catholic GIs, but "GI's throughout the United States!"

"Well, whatever they are, if they take exception to the fact that I am not a citizen and that I pay my taxes and that seventy percent of my revenue comes from . . . abroad, then I apologize for paying that 100 percent on that 70 percent."

"I think that is a very evasive answer, Mr. Chaplin, because so do those veterans pay their taxes too!"

"Yes?"

"Whether their revenue comes from elsewhere or not."

"The problem is—what is it that you are objecting to?"

"I'm objecting to your particular stand that you have no patriotic feelings about this country or any other country."

". . . Well, that's another question of opinion and as I say I think it rather dictatorial on your part to say as how I should apply my patriotism. I had patriotism during the war, and I showed it and I did a great deal for the war effort but it was never advertised."

There were questions about Chaplin's friendship with Hanns

Eisler, the unsympathetic nature of Henri Verdoux, the untoward amount of "levity" in the concluding scene with the priest. Finally, toward the end of the event, James Agee stood up and asked, "What are people who care a damn about freedom—who really care for it—think of a country and the people in it, who congratulate themselves upon this country as the finest on earth, and as a 'free country' when so many of the people in this country pry into what a man's citizenship is, try to tell him his business from hour to hour and from day to day and exert a public moral blackmail against him for not becoming an American citizen—for his political views and for not entertaining troops in the manner—in the way that they think he should. What is to be thought of a general country where those people are well thought of?"

"Thank you very much," Chaplin replied, "but I have nothing to say to that question."

It was less a press conference than a bullfight, with Chaplin afflicted by a dozen bleeding wounds. Things only got worse.

The usual columnists took the drab business the picture was doing as an opportunity to pile on. On April 12, Ed Sullivan led off his column with this: "The Marines who died at Iwo Jima, the World War II paraplegics, amputees and the blinded, must writhe at Charlie Chaplin's smug explanation that, 'I'm a very good paying guest in the United States' . . . to Chaplin, the USA is a boarding house, a motel or a roadside inn, where, in return for taxes, you get liberty, freedom of speech, jury trial, freedom of religion and everything else as some sort of room service."

Sullivan liked the analogy so much he used it again four days later. "On his 58th birthday, Charlie Chaplin, driven to the wall by this column and trying to salvage his $2 million flop picture, tells 100 newspapermen that he is not a Communist . . . tell that to the Marines who died at Tarawa." Despite the fact that there were many more South Pacific islands for Sullivan to reference, he dropped that trope while continuing his relentless attacks.

Chaplin tried to put on a brave face. He and Oona met James Mason and his wife at the Stork Club, where he did some of his party pieces from years past and enthralled his audience. He even submitted to an interview with Walter Winchell at three in the morning.

Oona sat there without saying a word, finally whispering "I want to go back to California. I miss my children."

AFTER FIVE WEEKS at the Broadway Theatre, Chaplin pulled *Monsieur Verdoux*, just about the same time that Loew's theaters announced they would not play the picture. The film had opened to $27,000 for its first weekend, but had slid down to $15,000 or less in its last week. Chaplin and United Artists decided to concoct a new advertising campaign and reopen the film in the fall. Chaplin hired Russell Birdwell on a six-month contract to design the new publicity blitz.

Birdwell had masterminded elaborate promotions for *Gone With the Wind*, as well as Howard Hughes's years of ballyhoo about Jane Russell and *The Outlaw*. Birdwell specialized in making news, and his contribution amounted to a bluntly combative question atop the new posters and ads: "CHAPLIN CHANGES! CAN YOU?" In other words, use the issues that had caused the picture to fail in New York to convert the picture into a success.

Birdwell's secondary focus was on de-emphasizing Chaplin and pushing Marilyn Nash as a star of tomorrow. Tom Waller, the national publicity manager for United Artists, wrote a memo laying out the reasoning: "As you know we have had [Marilyn] Nash in New York for the past two weeks with the sole purpose of using her through national channels to get over to the country the fact that she is in *Monsieur Verdoux*; that *Monsieur Verdoux* is a good picture; that *Monseur Verdoux* is Charlie Chaplin's picture; that Charlie Chaplin is a pretty good guy."

After the film had failed in New York, Congressman John Rankin gave a speech on the floor of the House of Representatives demanding that the Truman administration begin deportation proceedings against Chaplin because of his scorn for America and its institutions.

In June 1947, Congressman J. Parnell Thomas, chairman of the House Committee on Un-American Activities, told J. Edgar Hoover in a face-to-face meeting "that one of the first persons they wanted to inquire about [in prospective congressional hearings] would be Charles Chaplin." The FBI had long had at least one informant within the Los Angeles Communist Party and had a verified list of 287 former or current members of the Party in the motion picture industry, including all the members of the Hollywood Ten that were shortly to be called before the committee.

Although Chaplin was not among the former or current members, Thomas still planned to subpoena his testimony in the hearings scheduled to begin in September 1947. Chaplin promptly sent a defiant telegram to HUAC's chairman: "From your publicity I noted that I am to be 'quizzed' by the House Un-American Activities Committee in Washington in September. I understand I am to be your 'guest' at the expense of the taxpayers. Forgive me for this premature acceptance of your headlined newspaper invitation. You have been quoted as saying you wish to ask me if I am a Communist. You sojourned for ten days in Hollywood not long ago and could have asked me the question at that time, effecting something of an economy. Or you could telephone me now—collect. In order that you be completely up to date on my thinking I suggest that you view carefully my latest production *Monsieur Verdoux*. It is against war and the futile slaughter of our youth. I trust you will not find its humane message distasteful. While you are preparing your engraved subpoena I will give you a hint on where I stand. I am not a Communist. I am a peace-monger."

HUAC postponed Chaplin's appearance three times and then let the matter drop, probably because the 1947 hearings focused exclusively on men the committee knew had been or still were Communists.

Chaplin obviously sensed his picture's fate but was helpless to prevent it. On September 17, 1947, he sent a telegram to Gradwell Sears, the head of United Artists: "Tell Birdwell under no circumstances to quote me personally in the press. This blast of the Un-American Activities Committee at this time will do more harm than good both to me and to the picture. I am not by nature ignorant or one that asks for trouble. I told Birdwell specially not to drag in the Un-American Activities Committee in connection with my picture. It can only antagonize the public. Neither do I want politics of any nature connected with the picture. It is bad showmanship and will create the impression that the picture is dull and not funny.

Another item to tell Birdwell is to correct the radio spots. They are spoken too slowly. Under no circumstances release them in present form. They are too arrogant and egotistical. New ones should be made in lighter vein."

Monsieur Verdoux met the same fate in September that it had in April. In some cities, theaters ditched the UA advertising and did their own. A theater in Lincoln, Nebraska, advertised the film as "Charles Chaplin in his greatest and gayest comedy!" and added the tagline, "What will be the fate of these lovely girls in the hands of the Modern Bluebeard?" So much for truth in advertising.

October saw the film open in Chicago, New Orleans, San Francisco, Seattle, Toronto, and Portland. The receipts were dismal, and UA finally threw in the towel. *Monsieur Verdoux* earned only $325,000 in America, and barely nudged over $2 million worldwide, which meant Chaplin might have broken even. However you care to look at the picture artistically, commercially it was a catastrophic falling-off from the success of *The Great Dictator*.

It was official: Charlie Chaplin had his first flop.

It would be wrong to imply that only the hyenas of the press hated *Monsieur Verdoux*. Some of Chaplin's friends had serious problems with the picture as well. Aldous Huxley, who attended Salka Viertel's Sunday salons with Chaplin, called the film "an aesthetic mess. [Chaplin] passes from a mime about murder, which depends on not being taken seriously, to attempts at serious psychology . . . not conceivably a subject for comedy. One feels terribly sorry for Charlie— such talents, such a mess—in art no less than in life."

Even the state of Ohio piled on, with the Independent Theater Owners of Ohio sending out a special bulletin: "Last night, in her weekly broadcast, dear Louella [Parsons] wasted nearly two minutes of her time boosting Charlie Chaplin and his new picture. . . .

"And although Chaplin has been able to make a large fortune out of Hollywood, he thinks so little of this country that he has never become an American citizen. It is our fervent hope that American moviegoers will stay away from Chaplin's new picture in vast quantities, and will spend their money at the box office of those theaters showing Bob Hope, Crosby, Frances Langford, Joe E. Brown, and those many others who showed their patriotism by entertaining the boys and girls overseas, while Chaplin lolled around in luxury and profligacy and brought front page disgrace upon the industry."

Ohio had always been a problem for Chaplin. In 1923, the state board of censors bowdlerized Chaplin's *A Woman of Paris*. Chaplin shot it between August 1922 and September 1923 at a cost of $351,853. It made money in its showcase in Los Angeles, lost money in its showcase in New York. It earned $634,000 in its general release through United Artists, which means it eked out a decent profit after UA deducted their 20 percent distribution fee. Ohio censors cut five minutes, and titles were rewritten so that Edna Purviance became Adolphe Menjou's fiancée rather than his mistress, while her opulent lifestyle became the result of an aunt's bequest.

It wasn't just Ohio; in Maryland, Marie's lifestyle was the result of a successful career as an actress. In Pennsylania the censor made the story confusing by cutting the suicide which motivates the ending. Kansas merely cut all the scenes involving smoking.

But that episode had been a minor annoyance compared to the fusillade directed at *Monsieur Verdoux*. Within the meeting rooms of the Un-American Activities Committee, Chairman J. Parnell Thomas and chief investigator Robert Stripling pointed to the boycotts of *Monsieur Verdoux* and actor-singer Paul Robeson's difficulty in booking concerts as proof of the efficacy of the committee's efforts. These were times in which right-wing witnesses informed the committee of un-American elements in *The Best Years of Our Lives*.

THE TRUTH ABOUT right-wing attacks on Hollywood then or now is that movies are always more of an attraction than a target, if only because of their publicity value. For anti-Semites, Hollywood has always been full of Jews, which translated to foreigners, which translated to Communists. How dare these people think that the state of the union was their business?

Never mind that all of the Jewish moguls were staunch anticommunists. How could they not be? Most of them had gotten out of Eastern Europe one step ahead of a pogrom, and whether the pogrom was instigated by a tsar or Stalin made little difference in the outcome. The mere thought of officially sanctioned government prosecution meant that most of them were perfectly willing to throw valuable employees to the sharks at the first sign of trouble.

As far as the FBI was concerned *Monsieur Verdoux* was "anti-capitalist propaganda" because of Chaplin's explicit comparison of Verdoux's murders with crimes committed by nation-states. The Bureau decided to step up its surveillance of the movie industry by obtaining scripts of pictures in production through friendly workers in the movie industry. The great art director Richard Day slipped the script of Abraham Polonsky's *Force of Evil* to the FBI, to accompany the Bureau's wiretap of Polonsky's phone.

THE SCHOLAR CHARLES Maland has posited a reasonable hypothesis for the flamboyant commercial failure of *Monsieur Verdoux*. He theorized that the film broke Chaplin's "aesthetic contract" with the public by abruptly abandoning his established image of the lovable, indomitable Tramp in favor of a morally ambiguous character of rank cynicism. Indeed, the film's comedy works quite well, especially the scenes with Martha Raye and the garden party where Verdoux tries desperately to avoid her.

And it offers at least one brilliant dramatic scene, when Verdoux has to knock off one of his wives, the deeply unpleasant Lydia. Verdoux follows her upstairs to the hallway. She goes into the bedroom, while he's transfixed by the full moon shining through a window. "How beautiful, this pale Endymion hour," he sighs. Chaplin stiffens his body as he glides into the bedroom, the camera staying in the hallway while the music races to a crescendo. The scene slowly lightens to reveal early morning. Verdoux briskly emerges from the bedroom and descends into the kitchen, where he sets out two plates for breakfast, then remembers that he needs only one.

But *Monsieur Verdoux* was simply a bridge too far, too fast. Chaplin replaces empathy with an intellectualized contempt undoubtedly born of his own persecution. Linking murder with capitalism was an intellectual leap a war-weary world didn't want to make. As Georges Sadoul wrote, "They didn't understand why Charlot, whose heart they heard beat more than once in Verdoux's breast, was completely dominated by bitterness and despair, bordering on viciousness."

The critical opinion on *Monsieur Verdoux* would shift in 1964, when it was rereleased. In the wake of satirical black comedies such as *Dr. Strangelove*, Chaplin's film seemed to have been ahead of its time, and the 1964 reviews were largely a reversal of the negative 1947 ones. In the subsequent years, the prevailing critical opinion seems to have settled into a halfway point between the dismal 1947 reviews and the laudatory 1964 reviews.

With *The Great Dictator* Chaplin had illustrated the duality of man by playing two parts: the sociopath Hynkel and the good-hearted Tramp/barber. In *Monsieur Verdoux* he tries to blend two radically different personalities into one, and the result is that you never quite buy the character. Part of the time Chaplin is having fun with the idea of a conceptually lethal but occasionally fumbling boulevardier, while the rest of the time he plays the part straight, adding painfully soggy scenes with a wife and child. The character makes little internal sense.

Unlike the comparatively unified targets of *Modern Times* (regimentation amidst social chaos) and *The Great Dictator* (Fascism), *Monsieur Verdoux* is several different movies uneasily spliced together. Chaplin's intentions seem to have involved a Shavian comedy of killing and he makes some good points, although more in the manner of a debate than a movie—there are no characters who argue for the other side. More to the point, Shaw would never have worked so hard to make his hero sympathetic—moral superiority would have been enough.

After the awkward six minutes of exposition that begins the picture, the film settles down somewhat at the entrance of Verdoux, a self-confident, charming gray-haired roué. Verdoux swivels through crises with the same aplomb he does a room—a witty, overripe character who can move real estate or bodies with a practiced skill and carries a jeweler's loupe so he can gauge the merchandise.

The film slides into trouble whenever it gets serious. Marilyn Nash's character is impossible—a clumsily written and played prostitute who reads Schopenhauer. The grace and implicit physical wit of Chaplin's performance, as well as his very funny pyramiding frustration when he runs into Martha Raye's Annabella, is persistently undermined by the unwieldy support structure erected for moral points. Verdoux is played out in one scene, energetic in a following scene, depending on the exigencies of the plot.

And yet Chaplin's gifts as an actor invariably keep him interesting, and he has a knack for suggestive dialogue he managed to get past the Breen office. "I often wonder," Verdoux murmurs to Madame Grosnay, "who are you in the dark?"

Chaplin almost always manages an ending of profound beauty, and *Verdoux* is no exception. Henri Verdoux spends most of the film in a dither, his smooth seductions giving way to frustration and panic, but he waits for his execution with an eerie calm—turbulence is vanquished, serenity is restored. He tries rum for the first and last time, then proceeds to the guillotine with a strong suggestion of the Tramp's walk.

You have to give the film points for audacity, but it ends up feeling like homework. Beyond that, the 1947 audience must have felt psychologically buffeted in that Verdoux is a 180-degree reversal from Chaplin's previous character. The Tramp is stoutly independent and never capitulates to the world's expectations, let alone its judgments, but when Verdoux is cornered he promptly blames society for his predicament.

The reasons for this reversal are not hard to discern. Chaplin's childhood poverty left him with a furious, unyielding indignation about anything resembling established authority. In the early years of the Tramp, the character was a pure projection of Chaplin's id—an aggressive scrapper, a disturber of the peace, always groping for an advantage or a girl. At the same time, the Tramp is being played by a man who basically saw himself as a disadvantaged child.

As the historian Richard M. Roberts has noted, the character's great leap forward comes in *The Kid*, when the Tramp begins as socially irresponsible as usual, but is radically altered by the experience of tending a small child. *The Kid* seamlessly unites both halves of Chaplin's own personality—the abandoned child coexisting with an idealistic adult who keeps a wary eye on his bank balance.

In all the features after *The Kid* (*The Gold Rush, The Circus, City Lights, Modern Times*) the Tramp remains a softer, more romantic figure. He invariably tries to do the right thing. It rarely works out, but that's where the comedy comes from. The characterization of the Tramp as an irresponsible pest was banished, syncing up with Chaplin's own increasing security with his place in art and life, not to mention his increasing distance from the poverty that had damaged him.

But in the 1940s, Chaplin the man was again assailed by a hostile world eager to castigate him for his personality and politics. Chaplin's politics were always remarkably consistent, but America's politics underwent a nearly complete reversal after World War II. Before the war America was officially—and mostly unofficially—isolationist. When Russia and America became temporary allies, Chaplin continued to voice resolute anti-Nazi beliefs, and championed the Soviet Union as America's partner. But the right wing in America never believed in the Soviet Union as an ally, only as an enemy in waiting. That, and Chaplin's unorthodox sex life, lit the fuse.

When the war was over, Chaplin funneled his accumulated anger into a portrait of a renegade, albeit with a change of costume. But this time the wounds were fresher, the stakes were greater, and the character chillier; unlike the Tramp, Verdoux is not concerned with doing the right thing. He's a killer who believes the wrongs inflicted on him by the world justify misogyny and murder.

Chaplin had been a completely independent filmmaker for more than thirty years, an absolute ruler of his own creative island in the midst of Hollywood. His insistence on sketching the sets, writing every word of the script, directing all the action, and even composing the musical score meant that there was no one who could tell him he might be making a mistake.

Chaplin believed his fail-safe resided in the fact that, as he put it in 1940, "I am protected by being a charlatan. I don't think in terms of common sense and, to be honest, I don't search for truth. I search for effectiveness. Do you know why most writers fail in the theater? Because they try to write what is worthwhile rather than what is effective." But with *Monsieur Verdoux*, he violated his own principle and actively tried to be worthwhile by didactically pointing out society's moral failings.

With the anti-capitalist rhetoric of the trial sequence the grinding of stylistic gears becomes deafening. And there's something else evident only in hindsight. Simply put, it was much harder for Chaplin—or anyone else—to play the social underdog after World War II. The Tramp's emotional core was a dignified poverty, a conception derived from the Victorian era. Chaplin would describe the Tramp as "the spirit of the English—their loyalty, their sense of responsibility, their belief in what they think is right and just."

After World War II, that point of view was rendered archaic by existential cynicism, which Chaplin tries on for size with *Verdoux*. The problem is that cynicism was antithetical to Chaplin's belief system as an artist and a man, as proven by all the pictures he made before *Verdoux*, and all the pictures he made afterward.

In a different environment, Chaplin could probably have gotten away with the film, if only because of its originality, but coming after the Berry trials, *Monsieur Verdoux* was taken as a deliberate provocation, perhaps even a self-portrait. The failure was confirmed by the 1947 Academy Awards. *Verdoux* was nominated for Best Original Screenplay, but lost to *The Bachelor and the Bobby-Soxer*.

With the exception of Martha Raye, the film did nothing for anybody connected with it. A few years after the film was released, Raye was in Paris and wanted to buy a Dior dress. Her timing was off—there was a fashion show in progress and Dior wouldn't sell merchandise. But Pierre Balmain, at the time Dior's assistant, recognized her. "Madame Verdoux!" he exclaimed. Balmain kissed her on both cheeks and Raye was allowed to purchase anything she wanted.

Chaplin's own feelings about the picture gradually evolved until they matched the public's: "There was no identification with the audience," he said in 1966. "And that was a mistake. That was a mistake as far as the public not accepting it. There was no identification to the audience."

"You like it better now?"

"No, on the contrary. . . . I'm terrifically influenced by the public. . . . I have a profound respect for that. They don't know why [they don't like it, but] it's our business to know why."

As 1948 dawned, Charlie Chaplin's reputation was shredded and his most recent film was a critical and financial disappointment. He was unsettled, at times even angry, but not depressed. He was still an invulnerable.

Chaplin industriously set about writing his next film. If the clashing dialectics of *Monsieur Verdoux* had alienated his audience, he would seek to lure them back by making something completely apolitical. He would offer them a love story.

CHAPTER 12

Shortly after *Monsieur Verdoux*, Maurice Bessy once again visited Chaplin and found him muted but defiant. "The press went for me. . . . They want to cut me down to size, terrorize me. I know they're going to haul me off to Washington to appear before the Un-American Activities Committee, they'll threaten to deport me. But I'll go there with my head held high. I know how to speak, I can defend myself when I'm attacked. I'll tell them exactly what I think. I won't mince my words. My arguments are good ones and I've got right on my side. I'll make them listen.

"They want me dead, but they won't succeed."

Bessy asked him if he wanted to leave America. "It would be a sign of weakness for me to leave. Of course I should like to go to Europe, to France especially, to the South. But I'm an old man. I'm nearly sixty. I've worked here all my life. I love my dear house, my good old studios, where no one but me can work. I dare not leave this cruel place, where even a great man like [director D. W.] Griffith wasn't appreciated. You think you're going to find monuments and universities and museums in Hollywood, but all people think of is opening new restaurants."

There was more of this, some of it self-pity, some of it anger, but then he came around again to the central point. "I worked very hard on *Monseur Verdoux*. I threw it in their faces." There was one thing of which he was sure: "I've found happiness, true happiness. It took a long time and it's not been easy. But I am happy, completely happy."

By ALL ODDS the most vitriolic columnist of his period or, for that matter, of any period, was Westbrook Pegler, a merchant of hate who subsisted on a diet of rage seasoned with contempt. For years his favorite target had been Eleanor Roosevelt, but after World War II she was out of the White House. Pegler decided to pile onto an easier target.

Pegler wrote that, "In Hollywood there is some doubt whether Chaplin is a Communist in the sense that he has ever joined the party. My guess would be that he is not because party members as rich as Chaplin are subject to demands for money and Chaplin is notoriously cheap, so stingy in fact that an unfortunate 23 year old girl whom he had seduced and who was pregnant was run out of town like a victim of the Gestapo, with only a few dollars and a one-way ticket out of Beverly Hills."

Pegler was just warming up, but he got to the point: "And should he ever undertake to become a citizen for some reason of expediency, loyalty being out of the question, that record should be sufficient to thwart him on the protest of any citizen with a decent regard for the privilege of citizenship . . .

"I believe it is doubtful that [Chaplin] will be seen in a new movie in the United States, although, if we should deport him for cause after more than 30 years, he might be used by the Communists in some other land for missionary films to be shown in the Balkans and Latin America. . . . All matters considered, I do not understand why he has not been deported to his native England even though England might regard this as a deliberately unfriendly act. . . .

"Through two wars involving his native country, Chaplin has hidden in Hollywood and, through this one, when hundreds of other movie actors too old for fighting, traveled overseas with camp shows, Chaplin still stayed in Hollywood.

"His most noteworthy public activity during that time was his

merciless persecution of a girl less than half his age who was be-
trayed by her hopes of a career, and his subsequent appearance as
defendant in a trial which revealed him as a vicious old man, still as
nasty at 56 as he had been throughout his earlier years."

Pegler would eventually strangle in his own bile when he in-
dulged in anti-Semitism so rank that the only publishing outlet he
had was the John Birch Society. By that time, Chaplin was no longer
in America.

THE FBI FILE on Chaplin encompasses just under two thousand
pages and is notable for its lack of filter—everything is included,
no matter how ridiculous. There is hearsay, rumor, bountiful examples of guilt by association. The file even contains poison-pen letters
from vengeful citizens that close with admonitions such as "Send him
back but freeze his properties and cash!!!" J. Edgar Hoover wrote
back, dryly noting that "This Bureau has no jurisdiction over such
matters."

Anything, no matter how trivial, was fodder. Frank Taylor, a recent escapee from the publishing business, had become an MGM
producer. He and his wife founded the Westland School, a progressive elementary school following the theories of John Dewey, where
Oona Chaplin enrolled her daughter Geraldine. Chaplin allowed the
school to show *City Lights* as a fundraiser, which earned $2,000.
The Daily Worker ran a story about the benefit, which ended up in
the FBI file as yet another example of Chaplin's misbegotten social
sympathies. After Chaplin's reentry permit was rescinded in 1952,
the attorney general would cite the article about the benefit as proof
of Chaplin's un-American sympathies.

A 1947 dossier labeled "Confidential" gets down to cases:
"CHAPLIN has been accused on a number of occasions of being a
member of the Communist party. However, source whose reliabil-
ity has been well established as an authentic informant stated that
he has never been able to identify CHAPLIN as a member of the
Communist Party in Hollywood. . . . CHAPLIN'S bank account
was monitored . . . and there is no indication of contributions to the
Communist Party."

Chaplin's memberships were listed as being the Loyal Order of Moose, the Tuna Club of Catalina Island, the Screen Actors Guild, the California Yacht Club, the Los Angeles Athletic Club, the Santa Monica Swimming Club, and the Lambs Club in New York. Chaplin never joined the Directors Guild after it was formed in 1936, probably because he thought it was irrelevant as far as he was concerned. He owned his own studio as well as 25 percent of United Artists, and answered only to himself. There was, of course, the possibility of using his leverage within the industry to benefit creatives on a lower level, but he evidently dismissed that possibility.

A memo of August 24, 1947, confirms that the Bureau was funneling negative material about Chaplin to specific Hollywood columnists ("In connection with the material prepared for Hedda Hopper"). Chaplin's attendance at a concert of music by Dmitri Shostakovich is ominously noted. Occasionally anti-Semitism rears up—the files often refer to Chaplin as "aka Israel Thonstein," because of the incorrect entry in *Who's Who in American Jewry*. Note is made that Chaplin "speaks with a Jewish accent" (he didn't) and "uses his hands when talking" (he did).

The FBI didn't have to funnel anything to Billy Wilkerson, the conservative publisher of *The Hollywood Reporter*. In December 1947, Wilkerson wrote another one of his scathing editorials: "The wonder to us is that Washington hasn't long ago relieved Mr. Chaplin of his privilege of living in this country, working among us, banking millions of dollars while, at the same time, it becomes quite obvious that he is not satisfied with the conduct of our Government and continually criticizes its actions. Why should such an agitator be given the benefits he has received here? Why should the picture business be forever burdened with his actions? Why?"

Wilkerson was about profits at least as much as he was about politics. "Our ticket buyers are being influenced against us in a cause that's growing like a typhoon. That influence might well curtail everything that has made our industry one of the greats in the world. Any man or woman who, under the guise of freedom of speech, or the cloak of the Bill of Rights, or under the pseudo protection of being a liberal, causes things to be said, or who actually is involved with many of the conspiracies that have now infested this great land of ours, has no place among us, be he commie or what. He or she should be rushed out of our business."

Wilkerson's primary attack dog was Mike Connolly, the daily columnist for the *Reporter*. Connolly was the movie industry's version of Roy Cohn—a gay man who adopted the identity of a rabid attack dog for protective coloration. When he wasn't popping Benzedrine or downing multiple Manhattans at Musso & Frank's, Connolly would typically refer to accused left-wingers as "vermin" or "scummie." Connolly went so far as to publish new work addresses for people who had been driven out of the movie business, in the hopes of inciting picketing, bankruptcy, or both.

Two months after Wilkerson's column about Chaplin, the Los Angeles office of the FBI requested Chaplin's income tax records from 1940 to 1947, presumably looking for either donations to the Communist Party, or evidence of tax evasion.

That same month, an August 10 report indicated that the FBI was tapping Chaplin's phone and reading his mail—the report notes dinner invitations to Chaplin from Salka Viertel and five phone calls from Lion Feuchtwanger to Chaplin between August and October of 1945.

This level of investigation continued into 1949. In April, Hoover asked for "the current status of this investigation." After reading the results, Hoover rendered his verdict: "A review of this file at the Bureau reflects that no substantial information has been developed to date which would indicate that the subject has been engaged in espionage or other intelligence activities." On October 7, the Los Angeles office wrote Hoover and told him that "no new information of value has been obtained." They had a few more interviews to do, but if no significant information was derived, Los Angeles recommended that the Chaplin internal security case be closed.

Nevertheless, in 1948, two professional informants included Chaplin in their list of Communist sympathizers. Louis Budenz, a former managing editor of *The Daily Worker* who became a paid informant for Senator Joseph McCarthy, named about four hundred "concealed Communists," including Chaplin, James Cagney,

Edward G. Robinson, and Vera Caspary—the author of *Laura*. Budenz's testimony helped refocus the FBI's interest in Chaplin. Their new efforts centered on assisting the INS in establishing that he was a "subversive" in order to justify deportation.

Budenz told an FBI agent in New York that in 1936 Chaplin was "the equivalent of a member of the party." Budenz claimed that in the early 1940s the Party had discouraged Chaplin from applying for American citizenship because "it would raise the whole question of his being an alien, an attack on his personal life, and all sorts of things that might lead to his deportation."

The other informant was Paul Crouch, a member of the party from 1925 to 1942, who told INS officials that Chaplin was "a member-at-large of the Communist party . . . temperamental but loyal" to the Party. In Crouch's telling, to protect Chaplin officials had decided he should not be affiliated with any of the Party cells in Los Angeles. These two hearsay testimonies were the only evidence the FBI ever uncovered about Chaplin's affiliations, and there is some indication that Hoover remained convinced that Chaplin was a Communist.

At one point in 1948, there was a report that somehow managed to link Chaplin to the sale of thirty-six armored tanks to the Zionist Haganah forces in Palestine. Chaplin's name came up as someone who "had to be consulted on both the financial aspect and the general advisability of the proposed acquisition" of the tanks from a storage facility in Barstow, California.

These wild-goose chases went on for years, culminating in Senator William Langer introducing a resolution requesting the attorney general to determine whether Chaplin should be deported. This led Chaplin to take the highly unusual step of responding:

"I wish to state that this action is part of a political persecution.

"It has been going on for . . . years, ever since I made an anti-Nazi picture, *The Great Dictator*, in which I expressed liberal ideas. On account of this picture I was called to Washington for questioning as a 'War monger' by Senators Clark and Nye. This investigation fell through after Pearl Harbor.

"The persecution, however, increased, after I 'dared' to speak on behalf of Russia, urging the Allies to open a second front. For this I was bitterly attacked by reactionary columnists, using every device to discredit me with the public. I was called a 'Communist,' an 'ingrate.' I was accused of 'making money in this country without becoming a citizen.'. . . I believe that in a democracy I have the right to state that I am an Internationalist—which ideas I expressed in *The Great Dictator*.

"But the pro-Nazi reactionary elements continued their attack. Trumped-up charges were the results of all this, inspired by vicious lies written by certain 'sob' sisters, using as their tool, Joan Berry, who was played up as an 'innocent girl lured into immoral relations.' This point was particularly stressed in the Mann Act trial.

"Although my lawyers tried to introduce the fact that long before I met Joan Berry, she had been the mistress of several men, and long before I met her (unknown to me) she had a police record for shoplifting in Los Angeles—these facts and many others, of which my lawyer has proof—were not allowed under the rules of evidence. Yet, on the word of the same woman, and on her accusations, my liberty was jeopardized. I was indicted and compelled to stand trial. Later she accused me of being the father of her child. But the fact remains, I was acquitted of the Mann Act charge, and medical science has proved I am NOT the father of Joan Berry's child.

"However, the prosecution continues, the Berry case being used to attack my character, discredit me with the public and banish me from the country."

WITH THE FAILURE of *Monsieur Verdoux*, Chaplin's enemies could have been satisfied. He had been tripped up by legal malpractice in the paternity suit, and the public had deserted his most recent film. But the government wasn't done with him yet.

In August 1948, the FBI made Chaplin an official subject of investigation by finally establishing a Security Index Card. Beneath the request an X was placed by the category of "Communist." It was a procedural technicality that made it possible for other government agencies to investigate him—especially the INS. It was the culmination of an unspoken struggle between Richard Hood of the Los Angeles office and J. Edgar Hoover.

The effort began on September 9, 1946, when Hoover sent a memo to Hood asking the Los Angeles office to review the files on Chaplin and "give consideration to recommending the preparation of a Security Index Card." Nothing happened until March 1947, when a fourteen-page memo was sent to Hoover erroneously mentioning Chaplin's supposed alias of "Thonstein."

The report mostly focused on an earlier memo from the chief investigator in the Mann Act prosecution. Along the way attention had been paid to *Charlie Chaplin, King of Tragedy*, a biography published in Idaho in 1940. The quoted material focused on more than a dozen women Chaplin had been involved with over the years, then made a wild right turn by suggesting that, despite voluminous evidence to the contrary, he might be homosexual: "In passing, rumor has it that CHAPLIN is unnatural in his sexual relations and it has been said that he is a homosexual. The author of the book makes mention of this item when he states, 'CHARLIE, though essentially normal himself, would not be the creative person that he is and would not have an understanding . . . that it has been these exponents of the intermediate sex who have dominated art through the centuries.' "

Six months later Hoover again sent a memo to the Los Angeles office asking "that instructions contained in the Bureau's memorandum of September 9, 1946 be given attention at an early date." Once again there was silence from the Los Angeles office. In July 1947, the INS commissioner, Ugo Carusi, wrote Hoover inquiring as to whether the INS interviewing Chaplin with the ultimate view of deporting him would conflict with the FBI investigation. Hoover wrote back to assure Carusi that it would not be a problem.

A month after that, FBI assistant director Louis Nichols wrote Hoover's right-hand man Clyde Tolson, "The following might be an excellent item for Louella Parsons," citing a 1923 *Pravda* article to the effect that Chaplin was making a production in Russia and was a Communist. Nichols probably meant to funnel the information to Hedda Hopper, because Louella Parsons rarely red-baited Chaplin. Parsons, for instance, wrote that the blood test in the Berry case had proved Chaplin was not the father of the child while Hopper never mentioned that inconvenient fact. This dissemination of targeted leaks would continue to be the tip of the spear aimed at Chaplin's relationship with the American public. Besides Hopper, other columnists who were regular recipients of FBI leaks were Drew Pearson, Westbrook Pegler, George Sokolsky, and Walter Winchell, not to mention friendly members of Congress: James Eastland, Pat McCarran, Joe McCarthy, Richard Nixon, Karl Mundt, and J. Parnell Thomas.

Hoover's interest was piqued, because he responded, "We ought to check the original at the Library of Congress to make certain of this." After such checking, it was discovered that the story referred to the showing of two old Chaplin two-reelers in Russia, not to any planned production in Russia. Hoover was not pleased: "Certainly a much labored effort brought forth a miserable product," he wrote on the memo.

In July 1947, the INS contacted the FBI, telling them that Chaplin was considering a trip abroad and had applied for a reentry permit. The INS saw this as an opportunity for an interview that, should Chaplin perjure himself, could be used to deport him. Hoover gave the effort his blessing and sent the INS a copy of the Bureau's summary report on Chaplin.

Chaplin canceled his travel plans, possibly because he sensed the government's intentions. At the same time, the INS opened its own investigation.

In February 1948, an irate Hoover once again pressed Richard Hood for movement on a Chaplin investigation. On August 26, 1948, Hood finally capitulated and forwarded a recommendation that a Security Index Card be established for Chaplin. On November 2, the card was established for "Charles Spencer Chaplin, alias _____ Thonstein, Alien and Communist." Hoover notified other officials in the Bureau that Chaplin was now listed as an Alien Communist, which meant that in the event of a national emergency he could be detained. The Los Angeles office began an effort to determine "whether or not CHAPLIN was or is engaged in Soviet Espionage activities."

The pincer movement was beginning to close.

*   *   *

THE ACTOR AND producer Norman Lloyd used to propose an after-dinner game. Someone would throw out the name of an eminent personality he had worked with and he would give a one-word *précis* of that person. Orson Welles was "theatrical." Jean Renoir = "humanist." When Chaplin was mentioned, Lloyd would thunder "*Outsider! Immigrant!* Charlie lived in Hollywood, but he wasn't of it."

Lloyd was one of the young people that congregated around Chaplin in the late 1940s, largely because all his old friends were dead, dying, or afraid to be seen with him. Lloyd, who had played Cinna the Poet in Orson Welles's Mercury Theatre production of *Julius Caesar*, became a frequent tennis partner of Chaplin's at his house on Summit Drive.

Lloyd noticed that Chaplin was anchored by his wife and growing family but was otherwise quite isolated from show business hurly-burly. To keep current with what was going on in his business, he and Oona went to the movies a lot. His favorite movie of these years was *A Place in the Sun*.

Other times they went to the theater, or to dance. In New York, they attended a performance of *Stephen Acrobat* with Martha Graham and Erick Hawkins, which provoked only confusion and a few random boos from the audience. Graham remembered that Chaplin and "his ravishing young wife" came backstage. He told Graham that she had used her body as a "tragical instrument." She found "the childlike gleam in his eye . . . hypnotic," adored the "sense of play in his body movement."

Chaplin kept up with his growing family with a rigorous exercise regimen. "The bloodstream is like a river," he told a friend. "When it isn't in motion, it becomes stagnant and diseased." His favorite exercise was tennis. Chaplin's game was fast and stubborn. His forehand was stronger than his backhand, and he could be impatient; he preferred to put the ball away quickly rather than labor through an endless rally while waiting for someone to make a mistake.

Norman Lloyd said Chaplin could be beaten, primarily because he was too vain to wear his glasses on the court. All you had to do was lure him to the net with drop shots, then clobber him with passing shots. He ran for every ball, disliked losing, and never, under any circumstances, lost track of the score. Off the court, he was anti-smoking at a time when everybody smoked, and prescient in the bargain. "How's your cancer coming?" he would snap at Constance Collier, who smoked incessantly.

Collier and Chaplin had a mock-aggressive Min-and-Bill relationship, but Chaplin adored her and kept her on his studio payroll. As a boy in London he had watched from the gallery at His Majesty's Theatre as she played Cleopatra to Sir Herbert Beerbohm Tree's Antony. He had also seen her play Nancy in *Oliver Twist*, Portia in *Julius Caesar*. They hadn't met until 1916, in Hollywood, and thirty years later she was dependent on the kindness of friends. Collier lived in ravaged splendor with her companion Phyllis and a parrot reputed to have a particularly filthy vocabulary. Chaplin's loyalty to Collier was based on unstinting professional regard: "He thought she was a real actress," said Dan James.

Norman Lloyd and Chaplin played tennis three or four times a week, usually around five in the afternoon, after the heat was fading and the cool California night was on the ascent. "I know he played a very aggressive game," said Daniel Selznick, the son of David Selznick, who lived by Chaplin. "The balls from Chaplin's court regularly landed in the east garden of our house. After we got 10 or 12 balls I would take them back to his house. Oona would come to the door and thank me. She was beautiful and kind, with long dark hair. I thought she looked a little like Morticia in the Charles Addams cartoons."

Despite the fact that they were neighbors, David Selznick and Chaplin were not particularly friendly because of a spat that erupted during Selznick's time at United Artists. He had delivered fine pictures—*A Star Is Born*, *Rebecca*, *Since You Went Away*, etc.—but he had snatched *Duel in the Sun* away from the company in order to start his own releasing organization. United Artists was desperate for the picture, which had money written all over it. As a result of all this, a deep freeze had descended on the partners.

After tennis, Lloyd and Chaplin would sit in the tennis house for a chat and Lloyd would often be invited into the main house for a drink—Chaplin's favorite was a Scotch old-fashioned. Sometimes he'd have Lloyd call his wife, Peggy, to come over for dinner.

On Sundays, Chaplin would invite friends and their children to drop by about three in the afternoon. People who didn't play tennis would swim in the pool. At four, Watson the butler would appear carrying tea and pastries.

It was in this period that Chaplin's sons by Lita Grey, Sydney and Charlie Jr., became close to their father. "My father liked to play tennis," said Syd. "That's why I took it up. I played golf, but he said, 'That's an old man's game. Play tennis. If you beat me, I'll give you $100.' It only took me three months before I could beat him. I suckered him with drop shots. God, he was furious. 'That's not tennis,' he told me. 'You've got to hit it back and forth.' He never did give me the $100. Instead, he gave it to Bill Tilden to give me lessons in proper tennis. Tilden was a good teacher, but he liked young boys and couldn't teach at the L.A. tennis clubs anymore. My father let Bill use his court to give lessons so he could make a living. He liked Bill and felt sorry for him. That's the kind of man my father was.

"It was all about poverty. My father and my uncle Sydney were very poor as children. It influenced my father for the rest of his life. He would always get very depressed at Christmas. Gifts piled to the ceiling, and then we'd get the speech: 'When I was a boy, if I got an orange for Christmas, I was lucky.' And I would say, 'Well, Pop, I can bring you as many oranges as you want.' And then he'd glare at me. He wasn't amused. He'd come out of it after a while, but he never got far from what he had missed as a child. But if you think about it, he wasn't poor for long. He was making a good living in the theater by the time he was eighteen and he was a millionaire in his twenties.

"When I was little, I lived with my mother, and I didn't spend a lot of time with him. Then I went off to the war. After the war, we began spending a lot of time together, and that's when I got to really know him, and see how tortured he was by being poor as a child. He was a very decent man, really. His greatest pleasure was his work. He adored work, getting lost in a script for a year or two. He wasn't that interested in the social aspect of what was going on around him; he wasn't a man to go to ball games, if you know what I mean.

"The best thing that ever happened to him was marrying Oona. He was crazy about her, and she was very easy to be with. A nice woman, bright, well read. In my memory she's always reading Philip Roth. They eventually had eight children, and even with all the kids around, he was tied up with his work. They had a marvelous nurse, Kay-Kay, a Scottish woman who did a lot of the child-rearing. He liked children, but they'd come down after dinner having been bathed and combed. He wasn't the father you see on TV. But it was a marvelous marriage and all the kids turned out well.

"People called him a genius, but he thought of himself as a good workman, as someone who cared and had good taste. And a perfectionist. Always a perfectionist."

It was Sydney who led his father to the Circle Theatre, an enterprise begun in 1946 by some students from UCLA—young Sydney, Charlie Jr., Jerry Epstein, and William Schallert, who was studying music with Arnold Schoenberg but eventually became a ubiquitous character actor and the president of the Screen Actors Guild.

Throughout his years in Hollywood, Chaplin had maintained a fascination with the theater and was quite open about his expertise. "I don't know anything about religion," he said. "I don't know anything about politics. But there's one thing I know more about than any man in this country, and that's the theater. The theater is sheer magic."

He went on to describe an archetypal example: "Imagine an empty stage. Dim lights. It is night. Suddenly the shrill ringing of a telephone on stage shatters the silence. A door slams open stage right. A man enters briskly and hurries across stage to the telephone . . .

"'Hello-yes-when? Where?—right— OK— On my way.'

"He hangs up the phone, rushes off stage, the door slams. Silence, curtain. You see? The audience has been shown nothing. They don't know what has happened. But their imaginations, fired by the dramatic intensity, have taken over. They are sitting on the edge of their seats.

"Magic. That's the theater."

He explained that the audience had to be allowed to participate, not just look on like gawkers at an accident. Spark the audience's imagination, let them take off from that starting point.

Jerry Epstein's savings of $1,000 were the seed money for what became the Circle Theatre. It proved a good creative investment. The Circle would showcase the debuts of a roster of distinguished character actors such as Strother Martin, Schallert, and Kathleen Freeman, while Epstein would go on to be Chaplin's assistant on his next two films and produce *A Countess from Hong Kong.*

The Circle's first production was Elmer Rice's *The Adding Machine.* Sydney was in the cast, and Chaplin came to a performance. He loved the show and became the Circle's biggest publicist. For most of its existence, the Circle was housed in a converted drugstore on North El Centro, a residential street near RKO and Paramount. Chaplin gave the group permission to raid his prop room for anything they could use. There were stored the gears from *Modern Times,* bombs from *The Great Dictator,* chairs and sofas from *City Lights,* the table from the log cabin in *The Gold Rush.*

The Circle Theatre became a refuge for Chaplin at a time when he was otherwise isolated. *The Adding Machine* was followed by *Ethan Frome* and Saroyan's *The Time of Your Life.* When the troupe mounted Galsworthy's *The Skin Game,* they were flummoxed by the play's Victorian aspects. Watching a rehearsal of the second act, Chaplin turned to Epstein and asked, "Do you mind if I suggest something to the actors?" He quickly began redirecting the act and kept at it until two in the morning, at which point he moved on to the third act. Oona tried to shush him but Chaplin forged ahead. Just about the time the sun was rising, Oona said, "Charlie, these kids have to get some sleep, because they've got to do this again tomorrow night! They're going to open in four or five days."

"All right, all right," he grumbled. "Now remember everything I've told you." He and Oona got into his black Ford and headed back to Summit Drive.

"And then he'd come back the next night," remembered Schallert, "and we'd rehearse and he would say, 'Oh, dear, all wrong, all wrong.' And we would start over again, from the top. And he would keep us there all night and then come back the next night. 'No, all wrong.' And we would be staggering, rocking back on our heels, punchy from no sleep and trying to absorb everything. But Chaplin was the soul of patience and endlessly inventive."

Jerry Epstein said that the odd thing was that Chaplin "never took time to prepare himself by reading the text of the plays, yet he had an unerring sense of the next line. And he stressed the importance of making effective entrances and exits. 'It's very important to establish your character with something compelling the first moment you enter; that way, you have the audience in the palm of your hand. The same with your exit—you must make it memorable.' "

For Chaplin, it wasn't about the words, it was about imposing a performance rhythm that would give the play a heartbeat. "Keep it light, keep it clean," he would admonish the actors. "Only use your hands when you want to make a point—that's when it becomes effective."

Julian Ludwig, one of the actors at the Circle, remembered that "when he would show somebody how to do a part—which he tended to do on a number of occasions—he'd always have his hand on his heart, and if he liked [the] interpretation, he'd say, 'That feels good.' "

The Circle had no money to speak of, so the troupe became a part of Chaplin's extended family. At Christmas, Jerry Epstein was always invited along with Wheeler Dryden and his son Spencer, Chaplin's cousins Betty and Ted Tetrick and Amy Reeves, the widow of Alf Reeves, who had died in 1946. Other regulars included Constance Collier and Phyllis, young Sydney, and assorted children.

Sometimes the Circle cast and Chaplin would pull an all-nighter, emerging at dawn. Everybody would go to Hollywood Boulevard for pancakes and maple syrup as Chaplin enthused over the color of the sky. "Drunkard's blue," he called it. When they reached the restaurant, he would tell Epstein, "My fee for directing is 35 cents and a cup of black coffee."

In these early morning conversations, Epstein never sensed Chaplin had any particular jealousy about other comedians of his or succeeding generations. Chaplin said that when he started out at Keystone, the only performer that scared him was Chester Conklin, who Chaplin thought was the funniest man in the world. That didn't stop Chaplin from working with Conklin over and over again, culminating in appearances in both *Modern Times* and *The Great Dictator*. In other conversations, he would also cite Ben Turpin as hilarious.

He liked performers who could establish an emotional bond with the audience. Al Jolson, for instance, whose live performance he regarded as the most spectacular theatrical experience of his life. Among the younger generation, he thought Lucille Ball was talented and very funny.

Chaplin directed seven shows in all for the Circle, including James M. Barrie's *What Every Woman Knows* and *Rain*, based on the Somerset Maugham story, in which he took a particular interest, because, as he told the cast, "I saw Jeanne Eagels do it, and they did it all wrong!" He thought Reverend Davidson needed to be played as a sexual sadist, and that the atmosphere needed to be stifling. The audience for the Circle's production sat under a tin roof on which water was hosed to simulate the constant tropical downpour. June Havoc played Sadie Thompson, and Jerry Epstein said that Chaplin "ironed out all her mannerisms and made her simple, lovely and vulnerable. It was a beautiful, poetic production."

When it came to the Barrie play, he made the actors play against sentiment, demanding the lines be delivered hard, factually—no self-pity at any time.

Chaplin also suggested plays for the Circle. He was interested in directing *Othello*, even though he didn't really like Shakespeare. But he was intrigued by the play because he felt it was basically about sex, and most productions failed to emphasize the sexual connection between Desdemona and Othello. Outwardly, Desdemona was pale and pure, but Chaplin believed she was on fire for the Moor, and vice versa.

Constance Collier thought that interpretation was absurd. "Charlie, *read* the play! Look at what Emilia says: 'The sweetest innocent that e'er did lift up eye! Moor, she was chaste.' She's *innocent*, Charlie, not some harem harlot."

"I don't care what the lines say," Chaplin replied. "This is a play about rampant sex." Chaplin thought Sydney could play Othello, and he was circling Evelyn Keyes for Desdemona when she was yanked back by Columbia for a film. Without a sensual Desdemona, the idea died. For a man who didn't like Shakespeare, Chaplin spent a lot of time thinking about him. He thought Hamlet had to be played as mad. "This makes all the entrances, exits and soliloquies exciting—it keeps the audience on edge!"

He failed only once at the Circle, with Camus' *Caligula*. Jerry Epstein begged him to take over because nobody at the Circle could make heads or tails out of it. Chaplin wasn't much help. "What does *this* mean?" he kept asking. Since nobody had any better grasp of it than he did, he decided to add gags, which got laughs but rather negated Camus.

Bob Sherman, an actor in the company, said that "It was osmosis. Charlie's whole body would impart to you what he wanted you to do. When he gave the line readings, he didn't worry about the exact words. He'd say, 'And so and so and so and so,' concentrating on the choreography and the emotion. But Charlie's 'so and sos' were worth an hour of detailed instruction from any other director."

Chaplin was never credited on the programs for direction, because, Jerry Epstein said, "he was afraid the controversies then surrounding him would shift focus away from the accomplishments of the Circle." But word got around town and the theater was soon besieged by celebrities hoping to catch a whiff of greatness. Gene Kelly, John Garfield, Eleanor Powell, Otto Preminger, Glenn Ford—everybody came to the Circle.

Even Hedda Hopper came. She cornered Jerry Epstein after a performance of *What Every Woman Knows* and asked him, "Is it true Charlie Chaplin had a finger in this?" Epstein remembered that "her voice [was] drenched in vitriol." Epstein laughed it off, but it was an ominous echo of everything going on outside the walls of the Circle Theatre.

William Schallert believed that Chaplin's brand of instinctive genius was hard to communicate to other people, which is where the incessant demonstrations came in. "On the other hand, when he directed *What Every Woman Knows*, he managed to make something really magical happen. There Chaplin was wonderful and he was able to communicate everything perfectly. But sometimes I think it was all off the top of his head. He . . . didn't [always] know the play, whereas Constance [Collier] did. [The actress directed a production of *Twelfth Night* for the Circle.] Perhaps most importantly, though, Chaplin had a wonderful sense of choreography and how people should move—he had a special understanding about movement on the stage. When he would show us things it was almost balletic . . . so quick and light on his feet."

Directing *What Every Woman Knows*, Chaplin was specific about mood and style, vague about everything else. "Don't let it get doleful," he told Ruth Conte, playing a spinster daughter. "Make it very warm. It's cold outside, but you get a glow, a warm glow."

To the cast in general, he admonished, "You must not act. You . . . *must* . . . *not* . . . *act*. I must sharpen you here. No self-pity. Don't give the audience the impression that you've just read the script. It's phony now. We don't talk that way. Just state it. Don't make it weary. You're too young for that. Let's get away from acting. We don't want acting. We want reality. Give the audience the feeling that they're looking through the keyhole. This will be maudlin and sticky as hell if you act. The play is sentimental enough. Don't do it with broken hearts. Come on. If you get a tear in the voice, it's ruined. . . . Get the feeling of embarrassment rather than self-pity. I like that. I like that. It's more noble. Get all the murkiness out of it now. . . .

"Keep it simple! Too many gestures are creeping in. I don't like that. If the audience notices a gesture, you're gone. Gestures are not to be seen. And I'm a gesture man. It's hard for me to keep them down. Thank God I can see myself on the screen the next day. . . . Good exits and good entrances. That's all theater is. And punctuation. That's all it is."

Schallert remembered that Chaplin was particularly generous with the actors at the Circle. "He took us out to dinner a couple of times to a well-known Italian place on Melrose called Lucey's, and one night he had everybody connected with the Circle—including the stage hands and ushers—up to his house for dinner.

"He shared with us all, without holding back. He completely gave himself as fully as he could, and in a way, I don't suppose he had a choice about it—that's just the way he was. But he had a great generosity of spirit and once the fever of working was on him he couldn't resist it, and that's wonderful to see. A true artist at work is wonderful to see."

The Circle was eventually driven out of business by a combination of exhaustion and Equity demanding higher salaries, which was impossible because the theater only held 150 people.

Watching his son Sydney act piqued Chaplin's interest in the boy's obvious talents—he was tall, dark, and handsome, with a good voice and manner, a leading man in the making. Not only that, he could sing. Chaplin had Arthur Kelly write a letter redolent of *noblesse oblige* to Sir Ralph Richardson asking for assistance in getting Syd a spot at the Old Vic for a year or two of seasoning. "Any assistance that you could render in this matter would be greatly appreciated by Mr. Chaplin and myself," wrote Kelly.

There is no record of a reply from Richardson.

OUTSIDE OF THE Circle, there weren't a lot of places in California where Chaplin felt comfortable in these years. He had always been a loner, and now he was an ostracized loner. But for the first time in his life, he had a refuge besides work—his family. Oona Chaplin's home movies from the late 1940s are full of backyard frolicking with Geraldine, Victoria, and Michael, outings for pony rides for the kids, and trips to Catalina Island, long one of his favorite getaways. The kids are giddy and Chaplin is beaming. In one series of shots he's wearing a captain's hat and expertly rowing a dinghy. He lets the kids take the oars and they prove considerably less adept.

Back home on Summit Drive, Chaplin was an extremely decorous and polite host, all the more so because there were fewer people willing to be seen with him. The screenwriter Ivan Moffat told a story about taking Dylan Thomas to Chaplin's house. Moffat thought that by this time Chaplin had become "almost like a sort of English colonel in his attitude to the correct way everything should go." He would welcome people to his house, usher them to a chair with a sweep of his hand, then say, "Would you care for something on ice?" Oona was quite tolerant of her guests, but Chaplin liked everything just so and didn't like bad language of any kind.

Chaplin and Dylan Thomas got into a conversation about the pervasive hostility of the press and Chaplin asked Thomas for some advice. "What would you say to them?"

"Well," said Thomas, "there's only one thing you could say. Tell them to go fuck their bloody eyelids."

Oona didn't look up from her knitting, but Chaplin whirled around to see if any other guests had heard Thomas. It was all quiet on that front, so he returned to the conversation.

Thomas went on to say that his family in Wales always regarded Chaplin as their hero. Chaplin immediately placed a long-distance call to Thomas's relatives and had a talk with his admirers.

The next day Chaplin discovered that someone had urinated on his living room sofa. He thought that Christopher Isherwood, who was also at the party, was guilty, and Isherwood was henceforth banned from the house. Ivan Moffat thought it was a clear case of mistaken identity and that Dylan Thomas was the miscreant.

Propriety could be displaced by whimsy. Michael Powell was a dinner guest at Chaplin's house when the host began imitating a West Highland terrier trying to scare away an intruder with a fusillade of furious barking.

"White or black?" asked Powell.

"White," Chaplin said definitively.

Ivan Moffat liked Chaplin, but realized that he had been raised by wolves—he had no idea about things that other people had learned through early immersion in conventional society. Tipping, for instance. Chaplin took Oona, Moffat, and Moffat's mother to Chasen's for dinner. The bill came, Chaplin signed it, and the waiter stood there. Chaplin realized the problem, said, "Excuse me, so sorry," and pulled a fifty-cent piece out of his pocket. The waiter didn't move. Chaplin said, "Excuse me, I'm so stupid," and produced an additional quarter.

Moffat believed that Chaplin had always been psychologically isolated, which was emphasized when he told Moffat that he'd never really known happiness until he married Oona.

"But surely success and all that?" Moffat said.

"Success was wonderful and all-important in my life," Chaplin replied. "But I never felt the audience loved me. They only loved the

Little Tramp. When I went to London . . . and they mobbed me, the police had to keep them back. But it wasn't *me*, and if they'd known what I was, they wouldn't have liked me at all. Although they loved the Little Tramp, I had no personal relationship with the audience to make me happy, unlike many star actors who were personally loved by their public. I never had that, and although success was wonderful, it didn't in itself gratify or please me, or make me feel more at ease with the world."

ON APRIL 17, 1948, Chaplin was interviewed by John P. Boyd of the Immigration and Naturalization Service. It was more of an interrogation than a conversation; Boyd was polite, but the questions were relentlessly prosecutorial:

"Have you ever made any contributions to the Communist Party?"

"Never. . . ."

"Mr. Chaplin, I understand that you have been rather—that the press from time to time has indicated that you were more or less interested in Communist-sponsored movements in this country. Is that correct?"

"No, not Communist sponsored. . . . I am liberal and I am interested in peace, but by no means am I interested in Communism. I have always made that statement. As I say, I never need any front or any other name. I have never belonged to any political organization other than the things I have to belong to in accordance with my work."

"Did you ever address a communication to anyone in which you stated, 'Russia, the future is yours.'"

"Yes."

"To whom was the communication addressed, and the nature of it?"

"It was at the request of our Allies, which were the Russians at that time. They wanted some kind of message . . . for one of their anniversaries."

"To whom was the communication addressed?"

"I don't know. To Soviet Russia, something like that." . . .

"Do you consider yourself in sympathy with the cause of the Communist Party of the USA?"

"I know nothing about the Communist Party of the USA, nothing whatsoever. Does that answer you? . . . All this sort of association of Communist attached to me emanates from the fact that I was called up during the war to make a speech and deputize for Mr. Davies, who was the Ambassador to Russia, and he was to speak in San Francisco. He was taken suddenly ill with laryngitis, and at the last minute they called me up and asked me if I would go there for the rally and so forth and get money for the Russia thing, charity, or whatever it was.

"I went down there at the last moment. I made a speech. I felt very emotional that they were at Stalingrad and so forth and all this business, they had fought and died a great deal, and I made a talk, a eulogy of Russia and the Russian people, and then, from there they said, 'Good work,' and it was the thing to do, and we wanted unity, and there seemed to be other forces trying to divide us at that time . . . in all my speeches I said, 'We want Thomas Lamont [J. P. Morgan, U.S. Steel] to Harry Bridges [left-wing labor leader] we want that same unity, we have to win this war. I mean, that is the whole thing. . . .

"I am not antagonistic. I'll say that now. I don't feel this antagonism against Russia. I don't feel it at all. Perhaps I don't understand the situation, but I frankly must say that I still have hope, and I still believe it would be a very good job if we could make a deal with them and I believe we . . . would be more prosperous all around."

"What is your attitude toward the Soviet Government at this time?"

"The same as it always has been. I feel very grateful to them. What I read of the news, I don't see anything where they have committed any particular crime or outrage in our democracy."

"What is your reaction to the way Czechoslovakia was taken over by the Soviets?"

"Frankly, I don't know very much about the situation. I am very ignorant on the subject. From what I read in the papers, I still maintain I don't think Russia has done a damn thing. That is my own personal belief. What [have they] done in handling the thing? No soldiers were there. There was no bloodshed, and my summation and analysis of the situation, I think my common sense tells me that we didn't do much for [Czechoslovakia] at the time of the Sudeten business, and I frankly believe the press is trying to create a war and start and create a war with Russia, and I wholeheartedly disapprove of it, and I am sure that I am not a Communist and my name will never be connected with any Communist. I have $30 million worth of business—what am I talking about Communism for?"

"Do you think the Communist way of life is better than the American?"

"No. Of course, if I did, I'd possibly go there and live. At the same time, I am not antagonistic. I have never been antagonistic until if they were to invade America. I'd be the first to take up arms."

"Would you take up arms to repel—"

"Yes, to repel any invader that came to the United States. Another thing, they don't like anybody that speaks frankly, the press. I haven't any decent public relationships in this country. I despise the press, and they have always lied about me. They have tried to build me up as a monster, all this sort of thing. I have lived a very quiet, normal life. I am not an association man at all, but during the war I felt very strongly against the Nazi business and up to that time I was completely against the war, because I think it was an outrage, they made a deal with Hitler.

"When they came to the war, I flung my luck with the whole Allied movement for the one purpose of defeating the Nazis and the Fascists. Because I made a picture, I felt very strongly about it. I felt they were Communist and aboriginal, but all this racial business—I am not a Jew—nevertheless the mere picking on a minority of people incenses more than the ideology, more than . . . anything else—just that they were crazy; they were mad men. . . ."

"As a matter of fact, Mr. Chaplin, you are not a citizen of the United States, are you?"

"I am not."

"Have you ever applied for citizenship in this country?"

"I have never applied. From the time I was 19 I have always had a sense of internationalism and I feel it is coming closer every day, for the United Nations and the One World. . . ."

"Is that the reason you have never applied for citizenship in the United States?"

"Yes. I consider myself as much a citizen of America as anybody else, and my great love has always been here in this country. I have been here thirty, thirty five years. My children and everybody are as much a part of my—at the same time I don't feel I am allied to any one particular country. I feel I am a citizen of the world. I feel that when the day comes and we have the barriers down and so forth, so the people come and go all around the world and be a part of any country, and I have always felt that about citizenship. . . .

"It isn't true, what the press says. Seventy five percent of my revenue comes from Europe, you see, and this country enjoys one hundred percent of its taxation. My last picture, which they didn't release here, which had only limited release in the US, the whole of the income derives from abroad. It comes into this country and the United States gets the full taxation on that. . . . I could just as well make a picture in England, have it produced there, and take my taxes in England. . . ."

"Mr. Chaplin, do you care to make any further statement in connection with your political views or affiliations?"

"I have no direct affiliations in the sense or am I conscious that they are affiliations for any political objectives, especially toward Communism. I have no affiliations of that nature. . . . I am a liberal man and right now, I feel very strongly about [Henry] Wallace. I feel that Wallace is a very fine forthright man and I think he is a very good support of democracy and for the preservation of the American way of life and for that reason only am I interested in Wallace.

"As I say, all my, all my sudden political—oh, the political rumors about me all emanate more or less since the war on this idea of Communist. As I say, I don't deny the fact that I spoke and eulogized and extolled Russia, because I felt it was necessary to do so because I personally believe and honestly believed they were doing a splendid job and I believe if it hadn't been for Russia we might have had these

Nazis over here and I firmly believe that, and I don't see any reason for any antagonism now against Russia. . . ."

"According to press reports, you more or less have followed the Communist line for a number of years. What have to say in that regard?"

"That is such a generality to say, 'Communist line' followed because of the eventual success of our fight against Germany and against Hitler. Prior to that, I have not followed Communist lines. I have been Democratic. Naturally, I am progressive and I am progressive in the sense that I am not a Socialist, but I believe in proper people's unionism and I believe it is a good thing. I believe all that sort of thing that will alleviate . . . raise the standard of living of the American people and that is all: I'd like to avoid another Depression. . . ."

"Is there anything further you would like to say, Mr. Chaplin?"

"Yes. . . . The mere fact that I say I would want to see peace with Russia and the United States, whether that furthers the American Communist line, I don't know. Well, if it does, it is inadvertent. That is what I would say. But that isn't intentional. That isn't my object. I want to get on record and say that I am not interested in any subversive movement to overthrow the American government or any government, and I am not a politically active person. . . . I have no affiliations other than those that are outside of the political organization, like the friendship of Russia thing, you see.

"My only object is to preserve democracy as we have it. I think there are certain abuses to it, like everything else. I think there has been a great deal of witch burning. I don't think that is democratic. I know it seems very strange and rather bewilders me why I should be considered a Communist. I have been here 35 years and my primary interest is in my work and it has never been an anti-anything . . . maybe a critical comment, but it has always been for the good of the country. I don't like war and I don't like revolution. I don't like anything overthrown. If the status quo of anything is all right, let it go. In my sense of being a liberal, I just want to see things function in harmony. I want to see everybody pretty well happy, and satisfied."

This interview sat in the files of the INS until April 1949, when J. Edgar Hoover requested the FBI's Los Angeles office for an update on the Internal Security file on Chaplin. The Los Angeles office responded by forwarding a thirty-eight-page report, most of which was the INS interview.

That same month, Senator Harry Cain (R-WA), demanded that Chaplin be deported because he had sent a telegram to Pablo Picasso asking for support for Hanns Eisler, who was about to be deported. Cain termed Chaplin's actions "perilously close to treason."

Chaplin didn't seem to notice. A few days after Cain's threat made the papers, Chaplin issued a message for his sixtieth birthday. "Still alive, kicking and enthusiastic about life. The present is wonderful and the future has possibilities. My attitude in the struggle for peace is unswerving. We have learned that war accomplishes nothing but death, upheaval, want and the multiplication of human misery. That is why our efforts for peace must be unremitting. We must move and act with reason toward that end. Until peace, cooperation and understanding can be achieved among all nations of the world."

On November 9, 1949, Assistant Attorney General Alexander Campbell sent a memo to J. Edgar Hoover: "Please send to my office as soon as possible personal study copies of all of the Bureau reports on Charles Chaplan [*sic*] and especially am I interested in the field of subversive activities, any communist connections, associations or information concerning Communist Party activity, or front organizations membership and/or activity."

Seven weeks later, Hoover wrote back saying, "It was determined that there are no witnesses available who could offer testimony that Chaplin has been a member of the Communist Party in the past, is now a member, or that he has contributed funds to the Communist Party." Hoover went on to say that the FBI informant and future McCarthy staffer Howard Rushmore had alleged that he was present on one occasion when Chaplin paid dues to the Party. But Hoover made his doubts about Rushmore quite clear: "Rushmore has not been interviewed in this connection. Unless you specifically request an interview with Rushmore, this will not be done, and no further action will be taken in this matter."

The Bureau had already noted "the known unreliability" of Rushmore. Hoover sent out a memo telling staff that unless specifically directed otherwise they should avoid Rushmore. Hoover's instincts proved correct; Rushmore would murder his wife and commit suicide in January 1958.

It was all very strange. Despite Hoover's acknowledgment that Chaplin was innocent of any specific charges, he was always presumed guilty of being an apostate, and in this period of American history, that was enough. He remained under surveillance. In September 1949, the FBI was told that Anna Louise Strong, "a well-known Russian propagandist" was to attend a meeting at Chaplin's house. On the night of September 19, two agents planted themselves "in the vicinity of the Chaplin residence." No cars were observed coming or going, nor was there any sighting of Anna Louise Strong, and no evidence that any kind of meeting was being held.

In 1950, Senator Joseph McCarthy sailed into the Chaplin business with a State Department loyalty investigation that turned the Wisconsin senator from a backbencher with a drinking problem into a political star.

McCarthy was occupied with attacking a woman named Dorothy Kenyon when he began reading from a letter describing something called the National Council of American-Soviet Friendship. Senator Millard Tydings took the letter and began reading off the names of some of the threats to the Republic: Maxwell Anderson, Charles Chaplin, Aaron Copland, Norman Corwin, Jo Davidson, Albert Einstein, Lion Feuchtwanger, Lillian Hellman, Langston Hughes, Helen Keller, Rockwell Kent, Serge Koussevitsky, Maurice Maeterlinck, Thomas Mann, Pierre Monteaux, Eugene O'Neill, Elmer Rice, Paul Robeson, Leopold Stokowski ("leader of an orchestra," Tydings helpfully interjected), and Ernest Hemingway. Also along for the ride were several United States senators.

McCarthy was nothing if not a namedropper. Neither the FBI nor the Un-American Activities Committee had been able to nail Chaplin for anything beyond being a paying guest with liberal sympathies and a penchant for young women. Lumping him in with half of the intellectual elite of the West, Communists and non-Communists alike, was a new tactic.

In any case, the Bureau clearly didn't think they had anything on Chaplin. On February 7, 1950, it was recommended that the case against Chaplin be closed: "No information has been developed indicating that Chaplin has engaged in espionage activity or is so engaged at the present time." At the same time, it was recommended that the Security Index Card on Chaplin be continued—just in case.

Despite Chaplin's constant assertions of being an innocent liberal bystander, there always seemed to be a pathway to judging him guilty. In 1950, the Communist *People's Daily World* acquired a bootleg print of *The Circus* for a fundraiser in Los Angeles. It was news to Chaplin. He called his lawyer, who stopped the screening before it went on, but not before Hedda Hopper weighed in: "The Commie Daily People's World advertised that Charlie Chaplin's *The Circus* is being shown here for their benefit. While our boys die in Korea, Chaplin's picture is making money for the loyal Commie opposition."

The *Los Angeles Times* ran a retraction, but it was clear that the dogs would continue to bark.

Sydney Chaplin was considerably more pragmatic, not to mention less liberal than his brother, but family loyalty transcended politics. About this time Sydney wrote lyrics for a song that might have been intended for a revival of the Tramp:

> Life isn't the same
> Since I heard the name
> That pervades the hemisphere.
> I am in despair.
> It's everywhere
> This communistic scare.
> It really is appalling
> To hear this man named Stalin
> To hear him speak and prophesy
> That capitalism will surely die.
> To destroy my way of life,
> What a bore. I'll be sore
> Never again to see Flori-dor.
> Nor sip my scotch and soda
> Or follow the horses over the courses

On the downs at Saratoga.
I'll miss the Waldorf and Astor
Where I dine every night
At the back door.

Probably meant as a jokey variation on "Let the Rest of the World Go By," this lyric of exile and isolation carried more truth than either Syd or Charlie could have imagined.

A rare shot of Chaplin onstage circa 1912 (sitting at left, holding bottle).

Chaplin, Edna Purviance, and Chaplin's brother Sydney on the set of *The Immigrant* in 1917.

The momentous day when creators became partners in the movie industry: Douglas Fairbanks, Mary Pickford, Chaplin, and D. W. Griffith announce the formation of United Artists.

Always willing to help his brother, Chaplin posed on the set of *The Gold Rush* with Syd to promote his delightful performance in the 1925 version of *Charley's Aunt*.

Chaplin and Winston Churchill on the set of *City Lights*.

An anxious Chaplin during the shooting of *Modern Times*.

A production shot from *The Great Dictator*. Note the camera tracks on left. The building in the background with air vents on the roof is the Chaplin studio soundstage.

A charming photograph of Chaplin and Paulette Goddard that conceals the tension between them during the making of *The Great Dictator*. They split shortly afterward.

Chaplin and Orson Welles in October 1942, the night of the pro-Russian speech that would change Chaplin's life.

Joan Berry.

A stunned Chaplin moments after his acquittal on charges of violating the Mann Act. His attorney Jerry Giesler is on the left, holding Chaplin's hand.

Chaplin's use of his body to delineate character remained definitive even after sound altered the nature of movie storytelling. Compare the unhinged rage of Hynkel in *The Great Dictator* with the elegant, composed posture of *Monsieur Verdoux*.

For his portrait of a music hall comedian in *Limelight*, Chaplin dared to appear without comic makeup, inviting the audience to conflate him with Calvero.

Chaplin and Buster Keaton in the Twilight of the Comic Gods that forms the climax of *Limelight*.

Chaplin, Oona, and two of their children face photographers at London's Waterloo Station on September 24, 1952, after he was banned from reentering the United States.

Piles of film in the courtyard of the Chaplin studio after his banishment—open pickings for anyone who wanted them.

Chaplin *en famille* in 1960, with Oona holding their youngest.

Marlon Brando in a typical mood on the set of *A Countess from Hong Kong*.

Chaplin accepting his honorary Oscar in 1972.

PART THREE

"In his youth he yearned to be a musician but could not afford any kind of instrument upon which to learn. Another longing was to be a romantic actor, but he was too small and his diction too uncultured. Nevertheless, he emotionally believed himself to be the greatest actor living. Necessity made him turn to comedy, which he loathed, because it demanded of him an intimacy with his audience which he did not feel and which never came natural to him."

—From "Calvero's Story,"
a portion of the novel Chaplin wrote as preparation for *Limelight*

Chaplin's follow-up to *Monsieur Verdoux* was rigorously apolitical—the story of a comedian, of fear and nightmares and isolation; of the ultimate crisis of not being able to make an audience laugh; of the approach of old age and the apprehension of waning skills; of the possibility of accepting love from a young, ardent woman who believes in him. It was the story of a man named Calvero, or, if you will, Charlie Chaplin, filtered through the sentiment, melodrama, and setting of the Edwardian theater.

It would be a richly evocative summing up of Chaplin's creative and emotional life—a story about a once revered comedian who tries to win back the audience that has abandoned him. It wasn't a literal depiction of what had happened to Chaplin—the audience was bored by the older Calvero, while the audience had been actively hostile to the man who played Verdoux. But in its examination of the potentially destructive relationship between a performer and his audience it was dead-on.

It was also a wistful depiction of the man Chaplin might have been. When he was asked by Thomas Burke what his ultimate ambition had been as a young man, Chaplin replied, "Top of the bill in a West End music hall. That was all I wanted. That was the limit—the maddest dream—the most hopeless goal."

Chaplin began dictating what he initially called *Footlights* in September 1948, and didn't start shooting until November of 1951—three long years of bathing in memory and imagination, of painstaking preparation. It was always going to be a long film—the first draft script, which film historian David Robinson dates to late 1949, ran to 185 pages, while the final draft is 166 pages.

Chaplin sets *Limelight* in 1914. It was not a casually chosen date. Nineteen fourteen was the year Chaplin became a movie star as well as the year World War I erupted, thus ending the Belle Epoque. For Chaplin, 1914 was the year his life changed. For Calvero, his alter ego, it was the year of his deepest despair, of his rebirth, and, ultimately, of his death.

Although Chaplin wrote that a comedian named Frank Tinney gave him the basic idea for Calvero, there are more than trace elements of Chaplin's father in the character, not to mention Leo Dryden, the father of Chaplin's half-brother, Wheeler Dryden.

Leo Dryden was known as the "Kipling of the Halls" for his songs of sentiment and patriotic duty, such as "The Miner's Dream of Home," which was so popular it became an unofficial British anthem sung to usher in the New Year. Dryden had other popular songs, such as "Gallant Gordon Highlanders" and "Bravo, Dublin Fusilliers," but was gradually left high and dry by changing tastes. In the years before his death in 1939 he became an impoverished busker.

Chaplin's final draft was sometimes windy, deeply heartfelt, full of the philosophy he had evolved over his life. "Consciousness is desire," Calvero says in dialogue that got cut. "And desire is eternity, with life and death flowing through it—life and death, all one and the same thing, coming and going, coming and going."

The script has some fascinating diversions that Chaplin shot but ended up cutting. There's a long flashback of the dancer Terry as a child, where she discovers her beloved sister working as a prostitute to pay for Terry's ballet lessons. The result is a paralyzing trauma that leads to Terry's suicide attempt. And there is a backstage scene involving a group of German acrobats. A young performer misses a trick, and the chief acrobat brutally slaps him.

The script is bawdier than the film—when Calvero is onstage singing "The Sardine Song," there's a line about "Fin—in the fish world, that's slang for jail bait." Wiser heads prevailed. The script also confronts Chaplin's deepest fears more bluntly than the finished film: "I wasn't funny," Calvero says after bombing in a performance. "I've lost something. I believe I'm getting old. . . . I've lost contact. They were like strangers."

Chaplin solves the problem of how to integrate flights of physical comedy in a sound film by framing the comedy as a series of stage performances—Dan Kamin correctly pointed out that comedy is something "his character *does*, rather than something his character *is*."

Ultimately, the movie is about what defined Chaplin's life: a performer's devotion to craft. In steadying a girl with a shaky sense of her own gift, Calvero rediscovers his own passion and need for applause.

> TERRY: To hear you talk no one would ever think you were a comedian.
> CALVERO: I'm beginning to realize that. I can't get a job.
> TERRY: What a sad business, being funny.
> CALVERO: Very sad, if they won't laugh. But it's a thrill when they do. To look out there, see them all laughing. To hear that roar go up, waves of laughter coming at you.

By the time Calvero dies, he has seen Terry dancing once again, an assured performer commanding the stage. The torch has been passed.

For the legendary stage act in which Chaplin partners with Buster Keaton, Chaplin's script suggests who might have been his first choice for the part when he describes Calvero's partner as "putting on a Chester Conklin makeup." The particulars of the scene itself were left for rehearsal; the script merely describes it as "Calvero and his partner enter and proceed with their musical act."

It is a fiercely remembered film that takes place almost entirely in the quarter square mile of Soho, centering around the Empire and the Alhambra—the two great music halls of Leicester Square, environments so lofty Chaplin never aspired to play there. In fact, there are only two scenes that take place outside Soho—Calvero's humiliation at the office of his agent, and his disastrous booking at the Middlesex Music Hall, six blocks east of Soho.

Chaplin fills the film with autobiographical references to his own past. Calvero wanted to be a dramatic actor, not a comedian. He mentions many marriages as well as the loss of his adoring public. Nigel Bruce plays a kindly impresario named Postant, modeled on William Postance, the stage manager for a production of *Sherlock Holmes* in which Chaplin played at the Duke of York's Theatre in 1905.

To prepare for this voyage into his past, Chaplin did something extraordinary—he wrote a novel. The book survives in some three hundred pages in at least eleven different states, some incomplete, as well as random pages of what one scholar referred to as "digressions, variations and incessant rewriting." The novel is partly backstory for the shooting script, partly a fond but clear-eyed memoir of the era that formed Chaplin's performing soul.

The autobiographical elements that constitute the core of the film were made clear in a description of Calvero's stage costume. "His makeup was ridiculous: a small tooth-brush moustache, an ill-fitting derby hat, a tight swallow-tail coat, baggy pants and a large pair of old shoes." (In the film itself, Chaplin devised a completely different makeup for Calvero.)

There are lovely diversions in the novel, historical mini-essays recalled from Chaplin's childhood, as in this about a theatrical pub called the Queens Head: "Only in the daytime was the place noisy, then it was a bedlam of loud conversation. Actors and agents met and talked business over a glass of beer or would have lunch at the bar.

"At Christmas time, old men appeared that were never seen at any other time. They were a particular specie as far as the other actors went, for they only considered being 'of the profession' for a period of eight to ten weeks, during which they played clowns in the various Christmas pantomimes. The rest of the year they were engaged elsewhere at different occupations. Some were paperhangers, others waiters and others did odd jobs, filling in at anything, until the next Christmas pantomime season came around.

"Some of these old fellows had been stars and successful vaude-villians in their day, but had succumbed to the inevitable enemy, time, which had dimmed the comic spirit, but had left enough of it to enable them to enact the traditional clown in the Harlequinade, which was a conventional entr'acte introduced at the end of all pantomimes. It was childish, slapstick entertainment, not particularly funny but contrived mostly for the amusement of children.

"Calvero had degraded to this station in life. He was one of these old men."

Chaplin was quite aware of the autobiographical elements, psychological and otherwise. "Is *Limelight* the autobiography of Chaplin?" he scribbled in some notes that he later crossed out. "Those who know him intimately say it is. Certainly, in the story there are many episodes which, if not absolute facts, are certainly analogous to Chaplin's own life." Referring to himself in the third person could have been a distancing mechanism, a way of melding his own life with a fictional character. In other, scattered handwritten notes he wrote lines that could be either ideas for dialogue or notes to himself:

"The horror of poverty is the hopelessness of forever being imprisoned in it."

"The horror of poverty is its sense of confinement."

And this:

"The energy and trouble it takes to fight back, is too much of an enterprise."

"I can't give anyone enough importance to hate them—but there are many I dislike."

In late October 1950, Chaplin traveled to New York in order to discuss financing for his picture and to meet with Mary Pickford about United Artists. Both Sam Goldwyn and David Selznick had left UA, Goldwyn to release through RKO, Selznick to release his own pictures. As a result, UA had been atrophying because of a lack of product and steely disagreements between the two surviving partners, both of whom were enormously strong-willed and disinclined to compromise.

"I was never interested much in the whys and wherefores," Chaplin would airily offer about the company. "I left that to lawyers and managers. I never thought of United Artists as a money-making scheme. . . . It was a way of distributing my films." The domestic distribution fee for United Artist partners was set well below what other studios charged. UA, then, had been conceived as a service operation for its founders rather than an investment that would return profits.

Chaplin and Pickford had long since settled down to a disastrous war of attrition. Neither of them trusted the other, and neither would agree to a suggestion offered by the other. The result was stalemate amplified by the general decline afflicting the movie business in the postwar years. By the end of 1949, the company was losing $65,000 a week.

Pickford related a story that indicated the huge distrust between them. Chaplin was at the Sherry-Netherland, and refused to meet at the Pierre, where Pickford stayed—he thought she might have the room bugged. For that matter, he thought she might have his room at the Sherry-Netherland bugged as well. They finally agreed to meet in Central Park. Chaplin chose a bench with no shrubbery behind it, so no one could be eavesdropping. The conversation was getting into deep corporate issues of money and trust when a street sweeper came by.

"Put 'em up!" he ordered. Chaplin and Mary Pickford raised their legs while the street cleaner brushed beneath them—a scene worthy of a Chaplin movie.

While Chaplin was in New York, Sydney wrote a long letter to Arthur Kelly, Chaplin's man at UA, about his brother's plans. As always, Sydney seemed to think that Charlie had just set foot in Hollywood and was an innocent surrounded by sharks:

"When [Charlie] told us he was going to the banks for a loan, I warned him that they were nothing more than glorified pawnbrokers & that they would insist upon a pound of his flesh as collateral. I told him they might even accept the negative as a guarantee for the loan, but beware if they ask you to personally endorse the note. They will take your eye teeth if they don't get their loan back from the film rentals. If you deal through a bank, you might as well use your own money because you will be paying interest on a loan while your own money lies idle in the bank. . . .

"If he has to make the picture, he should take a partner who would be willing to take all the financial risks for a percentage of the profits. How about [20th Century-Fox chairman] Joe Schenck?

He might make arrangements with the Fox Co., the picture could be made in their studio at a much lower cost than in his own studio, as they . . . no doubt have lots of standing sets that could be quickly changed to suit Charlie, they have all the supporting artists he needs, plus a good publicity dept. that could put out plenty of material that would dispel the bad public feeling that is killing the value of his pictures in the U.S.A. Personally I would like to see him work in one of the big studios as he is terribly handicapped when he has to get together a crew of his own."

Syd's instincts were good. Chaplin did have to build each new picture from the ground up, because he maintained only a skeleton staff during the long gaps between movies. The lack of any staffing continuity between pictures kept his overhead low, but it also made hiring for a new picture a catch-as-catch-can process.

Syd went on to suggest Howard Hughes as a (highly unlikely) financial partner for *Limelight*, and concluded by reiterating, "for heaven's sake keep Charlie away from the banks." Ultimately Chaplin went ahead with a plan that preserved his autonomy—he self-financed *Limelight* at a cost of $900,000 and shot it in the studio he had built in 1918.

IN JANUARY 1951, while still fine-tuning the script for the planned start of shooting in November, Chaplin began to compose the musical score and started looking for a young actress to play Terry. The schedule outlined a shoot of thirty-six days—an extremely ambitious plan considering the length of the script and the fact that the film included a ballet. In fact the film took fifty-five working days to make.

Nothing was too insignificant to be worthy of his interest. "When both script and music were ready," recalled Chaplin's son Sydney, "there was the choreography of the dances to work out, the costumes to be designed, the casting to be finished. Every day of the film was father's concern. If he'd had the time—for he certainly had the energy and inclination—I believe he would [have] himself made the shoes and sewn the skirts."

In January 1951, the journalist Ezra Goodman took a tour of the Chaplin lot with Rollie Totheroh as his guide. "He should be starting his next picture soon, though I don't know exactly when," Totheroh said. "It'll be about a music hall clown."

There were two stages, one 100 by 275 feet, another 130 by 75 feet. The prop room still held the giant wooden gears from *Modern Times*, the baby carriage used in *The Kid*, snowshoes from *The Gold Rush*, the defendant's stand from *Monsieur Verdoux*, the insignia of the double cross from *The Great Dictator*.

The small back lot still had the standing street set that had been built for *City Lights*. One side of the street had been redressed as the ghetto from *The Great Dictator*; the other side had been converted to the French street of *Monsieur Verdoux*. Parked by the sidewalk was the streetcleaner's brush and wagon from *City Lights*.

It all made a kind of sense. Chaplin had been a child whose possessions and security had been taken from him. With money and success, he meant to keep what was his as long as possible.

Besides, you never know when an old prop can be fixed up and used again.

FOR THE PART of Terry, Jerry Epstein remembered that "[Chaplin] interviewed every ingénue in Los Angeles, including Marilyn Monroe, but with no luck." Chaplin wanted a girl with a melodious voice; with all the girls he tested, he would close his eyes and listen to their voice. For a while it seemed an actress named Barbara Bates would get the role. He rehearsed with Bates for a full week before abruptly changing his mind and telling his casting director to hire Claire Bloom.

Chaplin's casting instincts were not always spot-on—he was right about Virginia Cherrill and Paulette Goddard, wrong about Marilyn Nash. But he triumphed by choosing Bloom for his leading lady in *Limelight*.

The process had begun with an ad in the trade papers: "WANTED: Young girl to play leading lady to a comedian generally recognized as the world's greatest. Must be between 20-24 years of age. Stage, ballet experience preferable but not necessary. Apply Charles Chaplin Studios, Hollywood."

None of the applicants set Chaplin afire until Arthur Laurents recommended the nineteen-year-old Bloom, whom Laurents had seen onstage in London. Bloom was darkly beautiful and already had classical experience, although she had only made one minor film. After being prodded by Chaplin, Bloom sent some stills, then got a one-week leave from a play called *Ring Round the Moon* to come to New York, where Chaplin tested her.

She was good and took direction well, but Chaplin stalled. After what Bloom remembered as four months, during which he temporarily shifted his enthusiasm to Barbara Bates, he came back to Bloom.

After signing to do the film—her salary was $15,000 plus expenses—and spending some time with the family, Bloom realized why Chaplin had hired her.

"He wanted the girl to be like Oona," Bloom remembered. "I think that what particularly excited Chaplin about the *Limelight* story was that at long last the damaged girl was to develop into a mature woman, strong, independent, completely in command of her powers. . . . The example of Oona—of her loving devotion and her quiet strength—was responsible for finally erasing the image of the broken womanhood that his mother's suffering had imprinted on his artistic conscience."

Before the cameras rolled, Chaplin rehearsed for two full weeks, first on the lawn of his house with Claire Bloom and Jerry Epstein from 11 a.m. to 4 p.m., then on the sets as they were built. Since Chaplin thought both he and Bloom needed to lose a few pounds, lunch was forbidden.

"I remembered each way he did it," Jerry Epstein said, "and would remind him of the gesture he left out, or how he did it, and where he turned. He loved it. He loved it because his whole thing was technique. He said, 'Learn your technique and then forget it. It is second nature then. Then you can do what you want.' "

Every detail of the film's physical presentation was present in his head. He escorted Bloom to the costumers and told her, "My mother used to wear a loose knitted cardigan, a blouse with a high neck and a little bow, and a worn velvet jacket." Rough duplicates were found for Bloom.

She would recall that the entire film constituted an attempt to, first, recapture his past, then reshape it, redirect it: "The dressing rooms, the boarding houses, the agents' offices, the pubs, all the melancholy landmarks of his lonely apprenticeship. . . . Nothing was left to chance. There was no such thing as chance. There was only his genius."

On days when the rehearsals went either very well or very badly, Chaplin would call a break and take Bloom, Epstein, and Oona for lunch at the Farmers Market. Bloom gradually became aware of how unpopular he was. Once, when she was being driven to Chaplin's studio, the cab driver asked her, "Is that guy still allowed to make films here?" Chaplin would tell her that the only Communist activity he'd ever engaged in was his daily perusal of the stock market returns in *The New York Times*. The difference between him and the Communists, he explained, was that he wasn't reading them hoping for a crash.

Chaplin plowed through sets of *Punch* and *The Strand* magazines, marking scores of images for the art director Eugene Lourie—staircases and apartments, the clothes, how people carried themselves on the streets. He worked on the script obsessively; at one point the mimeograph company gave up at the incessant flood of new pages and informed the studio that "We don't want his script or money."

He composed most of the musical score before production, either humming the themes to arranger Ray Rasch, or plinking out the notes on a piano, playing by ear, always in the key of F.

Filming got under way on November 19, 1951. Chaplin's habit of economizing disappeared when it came to quality. His attitude was summed up by an exchange with assistant director Robert Aldrich. At one point, Aldrich said to an aide, "If anything goes wrong technically give me a signal." Chaplin stopped and corrected Aldrich: "We'll stop if anything goes *esthetically* wrong."

Bloom realized that much of Chaplin's acting was filtered through movement, timing, beats. Eugene Lourie told Kevin Brownlow how important the dimensions of a set were for Chaplin: "I always started with a floor plan because the float line is where the actor will move, and where the camera will move. For [Chaplin], the float line was very important, because he directed his actors almost like dancers. In fact, the first set I built for him was put into use almost immediately because he wanted to rehearse with Claire Bloom. . . . So I had to build Calvero's small apartment, two rooms. And he started to rehearse every day from ten o'clock to four.

"The second day, he said, 'Mr. Lourie, is it possible to enlarge the room a little bit? I need about 18 more inches between the door and the stove. You see, I need to take one more step.'" Lourie's walls always had a few extra feet on either side so they could be expanded for just such an eventuality. He told Chaplin the enlarged set would be ready by the next morning. "[After] that day, our relations were much better."

The first day of shooting involved Calvero's apartment, and the actors on call were Chaplin, Claire Bloom, Wheeler Dryden, and Marjorie Bennett. Their task was to film all their entrances and exits out of sequence. They would perform a scene, then change their costumes to film another scene from a different part of the film. The lack of continuity could have made it difficult for the relatively inexperienced Bloom, but Chaplin's extensive rehearsals made it possible for them to jump around without trouble.

After three days of shooting, Chaplin made the decision to once again replace Rollie Totheroh with Karl Struss, who had shot *The Great Dictator*. As Struss remembered, "Rollie still couldn't light." Struss gave the film deep blacks, a multitude of grays, and crane shots that made the film seem more luxurious than the budget seemed to allow. Struss and Lourie took special pains with a miniature of London designed by Lourie that could be seen out of Calvero's window, where Chaplin planned to shoot several close-ups. The miniature contained walls, chimneys, hanging laundry, even tiny garbage cans. Both Struss and Lourie thought it was a thing of beauty. Chaplin came out of his bungalow, looked at the camera setup, and said, "The camera's too high. Lower it four inches."

"Four inches!" snorted Struss twenty years later. "So we gave him what he wanted. It took another hour to lower that camera four inches." Chaplin ended up using retakes for most of the shots, and the miniature is never seen in the finished film.

To a great extent, it was still a one-man show. When they needed a sound effect of scenery being moved, Chaplin was one of the men pushing, shoving, and muttering.

Struss noticed that "Charlie mellowed in between *Dictator* and

Limelight. Oona seldom came on the set, but Charlie had changed—quieter. Charlie's studio was pretty well equipped, except it was cold in winter; the heating wasn't any too good. Charlie devoted a lot of time to coaching Claire Bloom, more than the other actors. He treated her very well, showed her respect. Of course, he wasn't married to her!"

As always, Bloom was expected to replicate Chaplin's performance of her part. The long dialogue scenes between Calvero and Terry were completed by the end of the second week of filming. Chaplin then moved into the flashback scenes between Terry, her sister, and mother, which were eventually cut. By December 19, Chaplin was only five days behind schedule, and the film was targeted to be completed by January 8. The street scenes were shot on the New York brownstone street at Paramount, and the company moved to the Selznick/Pathé studios in Culver City to shoot the extensive theater and ballet sequences.

Chaplin has often been criticized for his methodical visual style, but he throws off a stunning shot that encapsulates the magic of the theater. Between acts of the ballet, he cuts to an overhead shot. The ceiling of the stage set flies up, the flats are lugged off, the new set is quickly assembled, the dancers take their positions and the curtain rises. The problem was that Chaplin had recorded the music score in advance, and he had written exactly eighteen seconds of music for the shot. He asked Eugene Lourie to rehearse the dismantling and construction of the set to make sure it took eighteen seconds. Lourie thought it was possible it might run a second or two shorter, or maybe longer.

Chaplin shook his head. "If the timing is right, we can use it. If not, put the set back together again." Lourie remembered that "the first take was good, and that was that." It's a transporting moment that captures all the magic of the theater—cardboard and crudely carpentered wood magically embodying a poeticized reality. It's as if Michael Powell took over directing for one shot.

Seventy years after the experience of making *Limelight*, Claire Bloom was still happy to talk about it. "I'm never sick of it. It was such a great experience, such a wonderful introduction to the world of movies.

"For Charlie, it was all about the actor. He was a very concrete director. 'Look here, say the line, then do this.' And then he would demonstrate the moment for me so beautifully I knew I could never equal it. He wanted to give me a very specific sense of what I was to communicate. I remember him saying that he had me wearing a shawl because his mother had worn the same kind of shawl. He wanted to give the sense of a woman who was always cold without anything cliché like shivering. He wanted the little details that made a character evocative.

"George Cukor is rightly known as a great woman's director. He entered into the feelings of being a woman. He completely understood emotionally a woman's psyche. Chaplin did too. That's part of the job of being a great director.

"In a sense, working with Charlie, making *Limelight*, having such a glorious experience, gave me the wrong idea about the business. Being an actor is so difficult, and there's the horrible dependence of waiting for someone to call you for this, that or the other. The whole game makes me quite sick. I wish I'd been a bricklayer; I wish I'd had a Plan B."

Young Syd Chaplin had worked for his father at the Circle Theatre, so he knew what he was getting into by playing a romantic young composer who falls in love with Terry. Sydney remembered it as a predominantly positive experience. "Sometimes Pa would be conventional in his shooting, but he did few close-ups compared with most movies. Most movies are always cutting to a close-up of Ingrid Bergman, but he figured a close-up was incredibly powerful and he didn't want to have a bunch of close-ups. What he did do was shoot a lot of takes. He'd look at the footage the next day and if he didn't like it, he'd redo it. And keep redoing it until he liked it."

Norman Lloyd had a slightly different take on Chaplin's treatment of his son. Lloyd remembered that Chaplin treated Buster Keaton, Nigel Bruce, and, for that matter, Lloyd, with the utmost respect and consideration, but to Claire Bloom and Sydney Chaplin, "he was hell on wheels. The only way he could direct was to act, so he would get up and act their parts. He played the leading man straightforwardly, but he acted the woman fantastically. His body expressed everything about the meaning of the scene and its emotional level, more strongly than what he said. He could translate it more specifically with movement than with words."

The problem was a native impatience that had not been diminished by age or experience. "Charlie would not sit in a chair; he squatted right under the lens and acted the scene, back and forth, back and forth with increasing anger as he felt he wasn't getting what he wanted. . . . [Bloom and Sydney] were constantly aware of all this movement, which would ruin their concentration; then he would sail into them, shout at them and show his impatience."

Lloyd said that Chaplin had a naturally combustible temperament, "a mixture of darkness and melancholy, great lightness, brilliant humor and savagery. Charlie had the gift of going all the way. I believe that if he had wanted to, Charlie could have killed a man—but not a butterfly.

"It was fascinating to watch him. As a director, he was basically an actor. He instructed the cameraman, 'Get me in the cross-hairs and stay with me.' He knew he was the star, the money, the primary interest. Every take in which he appeared was printed; he permitted himself this luxury, he said, because he had no one standing behind the camera for him. The only way he could get a perspective on it was to look at it the next morning in the projection room. Not a frame was cut until Charlie came into the cutting room. . . . Often he would take a look from one take, a gesture from another, and a walk from a third take to complete a scene. He needed that freedom, so no sequence was cut without his being there."

All this drove Robert Aldrich mad. Aldrich had been Jean Renoir's assistant on *The Southerner* and had been recommended by Norman Lloyd, who acted in the Renoir picture. "It's his money," Aldrich told Lloyd, "but we're wasting time. He can't direct. He's the greatest actor in the world, but he can't direct." Aldrich thought Chaplin's style was hopelessly old-fashioned.

Claire Bloom's big scene, when the heretofore crippled Terry begins to walk, was shot at least forty times. Whenever they would finish a scene early, Chaplin would grab Bloom and say, "Come on, we're doing your big scene again. It could be better."

Despite the pressure Chaplin put on Bloom, she never flinched, never complained. If he thought she went over the top, he would snap, "You're working for Charlie Chaplin now—no Shakespeare, please!" Chaplin's son Sydney said that Chaplin consistently raved about her to anyone that would listen, putting her forward as a role model for the profession: "Her ability and technique to follow my direction is fantastic!"

Just before the move to Culver City to shoot the theater sequences, Chaplin was told that Buster Keaton was having a hard time and was available. On impulse, Chaplin told Jerry Epstein to offer Keaton $1,000 for a few days' work as Calvero's assistant in the climactic comedy scene.

In fact, Keaton was working steadily, but mostly in television, which Chaplin despised and rarely watched, so he was unaware of Keaton's tentative comeback after years of alcoholism. Keaton's agent thought the fee was low, but Keaton told him that he would be willing to work for Chaplin for free.

Keaton's first day on the film was December 22 and he showed up wearing his traditional porkpie hat. Chaplin took him aside and told him, "We're not playing our old characters now. I'm not playing the Tramp; you're not playing Buster." Keaton quietly put together another costume, after which Chaplin and he went to work devising their comedy sequence.

The addition of Keaton provoked a decision to devise a lengthy scene showcasing their act, which disrupted Chaplin's carefully planned shooting schedule. The cast list compiled in mid-November, just before the picture began shooting, lists twenty-four parts, from Calvero all the way down to call boys. There is no mention of the character played by Keaton, nor does the character exist in Chaplin's preparatory novel *Footlights*. The final shooting script has Calvero introducing the act as "Igor Fiddleoffsky at the piano and I on the violin" although he cut the dialogue in the film.

Obviously, Chaplin decided to expand Keaton's part after hiring him for what was originally intended to be a bit. The Saturday that Keaton reported for work, Chaplin shot the dressing room scenes with him. So far, so good. Chaplin shut down shooting for a few days before Christmas, then started up again on December 26.

The next day involved Calvero's death scene, with Keaton standing over Chaplin's inert figure and surreptitiously whispering instructions not to breathe, not to move, because the camera was still tracking away from them. It's a startling scene because Chaplin somehow contrives to actually look dead, in contrast to the standard movie death scene, where an invariably healthy-looking actor holds their breath.

On December 27, Melissa Hayden and André Eglevsky arrived and began rehearsing the ballet. That same day, Chaplin added days to the production schedule to accommodate the shooting of the comedy routine that was beginning to form.

Melissa Hayden had begun her dance career with Boris Volkoff's Canadian Ballet and then went to New York and the corps de ballet at Radio City Music Hall. From there she moved to the American Ballet Theatre and, in 1950, the New York City Ballet, where she was the prima ballerina until her retirement in 1973.

Similarly, André Eglevsky had been the *premier danseur* with George Balanchine's American Ballet, the forerunner of the New York City Ballet. With a few timeouts for brief stints with other companies, he remained with Balanchine until he retired in 1958. Eglevsky was muscular, commanding, loved the girls, and was a superb dancer. Hayden was involved through Eglevsky, her former dance partner, whom Chaplin had seen dance in Los Angeles.

Hayden had her first meeting with Chaplin after a red-eye flight that got her to Los Angeles about six weeks before the film started shooting. "This was all an adventure for me," Hayden remembered. "I was very nonchalant." When they arrived at the Selznick studio in Culver City, where the ballet scenes would be shot, "a very little man" with white hair and dancing blue eyes greeted them. "I remember looking at his tiny feet. He was excited about meeting André, not me. He had a good idea about the ballet; it was a takeoff on 'Giselle' in a way, the second act. And he started to tell us about it."

They all went to lunch at the Brown Derby, where Charlie's brother Syd joined them. "Not only was Charlie looking me over, Syd was looking me over." They all went back to the studio and Eglevsky and Hayden got into their rehearsal clothes and prepared to improvise. "When you're not prepared for anything, you use the experience you already have as a performer. Since I had danced with André in a number of pieces, [André] said, 'Do this step from a Balanchine, then this step from *Sylphide* and Fokine.' And we put to-gether a *pas de deux* by talking with each other. And Chaplin would say, 'Good, good, good. This is wonderful!' "

After an hour of improvisation, Hayden was growing restless. Chaplin liked what they were doing, but Hayden didn't think he liked her. "I'm stopping, I'm tired," she told Eglevsky. "You speak to him and ask him if he likes me. If he likes me, that's okay, I'll do it. If he doesn't . . . *finis*, right now.' He hadn't looked at me; I felt like anybody could have been doing this. Somebody had to show an interest in me personally. You see, André and he had met before. André had the job; I was the one auditioning."

Eglevsky talked to Chaplin, and Chaplin was agreeable. He told Eglevsky he would call Hayden's agent. She asked for the same money Eglevsky was getting, which was fine with Chaplin.

Hayden thought Chaplin's choreography credit was ridiculous. "He didn't choreograph a thing; he didn't know anything about ballet. Maybe he took credit for what he was suggesting. All of our dances derived from the two of us, André and myself. And in the montage, I did that all myself. The montage took two or three hours. He just kept saying, 'Do it again!'

"I'm sure Chaplin knew about dance—he loved ballet, although he never spoke about other dancers. But we're talking about classic ballet. I don't know if he was ever in a ballet studio, but he could use the vocabulary of classical ballet, pliés and so forth, although he would mispronounce the word.

"I danced with Balanchine and Ashton. That is a kind of vocabu-lary, a kind of choreography and inventiveness that belongs only to the world of ballet. I don't think he had that particular experience. He was a vaudevillian, and a lot of vaudevillians knew a little or a lot about dance, but not in a classical form. He wasn't trained in that."

Hayden watched Chaplin rehearsing and shooting with Keaton and was amazed at the change in him. "He was very intense and his whole personality changed from what it had been with me. I never saw him shooting with anybody else. It was really intense, and I was amazed. That was the first inkling I had of what the movie was about, and of what he was about. He was very one-on-one in the circumstance of working with that person. He was *very* tunneled, and he gave you the energy he wanted to get back."

As Chaplin worked with Hayden, he got friendlier. One day he put a car at her disposal so she could go shopping. "He was basically a shy man. . . . He invited us to his house, and for André he had piroshky and borscht. And we met all the children. I figured he must have liked us to invite us to the house. Oona was charming; the children were adorable and they were all in the film."

Shooting the ballet lasted from December 29 to January 7. Keaton was usually on the set but not working. Melissa Hayden said that he sat quietly carving a miniature of New York City's 125th Street subway station for his model railroad layout.

Claire Bloom remembered, "Keaton was 56 when he made *Limelight*, but gave the impression of having suffered through a life twice that long. . . . His reserve was extreme, as was his isolation. He remained to himself on the set, until one day, to my astonishment, he took from his pocket a color postcard of a large Hollywood mansion and showed it to me. . . . In the friendliest, most intimate way, he explained to me that it had once been his home. That was it. He retreated back into silence and never addressed a word to me again."

With the ballet sequence completed, Hayden and Eglevsky left for New York on January 7 and for the next five days Chaplin and Keaton rehearsed and shot their routine. Keaton's last day was Saturday, January 12, and the two men put in a ten-hour day to complete the sequence.

Claire Bloom remembered that Chaplin treated Buster Keaton with "respect, actually a mutual respect. Chaplin was definitely the boss, but both of them were very creative together. Chaplin wouldn't have hired Keaton if he hadn't admired him, but don't forget that . . . it was Chaplin's studio, his film and his money."

Chaplin took his time with the sequence—all told, Keaton was on set for at least fifteen of the fifty-five days the film took to make. Bloom believed that the rumors that Chaplin cut some of Keaton's best material were absurd. "There was stuff cut from both of them. It was a very long sequence and it was equally divided between them. Frankly, I think that's a malicious thing to say."

Jerry Epstein concurred. Keaton struck Epstein as a sad, isolated man, barely speaking unless spoken to. "He seemed anxious to prove to Charlie that he hadn't made a mistake in casting him. There was a rapport between the pair, but it was all on a business level. Neither reminisced about the 'good old days.' . . . There was work to be done, and they both attacked their parts like the pros they were.

"Charlie cut some of Keaton's gags. . . but he cut just as many of his own best laughs." Epstein pointed out that some of Keaton's biggest laughs came because of Chaplin's edits. "The shots of the music sheets slipping off Buster's piano were all . . . a single take; it was Charlie who decided to make it into a running gag. Every time you cut to Buster, he's still battling with the tumbling music sheets. The cutting built the sequence and made Keaton's routine outstanding."

With the pas de deux between Chaplin and Keaton completed, shooting was over, except for four days of retakes in May that were added to the schedule against the better judgment of Lonnie D'Orsa, the production manager. One of the days was taken up with Norman Lloyd, who was called to redo his speech outlining the plot of the ballet. Chaplin worked Lloyd through nearly thirty takes on May 5. Chaplin finally okayed take 26, after rejecting others as "Bad intonation—too pausy," or "too recitey."

"I thank God Claire Bloom is back in London," D'Orsa complained. "Had she been around there would have been no end to it. At least he can't think up new versions for the Bloom scenes." In fact, one of the retakes was a long shot in which Oona Chaplin, hair covering her face, doubled Bloom lying in bed.

Chaplin edited the picture until the first week of August, and by the time it was finished he had few doubts about its quality or eventual success. Chaplin was calling the picture a "hymn to humanity" and told a reporter "It's great, my best, a renaissance." Then he ruefully added, "I thought the same about *Monsieur Verdoux*."

"You know they will love you in England," the reporter said.

"But what about this country?"

It had been a long script and it was a long film—145 minutes. The structural problem was the routine with Keaton at the end of the film. What had been intended to be a cameo taking up one or two days of shooting had expanded into two weeks of rehearsal and shooting. The result was an uproarious comic Twilight of the Gods surpassing the ballet that had been designed as the film's emotional centerpiece.

To make room for the Chaplin/Keaton sequence, Chaplin made some trims that Jerry Epstein always regretted. Out went the flashback sequence of Terry as a child. Out went a sequence where Calvero tries to jolly Terry out of her depression. "Calvero performs music hall acts for her with his derby and cane," remembered Epstein. "He made believe the sliding door [in Calvero's apartment] was the proscenium. Her character won't laugh and she says, 'I laugh on the inside.' 'That doesn't help me,' Calvero says."

The trims didn't end there, didn't end even after the picture was released. While the film was still playing in London, Chaplin ordered the removal of a sequence involving Claudius, an armless performer who offers Calvero a loan. Calvero has to reach into the man's jacket pocket to get the money. It's a good scene centering on Calvero's humiliation, and Chaplin obviously wanted to cling to the scene—he instructed the cameraman to hold on to the footage.

BY THE SUMMER of 1952, Chaplin was beginning to preview *Limelight*. He showed it to James Agee, who had become a family friend. Agee responded with two pages of handwritten notes that delve into the picture in granular—and largely irrelevant—detail: "On flea number hold [off-screen] laughter longer, over pan over empty theater at end maybe going into echo filter soon after this shot starts; and cut sharp to silence over C's watering face—or fade over this face. As is, the live audience laughter lasts so long as to kill the point. . . ."

Chaplin mostly kept the film the way it was.

Throughout the shoot, the meld between the old husband and the young wife had been something to bask in. Each day at lunchtime Oona would arrive with cottage cheese and pineapple, or hardboiled eggs—Chaplin believed a hearty lunch left you sleepy in the afternoon. They would sit in Chaplin's dressing room, contentedly nibbling until it was time for the afternoon's work.

Limelight was the work of a man who had found contentment in both his work and his life. He was so sanguine he even brought his old friend Harry Crocker back to work as a publicist for the picture.

Crocker had initially gone to work for Chaplin in October 1925 as a replacement for Harry D'Arrast, who had been hired away to direct at Paramount.

In his nearly four years with Chaplin, Crocker observed an immeasurably stubborn man whose pride often forced him to "argue that four plus four equaled nine, or to insist . . . that a curved line was the shortest distance between two points." Crocker believed that it was Chaplin's basic obstinance that led him into crises—with the government, with reporters, with women. He did as he pleased.

Presiding over his own studio as an Emperor gradually led to imperial behavior that damaged his relationships with the press, with exhibitors, and with the public. A childhood with no power whatever bred a man who needed the prerogatives of power as much as he did air. And that same certainty led him to persevere in the face of obstacles that would have shriveled and defeated most filmmakers.

By the early 1930s, Crocker believed, "Chaplin was withdrawing more and more into a world of his own. In this world there were to be two sets of laws: those which controlled all other men, and those with concern to Chaplin."

Crocker was part of the Crocker banking family, an amiable man everybody liked, and he convinced Chaplin that he could catch an audience for his new picture with honey. It was Crocker who arranged for *Life* magazine to do a major pictorial on *Limelight*, for which the great photographer W. Eugene Smith spent weeks on the set. Chaplin's willingness to alter his preference for a closed set was part of an emotional shift caused by his happy marriage.

At long last, Charlie Chaplin gave every sign of being a contented man.

CHAPTER 14

It was clear that releasing *Limelight* in America was going to be yet another uphill struggle. On August 24, 1952, Max Youngstein of United Artists wrote a memo outlining the headwinds the picture faced:

1. Danton Walker, Leonard Lyons and Earl Wilson are the only columnists who will mention Chaplin favorably. . . .
2. Walter Winchell, Dorothy Kilgallen, Ed Sullivan, Frank Farrell and Hy Gardner are on the antagonistic side. . . . Sullivan, Kilgallen and Farrell have close working connections with the Catholic War Veterans and will refuse, absolutely, to mention Chaplin except in an unfavorable light. Winchell, in addition to being with the Hearst press, is personally peeved with Chaplin.
3. In addition to the columnists, all of the Hearst papers we have contacted are definitely turning thumbs down on Chaplin stories, or favorable mention of any kind.

Youngstein said that Hy Gardner was a member of the American Legion and a negative article about Chaplin was scheduled to appear in the Legion magazine just about the time the film premiered. "We have also received word from a very good source that the Catholic War Veterans will picket *Limelight*. . . . There is no longer any doubt in my mind that we are going to run into serious boycotting, picketing and other difficulties.

"Although I have had different ideas in the past three weeks, I am now recommending that in view of the facts that have been disclosed, we are only to open New York and concentrate on building up the New York campaign and the New York business to such heights that no exhibitor can refuse, for selfish reasons, to play the picture once he knows that it is doing absolutely top business. . . .

"I would also like to recommend a meeting with Cardinal Spellman and try to find out just what can be done to solve the problem."

THE MONTH BEFORE Youngstein's memo, J. Edgar Hoover sent a memo to the Los Angeles office of the FBI regarding Chaplin's recently issued reentry permit. "This permit gives no guarantee that he will be allowed to return to the US once he leaves. Los Angeles is requested to be on the alert for any information that may indicate the subject is contemplating a trip abroad. Any information concerning the subject and his activities in relation to moving or taking a trip should be forwarded to the Bureau immediately."

The crucial meeting between Hoover and Attorney General James McGranery took place on September 9. Despite Hedda Hopper's strenuous pleadings, there is nothing in Richard Nixon's communications with either Hoover or McGranery to suggest that he had anything to do with the final act of the drama, perhaps because by this time Nixon was fully engaged in the task of running for vice president alongside Dwight Eisenhower.

McGranery had been appointed to the attorney general's job five months earlier by President Truman, who was beset by voter discontent about the stagnant situation in Korea as well as Joe McCarthy's charges that his administration was soft on Communism.

McGranery was a former three-term congressman who had been judge of the U.S. Court for the Eastern District in Pennsylvania since 1946. Before that he had been an ardent New Dealer, as well as a devout Roman Catholic who was a Knight Commander of the Order of St. Gregory, a Knight of the Holy Sepulchre, and Private Chamberlain of the Cape and Sword.

At the September 9 meeting, McGranery "stated that he was considering taking steps to prevent the re-entry into this country of Charlie Chaplin. The Attorney General . . . stated that Chaplin and his wife were taking a tour of the world and would return to the United States sometime in the spring, at San Francisco, California, and he had in mind taking the steps which would prevent his re-entry into the United States because of moral turpitude."

Hoover obviously thought this was a capital idea. He prepared a memo directing the Bureau to "prepare a memorandum of all information in our files concerning Charlie Chaplin and that it be transmitted to the Attorney General for his information."

Two agents began to review the seven volumes of material the Bureau had accumulated during the Joan Berry case, as well as six volumes of internal security files. Three more agents worked full-time in the preparation of the document for McGranery. The result was a twenty-page summary sent to the attorney general on September 18.

The next day McGranery issued the order revoking Chaplin's reentry permit. McGranery thought so little of his decision that he didn't bother noting it in his daily appointment diary.

The précis of the report stated, "As early as 1923, Chaplin received favorable mention in 'Pravda,' the official organ of the Communist Party in Russia. His name has been frequently mentioned in connection with Communist activities since that time, but no proof has been developed to reflect actual membership in or contributions to the Communist Party. His associates have included known Communist Party members. He has been connected with or supported sixteen cited organizations and publications. He was active in defense of Hanns Eisler during the deportation proceedings against Eisler in 1948."

The problem for McGranery and Hoover was that, as one FBI memo stated, "at the present time INS does not have sufficient information to exclude Chaplin from the United States if he attempts to re-enter. . . . [The] INS could, of course, make it difficult for Chaplin to re-enter but in the end, there is no doubt Chaplin would be admitted."

The administration's position would be binding under the McCarran-Walter Act, which had been passed over Harry Truman's veto and gave the government wide latitude for exclusions and deportations. But the McCarran-Walter Act wouldn't take effect until December 24, 1952.

"[Assistant Commissioner] Farrell expressed the view that if Chaplin's lawyer was astute, he would have Chaplin return to the United States before the effective date of the new law. Under the new law, INS hopes to exclude Chaplin on moral grounds."

The FBI's strategy was not new and in fact had already been outlined in an article in *Variety* a full two years earlier, on September 27, 1950. The article stated that Chaplin was a problem for the INS rather than the State Department, noted that a reentry permit was no guarantee that he would be able to come back to America because some reentry permits had been withdrawn after "an alien left the United States."

As memos flew back and forth, the decision was made to provisionally justify Chaplin's exclusion because of the abortions Joan Berry alleged he had paid for. The FBI believed that if Chaplin "denies the charge and INS is able to establish it, he will be committing perjury and on the basis of the charge alone, he will be mandatorily excludable under the Immigration and Nationality Act. . . . Any attempt now or later to exclude Chaplin for security reasons would end in a 'rhubarb' . . . attendant with a great deal of unfavorable publicity if attempts were made to exclude Chaplin on security grounds alone."

On the bottom of one memo, Hoover scrawled "We should get started *now* to get our phase of this case lined up."

Together, Hoover and McGranery made the tactical decision to revoke Chaplin's reentry permit after he left the country. There is no indication in either McGranery's or Truman's papers that the decision was run past the president, but it's possible that Chaplin's public support of Henry Wallace during the 1948 campaign was sufficient to render him persona non grata in Truman's eyes.

Hoover was concerned about the possibility of Chaplin forcing the issue and returning before the McCarran-Walter Act went into effect. Wanting some insurance, he once again pressured the Los Angeles office to find hard evidence connecting Chaplin to the Communist Party. In October 1952, weeks after Chaplin was barred from reentering the country, Hoover wrote to the Security Division of the State Department and copied the director of the CIA. Hoover explained that Chaplin had left the United States and could "possibly be denied admittance to this country upon return." He said that the FBI was not requesting a CIA or State Department investigation, but he did ask them to forward "any information concerning subject's activity that may come to your attention." There is no indication that either agency launched a serious investigation of Chaplin, but the American embassies in Belgium, England, France, and Switzerland began surveilling Chaplin.

The Los Angeles office of the FBI repeatedly told Hoover that most of the material collected by the agency in the past had come from sources that had either disappeared or were unreliable, i.e., wouldn't hold up if Chaplin chose to press the issue. In a memo of October 21, 1952, Los Angeles told Hoover that they did have information from a "reliable source" that Chaplin wasn't a member of the Party, and then offered a backhanded, but not inaccurate appraisal of the overall situation: "The CP [Communist Party] likes CHAPLIN when he comes out and takes a stand for issues the CP thinks are correct, but they dislike the independent way in which he does it."

WHILE THE GOVERNMENT was making its plans, *Limelight* premiered in New York on October 23, 1952, to excellent reviews. Melissa Hayden attended and remembered, "Well, I loved it. And I thought the dance sequences were wonderful. I thought it got a little corny at the end. I remember sitting there and thinking, 'OOoooohhh.' And I've seen it again over the years and it's not corny, it's quite touching. See what maturity does to a person? It widens their empathetic response. I'm a cornball myself now. I cry at any movie that's at all sad."

There was talk at the time that *Limelight* was going to be Chaplin's last film, and it would have been better if that had been the case. The film has weaknesses, but as one critic wrote, "It's overlong, shapeless, overblown, and a masterpiece. Few cinema artists have delved into their own lives and emotions with such ruthlessness and with such moving results."

Along with *Ikiru* and *Umberto D.*, *Limelight* is one of the great films about old age, traditionally a lethal stage for comedians—physical virtuosity has a short shelf life, as the careers of Harry Langdon, Jerry Lewis, and Danny Kaye attest. Stand-ups, on the other hand, can work until they drop, and usually do.

Norman Lloyd thought he knew why the picture was such an emotional experience: "It is the deepest story of Chaplin and Oona, told in theatrical terms." Chaplin's contentment in his marriage and family translated to a deeply moving and ultimately serene fictional representation.

A few years before *Limelight*, Chaplin had given Norman Lloyd $3,000 to buy the movie rights to Horace McCoy's novel *They Shoot Horses, Don't They?* The plan was for Chaplin to produce and Lloyd to direct. They had several script sessions, during which both Chaplin and Lloyd realized that the book didn't have a plot. Nevertheless, Chaplin had attended dance marathons during the Depression and found them fascinating. He thought his son Sydney could star, and perhaps that young actress who had made a splash in *The Asphalt Jungle*—Marilyn Monroe.

One of the narrative threads Chaplin devised was a friendship between the male lead and a seagull he would feed during meal breaks from the marathon, which Chaplin planned to shoot on the Santa Monica pier. "[The boy] built up a friendship with the gull who would wait for him—or he would scan the skies for the bird," remembered Lloyd. The problem was that Chaplin was increasingly preoccupied by *Limelight*. *They Shoot Horses, Don't They?* was tabled until after he completed *Limelight*.

With *Limelight* edited, scored, and previewed, Chaplin and Oona boarded a train for New York on September 6, 1952. Jerry Epstein saw them off at Union Station. On September 17, Chaplin and his family sailed from New York for London. Two days later, he received the cable informing him that his reentry permit had been rescinded.

Chaplin's plans for *They Shoot Horses, Don't They?*, not to mention for the rest of his life, were forced to undergo a precipitous change.

CHAPTER 15

With Chaplin out of the country and forced to play defense from a distance, the jackals once again descended.

Hedda Hopper: "There are hundreds of people in Hollywood, maybe thousands—stars, directors, producers and all those wonderful people we call little people, those workers behind the camera, the electricians, cameraman, props—who approve McGranery's statement that before Charlie Chaplin can return to these United States he will have to pass the board of immigration. . . .

"No one can deny that the little man with the floppy pants and the big shoes and the derby hat and the cane is a good actor. He is.

"But that doesn't give him the right to go against our customs, to abhor everything we stand for, to throw our hospitality back in our faces.

"He's done nothing for either the first World War or the Second World War effort. Mr. Charlie Chaplin has held onto all his blood, as well as his money. The great Mr. Winston Churchill said that to win the second World War would take blood, sweat and tears. If Charlie Chaplin ever read that statement he didn't obey Mr. Winston Churchill's summons.

"I've known him for many years. I abhor what he stands for,

while I admire his talents as an actor. I would like to say, 'Good riddance to bad company.' "

Again she asserted that Chaplin did nothing for the American
effort in World War II, without mentioning that Chaplin had bought
$241,000 worth of war bonds in 1941 and had made similar pur-
chases for each succeeding year of the war.

Privately, Hopper was exultant: "Have you ever known such timing as the Chaplin thing," she wrote a friend. "Even Pegler quoted
me in the column he devoted to our dear Charlie; and now the little
comic has gone from our shores forever. The Immigration Department has been holding its breath for three months, afraid it would
leak out and he would cancel his trip. Chaplin was so high and
mighty that he arranged his trip through the Justice Department. The
Immigration boys have been waiting for him for forty years. I don't
think he's going to like those English rations, do you?"

Ed Sullivan reprinted a 1940 column in which he took *The Great
Dictator* to task for its "last speech to the audience, in which he
expressed himself on such related themes as liberty and greed. This
was a series of clichés. Perhaps if Chaplin had asked a Msgr. Fulton
Sheen to sum up for him and prepare a brilliant summation, this last
speech would not have been off-key. What was needed here was a
magnificent mind as a constructionist. Chaplin said only the usual
things and they fell flat."

Similar columns about Chaplin were written by Westbrook Pegler
and Walter Winchell. They all had a peculiar way of making the
same slanted or false points. Hopper et al intentionally ignored the
millions of dollars Chaplin had raised during his Liberty Loan bond
tour during World War I, the speeches he had made during World
War II at the request of the White House, his war bond purchases, or
the fact that his eldest sons saw combat in World War II.

They also willfully ignored his private charities. Chaplin's payroll
reveals an interesting group of pensioners. He paid Edna Purviance
$100 a week, while $50 a week went to Constance Collier. (Besides
the stipend from Chaplin, Collier survived through the generosity
of Katharine Hepburn and George Cukor.) Most of Chaplin's other
donations went to show business charities, such as the Actors Fund.

Where information was lacking, Hopper invariably chose disinformation. In October 1947, she had run an imaginary item to the effect that Victor McLaglen was going to Argentina to make movies with Chaplin. An appalled McLaglen sent a telegram the next day: "Dear Hedda . . . I am not going to Argentina to make pictures with Charlie Chaplin. I am not on Charles Chaplin's band wagon. I have not seen or talked to Chaplin for many years. Unlike Chaplin I have been an American citizen for going on two decades. . . . I am jealous of my reputation for good citizenship and because of that I ask you to correct the impression created in your column."

On October 30, 1952, possibly as a tactic to deal with the INS in case Chaplin decided to return, Chaplin's attorney Loyd Wright had the studio compile a list of Chaplin's cash gifts from 1940 to 1951, exclusive of his direct family. The gifts included $2,500 to the Democratic National Committee, $115 to Medical Aid to Russia, $200 for *New Masses*, $100 for the Hollywood Strikers Defense Fund, $200 to the Union for Democratic Action, $2,000 to the Progressive Party, $235 to the Circle Theatre, $1,500 to Georgia Hale, $1,170 to Paulette Goddard, $1,337 to Constance Collier, a smaller amount to her companion Phyllis Welbourn, $4,500 to Oona's mother, and about $25,000 to members of the extended Chaplin family.

WHILE AMERICA WAS lining up in something perilously close to lockstep in condemnation of Chaplin, the London papers defended their native son. The *Observer* wrote, "Should American authorities really intend to revoke his permit—because of random imputations and not on the basis of judicial verdict, they would be acting rather shabbily and with little sense of logic." Another paper wrote, "The simple fact is that Charlie Chaplin is the most scarifying example yet of the way in which the West—and America in particular—is moving away from its much vaunted belief in personal freedom and political democracy into a state of totalitarian oppression."

On October 12, less than a month after the revocation of Chaplin's reentry permit, the American Legion, 2.5 million members strong, passed a resolution urging American movie theaters to boycott *Limelight*, as well as every movie in which Chaplin had appeared. At the same time the Legion honored Attorney General James McGranery with a plaque. In return he praised the organization, saying that the Legion "has sounded the bell of liberty and prepared the spiritual armor needed by all who fight against the godless serfs of the Soviets."

The Legion's magazine published a story about Chaplin asserting that his films constituted nothing less than a sustained assault on democratic ideals: "*Modern Times*, which satirized the capitalist machine age, showing the alleged horrors of workingmen's lives, is one of the few non-Soviet films constantly on exhibition in the Soviet orbit." Chaplin had, said the article, long used "film as a propaganda medium." Even his "seemingly inoffensive slapstick two-reelers were made with a view toward defying authority."

The Legion, in league with Ward Bond and Roy Brewer of the Motion Picture Alliance for the Preservation of American Ideals, managed to convince Loew's theaters as well as Fox West Coast theaters to cancel their bookings of *Limelight*. Despite laudatory reviews and strong business in New York City, the film was met with pickets in Philadelphia, Washington, D.C., New Orleans, and Cleveland.

On top of the picketing, the Legion passed a resolution urging "the distributors of the film *Limelight* to withdraw its presentation until the issues are determined; And Be It Further Resolved, that the American Legion commend the Justice Department for its desire to investigate Charlie Chaplin's eligibility to return to the shores of the United States."

Typically, the Legion would mount a picket line at theaters the day *Limelight* premiered so that no timely defense could be organized. After that, accusations about Chaplin's life and politics would be passed around without any factual evidence being presented. An example of the Legion's activities took place in Cleveland, where platoons of pickets worked from 1 p.m. to the last show at night.

United Artists tried to finesse the pressure groups. UA's Robert Benjamin told both the American Legion and the Catholic War Veterans that the company had agreed to handle *Limelight* after Chaplin got his reentry permit but before the attorney general's rescinding of it—a very fine shading of the truth.

Lloyd Gough, the Legion's national commander, wrote that, "We are continuing our collective effort for Americanism and adequate national security. If you carry this thinking to its logical conclusion, you will permit Communists to write books, to paint murals, to infiltrate every branch of educational and cultural life. We have never criticized Mr. Chaplin's art. But an individual cannot be disassociated from his political beliefs. If we patronize those who are Communists, or Fascists, or those who have been members of front organizations, we are inadvertently helping totalitarian causes."

UA tried an end-around. Chaplin's attorney Loyd Wright contributed some of his client's money to an American Legion cause, although the money was handed over under the name of United Artists. Beyond that, UA gave some thought to arranging a détente with New York's Francis Cardinal Spellman through what were decorously termed "economic incentives." A UA publicity manager named Joel Rose suggested that a showing of *Limelight* could serve as a fundraiser for one of Spellman's favorite charities, such as the New York Foundling Home. "Chaplin can write a letter to the Cardinal suggesting the benefit premiere, saying he is interested in the project because of his own six children. . . . These suggestions may be obvious, but I don't think we can be subtle in this situation."

UA seems to have ignored Rose's proposal. Despite stellar reviews, by February 1953 *Limelight* had played in only about 150 of the 2,000 theaters in which it had been scheduled. It ended up earning $1 million in America, three times the domestic return of *Monsieur Verdoux*—considering the headwinds, a minor triumph.

Limelight had its European premiere at the Odeon on Leicester Square. The event was a benefit for the Royal Society for the Blind and was attended by Princess Margaret, with a crowd estimated at more than six thousand outside the theater. The Odeon was built on the site of the Alhambra Music Hall, which had been torn down in 1936. The last ballet company to appear at the Alhambra was the Ballets de Monte Carlo, featuring the dazzling young André Eglevsky.

The night of the premiere, Chaplin was beset by nerves. At 4:45 p.m. Harry Crocker got a panicked call from Chaplin's room. He found Chaplin in his shorts, yanking at his collar and swearing. It seemed that his shirtmaker was "a thief and swindler" because his collar was too tight. Crocker rushed out in the rain to purchase collars a quarter of a size larger. He then had to lend Chaplin a set of shirt studs, as Chaplin had forgotten to bring his own.

Chaplin made a brief speech before the film, telling the crowd that he would be leaving the theater after the movie started, "because I know that I would be under the scrutinizing eyes of those who love me. I feel more at ease with those who detest me . . . because hate is a challenge. As Oscar Wilde said, 'Each man kills the thing that he loves.'"

Noel Coward came to the premiere with Vivien Leigh and they sat with Charlie and Oona. In his diary, Coward noted that "Charlie wonderful at moments but picture too long and too trite. His great genius has always been to make us cry with his comedy. In this story, he tries to make us cry with his tragedy and doesn't quite succeed."

Coward aside, the European reviews were rapturous. Of the London critics, only C. A. Lejeune had some reservations: "The fire still glows, but now it seems the fire of winter; as though the old Charlie had turned his back for the last time on the people who laughed with him, and, in a gentle mockery of the Chaplin fade-out, softly and silently faded away."

The Chaplin family traveled to Paris for the French premiere on October 30. Chaplin was feted at a dinner with Pablo Picasso, Jean-Paul Sartre, and Louis Aragon. After that, Chaplin and his party dined at the Tour d'Argent. Claude Terrail took them on a tour of the wine cellar with an aperitif in an underground wine-tasting room. Terrail chose a bottle of Oporto 1803 and gave Chaplin a bottle of Cognac from 1778.

Word came that Picasso wanted a private meeting with Chaplin. Picasso was further to the left than Chaplin, but Harry Crocker thought that his eminence was worth the risk. Crocker invited Picasso to come to the Ritz at 7:30 p.m. Crocker would check out the lobby at 7:15. If any reporters were there, Crocker would signal Chaplin to take a walk in Place Vendôme, where the reporters would follow. With the lobby empty, Crocker would bring Picasso up to Chaplin's room.

As it happened, there were no reporters around at 7:15, so the meeting went off without a hitch. After the two men had talked for a few hours, Picasso invited Chaplin to his atelier. Chaplin was surprised by how casually Picasso stacked art all around the room—his own work, as well as paintings by Renoir, Roualt, and Matisse were unceremoniously leaning against walls.

When Chaplin returned to London, he found a letter from Ben Hecht: "I came out of the Astor Theater full of elation and gratitude. I was elated by the wild human life of your movie, and I was grateful that there was one man still left in the arts whose spirit was unfouled by politics. The audience (a packed house) loved you as if you were their child." Vittorio De Sica chimed in with a telegram of devotion to both the film and its creator.

A week after the London premiere, *Pravda* announced the comforting news that "Chaplin was not a communist; in fact, some of his works are regarded as positively reactionary." In particular, the paper singled out *New Times* [apparently *Modern Times*] and *City Lights* as "distasteful to Russian ideals," while America's recent actions were evidence of "the brown cloud of fascism settling down over the United States."

Limelight played in New York for twelve weeks, the same lengthy run that *The Great Dictator* had amassed. It also ran at the Odeon in Leicester Square for twelve weeks and set box office records, a response that was duplicated throughout Europe. It eventually earned $7 million in foreign rentals.

Chaplin's own final word on the picture was one of deep, deserved satisfaction: "The film is very, very good," he said in 1966. "A beautiful, poetic finale. . . . There's a lot of beauty in that picture."

CHAPTER 16

Despite his public defiance, there were times when Chaplin would admit to feelings of loss. Harry Crocker recalled a lunch the two of them had at a London restaurant. The food was excellent, but Chaplin was quiet. Crocker knew his friend and didn't intrude, when Chaplin suddenly broke the silence: "Harry, you know I want to go home!"

As *Limelight* made its triumphant way around the world, Buster Keaton gave an interview about Chaplin and stoutly stood up for his friend despite the fact that their politics were different. Keaton's biographer James Curtis says, "Keaton was quite fond of Chaplin, even though politically he seemed to lean more to the right than Charlie."

"I have known Chaplin since 1912," said Keaton. "I remember twenty years ago he was asked if he was a Bolshevik. Today he is questioned about communism. To tell the truth, I believe that Charlie does not know what a political party is—only has he voted to serve Art.

"But he has always been on the side of those who suffer against those who have everything. He is for those who think that everyone should have enough to eat, and can sympathize with anyone who has been hungry and can remember. . . .

"Why shouldn't he be allowed to return to the United States? He has done nothing illegal. There is nothing he can be blamed for. He pays his taxes and keeps the peace." To the end of his life, Keaton always stood up for Chaplin, as both an artist and coworker.

IN HINDSIGHT, IT can be seen that Chaplin was the most prominent victim of the Red Scare. In the late 1940s and early 1950s, fear was everywhere. The triumph of World War II had been eclipsed by China turning Communist and the brutal stalemate of the Korean War. The dawn of the nuclear age was reflected in the sudden proliferation of film noir, a bleak showcase for worldly women and would-be wise guys who think they have all the moves, right up to the moment when they don't.

In 1950, Senator Joseph McCarthy gave a speech in Wheeling, West Virginia, that asserted the State Department was infested with Communists. Not only that, he had all the names. McCarthy didn't have any names, but the public believed that he did. As one journalist put it, "He was a political speculator, a prospector who drilled Communism and saw it come up a gusher." Harry Truman privately referred to McCarthy as a pathological liar.

That same year, J. Edgar Hoover devised a plan that would have suspended habeas corpus and allowed the detention of twelve thousand men and women, predominantly American citizens, who were "found to be potentially dangerous to the internal security through investigation."

Noir was the creative response to an atmosphere redolent of fear. There's a noir called *The Dark Corner* where the detective says, "I have a feeling something is closing in on me. I don't know what it is." Prophetic words . . .

As the historian Kenneth Weisbrode wrote, "The reactionary tendency is not so much a failure to manage fear as it is, especially in America, an alternative means of offense [pretending] to be a defense."

In retrospect, it's clear that *The Great Dictator*—the definitive example of premature antifascism—and *Monsieur Verdoux* were consecutive provocations which, along with Chaplin's perceived sexual transgressions, tipped the public scales. But then, Chaplin's entire career was a series of provocations both subtle and overt.

FOR A TIME, it was assumed that Chaplin would come back to America, if only to reclaim his fortune. On October 15, almost a month after the banishment, Ed Sullivan led off his column with this: "Immigration Dept. investigators are calling on Broadwayites and interviewing performers who knew Charlie Chaplin in the old days. They are trying to put together a portrait that will aid Attorney General McGranery when Chaplin is examined at Ellis Island."

Luckily, Oona Chaplin was an American citizen and could come and go as she pleased. Chaplin began withdrawing his investments from E. F. Hutton and had them funneled to the Swiss Bank Corporation on Nassau Street in New York.

Chaplin's roster of holdings provides conclusive proof that he was probably the most conservatively minded capitalist ever to be accused of Communism. He owned $50,000 in United States Treasuries, $150,000 in United States Savings Bonds, and $55,000 in United States Defense Bonds. His stocks included Kodak, General Electric, AT&T, Bank of America, Standard Oil, Texas Gulf Sulphur, Paramount Pictures, Principal Theatres, Eastman Kodak, General Electric, General Foods, National Distillers, R.J. Reynolds Tobacco, Southern California Edison, Standard Oil of New Jersey, Trans-America Corporation, United Fruit, F.W. Woolworth, and nearly all of the Chaplin Studios Inc.

On November 14, Jerry Epstein received a telegram from Oona. She was coming to New York and asked Epstein to meet her at the Sherry-Netherland. The day Oona left for America Chaplin was frantic. "I shouldn't have let her go," he told Harry Crocker. "If anything happens to the plane, I shall never forgive myself! I shall go straight out the window. Nothing—fame, money—nothing means anything but her. I should never have permitted her to fly! Check the airport."

Oona's plane had an uneventful crossing and actually landed early. "Thank God!" Chaplin told Crocker, then quickly recalibrated. "While waiting for news—I have been up since six a.m.—I ran over some gags. I've a wonderful comedy idea, not for my character; it'll have to be a dignified bank president sort of fellow." A few minutes later, he had become an efficiency expert, telling Crocker, "We must economize; there is now no need for you to have an office suite or secretary; we must count our pennies."

Oona made her way to California and began the process of closing down the house and Chaplin's other properties. The Chaplin butler told her that the FBI had called at the house twice and interrogated him. They wanted to know what kind of man Chaplin was, if there had been any wild parties with nude girls, etc. When the butler told them that Chaplin lived quietly with his wife and children, the agents tried to bully him, asking about his nationality, how long he had been in America, and demanding to see his passport.

Back in New York, Oona and Epstein had dinner at Manny Wolf's Steak House on Third Avenue. As they were having dinner, someone in the next booth recognized her and began making remarks about "Commie Red." She laughed it off. On November 27, she flew back to Europe.

That same day, Chaplin instructed Harry Crocker to write a letter to his attorney Loyd Wright. "Mr. Chaplin says that the FBI and the Bureau of Immigration have all his statements [about politics] on record under oath, and he will not make affidavits or statements which look as if he was kowtowing to anyone.

"He also would like you to send a more full description of what it is that you think necessary for you to do concerning his return. He refuses to make any attempts to placate any groups; he would rather live abroad."

Two days later, Chaplin received a letter from an old acquaintance:

My dear Mr. Chaplin, I have a private cinema at Chartwell and last Thursday had the great pleasure of seeing *Limelight*. I must congratulate you cordially on this masterpiece, which we all watched with mingled emotion and amusement. According to Plato, Socrates said that the genius of tragedy and comedy was essentially the same and that they should be written by the same author.

I am glad you have had such a cordial welcome home in your hard-pressed native land.

Yours sincerely,
Winston Churchill.

IN NOVEMBER 1952, Dwight Eisenhower defeated Adlai Stevenson for the presidency, and after his inauguration named Herbert Brownell to replace James McGranery as attorney general. A month after that, Henry Luce weighed in with an editorial in *Life*. Basically, he called on Brownell to take note of the difference between someone who conspires to overthrow the government and a heretic. "Heresy is not a crime in this country; it is every citizen's guaranteed right." Luce went on to write, "Attorney General McGranery seems to suspect [Chaplin] of being 'unsavory.' If he means morally unsavory, many an alien denizen of Hollywood will not dare to go abroad again; if he means politically unsavory, then the conspiracy-heresy test becomes applicable. The law is pretty clear against conspirators. Unless Chaplin can be proved to be one, then the Europeans who are howling at our cultural barbarity on his account are right."

Just before Christmas, James Agee wrote to Chaplin and his wife. "All this McGranery filth is sickening and infuriating, beyond any words, even unprintable." Agee went on to ask if Chaplin had seen Luce's pro-Chaplin editorial. "The thought of you being in any way beholden to that eminent libertarian Henry R. Luce is a little preposterous," he wrote, although he was obviously surprised that Luce's conservative politics made room for the editorial, which ran on the heels of the spring publication of W. Eugene Smith's epic photo essay about the making of *Limelight*.

"I've been wondering, of course, from the start, whether there is any useful thing I could do, and if so, what. The best idea I can get is the drafting of a statement, or petition, probably more useful to send to Brownell than McGranery, urging that you be permitted to return without any detainment whatever. . . . If you think there's any point in the idea, please let me know, and I'll do anything I know how, and get the best help I know how."

OVER THE NEXT few years, reputable publications published wild disinformation about Chaplin with impunity. *The Saturday Evening Post* ran a long story in which the author cited "a close friend in London" who claimed that Chaplin had fathered a child out of wedlock, said illegitimate child having become a famous starlet. The author also alleged that Chaplin had incurred the wrath of Harry Truman by doing a takeoff on Bess Truman trying unsuccessfully to launch a battleship. The story was printed despite Truman stating that Chaplin had never done any such thing.

The ongoing cannonade of lies was met by resounding silence from the Hollywood A list. The only defenses of Chaplin came from Cary Grant, William Wyler, and Sam Goldwyn, the last of whom tried to counter the slander with a strong statement: "In my opinion, Charlie Chaplin is the greatest artist we have ever had, and we have no one to take his place. I feel he is certainly not a Communist. I have known him well for over 20 years. We have had many disagreements, as he has decided views. He is a Liberal, but he is no Communist."

By necessity, Chaplin began formulating a plan for the rest of his life. The primary question was where to live. He had been contemplating alternatives for some time. In 1951, his brother Sydney wrote him from St. Moritz, offering Charlie alternatives to living in Hollywood, mostly centering on matters of taxation. There was Monte Carlo, but Syd preferred Switzerland, specifically Montreux, which Sydney thought "one of the most beautiful resorts." He went on to give specific information about Swiss bank accounts and how to avoid having the studio in Hollywood attached by the authorities— just in case.

Chaplin and Oona thought about buying a house at Cap-Ferrat called Lo Scoglietto, but decided against it after learning that the house had once belonged to Queen Frederica of Greece—a Nazi sympathizer. (The house eventually became the home of David Niven.)

After giving some thought to London, Chaplin followed Sydney's enthusiasm for Switzerland and began circling.

When Chaplin purchased the Manoir de Ban in Corsier, near Vevey, he had been the center of one firestorm after another for ten years and "was in a mood to hide away," as Harry Crocker put it. Chaplin needed peace and quiet, and he got it. The Manoir was situated on thirty-seven acres, had three stories, twenty-three rooms, and cost a reported $100,000. It came with an orchard that produced cherries, plums, apples, and pears, and had a serenely beautiful view of Lake Geneva and the mountains. The family moved in early in January 1953—barely four months after Chaplin's banishment, a mark of how determined he was to retake control of his and his family's life.

Chaplin unpacked the crates of books that were shipped from Beverly Hills and placed them on the library shelves himself. A new phonograph was installed in the library, so he could listen to music while he worked on scripts.

Then there was the matter of refurbishing the Manoir for his growing family and his guests. He didn't care for the furniture that came with the house—too formal—so decided to use much of the furniture from his Beverly Hills house. He installed a tennis court and a swimming pool as well as a separate building for the help—the children were domiciled on the top floor of the house, where the help used to be. The alterations included rooms for guests.

"Of course, it is the usual Oona and Chaplin style," Chaplin wrote his brother, "and whatever taste, good or bad, it is not Louis XVI! Since living here we have bought some more porcelain, which cost me a pretty penny! I won't even tell you the price, but it is beautiful, and considering the few years I have left, money well spent.

"I cannot tell you how happy I am living in Switzerland; it is like a ton weight off my shoulders: no fears, no blackmail, no hate, no politics. Whatever fantasy the European press writes about one may be irritat[ing], but it is not the vicious, sinister, murderous attack of the American press." He went on to tell Syd of some fragmentary ideas he had for the picture that would become *A King in New York*. He told Syd, "It will be a musical."

He would spend the rest of his life in peace and comfort at the Manoir. Oona and the staff became expert at preparing Charlie's favorite dishes from his childhood—tripe and onions, steak and kidney pie, stew with dumplings. Other favorite foods, such as the Almond Joy candy bars he had grown fond of in America, had to be brought by visitors, who were told to bring as many as their baggage would allow.

The basement of the Manoir was refurbished as a storage area for the files and memorabilia that Syd would ship from Hollywood, and the films eventually followed. The house at 1085 Summit Drive was sold.

It was a new chapter in the life of Charlie Chaplin.

WHILE CHAPLIN WAS shooting *Limelight*, he and Mary Pickford handed over management of United Artists to a management group headed by Arthur Krim. The company was still starved for product, but Krim and his crew got lucky. Stanley Kramer owed UA a picture on an old contract, and Columbia, for whom he was now working, suggested that Kramer give UA "the western without action." *High Noon* grossed $12 million worldwide. That put the company on firm footing for the first time in ten years, and that footing was solidified when UA put up money for American distribution rights to a film John Huston was shooting independently: *The African Queen*. By the end of 1951, UA was running in the black, and would become the most creatively innovative studio in Hollywood for the next twenty-five years, until it was smothered by the catastrophe of *Heaven's Gate*.

Chaplin held on to his 25 percent of United Artists until February 1955, when he phoned Arthur Krim. If UA could wire him $1.1 million within five days, Chaplin would sell his piece of the company. The deal was done—it was Chaplin's last holding in America. Mary Pickford held on to her 25 percent for another year, by which time United Artists had become even more successful. Her 25 percent brought her $3 million.

Having taken care of all family business, Chaplin could settle down to the rest of his life. As always, he was full of plans for his next film. He had the wife and family he had always wanted, he had all the money he would ever need, and he had all the time in the world.

There was only one problem: Chaplin's forced exile destroyed him as an artist.

CHAPTER 17

Chaplin's initial public responses to his banishment had been dignified, befitting a cultural elder statesman. As America receded into the distance and his life began to stabilize, Chaplin's private responses were something else. "Firstly, I am so glad to be out of that stink-pot country of yours," he wrote James Agee. "I should have done it in 1930 when I was over here the last time. . . .

"To be over here, away from that torrid atmosphere, is like stepping out of the death house into the free sunlight. Occasionally, someone sends us a New York [Herald] Tribune—its dark news makes me shudder: it's nothing else but [John Foster] Dulles' vomit all over the front page and the belly-aching about the charity they are giving to the world. Oh, what a stink-pot country! As the negro says about living in Paris: 'Colored folks is quality here,' so I say about Europe: 'Charlie's the tops.'"

After imparting some news of the family, Chaplin did a 180: "Strangely enough, I am not the least bit bitter, neither is Oona. . . . As for LIMELIGHT, it has been a tremendous success over here, and has grossed more than any other picture bar GONE WITH THE WIND so they tell me."

Chaplin's old friend Salka Viertel was renting a room to Agee, and Chaplin was glad that she had some support because Viertel was also having trouble with the authorities. "What bastards they are! Seems all the decent people are getting it in the neck. . . . Give her my love." Agee had mentioned to Chaplin that his new script (probably *Night of the Hunter*) verged on poetry, to which Chaplin responded, "I don't think you could write anything without it having that flavor. So let us have more of it." He proceeded to invite Agee to come to Switzerland for a visit.

Agee never got to Switzerland. He died from a massive heart attack in the backseat of a New York cab in May of 1955. He was in debt, without insurance or savings, and with a wife and three children. Friends organized a fund to support his family. Chaplin and John Huston each chipped in $1,000.

FIVE MONTHS AFTER moving into the Manoir de Ban, Chaplin wrote Loyd Wright a short letter enumerating what needed to be done regarding the cancellation of his remaining business arrangements:

1. Any lease in existence between myself personally and the Studio Company concerning 1085 Summit Drive.
2. Any arrangement whereby I lease the studio myself at a certain set price, whether written up on the books or paid by me, should be immediately cancelled out.
3. Any salary that has been written up on the books, or paid to me from the Chaplin Studios, Inc., should be cancelled out immediately.
4. Any employment contract that I might have with the Studio company should also be cancelled out.

    I would like to sell the studio for $650,000 cash, for which I understand we have an offer, and pay whatever taxes I have to pay, as I cannot continue the upkeep for another year, and who knows what will happen after that; also, I wish to cut my ties with America.

Best wishes . . .

Chaplin felt that, in a strange way, he had seen it all coming, as an inevitable response to his temperament rubbing up against that of his adopted country. "I am the same person I always was," he told the journalist Cedric Belfrage. "Always a rebel and partly a gypsy. At 12, in the East End of London, I was furious if the King was going by in procession and I was prevented from crossing the street. I didn't like the class lines that held down poor people like myself and, when I went to America 45 years ago, I felt I'd rather sling hash there than be a Lord Peabody in England.

"But then I flip-flopped into success from being a frightened, lonely person, and it was the greatest thing that ever happened to me. . . . Success brought life into focus and showed me the hollowness of men who run the world and of their solemn pronouncements. Overnight, people were coming to me for my opinion on things I knew nothing whatever about. I began to wonder, if they ask me for my opinion, whom won't they ask, and why should I believe the others know any more about it than I do?

"Then I was sought out by Rockefellers and Vanderbilts and, realizing that America had its own kind of aristocracy and snobbery, I knew I wasn't able to be a patriot anywhere in the sense they talk about. I had learned that a man must depend on himself. The only thing you can believe in is yourself—you must fight for what you want.

"I don't believe in any country 'right or wrong,' and all this talk about being grateful to America or any other country for opportunity is nonsense."

On April 10, 1953, Chaplin formally turned in his reentry permit in London, after which he issued a statement: "I have been the object of lies and vicious propaganda by powerful reactionary groups who, by their influence and by aid of America's yellow press, have created an unhealthy atmosphere in which the liberal-minded individuals can be singled out and persecuted. Under these conditions I find it virtually impossible to continue my motion picture work, and I have therefore given up my residence in the United States."

That event stimulated another flurry of exuberant calumny. In a column following Chaplin's statement, Hedda Hopper published a flamboyant series of lies about the circumstances under which he left

America: "When I heard that Charlie Chaplin had slipped out of the country without squaring his income taxes, I inquired into the situation and discovered that foreigners who work here must pay back taxes before being permitted to leave the country. . . . Chaplin must have planned his exit very carefully to get the utmost in sympathy and privileges in the new country of his adoption."

Hopper went on to position herself within a supposed quarrel within the Chaplin family: "I can't understand why Charles Chaplin Jr. isn't getting more work. He's good-looking, a good actor, and doesn't share his father's political views. Several times when Harry Bridges dined with Charlie, both Chaplin boys left the house. . . . Let's give the kid a break."

Psychologically, Chaplin was now a man without a country. When the Chicago columnist and broadcaster Studs Terkel wrote him a fan letter, Chaplin replied that Terkel should keep his admiration to himself—the name Chaplin was anathema in America.

To correspondents like Terkel, Chaplin mostly kept his counsel; to old friends like Lion Feuchtwanger, it was another story: "Oona and I are always glad to hear from you in the distant, remote country of California. It is so wonderful to be away from that creepy cancer of hate where one speaks in whispers, and to abide in a political temperature where everything is normal and contrasted to that torrid, dried-up, prune-souled desert of a country you live in. Even at its best, with its vast arid stretches, its bleached sun-kissed hills, its bleak sun-lit Pacific Ocean, its bleak acres of oil derricks and its bleak thriving prosperity, it makes me shudder to think that I spent 40 years of my life in it."

Chaplin went on to mention that he had recently had a conversation with India's prime minister Jawaharlal Nehru, and had just missed seeing Thomas Mann. Chaplin agreed that Lord Mountbatten had done a splendid job in handing back India to the Indians, "the merit of which I do not quite understand from the English point of view!"

The correspondence went on for years. Feuchtwanger congratulated Oona when she turned in her American passport in solidarity with her husband, and sent Chaplin a copy of *The Execution of Private Slovik*. Oona did most of the corresponding, but Chaplin would write PS's: "Lion! Martha! When are you coming? We are waiting for you. Charlie."

He didn't talk about it in letters, but Chaplin had some difficulties accommodating himself to Switzerland. In a 1953 letter to the Feuchtwangers, Oona noted that too much snow made Chaplin claustrophobic and depressed, so much so that he would threaten to take a trip to Marrakech just to break the monotony.

It wasn't all anger and exile. In August 1953, the Labour Party of Chelsea asked Chaplin to stand for Parliament. As the chairman of the party wrote Chaplin, "The philosophy shown in your great films is shared by our party, and that in the event of your election, your presence in the House of Commons would not only enliven the proceedings, but also contribute greatly to its deliberations."

Four days later Chaplin wrote back declining the opportunity: "Even if my qualifications were to warrant such an honour, I'm afraid I could not devote the necessary time as I am at the moment engaged in producing a motion picture, which work will take me at least a year to complete."

IN NOVEMBER 1953, Eugene O'Neill died, supposedly uttering the furious last words, "Born in a hotel room and Goddamn it, died in a hotel room!"

O'Neill was as vicious in death as he had been in life: his will contained this provision: "I purposely exclude from any interest under this will my son Shane O'Neill and my daughter Oona O'Neill Chaplin and I exclude their issue now and hereafter born."

Through a revision of the copyright law, years later Oona and Shane did in fact inherit a piece of their father's estate. She promptly gave her share to her brother, who was by that time an indigent drug addict. Both Shane O'Neill and Eugene O'Neill Jr. would eventually commit suicide. That Oona avoided that fate may be in large part due to her marriage to Chaplin. A man who had never been faithful to any woman had been converted into a slavishly devoted husband who grew anxious at any absence of his wife that extended past a few minutes. As for Oona, adoration was the precise antidote required after years of her father's malicious rejection.

All of 1953 and some of 1954 was taken up with winding down Chaplin's affairs in America. He couldn't stop himself from tweaking America whenever he got the chance. In May 1954, he and Dmitri Shostakovich were proclaimed winners of the World Peace Council, sponsored by Russia. The award came with a check for $14,000, which Chaplin promptly donated to charity, but not before the heretofore friendly *New York Times* criticized him for cooperating with a regime that "[served] the purposes of a brutal and tyrannical imperialism."

There were meetings with Chinese premier Chou En-lai in 1954 as well as Soviet premier Nikita Khrushchev. The last time the cinematographer Karl Struss saw Chaplin was in 1954, when they ran into each other in Rome. The two men and their wives had a leisurely lunch. "It was a lovely afternoon, and I remember Charlie with great affection," said Struss. "I don't use the word lightly, but he was a true genius, and a warm, wonderful man as well."

While Charlie was settling down in Switzerland, Sydney and his wife, Gypsy, were putting down roots at the Bermuda Apartments on Wilshire Boulevard, on the border of Beverly Hills and Westwood. They would stay there seasonally through the 1950s, as Charlie's American infrastructure was slowly closed down. Sydney acted as his brother's agent on much of this, down to details such as selling off the liquor in the house on Summit Drive for what Syd said was a 15 percent discount.

Syd was extremely responsible when handling Charlie's affairs, but his brother continued to be an indifferent correspondent, which drove Syd batty: "I have been waiting & hoping to get an answer from you to the letter I sent you a week ago. I told you that we had to get all the equipment from the time the escrow opens. It is MOST IMPORTANT that you give us instructions as to what you wish sent over to you & what should be sold or put into storage here."

The Chaplin studio on La Brea was a valuable piece of real estate, but the matter of the equipment inside it gave Syd a lot of grief. Among many other pieces, there were 35mm Mitchell and Bell & Howell cameras, a playback machine, a camera boom, etc. An appraisal set the price for all the equipment at $30,000, which Syd thought was too low by half.

Chaplin finally wrote back to say that any equipment he needed for future movies could be rented in London, so Syd should sell the hardware for whatever he could get. Charlie told Syd that he wanted all the files on the films, and all the trims from *Limelight*, as well as unused sequences from other films. "Now as to my papers on biographical matter, all the early photographs and stills should be shipped and any interesting correspondence such as Einstein's letters etc. should be shipped but a lot of it could be eliminated I am sure.

"Thank you for all the trouble you have gone to. I cannot tell you what a Godsend you have been. Being on the job at this time has been a great help to me and I won't forget it."

Syd sold all the studio equipment for $12,500, holding out the two cameras and the boom. The boom was rented out and brought in what Syd characterized as "a good return on your investment." Syd told Charlie that he thought Wheeler Dryden should be put in charge of all the biographical material—"The girls in the office were surprised when I told them your press clipping books were to be retained. . . . Good God! What do they think so much time was spent on these books for? . . . How does Churchill write his biography? From filed material. One cannot carry all that detail in one's mind or memory. The office does not think about your posterity & neither do you, but the public does & will continue to do so long after you have shuffled off."

Eventually Chaplin unloaded his beloved studio to a New York real estate firm for $655,000, including a big frame house that had fronted on Sunset Boulevard where Syd lived whenever he was in town.

As the film vault was cleaned out, hundreds of film cans were piled up in the courtyard of the studio. The film pirate Raymond Rohauer backed up a truck one night and stole a huge cache of Chaplin outtakes, which decades later were accessed by Kevin Brownlow and David Gill for their documentary *Unknown Chaplin*.

Wandering through the empty studio was like wandering through an obsolete summer hotel. The leading lady's dressing room, built for Edna Purviance, most recently occupied by Claire Bloom, was roomy but archaic—faded maroon drapes and wicker furniture. On the sidewalk leading to the soundstage a block of concrete recorded

Chaplin's signature and the date the studio opened: January 21, 1918—it gave Sid Grauman the idea of having star signatures and hand and footprints in the forecourt of his theater that opened in 1927. Other than the concrete slab, the only obvious sign of Chaplin's ownership of the property had been a brass plaque that said "Chaplin Studios," but that was stolen after the lot was vacated. In later years, the studio served as, variously, the production headquarters for the Perry Mason TV show and of Herb Alpert's A&M Records. Today, it houses the Jim Henson Company—Kermit the Frog, costumed as Chaplin's Tramp, adorns the studio chimney.

SYD REMAINED THE enthusiastic protector of his little brother, up to and including his opinion of *Limelight*: "Yesterday we had the good fortune to attend a private showing of the picture & we think it is a 'Masterpiece' & the greatest Charlie has ever made. There are no superlatives I could use to do justice to it. It was so well acted, so beautifully balanced between laughter & pathos. Gypsy & I cried like kids, so much so that we waited for everyone to leave the room before we left our seats. You did an excellent piece of acting Charlie & so did Clare [*sic*] Bloom, she is a great little actress & you made an ideal choice when you picked her for the part."

A month later, Sydney went on to say that *Limelight* had awakened his own nostalgia for show business; he wondered if he had made a mistake by quitting. "I console myself with the thought that I am Charlie Chaplin's brother, which is my usual form of introduction & which does not arouse in me the slightest thought of jealousy. I glory in your success, bask in your 'Limelight.'"

AS ONE WRITER noted, Chaplin never forgot about "the country that had made him rich, famous and unhappy." Although his wealth immunized him from the most crushing circumstances of the blacklist, he remained very conscious of his own psychological wounds. There's a hilarious picture of Chaplin taken in the 1950s. His head is peering around a corner somewhere in France, and on his face there is a look of wide-eyed panic. He captioned it "Hiding from McCarthy."

He might not have been so amused had he known that the FBI and the State Department were monitoring his mail as well as observing visitors to the Manoir. The FBI was particularly alarmed by a lunatic report in a Swedish paper that Chaplin was going to adopt the children of Julius and Ethel Rosenberg. Chaplin responded to the report by terming it "without foundation and absolutely ridiculous," but the New York office of the FBI stamped it "Do Not Destroy—Pending Litigation."

As his time in Switzerland stretched on, an alteration gradually took place—his politics weren't exactly growing more centrist, but they were definitely receding in importance. He inveighed against the Russian Iron Curtain, which prevented, among many other things, the free exchange of ideas and travel. Chaplin wanted open frontiers, with a minimum of passports, currency controls, or restrictions.

Perhaps it was just a case of the dust beginning to settle. Max Eastman, Chaplin's old friend from the 1920s, wrote a column attempting to put the whole thing in perspective. Although Eastman had been a Socialist in the 1920s, he had migrated to someplace right of center.

"My primary indignation is against the Department of Justice for pulling a dirty trick on a great artist. If there was anything unlawful in Charlie's conduct, he should have been investigated or indicted while he was resident here. It should have been a dignified judicial proceeding, not a quick trick pulled by the immigration authorities. . . .

"He once said to me years ago—and I noted it down because I was studying the varieties of humor at the time: 'Of course I am essentially American. I feel American, and I don't feel British—that's the chief thing.'

"My second indignation, equally strong, is directed against my once very astute and highly intelligent friend, Charlie Chaplin, for getting taken in by the gigantic lie campaign of Communists. He is not a conspirator; he is not a party member. He has neither the firmness of belief nor the force of character for that. He is a dupe. . . .

"I know from remarks he made when we last dined together in

New York, a few days before the premiere of *Monsieur Verdoux*, that he has swallowed about one half of the religion of Russia worship. When he told me that his legal persecution in the notorious paternity suit was due to the fact that America was going fascist and that he had attacked Hitler in his wartime film *The Great Dictator*, I just gave up.

"'If that's your opinion,' I said, 'let's not try to talk politics, because to my mind it's crazy.' He agreed, and we spent a pleasant evening of reminiscence and philosophical speculation.

"To sum it up, I'm disappointed in Charlie because of his political stupidity, and I'm ashamed of the United States Government for its unseemly behavior toward him."

Eastman would expand upon the citizenship question that was relentlessly used as a bludgeon by Chaplin's enemies: "His not becoming an American citizen . . . was due to an indifference to political institutions, not a preference for one or the other. Had he been born in America and made his career in England, he would not have bothered to become a British subject. That is a fact which perhaps only artists and anarchists can understand."

CHAPLIN'S FRIENDSHIP WITH Clifford Odets led him to write two of his extremely rare personal letters, the first in September 1953: "Life in Switzerland is really pleasant and can be anything you want it to be. One can rub elbows with the illustrious, the rich and the artistic, and politically one can agree to disagree with all of them—so different from the master-minded Americans that want to castrate you for having an opinion that differs from theirs."

Six months later, Chaplin again wrote Odets, this time in condolence—Betty Odets had died suddenly. She and Odets had divorced in 1952, but had remained close. Chaplin responded to her death with fatherly concern and a call to Odets's higher responsibility as a parent and artist.

"Now that it is all over, what is important is the effect it has on those near and dear to her; the effect it has on you in particular. Such sad events can only enrich the artist; can make him feel more the poignant depths of this magnificent and tragic thing called life. Passing events, these days, are like a dream, to the unfeeling they come and go like the wind and the rain. To the artist with character they leave an indelible impression of goodness, of matured understanding and a deeper pity, and the problems, whatever they are, if we survive them, build up our spiritual defences and give us a fibrous toughness to cope with it all.

"You are still young, Clifford, and you have those lovely children—yes, they are a responsibility, but they are also a blessing. They will enrich your work, they will give you a soberness and the calm of greatness necessary to all great work, all of which, I know, you are capable. A great climax has come to you much earlier than it does to others and being what you are it will set you out into the new paths which will enrich your creative work. What I am trying to say is what you already know—that life is a tragedy but that it also has its attending joys."

Now that Chaplin's life was once again settling down, he returned to neglecting his brother. Sydney and his wife lived in Los Angeles or Florida in the winter, Nice or Montreux in the spring and summer. Sydney wrote a friend in January 1954, "I hear little or no news from Charlie, now all his business is taken care of. I am rewarded with his silence which is golden." Sydney was soon invited to the Manoir and his once or twice yearly visits were always eagerly anticipated by the children, if only because he was so different from their father.

By the time he was middle-aged, dignity had begun to afflict Charlie Chaplin, but Sydney was never one for dignity. Rather, Sydney was *fun*. He enjoyed singing mildly racy music hall songs to the children and would then suggest they repeat them to their father, who usually responded with sputtering displeasure. The Chaplin children regarded Sydney as raffish and entertaining. He drove a Cadillac, slicked his hair back, smoked cigars, and his second wife, Gypsy, wore Chanel suits accented by gaudy jewelry.

"We *loved* Sydney," said Geraldine Chaplin. "He was very playful. He never owned a house, always lived in a hotel. He thought if he owned a house, he'd die in it. It was too much responsibility for him."

Responsibility, financial and otherwise, carried great meaning for Charlie Chaplin. When Oona's girlhood pal Carol Marcus—now Carol Saroyan—came for a visit, she was being pursued by Kenneth Tynan. Chaplin responded with a speech worthy of a Galsworthy novel. "My dear," Chaplin told her over a dessert of fresh strawberries and crème fraîche, "the man is a theater critic. I mean you must try to be realistic. You must ask yourself the question: How much could a theater critic possibly earn in a year? I'm only thinking of your good. You know that."

Chaplin had also advised her against leaving William Saroyan, while Oona had been all for it. "He's impossible," had been Oona's pithy summation. Carol dodged disaster with Tynan and would find happiness with Walter Matthau.

AFTER THE DUST settled from his relocation, Chaplin spent some time thinking about reviving *Shadow and Substance*, and he was also circling the project that would become *A King in New York*. He wrote Clifford Odets about both the past and the future: "It is a little king who goes to America under a nom de plume in order to escape assassination and becomes involved in all the ramifications of American life. It is a satire on Americans and the *modus operandi* of the day. Will let you know more about it later.

"In finishing my affairs, I brought over my staff Miss Runser and my camera man Rollie Totheroh, who have been with me for 30 odd years—Miss Runser, completing my accounts and Rollie, looking over my film and negatives etc. It was a moving experience having them here completing the finality of something which has been a part of their life and my own for 35 years. Of course reality is more poignant than what we theatrically contrive.

"On the last night before he left for America, Oona and I took Rollie out for dinner, after which he had to catch a train. It was all hurried and commonplace. We tried to avoid the goodbyes, but as he turned his back to me to get into the taxi, I knew this was the last I would see of him. I understand afterwards that he was drunk until he got back to New York."

He had one last letter from Rollie Totheroh: "My dear Charlie,

I seem to be living in a different world. Had a cry to myself after I waved goodbye to you and Mrs. Chaplin from the taxi, realizing perhaps it would be the last time I would see the one I have been so close to all these years. . . .

"I know that Mrs. Chaplin and you realize how much I enjoyed being with you and our conversations at the most enjoyable dinner I have ever had. One thing I know and it gives me comfort to realize no one can ever take away from me the honor of being so close to the most wonderful person that I have known."

After telling Chaplin that he was going to ship the Spanish, Italian, and German dialogue tracks for *Modern Times*, the foreign versions of *The Great Dictator*, and the B negative for *The Circus*, Rollie closed: "Please keep well and be happy, Charlie. If there is anything I can do to help in the future please let me know. Give Mrs. Chaplin and the children my love."

On March 30, 1954, Chaplin shipped severance checks to California for Rollie Totheroh, Edna Purviance, and seven other members of the studio staff. The total of the severances came to $71,502.

One of the seven, Lois Watt, wrote to Chaplin a few months later telling him that Wheeler Dryden seemed more lost than any other of the studio employees. "Have not talked to Edna since the day I took her to the unemployment office to see about her sick disability check. She is not at all well but tries to be cheerful."

Edna wrote Chaplin to thank him for "your friendship down the years, and for all you have done for me. In early life we do not seem to have so many troubles and I know you have had your share. I trust your cup of happiness is full with a charming wife and family."

Her last letter to Chaplin was dated November 13, 1956:

Dear Charlie, Here I am again with a heart full of thanks,
and back in hospital (Cedars of Lebanon) taking cobalt x-ray
treatment on my neck. There cannot be a hell hereafter! It all
comes while one can wriggle even a little finger. However, it is
the best known treatment for what ails me. Hope to be going
home at the end of the week, then can be an outside patient (how
wonderful!). Am thankful my innards are OK, this is purely and
simply local, so they say—all of which reminds me of the fellow

standing on the corner of Seventh and Broadway tearing up little bits of paper, throwing them to the four winds. A cop comes along and asks what was the big idea. He answers: "Just keeping elephants away." The cop says: "There aren't any elephants in this district." The fellow answers: "Well, it works, doesn't it?" This is my silly for the day, so forgive me.

Hope you and the family are well and enjoying everything you have worked for.

Love always,
Edna

Edna Purviance died in January 1958. "And so the world grows young," observed Chaplin. "And youth takes over. And we who have lived a little longer become a little more estranged as we journey on our way."

AND STILL AMERICA bedeviled him, helped by the steady procession of falsehoods printed in theoretically reputable magazines. The national Sunday supplement *This Week* printed an article stating that Chaplin had let his employees go without severance, that *Limelight* was every bit the failure that *Monsieur Verdoux* had been, and rehashed the Joan Berry case.

There were too many of these articles to respond to; Chaplin chose to vent in a sentence or two: "I no longer have any use for America at all. I wouldn't go back there if Jesus Christ was President." For the most part he assumed a dignified silence until he could answer his critics in his chosen arena.

There was the continuing matter of his legally mandated support for the child that was not his. The blood tests that had been minimized during the trial were now full proof of both paternity and nonpaternity in California, which was a further irritant. "As you know," Chaplin wrote Loyd Wright on March 10, 1954, "as of the first of the year I have put up $5,000 to take care of the Barry case and I do not intend to be blackmailed, abused or intimidated any further by this disgusting old shyster lawyer—I will not put up any further with his legal gangsterism. From the 'Examiner' clippings, I note that he says the child cannot be seen as it is in private school and its identity cannot be revealed. Being 6,000 miles away, how do I know that this child exists? I assume that you have seen it from time to time and can swear to its identity—and that he will swear to its true identity if I am to continue these payments. What's more I shall require a monthly statement as to what expenses are incurred for the child.

"I shall want a sworn statement from him on how this money is spent since the amount originally imposed upon me has been increased; and I shall want every detail itemized every month and sent to me personally. As to what this old man [Joseph] Scott vomits on the front page of the 'Examiner' or any other dirty rag—for all I care he can wipe his nose with it!"

There was more. He told Wright that he wanted his opinion about reopening the case in California. "It seems that you told [Arthur Kelly] it was impossible for me to win this case in spite of the blood tests, therefore, will you send me a copy of the new Californian statutes concerning blood tests in paternity cases and also a photostat copy of both the blood tests." The lawyer managed to wait out the storm until it passed.

When it came to his movies, no detail was too small. Chaplin wrote Arthur Kelly about the trailer for a reissue of *Modern Times*. "I am not particularly impressed by it. In the first place, I believe it gives away too much of our gags, especially if they want to use the stuff over television, which I would positively refuse. I think they can make a titillating trailer without giving away or using our best scenes."

As for fellow victims of the blacklist, he remained responsive. "I want to thank you and tell you how deeply I was moved by your recent message supporting the struggle now being waged to restore my right to a passport," Paul Robeson wrote.

"I recall that in his epic poem, 'Let the Railsplitter Awake,' Pablo Neruda . . . noted with sorrow that in the United States, 'Charles Chaplin, last father of tenderness in the world, is defamed.' But I also remember that fascists everywhere hated you for your anti-Nazi film, *The Great Dictator*. Well, Hitler and his gang are gone, but Chaplin and his art lives on! And your name will be honored—yes, here in America, too—long after McCarthy and his kind are buried in oblivion."

CHAPTER 18

Chaplin would tell the English novelist and playwright J. B. Priestley that the idea for *A King in New York* stemmed from an idle examination of a hotel register near Vevey, which made him realize how many ex-kings stopped in Switzerland. "At first I thought in terms of a charming melancholy light opera like something by Franz Lehar. Then I realized I had to make people laugh. So I thought of a natty little king with a lot of eccentricities and a good deal of money going through America on an official visit.

"That was all right. But I had only the opening scene and there were no more clothes to hang on the line. I went swimming. It is after swimming that I get ideas. Then slowly the thought came to me of how Kings had to lay corner-stones and inspect guards of honor and visit progressive schools and so on. After that it was easy."

After finishing the script, Chaplin decided to self-finance the picture, but the question of distribution was an open matter. By this time he had sold his percentage in United Artists, but there was still a long-standing business relationship, so he offered the picture to UA. Executives Max Youngstein and Arnold Picker flew to London to meet with Chaplin at the Savoy. The script was read to them, and their reaction was muted—they had been hoping for a gentle love story along the lines of *Limelight*. They said they would make a distribution decision after they saw the finished film.

Chaplin set the budget for *A King in New York* at £127,000, or $355,000—less than 40 percent of the budget for *Limelight*. He only charged £300 for his script and £1,024 for his direction. The film's final cost was £137,225.

For his leading lady, Chaplin had tentatively decided on the ravishing Kay Kendall, but when he saw *Genevieve* he was bored by the film and thought Kendall was too English to successfully play an American. Instead he cast Dawn Addams, charming and beautiful but not particularly funny. As word of the film began to circulate, Chaplin's enemies in the press pounced. "If Dawn Addams doesn't get out of doing *A King in New York* with Chaplin," wrote Mike Connolly in *The Hollywood Reporter*, "she might as well throw in the towel as far as her Free World career is concerned. Don't appear in that film—or you're dead."

For the character of Rupert, a child who is forced to inform on his own parents, Chaplin cast his son Michael. "I had a wonderful time working with my father on *A King in New York*," he remembered. "I was in a boarding school—which I hated—and I was taken out of it to work in the film. It was the only time, really, that I had a relationship with my father—with him coaching me and acting with him. I was able to become part of his creative world. . . . I recall the advice he gave me on acting was, 'What you have to try to achieve is to be as natural as possible.' It was a wonderful time."

Chaplin was still prone to sudden enthusiasms. He and Jerry Epstein, who Chaplin hired as his assistant on the picture, went to a pantomime at the Golders Green Hippodrome. They fell in love with a window cleaning routine done by George Truzzi and Lauri Lupino Lane. It must have brought memories of the Karno company flooding back, and nothing would do but that Truzzi and Lane do their act in *A King in New York*, thereby adding a few minutes of extraneous slapstick to a film that could ill afford it.

Where *Limelight* had been a happy shoot, simultaneously mellow and exuberant, Jerry Epstein remembered *A King in New York* as uncomfortable. "Charlie felt like a displaced person working at Shepperton. He was used to his own studio and his own staff: his office manager, gateman, even his studio cat—everyone who had made the Chaplin studio in Hollywood so friendly."

But at Shepperton, there were no familiar faces, and very few happy ones. When Chaplin moved a chair on the set one day, a strike was immediately called because he was doing the prop man's job. Chaplin was infuriated and told Epstein, "They're going to kill the goose that laid the golden egg."

When the picture was cut and scored, the United Artists executives flew in to take a look. They didn't like it and wouldn't distribute it. Arnold Picker took Jerry Epstein aside and told him he should take his name off the picture, that it would not do him any good when it came to finding work in the movie business. UA's refusal forced Chaplin to sell the picture territory by territory.

The odd thing about A King in New York is that, while Chaplin was ostracized for his presumably radical politics, in the film he views America from the viewpoint of an appalled conservative royalist. Other than spasms of reactionary politics, in Chaplin's view America is mostly guilty of bad manners and worse taste. "I know it's beneath your dignity," exclaims Sid James as a New York huckster, "but there's fifty thousand bucks in it!"

Chaplin has some fun with random topics of the moment—tacky television, progressive schools, and other subjects that were bound to date. One exception: the sequence when the King gets a facelift that leaves him looking like Lon Chaney's Phantom of the Opera—by far the funniest thing in the movie.

Then there are the diversions—Chaplin does the "To be or not to be . . ." speech from Hamlet simply because he feels like it. The film has flashes—King Shahdov attempting to cope with a widescreen movie is funny, if irrelevant—widescreen movies were also the rage in Europe—and he gets vicarious revenge on the witch-hunters by dousing bloviating politicians with a firehose.

But Chaplin refuses to correct miscalculations born of his own nervousness about the film and the budget—in one scene Michael can clearly be seen mouthing his father's lines while waiting for his cue. "That was pointed out to Charlie and he didn't mind," explained Jerry Epstein. "We could have used other takes where Michael didn't do that, but Charlie liked those takes."

The film drifts into the same unspecific place and time in which Chaplin found himself in Switzerland. Film historian David Thomson's line about Chaplin being "unable to approach the world on any other than his own terms" was the entire point of the Tramp, but it's a problem for a film that sets itself up as a scathing comment on contemporary insanity.

The film ends with gentle disapproval rather than a stentorian condemnation—a fact the American press pretended not to notice. "It's too crazy here," King Shahdov says by way of farewell. "I'll sit it out in Europe."

It's one of those movies with no knack for basics. Characters are continually buzzing at the door, walking in the room and taking off their coats before they start the scene. It's a one-off in terms of Chaplin's career—*Modern Times* and *The Great Dictator* are as socially and politically relevant in the twenty-first century as they were in the twentieth, but the dated jokes and disgruntled attitude of *A King in New York* were already old-fashioned in 1957. It's a severe falling-off from *Limelight*.

The reviews were . . . mixed. The most penetrating analysis came from Kenneth Tynan in *The Observer*: "The curious thing about the new Chaplin film . . . is that it is never boring. It is seldom funny, sometimes hysterical and almost always predictable, but it is never boring. Some of it is wildly self-indulgent. . . . Many of the slapstick interludes are both ill-judged and perfunctory, and none of the backgrounds convey the remotest feeling of America. When it aspires to epigrams, the dialogue falls into a quaint, soggy prissiness; when it attempts 'real feeling' we find ourselves in the dread company of lines like 'To part is to die a little.'

"Yet, I repeat at the risk of boring you: it is never boring. How can this be? Is it Chaplin's genius that sustains our interest? Hardly, for except in fugitive snatches the film shows little evidence of genius at work. . . . There are few sequences on which a screenwriter of moderate skill could not have improved.

"And this, I think is the point: that no one has peered over the author's shoulder, warning him that this line may not go over in Huddlesfield or that that situation may give offence in Scranton. . . . The result, in the fullest sense of the phrase, is 'free cinema,' in which anything within the limits of censorship can happen. In every shot Chaplin speaks his mind. It is not a very subtle mind, but its naked outspokenness is something rare, if not unique in the English speaking cinema: a crude, free film is preferable any day, to a smooth, fettered one."

The loss of Chaplin's filmmaking and domestic soil clearly hobbled him. There was no reason he couldn't have taken on blacklisting in much the same way he took on Hitler, but the intimacy of what had happened to him robbed him of the objective fury that could have made his take on McCarthy effective.

"I don't think *A King in New York* would have been made if he hadn't been sent into exile," said Jerry Epstein. "It was a nervous production. He wasn't used to working in England. He enjoyed working in his own studio, but the studios in England had an entirely different atmosphere. Charlie just wanted to get that picture over with quickly; he felt he had a hot potato in his hands and he didn't want to overspend because he knew it wouldn't be shown in America."

The film was released in September 1957, and was not handled by the Rank circuit of theaters in England, either because they didn't want it or because Chaplin wanted too much money. Instead, the film was distributed in England by Archway, a much smaller concern. The film did all right in London's Leicester Square with over £4,000 in its first week, and it did well in Blackpool, Leeds, and Sheffield, but Lancaster, Derby, and Oxford were disappointments. Brighton did well enough to warrant a second week. "In some places the film has done excellent business," wrote Archway director A. M. G. Gelardi to Chaplin after the premiere week, "but, unfortunately, in one or two places, it has not come up to expectations. . . . It may be difficult to reach the figures of *Limelight*, nevertheless I feel that we will do very well throughout the country."

In fact, *A King in New York* did badly in England. Ultimately it earned about $1.6 million throughout the world, excluding America, where it wasn't seen until 1973, where it premiered in, of all places, Yellow Springs, Ohio.

Aside from the scattershot nature of the script, there are two observations that need to be made about *A King in New York*: the film shows how much Chaplin the filmmaker depended on the prodigious skills of Chaplin the performer. By 1957, Chaplin's body was only slightly thickened, but the sixty-eight-year-old comedian is no longer as amazingly spry as he was five years earlier in *Limelight*. He's still light on his feet, but in other respects he moves like a sixty-eight-year-old man. With its star slowed down, the film's overall brio, not to mention its impact, is inevitably lessened.

And there's one other thing: the film pulls its punches. Chaplin could be excoriating about America in private, but in *A King in New York* he ends on a note of benign forgiveness of the "this too shall pass" variety, as indeed it did before authoritarian politics revved up again in the twenty-first century—a bitch always threatening to go into heat.

Being forced out of America clearly disrupted Chaplin's source. Artists who live in Rome, London, Paris, Berlin, New York, or Los Angeles are in intrinsically lively, abrasive environments that work to their creative advantage. But Switzerland and its attendant "serenity"—the word Chaplin often used to describe his new environment—would prove disastrous for his creativity.

As Jerry Epstein noted, "Charlie drew from life. If he had stayed in America, he would have been more stimulated. Living in Hollywood, good, bad, or indifferent, would have been stimulating. Exchanging ideas, having people over for dinner and tennis. Living in the Alps amongst goats and sheep is not the most exciting thing. He used to go to London for all that, but even then he was a visitor."

When *A King in New York* was finally released in America, the distributors noticed that the film was too long to fit into a two-hour TV slot. They asked Chaplin if they could trim the film by a few minutes to accommodate TV. Chaplin told them to go ahead and didn't ask to see the result. Seven minutes were cut. Chaplin would never have permitted such mutilation in any of his other movies.

In another sign of his awareness of the film's indifferent quality, Chaplin spends pages of his autobiography stoutly defending *Monsieur Verdoux*, but never mentions *A King in New York*. His last word on the subject came in a pictorial volume about his life published in 1974. "I was disappointed in the picture. I meant it to be so up-to-date and modern but perhaps I didn't quite understand it. It started out to be very good and then it got complicated and I'm not sure about the end. . . . I feel a little uneasy about the whole film."

"I wouldn't want to do anything like that now," he said in 1967. "Although genuinely I had what I thought was a comic notion. Frankly, I got a good opening. I didn't know where the hell the story was going, but the opening was very good. I think perhaps I went overboard a little bit, because I got into politics and so forth. . . . There were certain things that were excellent. It's a very funny idea to do a comedy on honesty. As I say, I am influenced a great deal by the public. Not that they're completely right, but if something goes wrong, if they show the slightest indifference, that's [on] me."

NINETEEN FIFTY-SEVEN BROUGHT occasional amusement that transcended *A King in New York*. The gangster Mickey Cohen, formerly the muscle behind a series of gangsters and the kingpin of Los Angeles crime, had just finished doing time for tax evasion when he wrote Chaplin a fan letter. Years before, Chaplin and Oona had been dining at Romanoff's when Chaplin spotted Cohen and invited him to join them. Cohen apparently had a pleasant time, because he wrote Chaplin to tell him how distressed he was by the recent political unpleasantness:

"As I think you already know, I have been away for five years on my conviction of income tax evasion. I have been home now for quite a few months, and am once again beginning to somewhat get my bearings again. . . . I have been terribly upset and disturbed to learn upon my return home, of what has taken place with you, and your lovely lady, and your children in this country.

"I have actually had a difficult time believing it, or that it could happen to a decent person such as yourself and your wonderful wife and children. Things like that are to be expected to happen to such as myself, who have had to contend with such a terrible continuous blast of unwarranted notoriety (sic) 'by our so-called wonderful free press.' And with politics as it is practised [*sic*] in this most wonderful country today, it is not to be surprising that certain things should happen with the likes of myself. *But to such a great artist*, and person like you, Charlie, believe me it is completely beyond my comprehension."

Cohen closed by mentioning that "there are still a few persons 'in power' that are much indebted to me, and have expressed themselves in such manner, and although it was an impossibility to do anything for me personally, on account of the trend of the times . . . I am absolutely sure than I could be of much help to you, which I am willing to be at your beck and call. All you have to do Charlie, is for you to express your wishes to me." He signed off, "Your friend always."

Outside of ordering a hit on Hedda Hopper, it's difficult to see what Cohen could have done for Chaplin. In any case, Chaplin didn't respond to Cohen's offer.

To ADD INSULT to injury, the Internal Revenue Service came after Chaplin for his profits on *Limelight* up until 1955, despite the fact that the government had kicked him out of the country in 1952. As Chaplin put it, "I settled for an amount considerably less than their claim and considerably more than I should have paid." The actual amount was $330,000, which had risen to $425,000 with interest.

Antagonists such as former attorney general James McGranery remained on perennial alert for any signs of weakening among their coreligionists. In October 1957, a pseudonymous writer wrote a piece for the Catholic magazine *America* in which he called Chaplin "a veritable Leonardo da Vinci of the movie industry" and referred to *A King in New York* as a movie where "his personal convictions, views and even resentments are boldly impressed on every frame."

McGranery promptly wrote a letter of protest to the magazine's editor, who attempted to placate him: "In going carefully over this article, I feel that I must say that it did not strike me in the same way it did Mrs. McGranery and yourself."

As for the INS, they still kept an eye on him. As late as July 1959, they were conducting an "extensive investigation" so that they could exclude Chaplin should he try to reenter the country, on the grounds that he had "conspired to have one of his girlfriends to abort."

CHAPTER 19

"We grew up with a fantastic example of a happy marriage," Geraldine Chaplin remembered. "I saw my parents flirting like teenagers. Mother would sit on his lap and they would hold hands. I think most children don't see that with their parents. We always thought marriage meant that you fall in love, and you stay in love forever, until the end. Monogamy has meaning to all of us in the family.

"Daddy was very strict with us. When we were naughty there was a spanking. And he was quite hard to get close to. But mostly it was fun. We knew not to disturb Daddy when he was working, so we'd tiptoe through the house and then when he'd come out at around six o'clock for dinner, we could be with him a bit."

It was Geraldine who set herself on a career in show business. Her first passion was ballet, and she attended the Royal Ballet School in London. "I used to come home and moan to my father that I was a lousy ballet dancer. I remember sitting with him by the fire and him saying sternly, 'Look, if you're moaning that you're lousy, you're going to be lousy. But if you get up on stage and say to yourself that you're a million times better than Margot Fonteyn, then maybe the public will think so too.' "

Geraldine remembered that "Education was very important to

him. He used to tell us, 'Education is the only defense.' He wanted us to have the education he never had and become professionals: doctors, lawyers, engineers and architects."

Geraldine had initially been sent to a convent school where she was instructed in religion. She talked about it with her father, who told her, "I am so happy you believe. I would give anything to believe. It makes life so much easier, but I can't. I would love to believe, but I can't."

AFTER *A KING in New York*, Chaplin set to work on his memoirs, which he attacked with the same intensity he brought to scriptwriting, filming, or composing. He rose at dawn, went for a quick swim, ate breakfast, then kissed Oona and disappeared into the library. He worked on the book till lunch, then took a short nap. After that, he continued working till five when it was time for tea followed by tennis, then dinner.

His concentration was only broken when friends visited, or vice versa. Ella Winter was a legendary firebrand of the left wing, the widow of Lincoln Steffens, the wife of screenwriter Donald Ogden Stewart. Winter's political beliefs didn't stop her from living in a large, fraying Georgian mansion in Hampstead that had once belonged to Prime Minister Ramsay MacDonald. The house was decorated with an excellent collection of Paul Klees and populated by a random collection of visitors encompassing ex-Communists, independent radicals, and expatriate liberals. Among the regulars were Ingrid Bergman, Cedric Belfrage, John Collier, Constance Cummings, Sam Wanamaker, Kenneth Tynan, and Larry Adler. Chaplin would often stop by when he was in London.

Despite the political variations, there was a strong sense of community among the group, mostly because they were almost all exiled from America for one reason or another. The atmosphere was less religious than familial. One member of the group remembered that "You couldn't tell if the accusations concerning [Chaplin's] 'moral worth' or his politics or his taxes made him angrier. . . . He had been used as an example, exhibited as a warning to others, as though his work as well as his opinions should be a source of shame. . . . His fury at the country which had discarded him was as urgent as the impulses that suddenly turned him into a cat or a tree or a cocktail hostess in mid-conversation." He would repeat what he told a reporter for *Time* magazine: "I said to that young man, you can tell them that the only thing Charlie Chaplin likes about America is . . . candy bars! They can put it in an ad if they want to, put it on a billboard."

The guests at the Stewarts' put up with Ella's legendarily bad table because of the star-studded cast of characters. Because Ella was indifferent to food and wine, she thought everybody else was too—she would pour half-empty wine bottles into decanters and serve them as newly opened bottles.

Even this largely indulgent crowd were nonplussed by Chaplin's attitude toward money, which recalled Clifford Odets's suggestion that Chaplin should make a sequel to *The Gold Rush*, about the Tramp's difficulties after becoming rich.

"It's not true," Chaplin replied. "I like being rich." Harold Clurman understood the difference between the two men: "The point was that Chaplin had fulfilled himself through money, and Odets hadn't."

Since he was among friends, Chaplin would let himself go. He still averred that he was an anarchist rather than a Socialist, let alone a Communist. During one monologue he said that he thought an ideal society should consist of stores where people could walk in and help themselves to anything they wanted; money should be irrelevant because everything should be free.

Since everyone understood what Chaplin's expulsion had cost him emotionally, not to mention creatively, most of the people at these gatherings were supportive. But there were some who objected to what they regarded as a mixture of naïveté and hypocrisy. Graham Greene had supported Chaplin when he was sent into exile, and had generally been enthusiastic about Chaplin's films, but one Sunday afternoon he left the Stewarts' "because I couldn't bear to hear Chaplin talking such rot about politics."

Greene never called Chaplin on his opinions or state of mind, nor did anybody else. They understood that being shunned for who he was had inflamed the same indignation as had poverty.

When Ella Winter stopped by the Manoir, she noted that Chaplin talked about the American unpleasantness only in snatches: "What are they so sore about? There was a time when they put out the red carpet, literally, on every platform when I went from Los Angeles to New York—the crowd adored me . . . now all that nonsense. . . . Actually I'm a Puritan. I haven't had the time to live the lives some of them attribute to me—or the energy. . . . I hate governments and rules and—fetters. . . . Can't stand caged animals. . . . People must be free."

When he spoke of America in these years, he tended to speak of the country he had found in his youth, not the clenched fist the country became after World War II—"The days when I was touring America with Fred Karno's vaudeville troupe. Then I was having experiences that made the marvelous country come alive for me.

"I was just a kid out from England, with all sorts of fancies about the West and the frontier. So when we hit towns such as Denver, Tacoma, Minneapolis—places with rich American names—I felt I was right in the middle of a new and wonderful thing."

During 1958 and 1959, he took time off from writing his book to prepare new versions of *The Pilgrim*, *A Dog's Life*, and *Shoulder Arms* for a compilation he titled *The Chaplin Revue*. Eric James, the arranger who was assisting him on the musical score, found a batch of Chaplin biographies at the Manoir that Chaplin had amassed. Chaplin had written angry responses in the margins to what he felt were incorrect conclusions.

James was the last of Chaplin's musical amanuenses. He first worked with Chaplin in 1957, when he recorded the piano part for the score of *A King in New York*. The first take was supposed to be a rehearsal, but Chaplin was so pleased with it he told James no further takes would be needed. For the next twenty years, James collaborated on the scores for all of Chaplin's music.

NORMAN LLOYD AND Chaplin still co-owned the movie rights to *They Shoot Horses, Don't They?*, but Chaplin refused to respond to Lloyd's entreaties about the property. "In bitterness and anger at what he felt was the injustice done him, he absolutely would not answer any correspondence about *They Shoot Horses, Don't They?*," recalled Lloyd. "He just dropped it. He vowed never to make another film in the United States."

Lloyd regularly got inquiries about selling the property for a profit, but he didn't want to do anything without Chaplin's approval. And so the years went by.

THE PREVIOUS FIFTEEN turbulent years of Chaplin's life had left many of his old friends defensive, and some shocked. Stan Laurel wrote several letters during October 1957 that showed Chaplin was much on his mind.

"For people having troubles, I agree with you that Chaplin doesn't have any—financially, but nevertheless, he is a very unhappy man, & mentally troubled, you can rest assured, success & Worldly good don't insure happiness & content, & there are many others in the same situation. . . .

"I have to agree with you re Chaplin being mean & cheap, he never to my knowledge ever had any consideration to anybody—financially or otherwise, he never had any time for any of his closest friends who worked with him in the early days, regardless of whether they needed his help or not, so you can imagine his feelings & actions towards utter strangers, including his beloved Kensingtonites.

"I was closely associated with Charlie for 2 or 3 years, I was his understudy and shared rooms with him on many occasions, so am fully aware of his idiosyncracies, he was a very eccentric character, composed of many moods, at times signs of insanity, which I think developed further when he gained Fame & Fortune. I frankly believe . . . that this was hereditary, I understand both of his parents died in the asylum—at least I know definitely his Mother did, shortly after he brought her to this Country. . . . I frankly think he is to be pitied more than censored—to my mind, he is still the greatest artiste in his field, but unfortunately his ideals have run amuck & he has lost all sense of propriety."

Laurel was no stranger to a loss of propriety—he endured seven marriages to five women—but his feelings about his old friend were familiar to those habitually kept at arm's length by Chaplin's basic lack of need for other people. After the Karno days Chaplin and

Laurel had mostly run into each other on Catalina Island, where they both liked to take their boats. At those times, Laurel would be greeted like the old friend he thought he was, and they would spend convivial time together. But after they sailed back to Los Angeles, the curtain of silence would once again descend.

Life with Charlie. Or, rather, life without Charlie.

IN 1962, CHAPLIN received an honorary degree from Oxford University, and some American publications began making noises to the effect that ten years of exile was more than enough time to be politically rehabilitated. *The New York Times* editorialized that "We do not believe the Republic would be in danger if the . . . [Kennedy] administration lifted the ban that was imposed in 1952 and if yesterday's forgotten little tramp were allowed to amble down the gangplank of a steamer or a plane in an American port."

This provoked a flurry of similar sentiments, which caused J. Edgar Hoover to ask for a concise summary memorandum based on the Bureau's file. Clyde Tolson ordered the summary sent to James McGranery, who by this time was a federal judge in Washington, D.C., and was given to complaining that he had received unfair blame for rescinding Chaplin's reentry permit.

McGranery sensed public sentiment turning in Chaplin's favor, and began a backchannel attempt to quell the wave, giving off-the-record interviews to Catholic magazines calculated to support his position. The substance of McGranery's defense, which included him suggesting specific information to be included in articles, was that the FBI documents left him no choice but to subject Chaplin to a further investigation because of the law stating that only aliens of good moral character who subscribed to the principles of the Constitution could be admitted to America. In other words, rescinding the reentry permit was not a punitive extraction but a legal necessity.

He told one writer that what amounted to good moral character was sadly lacking in Chaplin's case, while he also objected to Chaplin's "deliberate effort to impress on the American people his concern, or apparent concern, for the advancement of communism." He included a copy of the Immigration and Nationality Act as revised through January 1962 as evidence.

The précis of the FBI file, helpfully forwarded by J. Edgar Hoover, was included in McGranery's defense, although the précis neglected to mention that Chaplin was not the father of Joan Berry's child.

McGranery's defense implied that previous attorneys general had been lax in the conduct of their office because they had neglected to bring the hammer down. What weakened McGranery's self-defense was the fact that Chaplin had been accused of many things, but convicted of none of them.

Which did not stop the Chaplin haters from writing McGranery with that combination of fury and illiteracy that is the invariable mark of zealots:

WHAT MORE CAN BE SAID ABOUT CHARLIE CHAPLIN? HERE IT IS HE IS A RED AND THE WORST. START THERE IN WASHINGTON WITH ALL OF THE ANTI-CHRIST. . . . YOU CHRISTIAN MEN ARE DUPES FOR THIS KIND AND THEY ARE LAUGHING AT ALL OF OUR CHRISTIAN MEN, TAKE THEM UP BEFORE IT IS TOO LATE.

SINCERELY . . .

NORMAN LLOYD FINALLY traveled to Switzerland for a visit with Chaplin. They talked about his autobiography, they talked about every subject under the sun, but Chaplin would not talk about *They Shoot Horses.* "He was in such a fury about how he had been treated by this country that he didn't want to consider coming back or making a picture here. I waited for him to talk about *Horses*; I didn't want to press him. That was a mistake on my part."

Because of an arcane copyright issue, Chaplin and Lloyd's American rights expired, although they still owned European rights. United Artists paid author Horace McCoy's estate $40,000 for the American rights, but Chaplin refused to make a deal for the European rights.

By 1966, Lloyd had had enough. He made an executive decision and sold the European rights for $15,000, sending half the profits

to Chaplin. They saw each other after that, but Chaplin never mentioned the book, or the money Lloyd had sent him.

ALTHOUGH IT HAD long been obvious that Chaplin didn't want to
work for anybody but Chaplin, he still got occasional acting offers.
John Huston offered him the part of Noah in Huston's film of *The
Bible*. After Chaplin refused, Huston played the part himself in a
charming performance centered on puckish amusement.

A more interesting proposal came from Alan Schneider and
Samuel Beckett, who offered Chaplin the film rights to *Waiting for
Godot*, with Chaplin playing all the parts. "I got a nice letter back
from Chaplin," remembered Schneider, "saying that he respected the
work, and was intrigued by the idea, but that he didn't do other
people's material."

NINETEEN SIXTY-FOUR BROUGHT a letter from an old friend. Upton
Sinclair sent Chaplin a flyer announcing an exhibit of Sinclair's papers at Indiana University's Lilly Library, and scribbled a note: "Dear
Charlie: I know you don't write letters, but maybe this review may
tempt you. Upton"

Sinclair knew his man.

"Dear Uppie," replied Chaplin:

It was heartwarming to hear from you after all these years, and
I was happy to know that you have celebrated your eighty-fifth
birthday, please accept my heartiest congratulations. . . .

You might know that I have mentioned you in my book as
being one of my mentors, and you are rightly so, for after meeting
you I read *The Jungle, The Brass Check*, and *Oil*, all of which were
a revelation to me—and revelation is knowledge. . . .

As you know, I don't write letters. I think one reason is that I
am not a natural letter writer; then again, there is the spirit of the
merchant in me—the thought that if I have to exert the energy
to write a letter I might as well do something creative; but this
mercenary reason must be put aside occasionally for a very old friend.

I have little news that you don't know about, and I think I know your attitude to this atomic era; my own reaction is that it is both exciting and depressing. But in spite of tumult—I am extremely happy with my wife and family. We live a very peaceful and interesting life in Switzerland and if I can keep going for another twenty-five years—as I hope you will—I shall be happily satisfied.

Yours as ever . . .

CHAPLIN READ SECTIONS of his memoir to Jerry Epstein on his visits to the Manoir. "How can you remember in such detail all the events of your childhood?" Epstein asked.

"How could I forget?" Chaplin replied.

The memoir, redundantly titled *My Autobiography*, was bought by the Bodley Head for a minimum payment of $500,000, after which the company sold the rights country by country—Simon & Schuster bought the American rights. The book was released in eight languages simultaneously in October 1964. The American edition was in its third printing by early November and was tied for first place on the best-seller list with Douglas MacArthur's *Reminiscences*. *My Autobiography* sold more than 27,000 copies in America by the end of the year and remained on the best-seller list through March of 1965. It has never been out of print since.

My Autobiography is a key document in the Chaplin canon, a rich, evocative melding of Dickens and *Vanity Fair*. Except for the fact that Chaplin's story had a happy ending, Calvero could have written it. As many critics have noted, the book's first third is superb—detailed and vigorously narrated, albeit with a strange chronological tic: Chaplin consistently shaves a year or two off his age during his theatrical infancy, possibly to make himself seem even more precocious than he actually was.

But after Chaplin becomes famous the book loses focus, becomes far less introspective, and slowly declines into rote recitations of who he met, both irrelevant (Lady Astor, Sir Philip Sassoon) and relevant (Churchill, Einstein). He never mentions *The Circus, A King in New York*, or most of his devoted coworkers and refuses to go into his marriage to Lita Grey. Dan James, Chaplin's assistant on *The Great Dictator*, realized the central irony of Chaplin's later life when he pointed out that "Chaplin had always positioned himself against wealth and stuffiness [although] he too became wealthy and stuffy. . . . The stuffy fellow comes out in that autobiography."

The memoir demonstrates that once Chaplin became famous his gaze shifted firmly toward the titled and famous who clustered around him and, on some level, provided much needed validation. His early years formed him completely, for good and bad. No later experience had an equivalent impact, so he filled the latter portion of his book with a sublimated snobbery that lent him a status his childhood had denied him.

The primary takeaway from the book is his remarkable self-containment. Outside of his mother and brother, he seems to have been devoted to only two other people: Douglas Fairbanks and Oona. His other friendships were matters of shared sympathies more than deep emotional bonds, and his relationships with his coworkers seemed mostly transactional.

But even with a friend as close as Fairbanks, Chaplin was capable of clinical objectivity. Talking about Fairbanks in 1966, he characterized him as "the most charming man you ever met. He was a marvelous man, a great man, the nicest man I ever met. And considerate, charming, enthusiastic. He was . . . interested in everybody. He'd say, 'You know, I like successful people,' and I knew what he meant. Without any envy at all, where I would be a little bit envious. I had my defenses up, but Douglas liked anybody that was a success. . . .

"Douglas was a limited actor. He wasn't a good actor. . . . He knew Shakespeare—yes, his conceptions were very good. He of course didn't have the voice to play in Shakespeare. There was no resonance. But he had a very fine idea about the whole thing."

The reviews of the autobiography were mainly laudatory, but Louise Brooks, who had had an affair with Chaplin in New York in the summer of 1925, read the book and was appalled. "I would have forgiven him everything if he had written a first-rate film book," she wrote to a friend. "This he did not chose [*sic*] to do because of his vulgar need to please. At least he has made me understand why I never liked him.

"When I met him again after New York at the Hollywood home of [producer] Arthur Hornblow, I did not speak but moved into a corner. From that lovely vantage point, I watched him do all his tricks—like a poodle—for Garbo, whom he had just met. She sat smugly on the arm of a chair leaning on the back, watching him under her lashes (like centipedes) with her slight contemptuous smile while her feet pawed idly at the slippers she had cast on the floor. He could not afford emotionally to remember her in the book. . . .

"Oh, the book has made me ill. His sex pride! His intellectual fatuity! All those babes knocking on his bedroom door. He still tries to pass off a crude bunch of lies to a world who would not know the difference. He grew to hate Paulette [Goddard], who was . . . a bitch in a ditch. . . . And he does not even mention Martha Raye, who was so magnificent in *M. Verdoux*, or Von Sternberg."

Brooks was just getting warmed up for a subsequent letter: "That such a barren little man could have produced such a monumental collection of work is beyond belief. I have been so busy defending him over the last decades that I had forgotten, until I read his book, how very vulgar and cheap he was. . . . His character becomes more and more Dorian Gray-ish—his films becoming more wonderful as he devolves into something frightful, vapid and crass. Another fine example of the missing link between genius and humanity!!"

Brooks's antisocial—and anti-Chaplin—personality disorder had somehow receded when she wrote a piece about him for *Film Culture* in 1969, which amounted to a retrospective love letter. She described him as "small, perfectly made, meticulously dressed, with his fine grey hair and ivory skin and white teeth, he was as clean as a pearl and glowed all over." She thought him "the most bafflingly complex man who ever lived." The article did not refer to what Brooks regarded as Chaplin's most bizarre affectation: his habit of painting his genitals with iodine in the belief that it would prevent venereal disease. That, and the image of his bright red erection, she saved for her friends.

Brooks believed that Chaplin's sexuality and creativity were closely aligned—Chaplin probably believed the same thing—and that "his Lolita obsession" had convinced him "that he could seduce a girl only with his position as director and starmaker." Beyond that, the article left the impression she admired him as a man, a lover, and an artist: "The truth is that he existed on a plane above pride, jealousy or hate. I never heard him say a snide thing about anyone. *He lived totally without fear.*"

Brooks's alcoholism obviously fed her irascible outbursts; her imperious personality provided an avoidance mechanism useful for diverting attention from a life she regarded as a monumental failure.

"[Louise] wrote like a dream," Roddy McDowall would say. "She was very succinct about her point of view, even if it wasn't particularly accurate."

CHAPTER 20

The rich late autumn of Chaplin's life was interrupted by the death of his brother on April 16, 1965—Charlie's birthday. Before heart failure killed him, Syd had memory issues for several years—his wife, Gypsy, had to take over their finances—and he had grown increasingly obsessed by impending death. Syd was eighty years old.

Perhaps as a partial distraction from the inevitable loss of the people he loved, Chaplin continued to welcome guests to the Manoir, among them the Russian film director Grigori Alexandrov and his wife. After dinner one night, they went into the music room, where Alexandrov's wife saw some of Chaplin's scores resting on the piano. "Oh, Maestro, it would be such an honor if you could let me have a sheet of your music for the Moscow Museum!" Chaplin picked up the music sheets and put them away. Then she saw some loose pages from a script with his notes in the margins. "Oh, Maestro, if this could be presented to the Leningrad Museum, it would be preserved forever!"

Chaplin stalked out of the room and motioned for Jerry Epstein to follow him. "Get rid of those damned Communists," he ordered Epstein. "They're all the same. They'll take everything that's not nailed to the floor!"

He could be severe with his children if he thought they were cavalier about being born into wealth. One day Michael was dragging a sweater along the ground, and his father ordered him to "Get that up off the ground! People had to work for that!" He would confide to friends, "I don't believe I deserve dinner unless I do a day's work." Oona was more openly affectionate and far less judgmental with the children, making sure to spend a part of every day with each of them.

Occasionally Chaplin would see a movie. He enjoyed *La Dolce Vita* and developed an enthusiasm for Roberto Rossellini. "I didn't realize how beautiful he was. I saw [*General Della Rovere*]. Very moving—beautifully cast. He's one of the great directors, no question. Handled with such good taste. Beautifully done."

Chaplin was not alone in Switzerland, which was home to a variety of show business tax exiles. Noel Coward was nearby, as were Yul Brynner, Van Johnson, and George Sanders and his wife, Benita Hume. The latter had been the widow of Ronald Colman before she married Sanders and was highly perceptive. When Noel Coward returned from a visit to the Chaplins' and noted that Oona had "sat perfectly still in a cardigan," it propelled Hume into a bit of Chekhovian poetry about stateless aristocrats etched with a touch of acid:

The Chaplins' house was perfectly gay
And filled with all the old guard again.
The actors re-acted every play,
They shouted and sang of the days that were hey
Wishing Irving and Tree and Pelissier
Were back on the scene to be starred again.
But Oona Chaplin sat perfectly still,
Perfectly still, in a cardigan.

Charlie leapt up with an *entrechat*—
And I must say came down rather hard again,
George sang "Because"—to not much applause,
Then the children did cartwheels—and one lost her drawers,
While Noel followed his secret heart again.
But Oona Chaplin sat perfectly still,
She sat perfectly still. In a cardigan.

* * *

WHEN CHAPLIN SPOKE of his youth, it seemed that some of the anguish had drained away, and what was left was a residue of his limited youthful ambitions. "I never wanted to make a lot of money. I wasn't interested in that. I just wanted to get away . . . from my very poor environment, that's all. I've never thought of money. . . . I'm careful, I've been brought up that way. The three of us lived on seven and six a week. . . . If we were to get a Sunday dinner, we were very happy about it. And it was a great occasion.

"No, success [was] to get away from this imprisonment—this poverty. . . . All I needed was five dollars a week. If I had an income of five dollars a week, I could travel over the damn world. I'll play my violin, I'll do a little begging and so forth—be a very romantic figure, or whatever. Take pity on me and give me a couple bob. That was my romantic conception of life. It was purely back to the gypsy, so to say."

Occasionally he would be asked about the possibility of reviving the Tramp, but he thought the world had moved on in ways that rendered the character impossible. "I don't think there's any place for that sort of person now. You know, [in] England, there was nothing but derelicts, old women and old men, sleeping out in this kind of weather. Papers wrapped around them. Have you ever been in the Salvation Army places? And those who were not fortunate enough to get into one of the places, had to sleep out. Well, the Tramp was very much of a universal thing.

"I think that the world has become a little bit more ordered now. . . . There's not the same humility now. They don't know what humility is. The thing became outdated in a way. It became something of an antique. It belongs to another era, and we've passed it. And that's why I couldn't do anything like that now—and of course, sound—that's another reason."

AFTER *LIMELIGHT*, CHAPLIN was off American screens for more than ten years. *Modern Times* was reissued in 1959 to considerable success—$2.1 million in world rentals—but it didn't play in

America. Neither did *The Chaplin Revue*, which earned more than $800,000 in Canada and Europe.

What renewed Chaplin's cultural currency was a retrospective of his work at the Paris Theater in New York that began in November 1963 as a sort of preview of the autobiography. The series began with *City Lights* and hit its commercial peak with *Modern Times* and *Monsieur Verdoux*, which finally found its audience.

Bosley Crowther of the *Times*, one of the few critics who hadn't completely loathed *Verdoux*, was converted into an enthusiastic partisan by the reissue, writing of his appreciation for "the amazing and engrossing transition this supreme comic artist here makes from his established and lovable characterization to one that offers a paradox."

The once despised film had the greatest success of the Chaplin features at the Paris—it ran nine weeks and earned well over half what the picture had earned in all of America in 1947. The retrospective in toto ran for eleven months—a great success.

With his public image once again in the ascent, Chaplin began thinking of going back to work. But there was still the issue of isolation. He liked a TV production of Pinter's *The Caretaker* ("very mysterious and interesting"), was amused by *Goldfinger* and appreciative of Sean Connery. But despite the fact that his daughter Geraldine was one of the stars, he thought *Doctor Zhivago* was "banal . . . that ridiculous scene when he writes a poem by candle light! And *Blow-Up* was so slow and boring. I wouldn't go on for hours to work up to an eventual strip-tease. Or pretend that this man doesn't notice a murder."

In 1965, Chaplin dusted off *Stowaway*, the script he had written thirty years before for Paulette Goddard. Rechristened *A Countess from Hong Kong*, the idea of a new Chaplin film enticed everyone. Chaplin originally wanted to cast Sean Connery as the star, but Universal was interested in financing the picture and they already had Marlon Brando under contract. Brando flew over to meet Chaplin. "Do you think I can play it?" Brando asked. "I don't think, I know you can," replied Chaplin.

Brando had been tied to Universal since selling them his production company in the aftermath of the commercially disastrous *One-Eyed Jacks*, and he agreed to burn off one of his commitments with the Chaplin picture. Chaplin had seen Sophia Loren in Vittorio De Sica's *Yesterday, Today and Tomorrow* and was struck by both her beauty and comic facility. He made a trip to London to talk to her while she was making Stanley Donen's *Arabesque*, and she agreed to make the picture without seeing the script.

Chaplin wanted his neighbor Noel Coward for the part of Brando's valet, who has one amusingly amorous scene with the leading lady, but Coward's schedule wouldn't allow it. Jerry Epstein was producing, and he suggested Peter Sellers, but Chaplin didn't want the picture overweighted with stars. The part was given to Patrick Cargill.

The film was financed by Universal to the tune of $3.2 million, with a generous fourteen-week schedule. Chaplin was paid $600,000 plus 20 percent of the gross in excess of $2.5 million, 30 percent beyond $8.75 million. Given the presence of Brando, Loren, and Chaplin, the film was eagerly awaited by everyone, which meant that everyone was crushed by the result.

Part of the problem was that Brando was an actor with a slow rhythm—he cherished his pauses, his character's apparent groping for the right thing to say. Chaplin's comedy—most comedy—has to be played briskly. A deeper problem was that Brando was never the incarnation of the comic spirit.

The final blow was the script—Brando hadn't actually read it until he arrived for the shoot. When he did read the script, he was struck with a sudden attack of appendicitis/laryngitis/terminal hesitance which caused him to miss the first three days of production. When the problem magically receded and Brando showed up, Chaplin strode over to him, grabbed him by the arm, and snapped, "Listen you son of a bitch, you're working for Charlie Chaplin now. If you think you're slumming, take the next plane back to Hollywood. We don't need you." With that inauspicious beginning, Brando settled into a sullen pout.

With Sydney, who had the second male lead, Chaplin was brusque at best, cracked the whip at worst. "For Chrissakes, come on Syd, Get some feeling into the lines. You're trying to make Sophia feel better. Show a little warmth. . . . For Chrissakes, what's wrong with you? Get the lead out of your pants!"

Brando's own father had been cruel to his family, and Brando was infuriated by his treatment of Syd. "From that moment on, Marlon, the champion of the underdog, refused to take Charlie's directions," recalled Jerry Epstein.

Brando was far more upset than Sydney, who implied that Chaplin was hamstrung by his deal with Universal. "He was always pretty tough," Syd said. "He was a perfectionist, he wanted things done just right. But *A Countess from Hong Kong* was Universal and it wasn't his money. He had a studio telling him what to do. They were insistent on schedules, on money and he'd never had that before in his life. He'd thought nothing of reshooting a whole week's work, and if he didn't like the reshoots, he'd do it all over again, and all he'd say was, 'This isn't Warner Bros.' money, you know.'"

Brando never directly confronted Chaplin, maintaining a grimly professional demeanor. When Brando didn't react fast enough to Chaplin's blocking, the director would grab his star and physically maneuver him into the desired placement, as if he was a piece of furniture—which, in a way, he was.

"Chaplin in his old age seems to feel physically forty-five," noted Penelope Gilliatt, who observed a day of shooting. "He keeps saying that this is a romantic film, not a comedy. He wants to make a film about love that simply happens to be funny, without anyone in the picture knowing it. 'Play for absolute realism, not for comedy,' he says again and again."

For a scene where Brando's character asks his valet to marry the stowaway, Chaplin told Patrick Cargill, "Don't denote anything on your face. Keep your voice up. Insist on the action." A moment later, he told him, "More polite. You're disguising your feelings by being very polite. . . . But before you close up, just a shade of shock on that line of Marlon's 'I'd like you to marry her.' It lays an egg a little bit. So long as you're not suave. A suavity here would kill the whole scene."

The cast and crew were surprised by how articulate Chaplin was in the moment, how specific his directions were. He had always worked from the outside in, directing like a coach imposing muscle memory on young athletes. Once the movements were firmly set, relaxation came and so did emotion. It was a method that was the antithesis of The Method, which is why the shoot was so hellish for Brando, who seems to have surrendered and given Chaplin what he wanted with a complete absence of conviction. "Do that line again, Marlon," Chaplin told him at one point. "'Oh, in about ten minutes.' Quickly. Take off the fat."

For the part of Brando's wife, Chaplin chose Tippi Hedren, whom he had seen in Hitchcock's *Marnie*. "Charlie wouldn't let the script out of England," Hedren remembered. "We all accepted without reading the script, just being told about the plot and characters. I asked Charlie to tell me about the part. He said I'd be playing the ambassador's wife, that I came in halfway through the movie and was in it for the rest of the film.

"When I got over to England, I was so excited I went right from the plane to the set. I said 'I need a script,' and everybody disappeared. So I sat down and started paging through the script, looking and looking. At the three-quarter point Martha entered and she has four scenes. That wasn't what I had been told.

"I broached Charlie about it and he invited me to dinner with him and Oona. Oona had the flu; she didn't want to deal with it. 'Charlie,' I said, 'why didn't you tell me it was a cameo?'

"'Because I didn't think you'd come.'

"And I thought to myself, 'Well, what can I say to that?'

"When Marlon finally got to England and read the script he . . . wanted out. There was a big problem and Charlie said, 'Very well, you call your press conference and I'll call mine and we'll see who gets the bigger crowd.'

"Marlon was only on the set when it was time to roll 'em. He was not openly hostile. The set was okay. And Charlie loved Sophia! There was no sense of rustiness with Charlie—he was completely in control. I would say he was 100 percent. We worked for a full day, but he would get noticeably tired late in the day.

"Charlie was very interesting. The Hitchcock films are macabre and totally different in tone than Charlie's, but Hitch had a wonderful sense of humor on the set. Charlie was very serious on the set. I was kind of surprised. Demanding? Yeah! He was excellent in his perfection."

What made the movie bearable for all concerned was Sophia

Loren, who adored Chaplin and responded with a performance of comic commitment and emotion that deserved a better script.

"It's a strange little movie," said Hedren. "It works best on TV, on the small screen. It lends itself to that. The film they should have released was a documentary of Charlie making the movie. *That's* where the film really was—Charlie acting out each role for each actor. And he was brilliant at it. Watching him *become* Sophia, then Marlon, then me, all within a few minutes, that's where the film was, but he wouldn't allow a film crew on the set. He didn't want to be bothered."

The problem with *A Countess from Hong Kong* partly involved the film, partly the expectations: Chaplin! Brando!! Loren!!! The movie is basically an archaic shipboard farce/romance in a year when the big hits were *Bonnie and Clyde, The Graduate*, and *In the Heat of the Night*. The reviews were generally brutal, with lots of variations on "Chaplin has lost it."

"A saddening experience for all lovers of Chaplin's works." *The Times* of London

"The direction is dull and unimaginative and the whole thing reminded me of a third-rate farce performed by an uninspired repertory company." London *Daily Express*.

"Mr. Chaplin is now trapped by his own legend." *Financial Times*.

"A fairy tale so hopelessly out of date . . . it is almost pathetic." New York *Daily News*.

"It is so bad that I wondered, at one point, whether Mr. Chaplin might not be trying to put us on." *The New York Times*.

Chaplin's response was defiant. "With my next film I won't open in London. I'll open in Kalamazoo or somewhere and leave London till later. I don't understand what's happening there now. I think they're swinging drunk. It's a peculiar sort of desperation, a somnambulism, a negation of art, or any sort of simplicity. When the swinging thing is over, what will they have left?

"If they don't like it, they're bloody idiots. Old-fashioned? What's old-fashioned about the story? It's about a multi-millionaire who gives up his lovely wife to marry a whore. What's so old-fashioned about that? I think it's rather current."

Public response echoed the critics. The film had cost just under

$3.1 million, but earned only a meager $1.1 million in American rentals. While he stood up for his film publicly, Geraldine Chaplin said the failure of *A Countess from Hong Kong* "destroyed" him. It was the last film in a movie career that began in 1913.

It was at this point that Paulette Goddard chose to emerge from the shadows. She had been married to Erich Maria Remarque since 1958 and lived in Switzerland on what she said was "a different mountain" from Chaplin. In May 1966, she sent a legal notice to Chaplin reminding him that they had a contract obligating him to use her on any picture he made after her contract with Paramount concluded. "Please take this as notice to you under Paragraph Third that the term of my Paramount employment agreement is ended." Since her Paramount contract had ended in 1949, and the contract between Goddard and Chaplin included the phrase "at his option" for her services, Chaplin did not bother to reply.

A Countess from Hong Kong provoked a last flurry of concern from the American government. Universal applied for a permit allowing Chaplin "temporary admission to the United States" for the purpose of publicizing the film. Immigration officials decided that "the denial of a visa sought for the above purpose would seriously mar the image of the United States throughout the world, particularly in Western Europe, and that [Chaplin's] world-wide renown as an artist would undoubtedly make the matter a *cause celebre* with the U.S. portrayed as vindictive and fearful." The INS approved the application, but Chaplin canceled the trip without ever picking up his documents.

"Do you have any desire to go back to the U.S.?" inquired a reporter.

"Between you and I, no. . . . I'm really not interested. I used to love it. I used to have the grandest time of my life in New York. What happened was the culture changed. I used to love those beautiful houses on Fifth Avenue. Then the Rockefellers set in—horrible. Before that there were these very human understandable houses of rich men."

It seemed to him now that the only times he had been absolutely happy were in the creative enclosure of his studio. "I never liked Hollywood. I liked Los Angeles more than I liked Hollywood. . . .

We create a world of our own. Mine [was] the studio in California. The happiest moments were when I was on the set, and I had an idea, or just a suggestion of a story, and I felt good and then things would happen. It was the only surcease that I had. In the evening, it was a rather lonesome place, you know, California, but it was always marvelous creating a comic world."

IN OCTOBER 1966, during post-production on *Countess*, Chaplin tripped over an uneven sidewalk at the studio, fell down, and broke his ankle. It seemed to be a small thing, but it was the first in what would become a long series of physical events that gradually enfeebled a man who had seemed indomitable.

The broken ankle put an end to his beloved games of tennis, but he still felt obligated to keep working. He reissued *The Circus*, the only Chaplin feature that hadn't been included in the 1963 Paris Theater retrospective. He confided that the reason he had never reissued it before was that fact that "I didn't think it was very good." The score included a theme song sung by Chaplin himself, rolling his R's like an Edwardian man of the theater. United Artists gave it a release in 1970 to minimal impact—$97,000 in American rentals.

Shortly after that, Chaplin let it be known that he was open to a deal for distribution of his library of films. His son Sydney tried to get the rights but his father rejected his proposal. Chaplin liked Syd, but he thought his son lacked a work ethic—Syd liked golf far more than he liked acting—and he probably didn't trust him with the family patrimony.

After more than seven months of negotiations, Chaplin cut a deal with Mo Rothman, a former UA executive who had worked on the original release of *Limelight*. "The essential element that Chaplin loved was money," remembered Rothman. "Once when we were negotiating the agreement . . . Chaplin danced for me. He pirouetted around his living room saying, 'They're very good pictures, Mo. They're very good pictures.'"

Rothman had to forage for the up-front money, but Chaplin trusted him. With the financial backing of Bert Schneider, the producer of *Five Easy Pieces*, *Easy Rider*, and *The Last Picture Show*,

Rothman paid Chaplin a $5 million advance against 50 percent of the profits for a fifteen-year lease, with a five-year renewal at Rothman's discretion. The deal included TV and video rights. According to *Variety*, Rothman and Schneider beat out Time-Life on the deal.

Rothman went to work doing what he did best: selling. A few weeks after the deal was signed, the Cannes Film Festival hosted a ceremony making Chaplin a Commander of the Legion of Honor. For a man who had been in the public eye for nearly sixty years, Chaplin was always touchingly tongue-tied at these occasions. "I've been over here all these years," he told the audience, his voice quivering with emotion, "but I still can't speak anything but English. I just want to say I'm so moved to know you've appreciated me not only in the past, but also in the present."

By 1972, the Chaplin films were playing in theaters, and, through rbc films, a company formed by Bert Schneider, in college auditoriums. Schneider also financed a documentary begun by Peter Bogdanovich but completed by Richard Patterson under the title *The Gentleman Tramp*. (Bogdanovich found Chaplin diminished and vague, while Chaplin took an immediate dislike to the young director.)

Walter Matthau and his family came over to Vevey to participate in the documentary. Oona had remained close with Carol Saroyan Matthau, as well as with Gloria Vanderbilt. Gloria had all the money in the world, while Oona and Carol had married well, but they were still bound together by the fact that they were all de facto orphans— sisters under the skin.

"My mother and Oona were absolute equivalents," said Carol's son Charles Matthau. "Lifelong best friends. I don't think they ever had an argument, which was not the case with my mom and Gloria. Gloria did not approve of my father at first. You see, when they got married, he wasn't rich or famous."

With Matthau, Carol had found the happiness that had eluded her with Saroyan. "I like the way that man takes his food," Chaplin said after watching Matthau eat at the Manoir. "You give me back my faith in life—watching you eat. I know you want more of this corn, Walter. Here, now have more of this corn."

Chaplin and Walter Matthau got along splendidly. "They were

very much kindred spirits," said Charles. "Both grew up poor; both artists; both funny; both made larger points than their humor; both loved classical music and Mozart."

Charles Matthau was seven or eight when he met Chaplin, and remembered that he "was very unassuming. He didn't have to tell you how great he was because everybody already knew it. The Chaplin kids were great. Geraldine was the most outgoing. Chris was very nice, down-to-earth. Jane was the same. They were all normal, well-adjusted kids.

"The difference between Charlie and Oona and my parents as parents was that I don't know that the Chaplins were as involved with their children. My folks and I were bonded together in our own universe. With Oona and Charlie it was more like they were bonded together; I don't think they were as close to their children as my parents were.

"I noticed something interesting about Charlie. He had this look he would give you. He would suddenly sort of stare at you and you suddenly realized he was processing you. *Appraising* you. I used to imitate that look for my father, and he would always laugh. He did a version of it at the end of *The Taking of Pelham One Two Three*. It's not until the guy coughs at the end that he realizes that's the guy he's chasing. And he does this look that's him imitating me imitating Charlie."

Chaplin cannily tied the reissue of his library of films with a series of personal appearances, and, after much urging by Mo Rothman, he agreed to return to America, where he would be given an honorary Academy Award. Before that, he traveled to Paris to kick off *Modern Times*. When a reporter asked him "*Parlez-vous français?*" Chaplin replied "*Je parle comme Francais com une vache Espagnole*," i.e., "Like a Spanish cow."

The next stop was Venice, for an open-air showing of *City Lights*, and then it was time for the return to the United States. "I'm going to America, I like America, and I'm prepared to be shot," he told a reporter.

But he was a different man than he had been twenty years before. He was eighty-three years old, his legs were wobbly, and sometimes he had to concentrate to remember what he wanted to say. What hadn't changed was his devotion to Oona. "She has made her love for him the center of her own life, with the result that he soon came to depend on her entirely," wrote the journalist Francis Wyndham. "If she leaves his side for a moment, he looks distressed, until her return. Himself a sensitive, proud, egotistic, touchy man, the essential artist, he marvels at those qualities which make her the ideal artist's wife: tolerance, intuition, selflessness, tact."

Chaplin was *proud* of her, of the qualities she had in abundance that he lacked. He would point out that Oona's reading overflowed with "discrimination and choice . . . . I read more the hack stuff myself. Still, I have nicer bindings."

These were years of relaxation, if not rest, and a certain ease. "In all those years of Hollywood, I never knew the rank and file of the stars. I always worked alone and I had my own studios. I was also very shy. But the Fairbankses always spoiled me. Douglas used to have all the celebrities at his house and that was very convenient for me because, of course, I wanted to meet them all. But I stood there and very rarely said anything. I was, I suppose, one of his showpieces.

"That was a very gay, al fresco sort of life then. I loved getting up with the sunlight and the days themselves were beautiful and clear. We all worked by natural light, of course; everything was very simple. There wasn't the grim reality of it. There wasn't the self-importance of it.

"I've never trusted the intellect. If it were all intellect, it would be a horrible world. I adore sentiment. I've done everything the way Noel Coward says, with a talent to amuse. But I don't correspond with anyone from those days, or in films anymore. In the first place, I'm a bad speller."

The swimming pool was now empty, and the tennis court had leaves on it. "It's amazing how quickly you lose things. . . . I don't mean I was really playing. I would stand in the center of the court and when someone hit a good shot I would call out, 'Well done!' "

As for the country that had banished him, "I like America. I always did. I have no ill feelings. That's politics, and when you live as long as I have, all politics look pretty foolish."

It was all so long ago. What was left was art . . . and success. "On a clear day, one can see the roof of one of the branches of the

Union of Swiss Banks," he pointed out to a visitor. "Believe in my old capitalists' experience. Money and beauty always get on well together. . . .

"Do you know in America there are still some people who say I'm Communist? Look around us! If I were Communist, I'd be a funny type of chap."

His daughters had been enthralled by Fidel Castro and what they called "the Cuban miracle," but Chaplin thought they were naïve. "How else do you expect them to imagine their father's struggle to achieve all the luxury they were born in? . . . My Cuban miracle was to see Mother die, not in a poor people's refuge in the heart of the slums drowned in London fog, but in the best private clinic in California, among the orange trees, with car and chauffeur, surrounded by a thousand and one attendants, under the attentive vigilance of her two boys who had become rich. At that time that was our way of protesting."

His life had finally achieved the serenity he had always avoided when young, when he was courting young women who had a way of introducing chaos into his life. "I cultivate my strawberries, my plums, my pears, my wife and children." His daughter Geraldine remembered that "He got up . . . with my mother brewing the coffee. He'd work till lunch, then work some more till 5:30 p.m. He didn't really talk about the old days in Hollywood, but he did talk about Doug Fairbanks. He *loved* him. His physicality, his *joie de vivre*."

He professed to be over the unpleasantness of the war years and what came after. "It was a dreadful time for me altogether. I'd become very unpopular with the press because I'd been very belligerent politically, which I'm not anymore. . . . I've wondered since whether I would have done it if I hadn't just made an anti-Nazi film with *The Great Dictator*. Or perhaps I was hypnotized by a live audience.

"I was accused of being Jewish when *The Great Dictator* came out, but you don't have to be Jewish to be anti-Hitler. And when *Verdoux* opened, the *Daily News* said, 'Charlie Chaplin slings Communism at us.' I've never read Karl Marx in my life! I've never been what people wanted me to be. It was the time of the McCarthy witch hunts; the man was an opportunist and a complete scoundrel."

He might have put portions of his past behind him, but he never made an equivalent claim for his childhood. He still considered himself to have been irrevocably damaged.

The idea that a man who clung so ferociously to his creative and emotional independence could ever have given fealty to a system in which power rested with the State was now justifiably seen as intrinsically absurd—not just by Chaplin but by the world. "The unpleasant things have faded," he told Alden Whitman of *The New York Times*. "They don't mean much now."

"He didn't miss anything about America, not really," said his son Sydney. "When he came back here in 1972 it was because they were re-releasing his pictures. It was purely financial. For one thing, he didn't care about the Academy Award. He didn't believe in all that stuff. It didn't have anything to do with the work, and work was his pleasure. The doing of it. Oona would say, 'Charlie, we can't keep the kids in the house all the time.' And he'd sigh and say, 'All right, let's go on a vacation,' but it was very hard for him to relax."

Coming back to America was a nerve-racking experience. His initial response to the offer of an honorary Academy Award was Absolutely Not. Where had all those people at the Academy been twenty years before when he was being slagged from pillar to post? Oona and Eric James spent a lot of time persuading him to go, and he began to weaken. Still, he remained concerned. What if someone took a shot at him? Worse, what if people booed?

In the last week in March, he and his party flew to Bermuda where he rested up for what was sure to be an exhausting week. On Monday, April 3, Chaplin walked slowly down the steps of an airplane to return to New York and America for the first time in twenty years. At the bottom of the ramp he shook hands with David Rockefeller and with the president of the Film Society of Lincoln Center. "Delighted, delighted," he said. He walked slowly past barricades that held back several hundred spectators and blew kisses on his way to the Plaza Hotel, where he was greeted by eight bottles of Dom Pérignon in his fourteenth-floor corner suite.

The next night, Chaplin attended a showing at Lincoln Center of newly scored prints of *The Kid* and *The Idle Class*, and accepted the plaudits of an audience that included Leopold Stokowski, Ethel Kennedy, Norman Mailer, and Paulette Goddard. He was also awarded the Handel Medallion, New York's highest cultural award.

After four days in New York, Chaplin and Oona flew to Los Angeles, where they were welcomed at the airport by Daniel Taradash, the president of the Academy of Motion Picture Arts and Sciences, and Howard W. Koch, the producer of the broadcast. As Koch remembered it, Chaplin came down the steps from the plane and greeted the welcoming party by saying, "It's so good to be back in New York." Taradash found that Chaplin was beginning to descend into old age. He would be "apt to go in and out of focus mentally, now lucid and charming, now hazy and remote."

The date of the Award ceremony was April 10, 1972, and out of respect the Academy decided that no Honorary Oscars would be awarded other than Chaplin's. They saved the moment for the conclusion of the show. "He came on just like an old man, but the audience went crazy," said Koch. "It was a smash, the whole place stood up. It's one of those great moments."

The ovation went on for minutes, and after it finally died down, an obviously moved Chaplin accepted the award: "To Charles Chaplin, for the incalculable effect he has had in making motion pictures the art form of this century." Chaplin proved he still had the showman's knack of getting a laugh when he put on a derby hat and did his old trick of flicking it in the air with his fingers—the same gag that had entranced the natives in Bali forty years before. The hat fell to the ground and Chaplin gave a perfect little philosophical shrug—sometimes the magic works, sometimes it doesn't.

When the ceremony was over, he was happy, almost jubilant. At long last, Hollywood and Charlie Chaplin had made their peace with each other.

"I'm tired, exhausted," he complained. But there were compensations. "Thought I was going to blubber like a big kid. I cannot cope with emotions anymore. It's very hard to respond to affection. I can respond to antagonism, but love and affection . . . the only thing I wish is that my children were here. Because they look on me as somebody rather commonplace and they could see what an important guy I am.

"You're not a hero to your own children. There's always a little restraint, a reserve they feel—which is rather sad. I'm an austere person; I'm not . . . not especially friendly. I think that's been due to the fact that all my life I've been on the defensive—with the exception of politics. I gave that up long ago. I don't think it matters how the world progresses.

"The world seems like a dream to me now. I don't relate to anything [in] it. . . . In America I wanted to get the feeling of yesterday. But it keeps slipping away from you . . . time progresses in spite of everything. In spite of oneself. It's mystic: to have lived before, yet you are not the same person. But you *were* the same person."

CHAPLIN WAS AWARE of what old age was doing to him, and it didn't bother him overmuch. As he had explained to a woman at a dinner party some months before, "My dear, I've had a series of small strokes and I don't remember a single thing about anything." In a burst of pragmatism, he told Oona, "Don't go all mushy on me. I'm 83, and I refuse to be swept into grief at time's passing. It won't do me a bit of good."

Walter and Carol Matthau threw a garden party for Chaplin on their lawn in Pacific Palisades. Among the attendees were Cary Grant, Danny Kaye, Oscar Levant, Rosalind Russell, Groucho Marx, and George Burns. The Matthaus had forgotten to invite Martha Raye, but that didn't faze her; she phoned and asked to be invited and of course she was. She arrived in a big limousine and Chaplin not only recognized her immediately, he was delighted to see his Maggie once again. Chaplin was fully present, recognizing nearly everybody.

Charles Matthau was there as well, taking it all in, talking to Groucho Marx among others. "Charlie was pretty frail physically, but I thought he was totally there mentally. There was only one guest he didn't recognize: Jackie Coogan. And Jackie teased him about it for the rest of the party."

William Schallert, one of the stalwarts from the Circle Theatre period, was there too. "Some of the old spark was gone, but he had a very sweet quality about him, and I had never thought of him as a sweet man—he had always been pretty feisty and prickly."

Chaplin's enemies were now fewer in number, but they were still

around. The *Los Angeles Times* ran an article with the headline
"They Haven't Given Up—Letter Writers Assail Chaplin." Hundreds
of letters had been sent to the paper protesting Chaplin's triumphant
return. Most of the letters seemed to be written by the elderly. The
quoted letters called Chaplin, among other things, a "traitor," "Comrade Charlie," and "an insane Revolutionary Zionist."

To mark Chaplin's return to Hollywood, a sidewalk brass star
bearing his name was finally installed on Hollywood Boulevard,
but it had already been defaced at some point before the unveiling.
The Chamber of Commerce had to hire a twenty-four-hour armed
guard to protect it. The Chamber also received derogatory letters
about Chaplin, one of which complained that he was friends with
the North Vietnamese.

Driving through Los Angeles, Chaplin was stunned by the spreading of the city in the twenty years since he had last seen it. "It's nothing but banks, banks, banks," he said. Chaplin was driven past his
old studio, but he didn't want to go in. He had been supremely happy
there, and now there were too many memories. It was all so long ago.

James McGranery was unable to protest the public, social, and
artistic resurgence of Charlie Chaplin. He had died of a heart attack
in December 1962 in Palm Beach, just a few months after giving deep
background interviews justifying Chaplin's banishment. Hedda Hopper, Chaplin's primary antagonist in Hollywood, had died in 1966.
A month after Chaplin's return to America, J. Edgar Hoover died.

Time had defeated Chaplin's enemies.

Geraldine Chaplin believed that the Oscar ceremony, and the attendant publicity "gave him a lot of extra years. He bounced back
from the *Countess from Hong Kong* disaster and received recognition. This is a man who, his whole life, even though he might not
have liked it at that time, was the most loved man in the whole
world. The most beloved. The mobs of fans were unprecedented.
Then suddenly to lose all that. You know, life in Switzerland . . . well
you could call it peaceful, I suppose, but you could also call it boring!

"Going to America and receiving that huge standing ovation suddenly brought everything back. Those people loved him again."

*   *   *

OONA CHAPLIN HAD come to believe that there were parallels between the lives of her husband and her father. Her father's life had effectively ended when his failing health made it impossible for him to continue writing, so she was determined that her husband be encouraged to work at projects that he was physically able to do.

Back in Switzerland, Chaplin embarked on the scoring of the other films he owned—*A Woman of Paris*, a number of shorts, and a score for the project Chaplin called *The Freak*.

He had been playing around with *The Freak* since 1969 as a vehicle for his daughter Victoria. It was a fable on his basic theme of society's inability to accept outsiders: in this case, a girl born with wings. She is first caged by society, then destroyed by her need to escape.

Chaplin wrote a complete script for the film, and a fair amount of preproduction took place—storyboards, music, and so forth. But in the wake of *A Countess from Hong Kong*, there weren't any studios interested in financing a new Chaplin movie, let alone one that was so far outside his métier. Chaplin vowed to finance it himself. Victoria Chaplin remembered that her mother was afraid of the picture—she knew that the special effects would be far too complex for her perennially impatient husband. "I don't want him to do it," she told her daughter. "If he goes through the ordeal, it will kill him. . . . I can have him alive, or have him die making the film."

Finally, Oona put a stop to it. "There is no film," she told Jerry Epstein. "I have to make the decision. He'll never survive this picture. If *The Freak* was an easy film I would let it go ahead. . . . If it was . . . a simple comedy, I wouldn't object. But this picture would kill him."

Victoria took advantage of her mother's decision by leaving the Manoir and marrying her boyfriend, with whom she founded the highly regarded *Le Cirque Imaginaire*. Chaplin was furious about both the film and his daughter, but it's impossible to disagree with Oona's decision—a younger Chaplin might have been able to pull the picture off, but he was eighty-three, and there was the depressing evidence of his last two pictures.

"He could have made it, but only with great difficulty," said Jerry Epstein. "He was getting much older, and he was so impatient on the set. His attitude was simple: nothing matters but the actor. He was impatient with the lighting, and the special effects would have made him very frustrated."

Chaplin was not so weak that he couldn't argue. In the case of Eric James, it was about music.

"There was no way you could win," said James in retrospect, "so it was far better to admit defeat and assert your own idea as if it came from him." James developed a habit of silently counting to ten in order to maintain his temper. James was more diplomatic than he had been at the beginning of their partnership, when he had told Chaplin his credit should read, "Music composed by Eric James, in spite of Charlie Chaplin."

James had a passive-aggressive streak. He insisted on a tea break in the afternoon. After nearly forty years in America, Chaplin had fallen out of the habit and would sit there nervously checking his watch.

Despite the revolving door of collaborators, Chaplin's music always sounded like Chaplin's music—an elegant, romantic counterpoint to the action on the screen, with a knack for melody that resulted in some hit songs: "Smile" from *Modern Times*, "Eternally" from *Limelight*, and "This Is My Song" from *A Countess from Hong Kong*. Chaplin's musical intentions derived from his days with the Fred Karno company—no matter how rough the hurly-burly on stage, the music Karno insisted on was not competitive but caressing—"wistful, gentlemen, wistful," Karno would tell the musicians as well as the actors.

James had brought Lambert Williamson into the fold to orchestrate and conduct the score for *A Countess from Hong Kong*. Williamson did a good job, but he was an alcoholic, which Chaplin would not tolerate. Williamson's problem became obvious one night at the Manoir, after which Chaplin took James aside and told him, "Don't bring this man here again." Despite the commercial and critical failure of *A Countess from Hong Kong*, Petula Clark's recording of "This Is My Song" made so much money that it paid for the score for *The Circus*. "Eric, we're off the hook," Chaplin rhapsodized.

*　*　*

CHAPLIN'S MEMORY OF his career was now spotty, but he still remembered his childhood vividly. Francis Wyndham, who worked with him on *My Life in Pictures*, remembered that "He would wander and sort of couldn't remember. We brought up batches of photographs from the basement for him to go through, and we tried to get him to make comments. There were a great many photographs of Paulette Goddard, and he'd point and say, 'Who's that girl? I never saw her.' And Oona and I got the giggles. It was nice she could laugh. . . . He was very sweet and he wanted to please one by remembering, but then he would sort of forget."

Beyond the vicissitudes of age, the underlying problem was that the only film Chaplin ever really wanted to talk about was the next one, and there wasn't going to be a next one.

With all the renown, with all the money, there was still a terrible vulnerability. Geraldine Chaplin remembered coming to the Manoir with her partner at the time, the director Carlos Saura. At dinner, Saura "began to go on and on about Keaton—how wonderful he thought he was—what a great filmmaker. My father got smaller and smaller in his chair. He was so hurt, it looked as if someone had stabbed him. He became very quiet, didn't say a word through the rest of dinner. Afterwards, we're sitting by the fire and talking about other things now. My father was looking at the fire, still not talking. Then he looked at Carlos in the eyes and said, 'But I was an artist. . . . And I gave him work.' He'd been thinking about it all during dinner."

THE CONVENTIONAL NARRATIVE of the 1950s was that Chaplin had left America, but in truth it was America that had left him. The wounds ran deep. The reentry permit business had cost him no end of trauma. Most importantly, leaving America had cost him his psychological and emotional home, which in turn robbed him of his creative momentum. In that sense, his enemies had won.

In 1975, three years after the return to America, Chaplin was finally knighted. There had been conversations about it as early as 1956, but England had backed off for fear of angering America. The

Foreign Office opposed a knighthood for Chaplin as late as 1969. As with the Oscar, Chaplin's initial reaction was resistance. "How would it look for the Tramp to be called Sir Charlie?" he groused. A call was placed to Switzerland from Prime Minister Harold Wilson's office, and Chaplin was told that the prime minister and everyone else in the cabinet would be disappointed if he refused. The next day he accepted his knighthood.

He was in a wheelchair by the time of the investiture. Queen Elizabeth tapped him on the shoulders with her sword and said, "Arise, Sir Charles Chaplin, Knight Commander of the British Empire." Rising wasn't going to happen, but he was able to stand outside Buckingham Palace and tell reporters, "I feel wonderful. I was most impressed with the ceremony. And now, I am going to get drunk." As he left, he assured the reporters that "I'll make another film. I'm still able to work."

BY FAR THE most successful of the 1970s reissues were the films with social and political relevance: *Modern Times* and *The Great Dictator* each returned about $750,000 in domestic rentals, while *City Lights* earned $443,000. (By way of comparison, a contemporaneous reissue of Disney's *Lady and the Tramp* earned $535,000 in America.) In France, the pattern was the same—*The Great Dictator* earned $608,000, compared to Hitchcock's first-run *Frenzy*, which earned $832,000.

More than fifty years later, the pattern holds true. In the twenty-first century, worldwide receipts from both theatrical and nontheatrical venues make *The Great Dictator* the most commercially popular of the Chaplin films, with *Modern Times* coming in second. The rest of the top five are *The Kid, The Gold Rush*, and *City Lights*.

Of the features, *City Lights* is undoubtedly the finest, a comprehensive work of devastating art—the definitive statement about the Tramp. But it is *The Great Dictator* and, especially, *Modern Times* that audiences respond to most strongly. In their time, critics complained that Chaplin was denaturing the beloved Tramp by injecting him into contemporary political reality, salted with complaints about a filmmaking style that had not appreciably changed since 1925.

But removed from the period criticism, Chaplin's style looks time-less and remarkably effective, and his sense of the swirling destruc-tion wrought by social patterns remains eternally prophetic. In the case of *The Great Dictator*, the unending struggle against authori-tarian impulses; in the case of *Modern Times*, a prescient sense of the assaultive jostling of the twenty-first century that is so much like the world when the film was made only more so: war, riots, regimenta-tion, brutality, drugs, and rigid bureaucracies.

Sydney Chaplin could never quite understand his father's inces-sant desire for work that only grew more difficult as he aged. "The most insecure man I ever met in my life was my father. I used to feel sometimes like picking him up—I was a lot bigger than him—in my arms and say, 'Pa, you made it! You did it! You got rich, you got famous, you did everything. Marvelous wife and kids. You made it!'

"But also, if he felt that way about himself he never would have made the pictures, either."

The last creative work Charlie Chaplin did was the musical score for his 1923 film *A Woman of Paris*. When Eric James arrived at the Manoir to work on the project, Chaplin told him, "Eric, I haven't got an idea in my head for this picture." James said he would start outlining some melodies and Chaplin could either nod or shake his head. "Eric, you seem to forget I'm getting old and I find I can't keep up with you! You think too fast for me!"

It was around this time that Chaplin awoke early one morning. He had been talking in his sleep, dreaming about his days in the studio in Hollywood, busy but inwardly serene under the warmth of the lights. ". . . And they are *beautiful*," he said, "and I'll never make them again."

Shortly after the score for *A Woman of Paris* was completed, James was back at the Manoir to work on an LP anthology of Chap-lin music. In the interim Chaplin had suffered another stroke and was mostly silent. When he heard James working with some record-ings, Chaplin gestured to Oona that he wanted to watch. As James placed the tone arm on a record, the needle slipped and an ugly screech erupted through the speakers.

"*Eric, don't fuck it about!*" Chaplin snapped. James and Oona both broke up at the only sentence Chaplin had uttered in days. Chaplin laughed as well, then once again fell silent.

In November 1977, Charlie Chaplin saw his last movie: Stanley Kubrick's *Barry Lyndon*. He sat there for hours, murmuring "Beautiful . . . beautiful."

Although Jerry Epstein relayed this anecdote, it seemed less than believable. What could three hours of gorgeously composed shots punctuating a dramatically placid costume film mean to an elderly stroke-ridden genius? But the proof lies in a telegram in the Kubrick archive: "CONGRATULATIONS AND THANK YOU FOR BARRY LYNDON STOP WE WERE ALL VERY MOVED BY YOUR BEAUTIFUL FILM AND HATED TO SEND IT BACK BEST WISHES CHARLIE OONA CHAPLIN."

CHARLIE CHAPLIN DIED at 4 a.m. on Christmas Day 1977. It made a certain bleak sense. As Oona told her children, "He always hated Christmas"—the day his only present at the workhouse was an orange.

Among the letters of condolence Oona received was one from Gloria Romanoff, the widow of the restaurateur Mike Romanoff. "One wonders if others can fully understand the depth of emotion involved in building a life with a unique man who is essentially a survivor against tremendous odds," she wrote. "Their love is a rare gift, encompassing as it does all the trust, caring and devotion most other men share with a multitude of women in their lives—mother, child, mistress, etc. When you are fortunate enough to have known this kind of oneness, you are truly blessed."

Romanoff went on to share a story her husband had told her about Chaplin. It seems that Romanoff had met Chaplin in Hollywood in the late 1920s, after which he had begun his peripatetic existence "fleeing from country to country for lack of citizenship papers." In the early 1930s, Romanoff was in prison in the French town of Grasse. Upon release, he was given the standard five francs and told to leave the country within forty-eight hours.

Romanoff's first move upon release was to walk to a small café and spend his five francs on a good breakfast. On his way out of the café, the breakfast came back up. There was nothing to do but start walking in the direction of Cannes. He arrived in front of the Carlton Hotel, where he was hailed from the terrace. It was Chaplin in the midst of his 1931–1932 world tour, having drinks with some friends.

Charlie invited Romanoff to join his group. When Romanoff informed him of his situation, Chaplin insisted he stay for dinner. Chaplin then put Romanoff up for the night and the next morning sent Romanoff on his way with what his wife termed "a generous loan. Michael never forgot that kindness and some years later when he returned to Beverly Hills he was able to repay the loan, but the sense of obligation always remained."

THREE MONTHS AFTER Chaplin's death, on March 2, 1978, two thieves dug up Chaplin's oak coffin and stole it. Seventy-six days later, on May 17, police recovered the unopened coffin buried in a shallow grave in a cornfield outside the village of Villeneuve, twenty-five miles from Corsier. The two thieves had been traced by the police after a ransom demand of $600,000, which was later lowered to $250,000. The grave robbers, a Polish refugee and a Bulgarian mechanic, spent time in jail then returned to obscurity.

Charlie Chaplin was reburied in the Corsier cemetery, this time in an underground concrete vault.

Oona Chaplin lived for nearly thirteen more years. Her husband had been the absolute focus of her life since she was eighteen, and now that focus was gone. "She was utterly cosseted and cocooned by Charlie," said her friend Kathy Parrish, the wife of the director Robert Parrish. "It was like she had been in a cast all her life and suddenly the cast had been removed and she did not know how to walk."

"Oona was a very lovely lady," said Charles Matthau. "I got to spend a lot of time with her after Charlie passed away. She would come and stay with us at our house for weeks at a time. She was very sad and lonely without him. They had such a beautiful relationship against all odds—the age difference and all that.

"She tried to put on a good front. My mother would tell me how depressed Oona was. She said Oona drank a lot, but I never saw it.

She never was drunk around me or acted goofy or in a depressed manner. She was always very sweet and polite and outwardly cheerful."

When Oona boarded a flight to London, a friend noticed she opened her purse and took something out. The friend looked closely and saw that it was one of Charlie's gloves. Oona held on to it for the entire flight, as if his hand was still inside it.

Oona O'Neill Chaplin died on September 27, 1991, and was buried next to the man who had defined her life, as well as the tragicomic currents of the twentieth century.

EPILOGUE

Charlie Chaplin's troubles of the 1940s and 1950s made a certain sense.

He was practically and emotionally a nonconforming outsider from another country and another time, a man completely of his own making who held himself above conventions in politics, in society. From the beginning he engaged in social commentary on a scale that transcended categories of left and right. The Tramp's meaning was as clear to the ordinary viewer as it was to intellectuals. By both birth and social inclination Chaplin and the Tramp both set themselves resolutely against the prevailing American grain.

Strike One.

The Tramp combined primal urges for sex and food seasoned with astonishing physical grace, as well as the defiant attitude of the eternal outsider. He simultaneously projected empathy and the subtle distrust of one who knows he can't fit in. He presented middle- and upper-class society—the bulk of the audience—as violent, erratic, often cruel and full of casual corruption.

Strike Two.

As with his screen character, Chaplin refused to pay lip service to people he despised, refused to go along to get along. He had the good fortune to reach his artistic maturity at the birth of mass media, which gave him fame and wealth, but he had the misfortune to live through a time when the lance of anticommunism was used to impale behaviors and politics regarded as deviant.

Strike Three.

David Raksin understood the core issue. "Charlie was a man who was envied to a point of paranoia by people who were simply not in his league. He was also so independent that a lot of the major people who ran studios . . . couldn't have his control, because he had his own studio—if he wanted to do a hundred takes, if he wanted to stop production for that day, he would do that—he was a law unto himself, and they hated him. And they . . . used to say he was a communist, you know. He was about as left-wing as John Wayne's right foot. And he always had compassion for people in trouble, and so they were after him. They wanted to get him, and eventually they did."

Alistair Cooke characterized Chaplin as "a vague nuisance and a tiresome talking point among the noisy patriots who never felt that the government's 'Loyalty' procedures proceeded far enough. Chaplin was all the more offensive in that he could never, after endless investigating, be pinned down as a criminal. He was simply turned in—by, we should remember, the Truman administration—as a useful sacrifice to the witches who were then supposed to be riding exclusively on the broomstick of Senator Joseph McCarthy. The Chaplin expulsion was a squalid episode in a shabby period."

Chaplin's otherworldly level of courage—or obstinance—enabled him to survive a childhood that would have corrupted or destroyed most people. That same obstinance led him to take control of his screen career when it was only weeks old, to assert dominion over his films, over Hollywood, over the world audience. That same unyielding belief in his instincts led him to sleep with whom he pleased when he pleased, and to conflate political discretion with cowardice. And it was that same refusal to capitulate that ultimately insured his survival as a man and an artist.

"I never saw Charlie depressed," Jerry Epstein said. "I saw him anxious, tense, but never down. I was always amazed how, in the face of adversity, he was able to pick himself up and get on with living. For him, each new day was a day full of challenge and promise."

Charlie Chaplin's life is an object lesson in perseverance, in the intrinsic value of a devotion to work. His greatest joy was being intensely alive in the act of creation. What he had done in the past was past, and the future was indistinct. Only the now mattered. "Don't wish your life away," he'd say when Oona or Jerry Epstein were anticipating some big event. "Enjoy the moment."

Chaplin understood that by World War II, the Tramp was more or less obsolete in terms of social reality, yet that stubborn little figure who refuses to compromise his independence has survived, perhaps because Chaplin's underlying preoccupations involved a passion for the life of the world.

David Robinson points out that when the Solidarity movement flowed through Poland late in the twentieth century, filmmakers displayed a selection of stills from their films in the great square of Gdansk. "They had to choose a centerpiece for the display of still pictures . . . something that would adequately represent the resurgent, independent human spirit. The symbol they chose was Charlie Chaplin's Little Tramp."

In the twenty-first century, nothing has changed. Volodymyr Zelensky, the president of the embattled country of Ukraine invaded by Russia in 2022, quoted the final speech from *The Great Dictator* to an audience at the Cannes Film Festival. He concluded by telling them, "the world needs a new Chaplin who will prove [to] us that cinema isn't silent. We need cinema to show that each time the ending will be on the side of freedom."

But there has been only one Chaplin.

IN SOME NOTES he made for *Limelight*, Chaplin wrote dialogue for Calvero that he didn't use in the film: "When I was young, I made the audience my slave. Later, as I got older, I began to lose confidence and I became their slave." Chaplin had the satisfaction of knowing that, in this respect, he was unlike Calvero—for better or worse, he never lost his creative nerve.

"I beg no apologies for any stand that I have ever taken," he said in 1966. "I'd rather not have that explained at all. And that's one's prerogative."

In the years he lived in Switzerland, Chaplin would go to Paris "in the months with R in them"—for the oysters. And there were regular trips to London. As early as 1921, in his first return to Europe after achieving fame, he had begun his habit of returning to his old stomping grounds for what he variously called "an emotional jag" or a "Dickensian prowl" through Lambeth, Kennington, Elephant, and Castle. As an old man, unrecognizable beneath his mackintosh and trilby, he would take a bus or even the Tube in order to revisit these places, or the Soho he re-created in *Limelight*. He might stay at the Savoy, but his London was defined by Lambeth on one hand and the West End theater district on the other.

East London had been nearly destroyed by the Luftwaffe, and South London's Lambeth had suffered as well. What the Nazis started, urban renewal in the 1960s finished, but there were still fragments of his childhood to be rediscovered. The Queens Head pub, where Chaplin had danced for pennies on the cellar doors, was still there. So were the gates and iron fence around St. Mark's churchyard, which Chaplin had reproduced as the site for the blind girl's flower-selling in *City Lights*. A lifetime before, Chaplin had waited there for his few, hurried, unsatisfying meetings with Hetty Kelly.

Sometimes Jerry Epstein would drive while Chaplin told him where to turn and when. He'd always go past the Three Stags pub on Kennington Road, where he'd last seen his father alive. Then it would be the gates of the Lambeth Workhouse, where he and Syd and their mother had all been domiciled. (The Queens Head, the Three Stags, and the walls of the Workhouse are still there. So is the iron fence around St. Mark's.)

At some point he would want to see the theaters where he had played as a boy. He would usually keep up a narration about the various places they passed, but when they drove past the Workhouse, he lapsed into silence. Then he might walk to the door of 3 Pownall Terrace, where he and his brother and mother had lived in a garret Chaplin reproduced in *The Kid*. Sometimes he would want to visit the towns he had played with the Karno troupe—Wapping, Stepney, Canning Town, Hackney.

"He never tired of these trips down Memory Lane," Epstein remembered. "He seemed to need these trips into his past to replenish his spirit."

In one sense, revisiting the impoverishment of his childhood was a way of measuring how far he'd come. In another sense, he was plugging into the sense of loss that provided the foundation of his work and character.

His daughter Geraldine remembered that "he didn't want to be recognized or greeted. He wanted the melancholy of being on his own. He never, ever, forgot his origins. They'd had a warm, comfortable house, and suddenly there was nothing, and the fear of nothing never left him. He'd always say to us, 'Study, study, study, because you can have all the money in the world and lose it.'"

He would tell the story about his mother bringing home Eva Lester, the music hall colleague who had sunk into squalor, which would set Chaplin to brooding about all the legendary comedians of his youth who had ended up in penury.

"What would have happened to me," he said one day, "if I hadn't gone to America?"

He transmuted an alcoholic father, an insane mother, poverty, and isolation into utterly singular art. The foundation of his work was the pain of abandonment seasoned by compassion and kindness—the best of humanity distilled into one bedraggled figure that his assistant Dan James ranked with Proust, Picasso, and Joyce as spokesmen for a world in constant transition.

To the end of his life, Chaplin's attitude toward America was a stew of conflicting memories and impulses. He often said that he never would have achieved a success in England remotely equivalent to what he found in America because of the class barrier. Americans, he said, never ask, "Where are you from? Are you public school?" They only care about what you can do and how well you can do it.

Jerry Epstein said that underneath the flashes of anger, Chaplin never lost his underlying affection for the country where he spent most of his life. America gave him opportunity, wealth, and position. If more than a decade of impeccably targeted character assassination nudged the public into thinking Charlie Chaplin was more trouble than he was worth, he believed the ledger still came out on the positive side. America had given him the one thing more important than his work, more valuable than his money—a pearl beyond price, a prize beyond imagination.

"After all," he would say, "that's where I met Oona."

ACKNOWLEDGMENTS

The circle finally closes.

It took me a long time to write a book about Charlie Chaplin. To be precise, slightly less than sixty years. I started collecting Chaplin films when I was twelve years old. My first purchase was an 8mm Blackhawk Films print of Chaplin's two-reeler *Easy Street*. It cost me $9.95—a small amount of money to affect a life.

I had seen clips of Chaplin in various Robert Youngson compilation films, but *Easy Street* was my first exposure to him uncut, at full strength. Try as I might, I couldn't see how he did it. I slowed the film running through my Argus projector down from eighteen frames per second to half that, to see if I could catch the split second when Chaplin transitioned from one expression to another, one emotion to another. I wanted to see if I could catch him in the moment of calculation.

It was impossible. He was quicksilver, shifting instantaneously from one mood to another. As with a world-class athlete, his physicality was perfectly synchronized with his imagination—there was no barrier between intent and expression. *Easy Street* led me to decades of collecting books and other assorted ephemera about him.

Ordinary comedians rise or fall on the strength of their jokes, and, to a lesser extent, their relationship with the audience. But great comedians have a special relationship to their material. Their specific personality, their attitude toward the jokes, makes everything they do feel customized. "Your money or your life" said to Jack Benny earns a continuing roar because he spent a lifetime molding a comic character who was pathologically cheap. The same line said to any other comic doesn't get a smile—nor should it.

Chaplin's gags have resonance not because they're always brilliant in and of themselves—although I treasure the sequence with the wood stuck in a grate that he cut from *City Lights*, not to mention the feeding machine sequence in *Modern Times*—but because of his singular attitude toward a world that presents him with difficulties. His attitude is the seasoning of the joke.

The dance of the bread rolls in *The Gold Rush* is seventy-five seconds of perfection, but what makes the scene hover in the mind for decades is its emotional impact, which is only possible because of the time Chaplin has devoted to preparation—the Tramp's isolation in Alaska; the party to which nobody comes, culminating in a moment in the spotlight that exists only in his dreams. Roscoe Arbuckle actually did a version of the bread roll dance first, years before Chaplin, but he tosses it off as a quick bit, a clever throwaway. Chaplin constructs a narrative foundation that gives the gag meaning, a grounding in emotional reality. In so doing, he gave comedy a soul.

Over the decades my passion for Chaplin gradually evolved from wonderment to accreting piles of research. Kevin Brownlow and David Gill's electrifying three-hour documentary *Unknown Chaplin* revealed Chaplin's arduous working methods in granular detail. All of this eventually led to my introducing Chaplin to my students at the University of Miami.

I always wanted to write about him, but bookshelves groan under the weight of books about Charlie Chaplin, and I didn't have an approach. What could be said about him that hadn't already been said?

And then it hit me. Focus on the process by which Chaplin segued from the status of beloved icon to despised ingrate; focus on him being converted from one of America's prized immigrants to a man without a country.

Kate Guyonvarch of Association Chaplin in Paris thought it was a good idea and the Chaplin archives provided the bulk of the research material unearthed here. Special thanks goes to my cherished friend, the brilliant Neil Brand, a great composer and silent film accompanist, not to mention London historian. Neil took me on a guided tour of Chaplin's Lambeth, from the buildings that housed the Fred Karno company to the Three Stags—the pub where Chaplin last saw his father in 1901, where Neil and I felt compelled to share a few pints.

Will Coates did his usual astonishing research, coming up with material neither I nor anybody else knew existed—among many other things, Joseph Scott's autobiographical justification of his tactics in Chaplin's paternity trial.

The FBI files on Chaplin extend to over 1,900 pages filled with invariably derogatory and often blatantly incorrect information based on dubious sources and hearsay. Nevertheless, the FBI leaked volumes of biased or incorrect information to friendly reporters, who used the FBI's misinformation and added disinformation of their own—a self-perpetuating feedback loop of distortion that gave me the spine of the narrative.

My thanks go to the family members, friends, coworkers, and historians who talked about Chaplin with me over the years: Peter Bogdanovich, Geraldine Chaplin, Sydney Chaplin, Frank Coughlan, Jerry Epstein, Tippi Hedren, Norman Lloyd, Charles Matthau, David Nasaw, David Raksin, Daniel Selznick, Karl Struss, Eddie Sutherland.

Jim Lochner helped illuminate Chaplin's friendship with Hanns Eisler. James Curtis enlightened me about the political differences between Chaplin and Buster Keaton. Robert Bader, the world's foremost expert on the Marx Brothers, figured out the precise date when Chaplin and Groucho Marx visited a Salt Lake City whorehouse, with very different intentions. Tracey Goessel was incisive on medical matters, hilarious on social matters, and always great company.

Dan Kamin and Hooman Mehran were always available to clear up abstruse points about our mutual subject, as was Lisa Stein Haven, whose books on Chaplin's 1931–1932 trip around the world and Chaplin's brother Sydney were endlessly helpful. Frank Scheide provided me with Dan James's memories of his years working on *The Great Dictator*. Glenn Mitchell, author of the invaluable *The Chaplin Encyclopedia*, helped define vague chronologies. And at the

Nixon Library, special thanks to archivists Dorissa Martinez and Carla Brewer, who were both enormously helpful as well as fascinated by my topic.

I count myself lucky that Bob Bender has been my editor at Simon & Schuster for more than twenty years. He is calm, funny, always enthusiastic, wicked smart, and, unlike a certain author, never loses grasp of the narrative. His associate, Johanna Li, backs him—and me—up with grace and good humor. The third member of my irreplaceable triumvirate is Fred Chase, whose copyediting invariably saves me from multiple catastrophes.

And of course, there is Lynn Kalber. My wife was by my side during the travels, the research, the writing and the editing, making it all possible as well as fun.

My gratitude toward you all.

—*Scott Eyman*
October 2019–May 2023:
Barcelona, Ibiza, Marbella, London, New York, Los Angeles,
Aspen, West Palm Beach

SOURCE NOTES

Academy: Academy of Motion Picture Arts and Sciences
CA: Chaplin Archive
FBI Chaplin: FBI file on Charles Chaplin
HST: Harry S. Truman Presidential Library and Museum
LOC: Library of Congress
RN: Richard Nixon Foundation/Presidential Library and Museum
USC: University of Southern California
Wisconsin: University of Wisconsin, United Artists Collection

Prologue

2 *"The enclosed about Charlie Chaplin"*: RN, box 354, General Correspondence, Hopper to Nixon, undated.

2 *"I agree with you"*: Academy, Hedda Hopper Collection, Nixon to Hopper, 5-29-52.

3 *"I'd like to run"*: Academy, Hedda Hopper Collection, April 1947.

3 *"The film . . . arouses"*: USC, Lion Feuchtwanger papers, box C1-B, folder 19, 8-8-52.

4 *Oona thought he was being silly*: Epstein, p. 10.

5 *That rebuilding was necessary*: Robinson, *The World of Limelight*, p. 217.

5 *"I like this kind of day"*: Ross, p. 21.

5 *"You know, in 1910"*: Ross, p. 32.

6 *"I thought to myself"*: Hayes, ed., p. 128.

7   *Crocker left the table:* Academy, Harry Crocker Collection, Charlie Chaplin, Ch. XVI, p. 9.

7   *"The hearing will determine":* LOC, James McGranery papers, press release, 9-19-52.

7   *"morals, health or insanity":* Robinson, *Footlights,* p. 205.

7   *"Every nerve in me tensed":* Chaplin, *My Autobiography,* p. 465.

8   *"Through the proper procedure":* Academy, Harry Crocker Collection, Charlie Chaplin, Ch. XIV, p. 10.

8   *"It might prejudice our case":* Academy, Harry Crocker collection, Charlie Chaplin, chapter XVI, p. 12.

8   *"had scorned citizenship":* Maland, p. 300.

8   *"An immigrant arrives":* CA, Chaplin undated notes, but 1952.

10   *"There is no way of knowing":* Bosley Crowther, "Under Suspicion," *New York Times,* 9-20-52.

10   *"Judge him in the only way":* Anthony Slide, "The American Press & Public vs. Charles Spencer Chaplin," *Cineaste,* undated.

10   *"what most Americans resented":* Ed Sullivan column, New York *Daily News,* 9-29-52.

11   *"Those who have followed him":* New York Times, 9-24-52

11   *the government had no grounds:* Flom, p. 227.

12   *"They were desperately trying":* Lita Grey Chaplin and Vance, p. 128.

12   *"take a run over":* CA, Chaplin to Chaplin, 4-22-52.

13   *"With his name and ability":* CA, Chaplin to Chaplin, 5-2-52.

13   *"I do not want to create":* Robinson, *The World of Limelight,* p. 206.

14   *The report revealed:* Timothy Lyons, "The United States vs. Charlie Chaplin," *American Film,* 9-84, p. 29.

15   *"I don't want the old rugged":* FBI, Ladd to Hoover, 8-6-47.

15   *"determine whether or not":* FBI, Special Agent Los Angeles to Hoover, 9-3-48.

Part One

19   "Chaplin was Chaplin": Powell, *A Life in Movies,* p. 172.

Chapter 1

21   *"Will arrive ten o clock":* Chaplin, *My Autobiography,* pp. 72–73.

22   *Under her stage name Lily Harley:* Anthony, p. 35.

23   *"The original and refined":* Mitchell, p. 46.

23   *All of those houses were destroyed:* Mitchell, p. 26.

24   *She and her boys were sharing a house with her mother:* Anthony, p. 39.

24   *Eighteen ninety-three also saw Mary Ann Hill:* "Order for Reception of a Pauper Lunatic," February 1893, Paumier and Robinson.

24   *From 1895 to 1898:* Weissman, p. 57.

25 *"The treatment took weeks and seemed like an eternity"*: Chaplin, *My Auto-biography*, p. 33.

25 *The abbreviation "syph"*: Anthony, p. 36.

25 *"Has been very strange in manner"*: Weissman, pp. 49–50.

26 *"Hannah had tertiary neurosyphilis"*: Goessel to SE.

26 *"a mignonne . . . with fair complexion"*: Anthony, p. 32.

26 *"riding with Mother"*: Chaplin, *My Autobiography*, p. 6.

27 *"I didn't feel the hurt so much"*: Richard Meryman interview with Chaplin, 1966, author's collection.

28 *defined "high-risk"*: Weissman, Ch. 4.

28 *"like a dream"*: Chaplin, *My Life in Pictures*, p. 40.

29 *"If Sydney had not returned"*: Weissman, p. 108.

29 *"a lunatic and a proper person to be taken charge of"*: Stein, p. 26.

29 *"For one reason, I could not spell"*: Chaplin, *My Autobiography*, p. 82.

30 *"Fred Karno mass-produced comedy"*: Anthony, p. 189.

30 *Karno was supervising*: Anthony, p. 195.

30 *"Syd arrived, accompanied by a young lad"*: Weissman, p. 145.

31 *"He always showed up"*: Mitchell, p. 168.

31 *"Fred Karno didn't teach Charlie"*: Weissman, p. 169.

31 *"I would go to the saloons"*: Chaplin, *My Autobiography*, p. 82.

31 *"To some of the company"*: McCabe, p. 47.

31 *"People through the years"*: McCabe, pp. 41, 47.

32 *"All of the pieces we did"*: Anthony, p. 196.

32 *"As I walked along Broadway"*: Chaplin, *My Autobiography*, p. 126.

32 *"Such cities as Cleveland"*: Chaplin, *My Autobiography*, p. 133.

32 *"Sometimes we won the affection"*: Chaplin, *My Autobiography*, p. 133.

33 *"We were in Salt Lake City"*: Marx to Anobile, 4-4-73. Tape courtesy of Robert Bader.

33 *His last engagement with the Karno company*: Marriot, p. 243.

34 *" 'Oh.' Sid I can see you!!"*: CA, C. Chaplin to Syd Chaplin, undated, but 1913.

34 *Interestingly, there is another surviving draft*: Paumier and Robinson, p. 69.

Chapter 2

35 *"The average actor"*: Weissman, p. 251.

35 *"this little modest actor"*: Eastman, p. 208.

36 *"I didn't have to read books"*: Chaplin, *My Autobiography*, p. 227.

36 *Dave Kehr noted*: Kehr, "Chaplin's World, and Ours," *Chicago Tribune*, 4-2-89.

36 *"You've always had all you wanted to eat"*: Academy, Harry Crocker Collection, Charlie Chaplin, Ch. I, pp. 11–12.

37   *"[The Tramp isn't] a character"*: Academy, Harry Crocker Collection, Charlie Chaplin, Ch. VI, p. 9.

37   *"Take it, Sydney"*: Stein, p. 69.

39   *"Have you any suggestions"*: Stein, p. 70.

39   *"I need you here to help me"*: Stein, p. 70.

39   *"Second thoughts"*: Stein, p. 79.

40   *"a little crazy"*: Eastman, p. 221.

40   *"My, you must be terribly fatigued"*: Academy, Harry Crocker Collection, Charlie Chaplin, Ch. XI, p. 39.

40   *"No, no! That's not shit-brown!"*: Lynn, p. 322.

41   *"Those poor little fish"*: Benedict Nightingale, "The Melancholy That Forged a Comic Genius," *New York Times*, 3-22-92.

41   *"cholecystitis"*: Vance, p. 195.

41   *"I have taken cocaine"*: Academy, Harry Crocker Collection, Charlie Chaplin, Ch. V, p. 10.

41   *They met in in the fall of 1908*: Anthony, p. 187.

42   *"The question of 'How is Hetty?' burned in the back of my brain"*: Academy, Harry Crocker Collection, Charlie Chaplin, Ch. VIII, p. 3.

42   *"It was nothing"*: Eastman, p. 242.

43   *"Well Honey Boy"*: CA, Purviance to Chaplin, undated. The Chaplin Archive has dated it as 1916.

43   *"March 1st 1915"*: CA, Chaplin to Purviance, 3-1-15.

44   *in his memoir*: Chaplin, *My Autobiography*, p. 221.

46   *"solicited, urged and demanded"*: Lita Grey Chaplin and Vance, p. 127.

46   *The divorce cost Chaplin $950,000*: Mitchell, p. 124.

46   *"I loved all the women in my life"*: Lita Grey Chaplin and Vance, p. xx.

46   *"Nothing. Not a single word."* Lita Grey Chaplin and Vance, p. xi.

48   *Her contract was for one year*: Hale, p. xx.

48   *"taxable stocks and bonds"*: New York Times, 7-8-32.

49   *The tour raised several million dollars*: Warren, p. 142.

49   *"I'd have gone to jail"*: Academy, Harry Crocker Collection, Charlie Chaplin, Ch. VIII, p. 11.

Chapter 3

52   *"You have what I consider"*: Warren, p. 153.

52   *"Charlie liked radical ideas"*: Eastman, p. 215.

52   *On the other hand*: Eastman, p. 215.

52   *"He is anxious about money"*: Academy, Harry Crocker Collection, Charlie Chaplin, Ch. XII, p. 22.

52   *"He impressed me"*: Eastman, p. 213.

53   *"Any perfectly free"*: Eastman, p. 214.

53 *"We . . . were as intimate"*: Warren, p. 171.

53 *"Charlie speaks of going away"*: Lynn, p. 233.

54 *After another letter*: Warren, p. 182.

54 *"Our friendship"*: Eastman, p. 216.

54 *When she got to New York*: Warren, p. 197.

54 *"We both admired her extravagantly"*: Lynn, p. 237.

54 *"The fact that we had both"*: Warren, p. 224.

55 *Eastman believed that she meant more to Chaplin*: Lynn, p. 237.

55 *"Chaplin never embraced radicalism"*: Wagner, p. 93.

56 *"Like Dickens, he came from the dregs of London"*: Jim Tully, "The King of Laughter," *Liberty*, June 1937.

57 *"It's easy to judge"*: Hayes, ed., p. 81.

57 *"gladly volunteered any and all information"*: Sbardellati, p. 18.

58 *"We are against any kind of censorship"*: FBI Chaplin, 8-15-22.

58 *"I think the party mentioned"*: FBI Chaplin, Hays to Burns, 9-6-22.

58 *"the name of the donor"*: FBI Chaplin, 1-10-23.

59 *"The most advanced revolutionist"*: Academy, Harry Crocker Collection, Charlie Chaplin, ch. VII, p. 22.

59 *"an uproarious time"*: Upton Sinclair, "The Chaplin Story—Gags to Riches," *Los Angeles Times*, 10-11-64.

60 *"the most interesting man"*: Eisenstein, p. 331.

60 *"Charlie and Pola Negri"*: Eisenstein, p. 333.

60 *"afraid of solitude"*: Eisenstein, p. 691.

60 *"For my friend Sergei Eisenstein"*: Eisenstein, p. 692.

61 *he refused to join the Hollywood Anti-Nazi League*: Maland, p. 162.

61 *"My next picture"*: Duncan, ed., p. 344.

61 *"I spent two years as a child"*: Haven, p. 48.

62 *"In the last few days"*: Haven, p. 206.

63 *"was just getting ready to hibernate"*: Haven, p. 176.

63 *ritual flagellation among young men*: Chaplin, *My Autobiography*, p. 399.

64 *"like landed aristocrats"*: Chaplin, *My Autobiography*, p. 398.

64 *"an original mind"*: Scheide and Mehran, eds., *Chaplin: The Dictator and The Tramp*, p. 62.

64 *"was not in the same league"*: Scheide and Mehran, eds., *Chaplin: The Dictator and The Tramp*, p. 64.

64 *"I wonder if they will laugh"*: Scheide and Mehran, eds., *Chaplin: The Dictator and The Tramp*, p. 63.

64 *"Natives worked four months"*: Chaplin, *My Autobiography*, p. 401.

64 *"He was dancing,"*: Al Hirschfeld, "A Man with Both Feet in the Clouds," *New York Times*, 7-26-42.

65 *"The future of Charlie Chaplin"*: Kamin, *The Comedy of Charlie Chaplin*, p. 137.

66   *"I think every man"*: Haven, p. 62.

66   *"Religion—organized religion"*: Haven, p. 215.

66   *"Do you know"*: Haven, p. 41.

67   *"Patriotism is the greatest insanity"*: Robinson, *Charlie Chaplin: 100 Years*, p. 23.

67   *he was paid $50,000*: CA, contract with *Woman's Home Companion*, 3-25-31.

67   *"Expect news from Mussolini"*: Haven, p. 126.

68   *"As I journey from Seattle"*: Haven, p. 144.

68   *"each nation to be given"*: Delage, p. 40.

68   *"This is the nucleus"*: Delage, p. 46.

68   *"I saw food rotting"*: Haven, p. 18.

69   *"Don't you want us"*: Duncan, ed., p. 341.

Chapter 4

71   *"Charlie has a story milling around"*: CA, Reeves to Syd Chaplin, 3-14-33.

71   *"I was shocked at the utter bewilderment"*: "Questions and Answer Concerning Mr. Chaplin," *New York Herald Tribune*, 2-7-36.

72   *"A factory whistle blows"*: Delage, p. 48.

72   *"The only two live spirits"*: CA, *Modern Times* Story Notes, undated.

73   *"the natural man"*: Kamin, *Charlie Chaplin's One-Man Show*, p. 114.

73   *"I am so glad to hear you are making rapid progress"*: CA, Syd Chaplin to CC, 11-29-34.

73   *"Don't sit in that clam chowder!"*: Delage, p. 108.

74   *Chaplin made over two hundred takes*: Duncan, ed., p. 358.

75   *"He felt"*: "The Music of Charles Chaplin," BBC Radio 2, 4-13-97.

75   *"If I were to take out citizenship papers"*: Karl Kitchen, "Chaplin Has Itch and He Scratches," Cleveland *Plain Dealer*, March 1935.

77   *"I loved the picture at once"*: Newsom, ed., p. 161.

77   *"There is a special kind of genius*: Newsom, ed., p. 162.

78   *"Sometimes we would use his tune"*: Newsom, ed., pp. 162–63.

78   *"I want a curry/ a ricy, spicy curry"*: Ransom, p. 165.

79   *"I'd stalk out of the rooms"*: Brownlow, p. 116.

79   *"What we need here is one of those Puccini melodies"*: Newsom, ed., p. 164.

80   *"We had the very great pleasure"*: Delage, p. 188.

80   *"It's now in the lap of the gods"*: "Questions and Answers Concerning Mr. Chaplin," *New York Herald Tribune*, 2-7-36.

81   *"Charlie is a brave and wistful Don Quixote"*: *Liberty*, 3-21-36, p. 28.

81   *The shortfall*: CA, Reeves to Chaplin, 12-18-36.

81   *Alf Reeves estimated*: Undated clipping, Hubbard Keavy, "Modern Times Still Earns $3,000 Per Week for Chaplin; Profits Run to $3,000,000."

81 *Chaplin's stock portfolio*: CA, Reeves to Chaplin, 12-18-36.

83 *"As you will have seen by the newspapers"*: CA, Reeves to Chaplin, 12-18-36.

83 *"All boats should be called* Panacea*"*: Comte, p. 174.

84 *"Well Charlie I saw your new picture"*: CA, Syd Chaplin to CC, 6-4-36.

86 *In July 1930, British International*: Haven, p. 166.

86 *"Syd was talented"*: Projections #2, 1993, p. 121.

86 *"I will always maintain my innocence"*: Haven, p. 167.

86 *BIP sued Sydney*: Haven, p. 174.

87 *"I read lots of articles in the press"*: CA, Syd Chaplin to CC, 12-10-36.

Chapter 5

89 *"[Chaplin] treated me as an equal"*: Bonnie McCourt and David Totheroh, "Getting Acquainted with 'Dinky Dean,'" *Limelight*, Winter 1997.

90 *"That's one of the worst traits"*: Konrad Bercovici, "Making a Movie with Charlie Chaplin," *McCall's*, March 1924.

90 *"The sets were tatty"*: Bessy, p. 414.

91 *"It's just a small studio"*: Bessy, p. 414.

91 *"This . . . room had peeling wallpaper"*: Brownlow, p. 156.

92 *"I don't think I'll ever wear my tramp costume"*: Bessy, p. 417.

93 *"I like to think I would have been arrested anywhere"*: Comte, p. 113.

93 *"Charlie, the genius"*: Hale manuscript, p. 163, author's collection

93 *"I'd never exchange"*: Hale manuscript, p. 151, author's collection.

Part Two

95 Clarence Brown's comment was made to SE.

Chapter 6

97 *"They go in for being crazy"*: Schickel, ed., p. 217.

97 *"Politically, I don't like"*: Transcript of Skelton/Fowler interviews, 4-24-51, author's collection.

98 *"Each is a distorting mirror"*: Robinson, *Charlie Chaplin: 100 Years*, p. 24.

98 *"It was as though"*: Michael Ventura, *LA Weekly*, 2-26-82, 3-4-82.

99 *as Dan Kamin points out*: Kamin, p. 125.

99 *"the son of Eastern European Jews"*: Duncan, ed., p. 383.

99 *"This little Jewish tumbler"*: Scheide and Mehran, eds., p. 5.

99 *"the creator and leader"*: Doherty, pp. 28–29.

100 *"It cannot be denied"*: Louvish, pp. 266–67.

101 *On January 27*: CA, Projection Log Book, 1939, p. 3.

102 *"Oh you bastard, you son of a bitch"*: Vance, p. 240.

102 *"Naturally a man in his position"*: Richard Meryman interview, 1966.

102 *"That is wrong"*: Hayes, ed., p. 92.

102 *"We have had some personal conversation"*: Duncan, ed., pp. 401–2.

103 *"There [is] no reason for our ever becoming"*: Beauchamp, p. 370.

104 *"At Yale, I had taken"*: Allen Eyles and John Gillett, "Donald Ogden Stewart: Writing for the Movies," *Focus on Film #5*, November-December 1970.

104 *"May I express"*: Blauvelt, p. 13.

104 *"The particular atmosphere"*: Scheide and Mehran, eds., *Chaplin: The Dictator and The Tramp*, p. 92.

105 *"the persecution of the Jews"*: Blauvelt, p. 21.

105 *"My dear Mr. Breen"*: Academy, Production Code Administration file, *The Great Dictator*, Gyssling to Breen, 10-31-38.

106 *"Regardless of how much we deplore"*: Welky, p. 228.

106 *"I was determined to ridicule"*: Chaplin, *My Autobiography*, p. 426.

106 *"During our conversation the President"*: USC, Jack Warner Collection, box 58, folder 5, Warner to Chaplin, 3-23-39.

106 *"Look, Charlie"*: Duncan, ed., p. 402.

108 *"Needless to say"*: Haven, p. 205.

108 *Sydney had done a similar scene*: Vance, p. 239.

109 *Jack Oakie was also on the ship*: Oakie, p. 71.

109 *"When I arrived"*: Haven, p. 210.

110 *"Oh, tell them to leave us alone"*: Haven, p. 208.

110 *"All right, comedian"*: Oakie, p. 75.

110 *"What's a makeup man?"*: Oakie, p. 77.

112 *Big Bertha, the huge cannon*: Comte, p. 235.

112 *"Charlie would get there"*: Struss to SE.

113 *"First picture in which the story"*: Delage, p. 1.

114 *"The Final Speech, 5 June 1940"*: Delage, p. 108.

114 *"With the condition of the world"*: Duncan, ed., p. 418.

115 *"A survey [Hopper] has made in Hollywood"*: RN, General Correspondence, Hedda Hopper folder 1956–58. Note dated 9-5-56.

115 *"He picked them up one by one"*: Academy, Harry Crocker Collection, Charlie Chaplin, Ch. XI, p. 23.

117 *On September 4, 1940*: Bessy, p. 405.

117 *Joe Breen's letter*: Lynn, p. 404.

117 *"To me, the funniest thing in the world"*: "I Made the Great Dictator Because I Hate Dictators," *Look*, 9-24-40.

118 *"It's the best part"*: Carlton Chaney, "Charlie Chaplin and *The Great Dictator*, September 1940, unsourced clipping, author's collection.

118 *"I just want to wish you"*: CA, Syd Chaplin to CC, 10-11-40.

118 *"the picture has had much advance"*: Review of *The Great Dictator*, *Variety*, 10-16-40.

119 *"The Great Dictator is one of those milestones"*: *Variety*, 10-23-40.

120 *"He didn't just scream"*: Scheide and Mehran, eds., *Chaplin: The Dictator and The Tramp*, p. 79.

120 *"There have been objections"*: *Variety*, 10-23-40, p. 4.

121 *"He steps up to the microphone"*: Quoted in "Cinema's First Genius," *Variety*, special section, 2003.

122 *"uneven . . . harsh at some moments"*: Karney and Cross, p. 107.

122 *"a curious mixture of humbleness"*: Herb Golden, "Chaplin Rebuttal to Critics," *Variety*, 10-23-40.

123 *"Historically, it was one"*: Scheide and Mehran, eds., *Chaplin: The Dictator and The Tramp*, p. 99.

123 *As for theoretical pro-Communist leanings*: Stephen Weissman, "The Little Tramp, Unlikely Hero," *Washington Post*, 4-16-89.

Chapter 7

126 *"Chaplin was not part of the general effort"*: Marta Feuchtwanger, "Chaplin as a Friend," *Los Angeles Times*, 1-15-78.

126 *"between April, 1945"*: Beverly Gage, "The Accidental President," *The New Yorker*, 3-14-22.

126 *"dangerous propaganda is . . . unloosed"*: Sbardellati, p. 37.

127 *"the most vicious propaganda"*: Sbardellati, p. 38.

127 *His lawyers prepared material*: Maland, p. 184.

127 *"the affidavits of Miss Goddard"*: CA, Walthall to Wright, 6-8-42.

127 *The Paramount contract*: CA, Chaplin-Goddard contract, 5-24-44.

128 *in 1939 Chaplin's salary*: *Motion Picture Herald*, 8-9-41, p. 31.

129 *"I am not a Communist"*: Flom, p. 149.

129 *"I dislike being told whom to kill"*: Chaplin, *My Autobiography*, p. 383.

130 *"were tired of having their industry"*: Sbardellati, p. 228.

130 *"The speeches enumerated"*: FBI Chaplin, 12-4-42.

131 *"We are fighting this war"*: FBI Chaplin, 12-4-42.

132 *"He was anxious"*: Schickel, ed., pp. 134–35.

132 *"after years of sly pretending"*: Maland, p. 194.

133 *"Germany for Germans!"*: CA, Trumbo to Chaplin, 10-9-42.

134 *In a private conversation*: Thomas M. Pryor, "Human Side of Chaplin," *Variety*, undated but 1989.

134 *Sydney shot him*: Richard Meryman interview, 1966.

134 *"for the standard American relationship"*: Stephen Weissman, "The Little Tramp, Unlikely Hero," *Washington Post*, 4-16-89.

135 *"he is regarded as stingy"*: FBI Chaplin, Hood to Hoover, 1-5-43.

Chapter 8

137 *Instead, she was arrested:* Maland, p. 198.

137 *"impressed at the enthusiasm":* Lynn, p. 414.

138 *"When Chaplin took to anyone":* Schickel, ed., p. 133.

138 *"[Berry] had played her cards":* Scheide and Mehran, eds., *Chaplin's Lime-light and the Music Hall Tradition*, p. 195.

139 *"I'll be goddamned":* FBI Chaplin, Memorandum for Mr. E. A. Tamm, 11-5-43.

139 *"I might add here":* FBI Chaplin, Berry interview, p. 4.

139 *She liked to accompany:* FBI Chaplin, Berry interview, p. 8.

140 *"In the meantime":* FBI Chaplin, Berry interview, p. 11.

141 *"I've got to have peace":* FBI Chaplin, Berry interview, p. 23.

141 *"We thought she was a tramp":* Duncan, ed., p. 432.

142 *"remained a mystery":* Eastman, pp. 236–37.

143 "He could not mold his personal life": Eastman, pp. 240–41.

144 *"Go out and call me":* Muir, pp. 58–60.

145 *"When I went to cash":* Totheroh interview with Timothy Lyons, p. 72, author's collection.

Chapter 9

147 *"was erratic, emotional, hard to talk to":* FBI Chaplin, Alf Reeves interview, 11-19-43, pp. 29–32.

149 *"There's nobody that knows Charlie":* FBI Chaplin, Tim Durant interview, 1-3-43, pp. 50–59.

Chapter 10

153 *she slugged Salinger:* Saroyan, p. 160.

153 *She had more serious relationships:* Scovell, p. 292.

154 *she referred to Ernest Hemingway:* Scovell, p. 90.

155 *"resolute, as though she had come upon":* Chaplin, *My Autobiography*, p. 420.

155 *"any kind of display":* Scovell, p. 119.

156 *"Her misery was as abject":* Muir, p. 69.

156 *"They clung to each other":* Vance, p. 262.

156 *"in accordance with the policy":* FBI Chaplin, Hood to Hoover, 1-17-44.

157 *"Chaplin and Oona O'Neill Wed":* New York Herald Tribune, 6-16-43.

157 *"With every front-page record":* Adela Rogers St. Johns, "Case Against Chaplin," *Photoplay*, September 1943.

157 *"He knew that he had had affairs":* Academy, Harry Crocker Collection, Charlie Chaplin, "Courage," p. 1.

157   *"Charlie never gossiped"*: Epstein to SE.

157   *On Christmas Day 1943*: FBI Chaplin, *Script* magazine, 1-8-44.

158   *"fairly good coverage"*: FBI Chaplin, Memorandum for Mr. A. Rosen, 1-15-44.

158   *On February 26, 1944*: FBI Chaplin, "Exclusive to Walter Winchell," 2-26-44.

159   *"That our first interest was to make a case"*: FBI Chaplin, Rosen to Tamm, 1-27-44.

159   *"incarcerated in a sanitarium"*: FBI Chaplin, Hood to Hoover, 1-12-44.

159   *"would not have any adverse"*: FBI Chaplin, lab analysis, 1-25-44.

159   *"Give immediate attention"*: FBI Chaplin, Hood to Hoover, 1-12-44.

159   *"Bureau does not desire"*: FBI Chaplin, Hoover telegram, 1-13-44.

159   *"advised agent that she talked"*: FBI Chaplin, Conroy to Hoover, 1-31-44.

159   *"Carr is considering"*: FBI Chaplin, Hood to Hoover, 1-25-44.

160   *"a little ingrate"*: FBI Chaplin, Pegler column, 2-20-44.

161   *"a friend of mine spent with the girl"*: Eastman, p. 245.

161   *"The following morning"*: FBI Chaplin, "Summary Status of Barry's Civil Suit Against Chaplin as Father of her daughter Carol Ann," p. 63.

162   *"Would my client"*: Duncan, ed., p. 435.

162   *"Chaplin was the best witness"*: All Giesler quotes from Jerry Giesler as told to Pete Martin, "The Chaplin Case," *Saturday Evening Post*, 11-21-59.

162   *"There lurked in the back of my mind"*: Chaplin, *My Autobiography*, pp. 464–65.

164   *"I think as time goes by"*: CA, Wright to Giesler, 12-5-44.

164   *"Had Chaplin lost his case"*: FBI Chaplin, "Security Information, Confidential," document of 9-18-52, quoting column of 4-6-44.

165   *"We discussed the possibility of [Chaplin] being deported"*: Timothy Lyons, "The United States vs. Charlie Chaplin," *American Film*, 9-84, p. 30.

165   *"There is no sound reason to deny"*: Roger M. Grace, "Scott Takes on Paternity Case Against Charlie Chaplin," *Metropolitan News-Enterprise*, 10-23-2008.

166   *"I knew Charlie Chaplin when he came to Los Angeles"*: Scott's autobiography was printed in the Congressional Record, 82nd Congress, Vol. 98, Part II, June 17, 1952, to August 18, 1952, pp. A3954–76. Unless otherwise specified, Scott quotes derive from this autobiography.

167   *"serving to build up an enormous"*: Lynn, p. 365.

167   *Florabel Muir got her exclusive*: Muir, p. 65.

169   *"Scott tore the principles"*: Muir, p. 70.

171   *"I admit the press"*: "Chaplin Trial Will Adjourn," *Austin American-Statesman*, 4-13-45.

171   *"Yes, they'll believe all your lies"*: "Chaplin Called to Testify," *Los Angeles Evening Citizen-News*, 4-12-45.

172 *"this pestiferous, lecherous hound"*: Roger M. Grace, "Scott Upstages Chaplin at 1944 Paternity Trial," *Metropolitan News-Enterprise*, 10-30-2008.

172 *"What is your duty as jurors?"*: Duncan, ed., p. 436.

173 *The first showed Chaplin*: "Jury Holds Charlie Chaplin Father of Joan Barry Child," *Los Angeles Times*, 4-18-45.

173 *"Scott," wrote Florabel Muir*: Muir, p. 70.

174 *"We feel that there has been a law"*: CA, Wright to Chaplin, 7-25-46.

174 *"he will undoubtedly serve"*: CA, Millikan to Chaplin, 11-4-46.

174 *In January 1947*: CA, Chaplin Studios to Loyd Wright, 1-28-47.

174 *Millikan wrote Chaplin*: CA, Millikan to Scott, 1-13-48.

175 *"Did I seek her out?"*: Academy, Harry Crocker Collection, Charlie Chaplin, "Courage," p. 1.

175 *"Joan Barry, Lovely—Vivacious—Captivating Ex-Protégé of Charlie Chaplin"*: Ad reproduced in *Limelight*, Spring 1997.

175 *"I do not feel any disloyalty"*: Duncan, ed., p. 451.

177 *"I hereby recognize"*: Berry's letters are all in the Chaplin Archive.

177 *"The fact that Miss Berry has been unable"*: CA, *Los Angeles Times*, 6-23-53.

178 *"In his brief reference to the paternity case"*: Father George Dunne, "I Remember Chaplin," *Commonweal*, 6-2-72.

178 *"I was full of religion"*: Vance, p. 373.

Chapter 11

182 *A Communist agent who in 1918*: Haas, p. 107.

182 *"My usual salary for a motion picture"*: USC, Hanns Eisler papers, Eisler to Lois Runser, 9-16-47.

182 *His sister Ruth Fischer*: Haas, p. 133.

183 *"a man like Charlie Chaplin, with his communistic leanings"*: John Sbardellati and Tony Shaw, "Booting a Tramp: Charlie Chaplin, the FBI and the Construction of the Subversive Image in Red Scare America," *Pacific Historical Review* 72, no. 4 (November 2003).

183 *"I am today demanding"*: Maland, p. 260.

184 *"I hereby sell, assign and transfer"*: CA, Welles contract, 7-24-41.

184 *"I wrote it"*: Biskind, p. 144.

185 *"He never wrote anything"*: Hayes, ed., p. 105.

185 *"An Original Story"*: Program in author's collection.

185 *It wasn't until ten days*: Duncan, ed., p. 446.

185 *"lavishly acted out every scene"* Mitchell, p. 194.

186 *"UNACCEPTABLE under the provisions"*: Lynn, p. 440.

187 *"We pass over those elements"*: Chaplin, *My Autobiography*, p. 473.

188 *"What have you against the Catholic church?"*: Chaplin, *My Autobiography*, p. 483.

188   *"Please change the word 'voluptuous'"*: Chaplin, *My Autobiography*, p. 481.

190   *"He'd entertain the troops"*: Lewis, pp. 162–63.

190   *"Chaplin believed that an allegiance to craft"*: Lewis, pp. 159–60.

190   *"director and/or associate director"*: CA, Florey contract, 4-24-46.

191   *"production supervisor"*: CA, Courant contract, undated, but 1946.

191   *Martha Raye was paid $2,500*: CA, Raye contract, 5-6-46.

192   *"I laugh at your shadow"*: Brian Taves, "Charlie Dearest," *Film Comment*, 4-88, pp. 66, 69.

192   *"With Martha Raye he gave no direction"*: Marilyn Nash interview, *Limelight*, Spring 1997, p. 5.

192   *"You can do anything if you don't have a vulgar mind"*: Comte, p. 252.

193   *"I thought that scene would never get done"*: "Monsieur Verdoux's Annabella, Adieu," *Limelight*, Winter 1995.

193   *"Long before he immortalized"*: Bessy, p. 214.

193   *"The mood of the text"*: Taves, p. 283.

193   *"He was very unhappy"*: Marilyn Nash interview, *Limelight*, Spring 1997.

193   *Florey saved some*: The sketches are reproduced in Bessy.

194   *"a series of simple ads"*: Davis, p. 50.

194   *"Verdoux is a very complex"*: Hayes, ed., pp. 98–99.

195   *"Wives, Lover, Passionate, Bigamy, Sex"*: Davis, p. 49.

195   *"I'd like to run every one"*: Academy, Hedda Hopper Collection, Hopper to Hoover, 4-7-47.

195   *"If you had your way:"* Academy, Hedda Hopper Collection, Hopper to Hoover, 8-7-47.

196   *"The picture wins in recollection"*: USC, Lion Feuchtwanger papers, box C1-B, folder 19, Feuchtwanger to Chaplin, 3-11-47.

196   *"There was an uneasy"*: Chaplin, *My Autobiography*, p. 489.

196   *"I should never have made"*: Epstein, p. 40.

197   *"They couldn't take it"*: Lewis, p. 165.

198   *"There's no use saying"*: FBI Chaplin, 4-29-47.

198   *The composer and actor Ivor Novello*: Mitchell, p. 197.

199   *Chaplin, she reported*: CA, Oona Chaplin to Lou Eisler, undated, but April 1947.

199   *As the Chaplins were leaving*: Scovell, p. 156.

199   *"Proceed with the butchery"*: Hayes, ed., p. 115.

201   *"The Marines who died"*: FBI Chaplin, Ed Sullivan, *Washington Times Herald*, 4-12-47

201   *"On his 58th birthday"*: FBI Chaplin, *Washington Times Herald*, 4-16-47.

202   *"I want to go back to California"*: Hedda Hopper, *San Francisco Examiner*, 4-16-47.

202   *"As you know we have"*: Wisconsin, UA office rushgram, 6-10-47.

202 *"that one of the first persons"*: Sbardellati, p. 128.

203 *"Tell Birdwell under no circumstances"*: CA, Chaplin to Sears, 9-17-47.

204 *"Charles Chaplin in his greatest and gayest comedy!"*: *Lincoln Journal Star*, 10-13-47.

204 *"an aesthetic mess"*: Lynn, p. 451.

204 *"Last night, in her weekly"*: Independent Theater Owners of Ohio, Service Bulletin #370, 3-17-47, author's collection.

206 *The great art director Richard Day*: Sbardellati, p. 154.

209 *"I am protected by being a charlatan"*: Hayes, ed., p. 95.

210 *The Tramp's emotional core*: I am indebted to my friend Neil Brand for this point.

210 *"Madame Verdoux!"*: Mitchell, p. 198.

210 *"There was no identification"*: Richard Meryman interview, 1966.

Chapter 12

213 *"The press went for me"*: Bessy, pp. 421–24.

214 *"In Hollywood there is some doubt"*: CA, Westbrook Pegler, "Columnist Attacks Chaplin's Record," *New York Journal-American*, 10-31-45.

215 *"Send him back"*: FBI Chaplin, 5-25-46.

215 *Oona Chaplin enrolled her daughter*: Wranovics, p. 75.

215 *"CHAPLIN has been accused"*: FBI Chaplin, "Summary Report," 3-13-47.

216 *Chaplin never joined the Directors Guild*: Email from Eric Gutierrez, membership representative of the Directors Guild of America, 10-29-21.

216 *"In connection with the material prepared for Hedda Hopper"*: FBI Chaplin, "Memorandum for the Director from Mr. Ladd," 8-24-47.

216 *"aka Israel Thonstein"*: FBI Chaplin, 3-13-47.

216 *"The wonder to us"*: FBI Chaplin, "Letter to the Director," 5-8-48, p. 2.

216 *"Our ticket buyers"*: *Hollywood Reporter*, 11-5-47.

217 *When he wasn't popping Benzedrine*: Wilkerson, p. 261.

217 *Connolly went so far*: Gary Baum and Daniel Miller, "The Hollywood Reporter, After 65 Years, Addresses Role in Blacklist," *Hollywood Reporter*, 11-19-12.

217 *"no new information of value"*: Maland, p. 270.

217 *Louis Budenz, a former managing editor of* The Daily Worker: FBI Chaplin, Special Agent in Charge, New York to Hoover, 7-14-50.

218 *The other informant was Paul Crouch*: Timothy Lyons, "United States vs. Charlie Chaplin," *American Film*, 9-84.

218 *At one point in 1948*: Lyons, "United States vs. Charlie Chaplin," p. 34.

218 *"I wish to state that this action"*: Tim Lyons, "The Great Dictator, or J. Edgar at the Wheel," *Limelight*, Spring 1997.

220 *"In passing, rumor has it"*: Lyons, p. 4.

220 *Hopper never mentioned*: Maland, p. 399.

221 *Besides Hopper*: Sbardellati, p. 167.

221 *On November 2, the card was established*: Timothy Lyons, "J. Edgar Hoover and the Little Tramp," *Flashback*, Indiana University Bloomington, 1990, p. 9.

221 *"whether or not CHAPLIN"*: FBI Chaplin, 9-3-48.

222 *"theatrical"*: Lloyd to SE.

222 *His favorite movie of these years*: Epstein, p. 52.

222 *"his ravishing young wife"*: Graham, p. 181.

223 *"How's your cancer coming?"*: Epstein, p. 52.

223 *"I know he played a very aggressive game"*: Selznick to SE.

224 *"My father liked to play tennis"*: Sydney Chaplin to SE. Unless otherwise specified, all quotes from Syd derive from this interview.

227 *"never took time to prepare"*: Epstein, p. 48.

227 *"Keep it light"*: Epstein, p. 48.

227 *"when he would show somebody"*: Scheide and Mehran, eds., *Chaplins Limelight and the Music Hall Tradition*, p. 85.

228 *"ironed out all her mannerisms"*: Epstein, p. 55.

228 *When it came to the Barrie play*: Epstein, p. 72.

229 *"What does this mean?"*: Epstein, p. 58.

229 *"It was osmosis"*: Epstein, p. 75.

229 *"Is it true Charlie Chaplin had"*: Epstein, p. 75.

230 *"You must not act"*: Ross, p. 15.

230 *"Keep it simple!"*: Ross, p. 19.

230 *"He took us out to dinner"*: Bonnie McCourt and David Totheroh, "His New Profession: Interview with William Schallert," *Limelight*, Winter 1998.

231 *"Any assistance that you could render"*: CA, Kelly to Richardson, 2-9-49.

231 *"almost like a sort of English colonel"*: Lambert, p. 229.

232 *Michael Powell was a dinner guest*: Powell, p. 205.

232 *Ivan Moffat liked Chaplin*: Lambert, pp. 230–31.

233 *"Have you ever made any contributions"*: FBI Chaplin, *Confidential*, Interview of Chaplin by INS, 4-17-48.

238 *Senator Harry Cain*: CA, "Deport Chaplin," 4-14-49.

238 *"Still alive, kicking and enthusiastic"*: CA, Chaplin 1949 birthday message.

238 *"It was determined that there are no witnesses available"*: FBI Chaplin, Hoover to Ford, 12-29-49.

239 *Hoover sent out a memo*: FBI Chaplin, 1-5-50.

239 *"a well-known Russian propagandist"*: FBI Chaplin, 1-5-50, p. 6.

239 *Senator Millard Tydings took the letter*: Hearings Before a Subcommittee of

the Committee on Foreign Relations United States Senate, 81st Congress, Second Session, S. Res. 231: A Resolution to Investigate Whether There Are Employees in the State Department Disloyal to the United States, March 8, 9, 13, 14, 20, 21, 27, 28, April 5, 6, 20, 25, 27, 28, May 1, 2, 3, 4, 26, 31, June 5, 6, 7, 8, 9, 12, 21, 22, 23, 26, 28, 1950. Chaplin's name is mentioned on March 8, 1950.

240 *"No information has been developed"*: FBI Chaplin, Turner to Whitson, 2-7-50.

240 *"The Commie Daily People's World"*: CA, Hedda Hopper column, "World Famous Clown Villain in Fat Man," *Los Angeles Times*, 7-29-50.

240 *"Life isn't the same"*: Fiaccarini et al., p. 278.

Chapter 13

245 *"Top of the bill"*: Anthony, p. 161.

246 *there are more than trace elements*: Anthony, p. 116.

246 *Leo Dryden was known as*: Anthony, p. 136.

247 *"his character does"*: The Comedy of Charlie Chaplin, Kamin, p. 190.

247 *the two great music halls*: Robinson, *The World of Limelight*, p. 98.

247 *there are only two scenes*: Robinson, *The World of Limelight*, p. 149.

248 *"digressions, variations and incessant rewriting"*: Scheide and Mehran, eds., *Chaplin's Limelight and the Music Hall Tradition*, p. 58.

248 *"Only in the daytime"*: Fiaccarini et al., p. 39.

249 *"Is* Limelight *the autobiography"*: Fiaccarini et al., p. 50.

249 *"The horror of poverty"*: Fiaccarini et al., p. 27.

249 *"I was never interested"*: Tino Balio, "Charles Chaplin, Entrepreneur: A United Artist," *Journal of the University Film Association*, XXL, 1, Winter 1979, p. 12.

250 *"Put 'em up!"*: Academy, Harry Crocker Collection, Charlie Chaplin, Sale of UA, p. 1.

251 *"When both script and music were ready"*: Fiaccarini et al., p. 120.

251 *"He should be starting his next picture"*: Limelight, Summer 1997, "Where to Make Movies," *Daily News*, January 22, 1951, *Daily News*, also January 29, 1954, *Citizen News*.

252 *For a while it seemed an actress named Barbara Bates*: CA, Henry Gris manuscript.

253 *"He wanted the girl to be like Oona"*: Vance, p. 284.

253 *"I remembered each way he did it"*: Scheide and Mehran, eds., *Chaplin's Limelight and the Music Hall Tradition*, p. 93.

253 *"My mother used to wear"*: Bloom, p. 101.

253 *"The dressing rooms"*: Bloom, p. 102.

254 *"The difference between him and the Communists"*: Bloom, p. 96.

254 *"We don't want his script or money"*: CA, Henry Gris manuscript.

254 *He composed most of the musical score*: CA, Henry Gris manuscript.

254 *"I always started with a floor plan"*: Scheide and Mehran, eds., *Chaplin's Limelight and the Music Hall Tradition*, p. 67.

255 *The first day of shooting*: Scheide and Mehran, eds., *Chaplin's Limelight and the Music Hall Tradition*, p. 20.

255 *"Rollie still couldn't light"*: Struss to SE.

255 *"Four inches!"*: Struss to SE.

255 *"Charlie mellowed"*: Struss to SE.

256 *"I'm never sick of it"*: Bloom to SE.

257 *"Sometimes Pa"*: Sydney Chaplin to SE.

257 *"he was hell on wheels"*: Lloyd and Parker, p. 131.

258 *"Charlie would not sit in a chair"*: Lloyd and Parker, p. 131.

258 *"a mixture of darkness and melancholy"*: Lloyd and Parker, p. 132.

259 *"Her ability and technique"*: Fiaccarini et al., p. 187.

259 *Keaton's agent thought*: Scheide and Mehran, eds., *Chaplin's Limelight and the Music Hall Tradition*, p. 23.

259 *The next day involved Calvero's death scene*: Norman Lloyd to SE.

260 *"This was all an adventure for me"*: Melissa Hayden to SE and Hooman Mehran. All Hayden quotes derive from this interview.

262 *"Keaton was 56"*: Bloom, p. 112.

262 *"respect, actually a mutual respect"*: Bloom to SE.

263 *"He seemed anxious"*: Epstein, p. 96.

263 *"The shots of the music sheets"*: Epstein, p. 96.

263 *Chaplin worked Lloyd*: Fiaccarini et al., pp. 191, 198.

263 *"I thank God Claire Bloom"*: CA, Henry Gris manuscript.

263 *"It's great, my best, a renaissance"*: CA, Henry Gris manuscript.

264 *"Calvero performs music hall acts"*: Epstein to SE.

264 *"On flea number hold"*: Wranovics, p. 122.

264 *They would sit in Chaplin's dressing room*: Epstein, p. 91.

265 *Crocker believed that it was Chaplin's basic obstinance*: Academy, Harry Crocker Collection, Charlie Chaplin, Ch. X, p. 2.

265 *"Chaplin was withdrawing"*: Academy, Harry Crocker Collection, Charlie Chaplin, Ch. X, p. 12.

Chapter 14

268 *"This permit gives no guarantee"*: FBI Chaplin, Hoover memo, 7-8-52.

268 *McGranery was a former*: Lynn, p. 487.

269 *"prepare a memorandum"*: FBI Chaplin, Belmont to Ladd, 9-18-52.

269   *"As early as 1923"*: FBI Chaplin, 9-16-52.

269   *"at the present time"*: FBI Chaplin, Belmont to Ladd, 9-30-52.

270   *"an alien left the United States"*: FBI Chaplin, 4-5-51, including *Variety* story of 9-27-50.

270   *"denies the charge and INS is able to establish it"*: John Sbardellati and Tony Shaw, "Booting a Tramp: Charlie Chaplin, the FBI and the Construction of the Subversive Image in Red Scare America," *Pacific Historical Review* 72, no. 4 (November 2003): 82.

270   *"We should get started now"*: FBI Chaplin, Belmont to Ladd, 9-16-52.

270   *Together, Hoover and McGranery*: FBI Chaplin, Belmont to Ladd, 9-16-52.

271   *"possibly be denied"*: Hayden to SE and Hooman Mehran.

271   *"The CP [Communist Party] likes CHAPLIN"*: FBI Chaplin, Los Angeles to Hoover, 10-14-52.

271   *"Well, I loved it"*: Hayden to SE and Hooman Mehran.

Chapter 15

274   *"Chaplin had bought $241,000"*: Academy, Harry Crocker Collection, Charlie Chaplin, Ch. XVII, p. 7.

274   *"Have you ever known such timing"*: Academy, Hedda Hopper Collection, Hopper to Koury, 9-22-52.

275   *"Dear Hedda . . . I am not going to Argentina"*: Academy, Hedda Hopper papers, McLaglen to Hopper, 10-24-47.

275   *On October 30, 1952*: CA, Watt to Wright, 10-30-52.

275   *"Should American authorities"*: Academy, Harry Crocker Collection, Charlie Chaplin, Ch. XVI, p. 19.

276   *"has sounded the bell of liberty"*: "Chaplin Must Prove Case," *New York Times*, 10-29-52, p. 32.

276   *"the distributors of the film* Limelight*"*: Wisconsin, UA Archives, American Legion to Arthur Krim, 10-14-52.

276   *"We are continuing our collective effort"*: *Variety*, 2-25-53, p. 4.

277   *Beyond that, UA gave some thought*: Davis, p. 58.

277   *"Chaplin can write a letter"*: Davis, p. 58.

277   *He found Chaplin in his shorts*: Academy, Harry Crocker Collection, Charlie Chaplin, Ch. XVII, p. 16.

278   *"because I know that I would be under"*: Fiaccarini et al., p. 220.

278   *"The fire still glows, but now it seems the fire of winter"*: Slide, "The American Press & Public v. Charles Spencer Chaplin."

278   *Claude Terrail took them on a tour*: Academy, Harry Crocker Collection, Charlie Chaplin, Ch. XVIII, p. 2.

278   *Chaplin was surprised by how casually Picasso*: Academy, Harry Crocker Collection, Charlie Chaplin, Ch. XVIII, p. 6.

279 *"I came out of the Astor Theater"*: Academy, Harry Crocker Collection, Charlie Chaplin, Ch. XVIII, p. 7.

279 *"Chaplin was not a communist"*: Academy, Harry Crocker Collection, Charlie Chaplin, Ch. XVII, pp. 18–19.

279 *"The film is very, very good"*: Richard Meryman interview, 1966.

Chapter 16

281 *"Harry, you know I want to go home!"*: Academy, Harry Crocker Collection, Charlie Chaplin, Ch. 1.

281 *"Keaton was quite fond"*: Curtis to SE.

281 *"I have known Chaplin since 1912"*: Fiaccarini et al., p. 290.

282 *"He was a political speculator"*: Frank, p. 217.

282 *"found to be potentially dangerous"*: Frank, p. 249.

283 *"Immigration Dept. investigators"*: Ed Sullivan column, New York *Daily News*, 10-15-52.

283 *"I shouldn't have let her go"*: Academy, Harry Crocker Collection, Charlie Chaplin, Ch. XVIII, p. 9.

284 *They wanted to know what kind of man Chaplin was*: Chaplin, *My Autobiography*, p. 504.

284 *"Mr. Chaplin says that the FBI"*: CA, Crocker to Wright, 11-27-52.

284 *"My dear Mr. Chaplin"*: CA, Churchill to Chaplin, 11-29-52.

285 *"Attorney General McGranery seems to suspect"*: Wranovics, pp. 127–28.

285 *"All this McGranery filth is sickening"*: CA, Agee to Chaplin, 12-52.

286 *The Saturday Evening Post ran a long story*: James P. O'Donnell, "Charlie Chaplin's Stormy Exile," *Saturday Evening Post*, 3-8-58.

286 *The only defenses of Chaplin came from*: Academy, Harry Crocker Collection, Charlie Chaplin, Ch. XVIII, p. 21.

286 *"one of the most beautiful resorts"*: Haven, p. 215.

286 *Chaplin and Oona thought about buying a house*: Comte, p. 328.

287 *"was in a mood to hide away"*: Academy, Harry Crocker Collection, Charlie Chaplin, "Manoir de Ban," p. 1.

287 *It came with an orchard*: Chaplin, *My Autobiography*, p. 514.

287 *"Of course, it is the usual Oona and Chaplin style"*: CA, Chaplin to Syd Chaplin, 3-17-54.

Chapter 17

291 *"Firstly, I am so glad to be out of that stink-pot"*: CA, Chaplin to Agee, 12-16-53.

292 *"1. Any lease in existence"*: CA, Chaplin to Wright, 6-3-53.

293 *"I am the same person I always was"*: CA, Cedric Belfrage, "Charlie Chaplin Looks at USA," *National Guardian*, 11-14-55.

293 *"I have been"*: Flom, p. 231.

294 *"When I heard that Charlie Chaplin had slipped"*: Hedda Hopper column, *Los Angeles Times*, 4-24-53.

294 *"I can't understand why Charles Chaplin Jr."*: Hedda Hopper column, *Los Angeles Times*, 3-12-53.

294 *the name Chaplin was anathema*: Louvish, p. 334.

294 *"Oona and I are always glad to hear from you"*: USC, Feuchtwanger papers, box C1-B, folder 19, Chaplin to Feuchtwanger, 9-2-53.

295 *"Lion! Martha! When are you coming?"*: USC, Feuchtwanger papers, box B3-A, folder 7, Chaplin to Feuchtwanger, 4-14-53.

295 *In a 1953 letter to the Feuchtwangers*: USC, Feuchtwanger papers, box C1-B, folder 19, undated but 1953.

295 *"The philosophy shown in your great films"*: CA, Hooberman to Chaplin, 8-16-53.

295 *"Even if my qualifications"*: CA, Chaplin to Hooberman, 8-20-53.

296 *"[served] the purposes of a brutal and tyrannical imperialism"*: Maland, p. 319.

296 *"It was a lovely afternoon"*: Struss to SE.

296 *Sydney acted as his brother's agent*: CA, Syd Chaplin to Charlie Chaplin, 11-3-53.

296 *"I have been waiting & hoping"*: CA, Syd Chaplin to Charlie Chaplin, 9-12-53.

297 *"Now as to my papers on biographical matter"*: CA, Charlie Chaplin to Syd Chaplin, 10-20-53.

297 *"a good return on your investment"*: CA, Syd Chaplin to Charlie Chaplin, 11-3-53.

298 *the only obvious sign of Chaplin's ownership*: Bob Thomas, Associated Press column, 1-22-55.

298 *"Yesterday we had the good fortune"*: CA, Syd Chaplin to Charlie Chaplin, 5-24-53.

298 *"I console myself"*: CA, Syd Chaplin to Charlie Chaplin, 6-27-53.

298 *"the country that had made him rich, famous and unhappy"*: John Sbardellati and Tony Shaw, "Booting a Tramp: Charlie Chaplin, the FBI and the Construction of the Subversive Image in Red Scare America," *Pacific Historical Review* 72, no. 4 (November 2003): 524.

299 *"Hiding from McCarthy"*: The picture is reproduced in Comte, p. 307.

299 *"Do Not Destroy—Pending Litigation"*: Timothy Lyons, "United States vs. Charlie Chaplin," *American Film*, 9-84, p. 34.

299 *He inveighed against the Russian Iron Curtain*: Academy, Harry Crocker Collection, Charlie Chaplin, "Manoir de Ban," p. 8.

299 *"My primary indignation"*: FBI Chaplin, Max Eastman, "2 Way Blast on Chaplin Case: Both U.S. and Charlie Wrong," *Brooklyn Eagle*, 5-18-53.

300 *"His not becoming an American citizen"*: Eastman, p. 244.

300 *"Life in Switzerland"*: CA, Chaplin to Odets, 9-2-53.

301 *"I hear little or no news"*: Stein, p. 220.

301 *He drove a Cadillac*: Stein, p. 220.

301 *"We loved Sydney"*: Geraldine Chaplin to SE.

302 *"My dear"*: Saroyan, p. 128.

302 *"It is a little king"*: CA, Chaplin to Odets, 3-11-54.

302 *"My dear Charlie"*: CA, Totheroh to Chaplin, 3-21-54.

303 *On March 30, 1954*: CA, Chaplin to Lois Watt, 3-30-54.

303 *"Have not talked to Edna"*: CA, Watt to Chaplin, 7-9-54.

304 *"And so the world grows young"*: Chaplin, *My Autobiography*, p. 527.

304 *The national Sunday supplement* This Week: CA, Louis Berg, "What Made Charlie Run," *This Week*, 12-12-54.

304 *"I no longer have any use for America"*: CA, Cedric Belfrage, "Charlie Chaplin Looks at USA," *Guardian*, 11-14-54.

304 *"As you know"*: CA, Chaplin to Loyd Wright, 3-10-54.

305 *"I am not particularly impressed by it"*: CA, Chaplin to Kelly, 6-16-54.

305 *"I want to thank you"*: CA, Robeson to Chaplin, 6-23-54.

Chapter 18

307 *"At first I thought"*: CA, J. B. Priestley, "King Charlie Does It Again," *Sunday Dispatch*, 7-28-58.

308 *They said they would make a distribution decision*: Epstein, p. 135.

308 *The film's final cost*: CA, Statement of Production Cost, *A King in New York*, 5-27-56–2-2-57.

308 *"If Dawn Addams"*: Duncan, ed., p. 496.

308 *"Charlie felt like a displaced person"*: Epstein, p. 137.

309 *"That was pointed out to Charlie"*: Epstein to SE.

311 *"I don't think"*: Epstein to SE.

311 *"In some places"*: CA, Gelardi to Chaplin re earnings, 9-25-57.

312 *"Charlie drew from life"*: Epstein to SE.

312 *Seven minutes were cut*: Scheide and Mehran, eds., p. 201.

312 *"I was disappointed in the picture"*: Chaplin, *My Life in Pictures*, p. 306.

313 *"I wouldn't want to do anything like that now"*: Vance, p. 365.

313 *"As I think you already know"*: CA, Cohen to Chaplin, 3-30-57.

314 *The actual amount*: Duncan, ed., p. 510.

314 *"his personal convictions"*: LOC, James McGranery papers, "Immigration and Naturalization File."

314 *As late as July 1959*: Duncan, ed., p. 510.

Chapter 19

315 *"'Look, if you're moaning that you're lousy'"*: Ivor Davis, Interview with Geraldine Chaplin, *US Airways* magazine, 5-97.

316 *"I am so happy you believe"*: Vance, p. 313.

316 *"You couldn't tell if the accusations"*: Sayre, p. 171.

317 *"I said to that young man"*: Sayre, pp. 155–56.

317 *During one monologue*: Sayre, p. 156.

317 *"because I couldn't bear to hear"*: Sayre, p. 157.

318 *"What are they so sore about?"*: Hayes, ed., pp. 120–21.

318 *"The days when I was touring America"*: Hayes, ed., p. 125.

318 *"In bitterness and anger"*: Lloyd and Parker, p. 140.

319 *"For people having troubles"*: Website "Letters from Stan," Laurel to Ed Patterson, 10-2-57 and 10-14-57.

320 *"We do not believe the Republic"*: *New York Times* editorial, 7-2-62.

320 *The substance of McGranery's defense*: LOC, James McGranery papers, document dated 7-23-62.

320 *"deliberate effort to impress on the American people"*: LOC, James McGranery notes, 7-18-62.

321 *"WHAT MORE CAN BE SAID ABOUT CHARLIE CHAPLIN?"*: LOC, James McGranery papers, Immigration and Naturalization papers, 10-2-52.

321 *"He was in such a fury"*: Lloyd and Parker, p. 140.

322 *"I got a nice letter back from Chaplin"*: Mark Matousek, "Understanding, Differently," *Village Voice*, undated.

322 *"Dear Uppie"*: CA, Chaplin to Sinclair, 10-19-64.

323 *"How can you remember"*: Epstein, p. 159.

323 My Autobiography *sold more than 27,000 copies*: Haven, p. 151.

324 *"the most charming man you ever met"*: Richard Meryman interview, 1966.

325 *"small, perfectly made"*: Paris, p. 109.

325 *his habit of painting his genitals*: Paris, p. 109.

326 *"that he could seduce a girl"*: Paris, p. 109.

326 *"[Louise] wrote like a dream"*: Paris, p. 471.

Chapter 20

327 *"Get rid of those damned Communists"*: Epstein, p. 160.

328 *"I don't believe I deserve dinner"*: Norman Lloyd to SE.

328 *"I didn't realize how beautiful he was"*: Richard Meryman interview, 1966.

328 *"The Chaplins' house was perfectly gay"*: Day, p. 689.

329 *"I never wanted to make a lot of money"*: Richard Meryman interview, 1966.

329 *"I don't think there's any place"*: Richard Meryman interview, 1966.

330 *"banal . . . that ridiculous scene"*: Hayes, ed., p. 143.

331 *he suggested Peter Sellers*: Vance, p. 332.

331 *Chaplin was paid $600,000*: Vance, p. 330.

331 *"Listen you son of a bitch"*: Duncan, ed., p. 519.

332 *"From that moment on"*: Epstein, p. 186.

333 *"Do that line again, Marlon"*: Gilliatt, p. 148.

333 *"Charlie wouldn't let the script out of England"*: Hedren to SE.

334 *"With my next film"*: Hayes, ed., p. 142.

334 *The film had cost just under $3.1 million*: CA, Statement of Production Cost, *A Countess from Hong Kong*, 12-11-66

335 *"destroyed"*: Geraldine Chaplin to SE.

335 *"Please take this as notice"*: CA, Goddard to Chaplin, 5-9-66.

335 *"at his option"*: CA, contract between Chaplin and Goddard, 11-30-43.

335 *"the denial of a visa"*: Timothy Lyons, "United States vs. Charlie Chaplin," *American Film*, 9-84.

335 *"Between you and I"*: Richard Meryman interview, 1966.

335 *"I never liked Hollywood"*: Richard Meryman interview, 1966.

336 *"The essential element that Chaplin loved was money"*: Vance, p. 355.

337 *Rothman paid Chaplin a $5 million advance*: "Chaplin's Features for Theatrical Release, TV, Cassettes; Rothman Deal," *Variety*, 5-12-71.

337 *Bogdanovich found Chaplin*: Bogdanovich to SE.

337 *"My mother and Oona"*: Charles Matthau to SE. All quotes from Matthau derive from this interview.

337 *"I like the way that man takes his food"*: Saroyan, p. 181.

338 "Parlez-vous français?": Don Cook, Cleveland *Plain Dealer*, "Modern Times to Paris, for French 'Understand' Chaplin," 11-21-71.

338 *"I'm going to America"*: William Wolf, "Charlie Chaplin Is Prepared to Be Shot," Cleveland *Plain Dealer*, 4-2-72.

339 *"She has made her love for him the center"*: Chaplin, *My Life in Pictures*, pp. 30–31.

339 *"discrimination and choice"*: Mark Shivas, "Remembrance of Tramps Past," *New York Times*, 12-12-71.

339 *"In all those years of Hollywood"*: William McWhirter, "Grand Rerun for Charlie Chaplin, *Life*, 12-3-71.

340 *"He got up"*: Geraldine Chaplin to SE.

340 *"It was a dreadful time for me altogether"*: Shivas, "Remembrance of Tramps Past."

341 *"The unpleasant things have faded"*: Alden Whitman, "The King of Comedy," *New York Times*, 4-4-72.

341 *"He didn't miss anything"*: Sydney Chaplin to SE.

342   *"apt to go in and out of focus"*: Lynn, p. 531.

342   *"Thought I was going to blubber like a big kid"*: Richard Meryman, "If Only My Children Were Here," *Life*, 4-21-72.

343   *"My dear, I've had a series of small strokes"*: Saroyan, p. 196.

343   *"Don't go all mushy on me"*: Saroyan, p. 213.

343   *Cary Grant, Danny Kaye*: Epstein, p. 205.

343   *"Some of the old spark"*: "His New Profession," William Schallert interview with Bonnie McCourt and David Totheroh, *Limelight*, Winter 1998.

344   *"traitor"*: Maland, p. 343.

344   *The Chamber of Commerce also received derogatory letters*: Tom Shales, "Forgive and Forget," *Washington Post*, 4-11-72.

344   *"gave him a lot of extra years"*: "Cinema's First Genius," *Variety*, special section, 2003.

345   *"I don't want him to do it"*: Vance, p. 353.

345   *"There is no film"*: Epstein, p. 203.

345   *"He could have made it"*: Epstein to SE.

347   *"He would wander and sort of couldn't remember"*: Scovell, p. 255.

347   *"began to go on and on about Keaton"*: "Cinema's First Genius," *Variety*.

347   *There had been conversations*: Vance, p. 357.

348   *"How would it look for the Tramp to be called Sir Charlie?"*: Jerry Epstein to SE.

348   *"I'll make another film"*: "Queen Elizabeth Knights Frail Charlie Chaplin, 85," Cleveland *Plain Dealer*, 3-5-75.

348   *Modern Times and The Great Dictator each returned about $750,000*: *Variety*, 5-9-73, p. 44.

348   *The Great Dictator earned $608,000*: *Variety*, 5-9-73, p. 226.

348   *The rest of the top five*: Kate Guyonvarch, email to SE, 11-3-20.

349   *"The most insecure man"*: From Peter Jones's documentary *Charlie Chaplin*.

349   *"And they are beautiful"*: Epstein, p. 209.

349   *"Eric, don't fuck it about!"*: Hooman Mehran, "His Musical Career," *Limelight*, Spring 1999.

350   *"CONGRATULATIONS AND THANK YOU"*: Kubrick archive, London. Chaplin to Kubrick, 11-13-77.

350   *"He always hated Christmas"*: "A Woman of Paris," Josephine Chaplin interview with Bonnie McCourt and David Totheroh, *Limelight*, Summer 1997.

350   *"One wonders if others"*: CA, Romanoff to Chaplin, 2-6-78.

351   *"She was utterly cosseted"*: Scovell, p. 279.

351   *"Oona was a very lovely lady"*: Charles Matthau to SE.

352   *When Oona boarded a flight*: Scovell, p. 280.

Epilogue

354 *"Charlie was a man"*: "The Music of Charles Chaplin," BBC Radio 2, 4-13-97.

354 *"a vague nuisance"*: Schickel, ed., p. 149.

355 *"Don't wish your life away"*: Epstein, p. 215.

355 *"They had to choose a centerpiece"*: Paumier and Robinson, *Charlie Chaplin 100 Years*, p. 31.

355 *"I beg no apologies for any stand"*: Richard Meryman interview, 1966.

357 *"He never tired of these trips"*: Epstein, pp. 11–12.

357 *"he didn't want to be recognized or greeted"*: Benedict Nightingale, "The Melancholy That Forged a Comic Genius," *New York Times*, 3-22-92.

358 *"After all"*: Epstein, p. 216.

BIBLIOGRAPHY

Anthony, Barry. *Chaplin's Music Hall*. London: I. B. Tauris, 2012.

Balio, Tino. *United Artists: The Company Built by the Stars*. Madison: University of Wisconsin Press, 2009.

Beauchamp, Cari. *Joseph P. Kennedy Presents: His Hollywood Years*. New York: Knopf, 2009.

Bessy, Maurice. *Charlie Chaplin*. New York: Harper & Row, 1985.

Biskind, Peter. *My Lunches with Orson: Conversations Between Henry Jaglom and Orson Welles*. New York: Metropolitan, 2013.

Blauvelt, Christian. *Hollywood Victory*. Philadelphia: Running Press, 2021.

Bloom, Claire. *Limelight and After*. New York: Harper & Row, 1982.

Brownlow, Kevin. *The Search for Charlie Chaplin*. London: UKA Press, 2010.

Chaplin, Charles. *My Autobiography*. London: Bodley Head, 1964.

———. *My Life in Pictures*. New York: Grosset & Dunlap, 1975.

Chaplin, Charles. Edited by Lisa Stein Haven. *A Comedian Sees the World*. Columbia: University of Missouri Press, 2014.

Chaplin, Charles. *Footlights*, with Robinson, David, *The World of Limelight*. Bologna: Cineteca di Bologna, 2014.

Chaplin, Lita Grey, and Jeffrey Vance. *Wife of the Life of the Party*. Lanham, MD: Scarecrow Press, 1998.

Comte, Michel. *Charlie Chaplin: A Photo Diary*. Gottingen: Steidl, 2002.

Coward, Noel. Edited by Graham Payne and Sheridan Morley. *The Noel Coward Diaries*. Boston: Little, Brown, 1982.

Crocker, Harry. *Charlie Chaplin: Man and Mime*. Crocker Collection, Academy of Motion Picture Arts and Sciences.

Davis, D. William. "A Tale of Two Movies: Charlie Chaplin, United Artists, and the Red Scare." *Cinema Journal* 27, no. 1 (Fall 1987).

Day, Barry. *The Letters of Noel Coward*. New York: Knopf, 2007.

Delage, Christian. *Chaplin: La Grand Histoire*. Paris: Jean-Michel Place, 1998.

Delage, Christian, with Cecilia Cenciarelli. *Modern Times*. Bologna: Cineteca di Bologna, 2004.

Doherty, Thomas. *Hollywood and Hitler, 1933–1939*. New York: Columbia University Press, 2013.

Duncan, Paul, ed. *The Chaplin Archives*. Cologne: Taschen, 2015.

Eastman, Max. *Great Companions*. New York: Farrar, Straus & Cudahy, 1959.

Eisenstein, Sergei M. *Beyond the Stars: The Memoirs of Sergei Eisenstein*, Vol. 6. London: British Film Institute, 1995.

Epstein, Jerry. *Remembering Charlie*. New York: Doubleday, 1989.

Eyman, Scott. *Five American Cinematographers*. Metuchen, NJ: Scarecrow Press, 1987.

Fiaccarini, Anna, Peter von Bagh, and Cecilia Cenciarelli. *Limelight: Documents and Essays*. Bologna: Cineteca di Bologna, 2002.

Flom, Eric L. *Chaplin in the Sound Era: An Analysis of the Seven Talkies*. Jefferson, NC: McFarland, 1997.

Frank, Jeffrey. *The Trials of Harry S. Truman*. New York: Simon & Schuster, 2022.

Giesler, Jerry. *The Jerry Giesler Story*. New York: Simon & Schuster, 1960.

Gilliatt, Penelope. *Unholy Fools*. New York: Viking, 1973.

Graham, Martha. *Blood Memory*. New York: Doubleday, 1991.

Haas, Michael. *Forbidden Music: The Jewish Composers Banned by the Nazis*. New Haven: Yale University Press, 2013.

Hale, Georgia. *Charlie Chaplin: Intimate Close-Ups*. Metuchen, NJ: Scarecrow Press, 1995. (Also, an early draft of the book in author's collection.)

Haven, Lisa Stein. *Charlie Chaplin's Little Tramp in America*. London: Palgrave Macmillan, 2016.

Hayes, Kevin J., ed. *Charlie Chaplin Interviews*. Jackson: University Press of Mississippi, 2005.

Kamin, Dan. *Charlie Chaplin's One-Man Show*. Carbondale: Southern Illinois University Press, 1991.

———. *The Comedy of Charlie Chaplin*. Lanham, MD: Scarecrow Press, 2008.

Karney, Robyn, and Robin Cross. *The Life and Times of Charlie Chaplin*. New York: Smithmark, 1992.

Lambert, Gavin. *The Ivan Moffat File*. New York: Pantheon, 2004.

Lang, Rocky, and Barbara Hall. *Letters from Hollywood*. New York: Abrams, 2019.

Lavalley, Al, and Barry Scherr, eds. *Eisenstein at 100*. New Brunswick, NJ: Rutgers University Press, 2001.

Leslie, Anita. *Clare Sheridan*. Garden City: Doubleday, 1977.

Lewis, Robert. *Slings and Arrows*. New York: Applause, 2000.

Lloyd, Norman, and Francine Parker. *Stages*. Metuchen, NJ: Scarecrow Press, 1990.

Louvish, Simon. *Chaplin: The Tramp's Odyssey*. New York: St. Martin's, 2009.

Lynn, Kenneth S. *Charlie Chaplin and His Times*. New York: Simon & Schuster, 1997.

Maland, Charles J. *Chaplin and American Culture*. Princeton: Princeton University Press, 1989.

Marriot, "A.J." *Chaplin Stage by Stage*. Kent: Marriot Publishing, 2005.

Marx, Groucho. *The Groucho Phile*. Indianapolis: Bobbs-Merrill, 1976.

McCabe, John. *Charlie Chaplin*. Garden City: Doubleday, 1978.

McElwee, John. *Showmen, Sell It Hot! Movies as Merchandise in Golden Era Hollywood*. Pittsburgh: GoodKnight Books, 2013.

Mitchell, Glenn. *The Chaplin Encyclopedia*. London: Batsford, 1997.

Muir, Florabel. *Headline Happy*. New York: Henry Holt, 1950.

Newsom, Iris, ed. *Wonderful Inventions: Motion Pictures, Broadcasting and Recorded Sound at the Library of Congress*. Washington: Library of Congress, 1985.

Oakie, Jack. *Jack Oakie's Double Takes*. San Francisco: Strawberry Hill Press, 1980.

Paris, Barry. *Louise Brooks*. New York: Knopf, 1989.

Paumier, Pam, and David Robinson. *Chaplin: 100 Years, 100 Images, 100 Documents*. Pordenone: Roy Export Establishment, 1989.

Powell, Michael. *A Life in Movies*. New York: Knopf, 1987.

———. *Million Dollar Movie*. New York: Random House, 1992.

Ross, Lillian. *Moments with Chaplin*. New York: Dodd, Mead, 1978.

Saroyan, Aram. *Trio: Portrait of an Intimate Friendship*. New York: Linden Press, 1985.

Sayre, Nora. *On the Wing*. New York: Counterpoint, 2001.

Sbardellati, John. *J. Edgar Hoover Goes to the Movies: The FBI and the Origins of Hollywood's Cold War*. Ithaca: Cornell University Press, 2012.

Scheide, Frank, and Hooman Mehran, eds. *Chaplin: The Dictator and the Tramp*. London: British Film Institute, 2004.

———. *Chaplin's Limelight and the Music Hall Tradition*. Jefferson, NC: McFarland, 2006.

Schickel, Richard, ed. *The Essential Chaplin*. Chicago: Ivan R. Dee, 2006.

Scovell, Jane. *Oona: Living in the Shadows*. New York: Warner Books, 1998.

Silver, Charles. *Charles Chaplin: An Appreciation*. New York: Museum of Modern Art, 1989.

Stein, Lisa. *Syd Chaplin*. Jefferson, NC: McFarland, 2011.

Taves, Brian. *Robert Florey, the French Expressionist*. Metuchen, NJ: Scarecrow Press, 1987.

Tereba, Tere. *Mickey Cohen: The Life and Crimes of L.A.'s Notorious Mobster*. Toronto: ECW Press, 2012.

Vance, Jeffrey. *Chaplin: Genius of the Cinema*. New York: Abrams, 2003.

Wagner, Rob Leicester. *Hollywood Bohemia: The Roots of Progressive Politics in Rob Wagner's Script*. Santa Maria: Janeway, 2016.

Warren, Beth Gates. *Artful Lives: Edward Weston, Margrethe Mather and the Bohemians of Los Angeles*. Los Angeles: J. Paul Getty Museum, 2011.

Weissman, Stephen, M.D. *Chaplin: A Life*. New York: Arcade, 2008.

Welky, David. *The Moguls and the Dictators: Hollywood and the Coming of World War II*. Baltimore: Johns Hopkins University Press, 2008.

Wilkerson, W. R., III. *Hollywood Godfather: The Life and Crimes of Billy Wilkerson*. Chicago: Chicago Review Press, 2018.

Wranovics, John. *Chaplin and Agee: The Untold Story of the Tramp, the Writer, and the Lost Screenplay*. New York: Palgrave Macmillan, 2005.

Zollo, Paul. *Hollywood Remembered: An Oral History of Its Golden Age*. New York: Cooper Square Press, 2002.

INDEX

Page numbers in *italics* refer to illustrations.

A&M Records, 298
Academy Award Theater, 185
Academy of Motion Picture Arts and
    Sciences, 342
Acheson, Dean, 2, 16
  see also State Department, U.S.
Actors Fund, 274
Actors Studio, 190
Addams, Dawn, 308
Adding Machine, The (Rice), 226
African Queen, The (film), 288
Agee, James, 6, 201
    CC's correspondence with, 285–86,
        291–92
    CC's friendship with, 264
    death of, 292
    Monsieur Verdoux defended by, 198
Agee, Mia, 6
Aldrich, Robert, 254, 258
Alexandrov, Grigori, 327
Alhambra Music Hall, 247, 277
Allen, Fred, 76
Alpert, Herb, 298

America, 314
America First movement, 102, 103,
    126
America Looks Abroad (radio show),
    CC's appearance on, 131–32
American Committee for Russian War
    Relief, CC's speech for, 128–30
American Communist Party, 58
  Hollywood Anti-Nazi League and,
    104
American Legion, 267, 275–76
anti-Fascism:
    of CC, 105, 126, 132, 207, 282, 306
    in film industry, 101, 105
    see also Fascism
Arabesque (film), 331
Aragon, Louis, 278
Archway, 311
Arden, Robert, 131, 158, 159
    FBI interview of, 138
    indictment of, 160
Army and Navy Intelligence, CC
    surveilled by, 14

Arno, Peter, 153
Arsenic and Old Lace (film), 198
Artists Front to Win the War, CC's speech for, 138
Arts and Crafts movement, 100
Asphalt Jungle, The (film), 272
Astor, Lady, 65, 323
Avedon, Richard, 6

Bachelor and the Bobby-Soxer, The (film), 210
Bader, Robert, 33
Balanchine, George, 260
Bali, CC's visit to, 63–64
Ball, Lucille, 228
Balmain, Pierre, 210
Barrie, Elaine, 140
Barrie, James M., 228
Barry, Gertrude, 147, 158
Barry Lyndon (film), 350
Barrymore, John, 140
Bates, Barbara, 252, 253
Baum, Vicki, 181
Beckett, Samuel, 322
Belfrage, Cedric, 293, 316
Bel Geddes, Barbara, 153
Benjamin, Robert, 276
Bergman, Henry, 78, 101, 189
Berry, Joan, 137, 156, 219
    abortions of, 139, 148, 149, 270
    arrests of, 137, 141
    CC's relationship with, 138–41
    Chaplin Studios contract with, 138, 139
    Getty's relationship with, 137, 138, 139, 140, 145
    gun of, 140–41, 169
    Hopper and, 141–42, 144, 156, 167
    instability of, 158–59
    letters to Loyd by, 175–77
    Sam Marx's relationship with, 140
    schizophrenia diagnosis of, 177
    Seck's marriage to, 175
    suicide attempt of, 140

Berry, Joan, paternity suit against Chaplin of, 4, 15, 147, 156–57, 161, 165–67, 210
    CC found liable in, 173
    exculpatory blood tests in, 15, 161, 165, 169–70
    retrial in, 172–73
    trial in, 165, 168–72
Bessy, Maurice, 90–92, 213
Best Years of Our Lives, The (film), 205
Bible, The (film), 322
Birdwell, Russell, 202, 203
Bloom, Claire, 82, 262
    in *Limelight*, 252–57, 258–59
Bloomer Girl (musical), 116, 190
Blow-Up (film), 330
Blumenthal, A. C., 137, 149
Bodley Head, 325
Bogdanovich, Peter, 337
Bond, The (propaganda short), 49
Bond, Ward, 276
Bonnie and Clyde (film), 334
Boyd, John P., CC interviewed by, 233–38
Brando, Marlon, 330–32
Brecht, Bertolt, 181
Breen, Joseph, 105–6, 167
Breen Office, *see* Production Code Administration (PCA)
Brewer, Roy, 276
Brice, Fanny, 107, 113
Bridges, Harry, 116
Brigadoon (musical), 190
British Board of Film Censors, 106
British International Pictures, 86
Brooks, Louise, 324–26
Browder, Earl, 130
Brown, Clarence, 95
Brownell, Herbert, 285
Brownlow, Kevin, 110, 254, 297
Bruce, Nigel, 131, 257, 248
Brynner, Yul, 328
Buchman, Sidney, 107

Budenz, Louis, 217–18
Bureau of Investigation (BOI):
  CC investigated by, 57–58
  see also Federal Bureau of
    Investigation (FBI)
Burke, Thomas, 245
  on CC, 92–93
Burns, William J., 58
Burroughs, Edgar Rice, 51

Cagney, James, 217
Cain, Harry, 238
Caligula (Camus), 229
"Calvero's Story" (Chaplin), *243*
Campbell, Alexander, 238
Cane Hill Asylum, Hannah Chaplin at,
  22, 25, 28–29
Cannes Film Festival, 337, 355
Cantwell, John, 167
capitalism:
  CC's accumulation of wealth under,
    150, 283
  CC's films as commentary on, 14–15,
    16, 36, 61, 187–88, 206, 209–10,
    276
Caretaker, The (Pinter), 330
Cargill, Patrick, 331, 332
Carnegie Hall, CC's speech at, 130
Carol Ann (Berry's daughter), 170–71,
  176
  child-support paid by CC for, 174,
    304
Carr (U.S. attorney), 159–60, 176
Carroll, Paul Vincent, 138
Carusi, Ugo, 220
Caspary, Vera, 218
Castro, Fidel, 340
Catholic War Veterans, 200, 267, 276
Central Intelligence Agency (CIA), 271
  CC surveilled by, 14
Chamberlain, Neville, 105
Chaney, Edward, 158, 172
  CC paternity trial testimony of, 169
  FBI interview of, 148, 149

Chaplin, Charles, *19*, *95*, *243*
  affairs and dalliances of, 44, 45,
    46–47, 48, 53–55, 60, 65, 93, 138,
    157, 324, 340; *see also specific*
    women
  America's evolving relationship with,
    4, 7, 13, 32, 48, 61, 68, 71–72,
    93, 178, 213, 236, 275, 287,
    291, 293–94, 296, 299, 304, 312,
    317–18, 347, 357–58
  antiwar sentiment and pacifism of,
    48–49, 59, 134, 203, 238
  as apolitical, 9, 48, 55, 59, 209
  around-the-world trip of, 61–64,
    65–67
  as attracted to young girls, 41–42,
    115, 157, 162, 239, 340
  as avid tennis player, 189, 222–24,
    287, 312, 316
  boat of, 83–84
  charities of, 56–57, 126, 274, 275,
    296
  charm and graciousness of, 48, 53,
    56, 77, 150, 191, 197, 231, 342
  children of, *see specific children*
  coffin of, dug up and stolen, 351
  communism disavowed by, 14, 15
  compassion and generosity of, 48,
    52, 55, 56–57, 63, 126, 138, 182,
    223, 230–31, 274–75, 281, 292,
    296, 351, 354, 357
  contempt for authority of, 59, 208,
    276
  economics as interest of, 66, 68, 150
  exercise regimen of, 222–23
  fame of, 21, 27, 35, 36, 48, 142, 157,
    298, 324, 349, 354, 356
  film studio of, *see* Chaplin Studios
  final illness and death of, 349–50
  first arrival in U.S. of, 5–6, 32
  half-brothers of, *see* Chaplin, Sydney
    "Syd" (CC's half-brother); Dryden,
    Wheeler
  Handel Medallion awarded to, 342

Chaplin, Charles (*cont.*)
  Hollywood house of, *see* Hollywood,
    CC's Summit Drive house in
  honorary Academy Award of,
    338–39, 341–42
  honorary Oxford University degree
    of, 320
  as impatient and obstinate of, 38,
    193, 222, 257–58, 265, 331,
    345–46, 354
  as indifferent to groups, 61, 105,
    126, 235, 300
  individualism of, 9, 38, 122, 198
  knighted by Queen Elizabeth II,
    347–48
  liberal political sympathies of, 61,
    135, 218, 233, 236, 237, 239, 240,
    278, 286, 293
  as loner and outsider, 38, 90, 222,
    231, 232, 233, 319, 339, 353
  loyalty of, 47, 91, 92, 223
  memoirs of, *see My Autobiography*
    (Chaplin)
  misidentified as Jewish, 99, 340
  music collection of, 78
  natural talent for performance of,
    29–30, 31
  New York City walks of, 5–7, 32
  paternity suit against, *see* Berry,
    Joan, paternity suit against CC of
  on patriotism and nationalism, 67,
    68, 129–30, 178, 200, 293
  physical and mental decline of, 336,
    342, 343, 345–46, 347
  as poor correspondent, 6, 29, 85,
    296
  as romantic, 16, 64, 143
  second front in World War II
    supported by, 4, 15, 128–30, 132,
    171
  as self-described anarchist, 59, 101,
    115, 116, 317
  as self-described atheist, 178
  on Shakespeare, 228–29
  as shy and self-conscious, 31, 32–33,
    35, 38, 41, 42, 90, 262, 339
  Switzerland home of, *see* Manoir de
    Ban
  in Third Liberty Loan campaign tour,
    48–49
  Tramp character of, *see* The Tramp
  two-tone side-button shoes of,
    31–32, 77
  UA cofounded by, *see* United Artists
    (UA)
  U.S. citizenship not sought by, 9, 75,
    166, 178, 183, 201, 204, 236, 300
  U.S. return visa granted to, 1, 8
  U.S. return visa rescinded by INS, 7,
    11, 14, 347
  wealth of, 27, 35, 36, 48, 75, 142,
    298, 324, 349, 354, 357
  wives of, *see* Chaplin, Oona O'Neill;
    Goddard, Paulette; Grey, Lita;
    Harris, Mildred
  work as greatest pleasure and
    primary focus of, 8, 35, 41, 224,
    335–36, 341
Chaplin, Charles, early years of, 23
  abject poverty and homelessness in,
    5, 21–22, 24–25, 27, 36–37, 41,
    62, 142, 208, 224, 329, 356–57
  odd jobs in, 27–28
  vaudeville work in, 25, 27, 29–30
Chaplin, Charles, films of:
  CC's complete artistic and financial
    control of, 38, 209, 354
  CC's directing style in, 89–90, 113,
    192–93, 226–30, 257–58, 331–33,
    334
  CC's ownership of, 37
  little guy against the system as
    recurring theme in, 9, 16, 36, 59,
    61, 81–82, 345
  1963 U.S. retrospective of, 330, 336
  rescuing of women as recurring
    theme in, 36
  The Chaplin Revue, 318, 330

The Circus, 4, 46, 182, 208, 240, 323, 336

City Lights, 4, 14, 57, 61, 72, 81, 90, 101, 103, 194, 208, 215, 279, 348

The Count, 39

A Countess from Hong Kong, see Countess from Hong Kong, A (film)

A Dog's Life, 56, 57, 318

The Gold Rush, 48, 76, 93, 138, 193, 208, 348

The Great Dictator, see Great Dictator, The (film)

The Idle Class, 341

The Immigrant, 14

The Kid, see Kid, The (film)

Limelight, see Limelight (film)

Modern Times, see Modern Times

Monsieur Verdoux, see Monsieur Verdoux (film)

The Pilgrim, 14, 318

The Professor (unreleased fragment), 110

Shoulder Arms, 101, 318

Sunnyside, 101

A Woman of Paris, 47, 57, 116, 205, 345, 349

Chaplin, Charles (CC's father), 22
alcoholism of, 24, 27, 357
American tour of, 24
child support shirked by, 24, 25
death of, 27
music hall career of, 23–24
unmarked grave of, 27

Chaplin, Charles (CC's son), 12, 101
CC's relationship with, 224
falsified birth certificate of, 46
World War II service of, 12, 134, 274

Chaplin, Chris, 338

Chaplin, Geraldine, 4, 121, 215, 231, 301, 315–16, 330, 335, 338, 340, 344, 347, 357

Chaplin, Gypsy, 296, 298, 301, 327

Chaplin, Hannah Hill, 40, 356

brought to U.S. by CC and Syd, 39–40, 340
CC's relationship with, 26–27, 39–40, 56
Dryden's affair with, 24
final illness and death of, 40–41, 340
Lily Harly stage name of, 23
mental illness of, 21–22, 24, 25, 28–29
syphilis contracted by, 25–26

Chaplin, Jane, 338

Chaplin, Josephine, 4

Chaplin, Michael, 4, 231, 328
in *A King in New York*, 308, 309

Chaplin, Minnie, 34, 85
death of, 85, 108

Chaplin, Norman Spencer, 45

Chaplin, Oona O'Neill, 7, 157–58, 199, 223, 226, 231–32, 328, 337, 341, 342, 349–50, 351–52
abiding love for and devotion to CC of, 155, 194, 253, 264, 288, 315, 338–39, 351
Carol Matthau's friendship with, 302, 337
CC's abiding love for and devotion to, 4, 55, 225, 232, 272, 295, 315, 324, 338–39
CC's children with, 4, 5, 15, 262, 272, 328, 338; *see also specific children*
CC's first meeting with, 155
Chaplin Studios avoided by, 194, 256
death of, 352
disinherited by father, 156, 295
early years of, 153–54
father's relationship with, 153–55
The Freak halted by, 345
intelligence and maturity of, 154, 155, 156
Summit Drive house closed down by, 283–84
U.S. passport relinquished by, 294
wedding of CC and 15, 151, 157

Chaplin, Sydney (CC's son), 12, 13, 46,
    101, 158, 227, 251, 259, 341
  on CC, 224–26, 349
  CC's relationship with, 224, 231, 336
  in *A Countess from Hong Kong*,
    331–32
  World War II service of, 12, 134,
    224, 274
Chaplin, Sydney "Syd" (CC's half-
    brother), 12–13, 37, 65, 66, 122,
    240–41, 260, 356
  adored by CC's children, 301
  apprenticeship at sea of, 25, 28
  on around-the-world trip with CC,
    63–64
  as associate producer on *The Great
    Dictator*, 108–9, 112
  birth of, 22–23
  CC's correspondence with, 12, 13,
    33–34, 73, 84–85, 87, 118, 286,
    287, 296
  CC's U.S. affairs wound down by,
    296–98
  childhood poverty of, 24, 28–29, 224
  death of, 327
  father's grave left unmarked by CC
    and, 27
  Karno's comedy troupe work of, 30
  lifelong devotion to and support
    of CC by, 21–22, 28–29, 38–39,
    108–10, 250–51, 296–98
  on *Modern Times*, 84–85
  Reeves's letters to, 71, 83
  16mm camera of, 63, 110
  Wright's suit against, 85–86, 118
Chaplin, Victoria, 4, 231, 345
Chaplin Studios, 13, 37–38, 90–92,
    216, 251–52
  CC as happiest at, 335–36, 344
  CC's salary from, 128
  CC's selling of, 292, 296–97
  CC's total control at, 216, 256, 265,
    354
  in FBI investigation, 147–48

  as increasingly dilapidated, 90–91
  mascot of, 56, 91
  Oona's avoidance of, 194, 256
  prop room of, 109, 252
  Reeves as general manager of, 47,
    69, 77, 90, 91
  selling of, 296–98
  Syd as manager at, 109–10
  W. Dryden as general assistant at, 44
  see also Chaplin, Charles, films of
Charley's Aunt (film), 85
Charlie Chaplin, King of Tragedy (Von
    Ulm), 220
Cherrill, Virginia, 47, 89, 252
Chicago Tribune, 8
China, Communist, 282
Chou En-lai, 296
Churchill, Winston, CC and, 65,
    284–85
Circle Theatre, 225–31, 257, 275, 343
  CC's directing for, 226–30
Citizen Kane (film), 154, 184
Clark, Petula, 346
Clark, Tom, 183, 218
Clinton, Hillary, 16
Cloak and Dagger (film), 195
Clurman, Harold, 317
Coe, Richard, 198
Cohen, Mickey, 144, 313–14
Colbert, Claudette, 128
Collier, Constance, 223, 227, 228, 230,
    274, 275
Collier's, 65
Colman, Ronald, 3, 328
Commonwealth, see Modern Times
    (film)
communism, Communists, 14, 104,
    195
  CC's disavowal of, 14, 15
  employed by CC, 115–16
  in Hollywood, 104–5, 195, 215
Communist Party, German, 182
Communist Party, Los Angeles, 203,
    218

Communist Party, Vienna, 182
Communist Party of the USA, 130
Congress, U.S., 102, 118, 126
    see also House of Representatives,
    U.S.
Conklin, Chester, 75, 227–28, 247
Connery, Sean, 330
Connolly, Mike, 217, 308
Conte, Ruth, 196, 230
Coogan, Jackie, 343
    in The Kid, 89
    misidentified as Jewish by Nazis,
    99–100
Cooke, Alistair, 91–92, 93, 120, 132,
    138, 354
Cooper, Gary, 65, 128
Corsier cemetery, CC buried in, 351
Countess from Hong Kong, A (film),
    16, 65, 344
    Cargill in, 331, 332
    commercial failure of, 334–35
    cost of, 331, 334–35
    critical reviews of, 334
    Epstein as producer for, 226, 331
    financial returns of, 335
    Hedren in, 333, 334
    Loren in, 331, 333–34
    script for, 331, 333–34
    Sydney Chaplin in, 331–32
Courant, Curt, 191, 192
Covarrubias, Miguel, 64
Coward, Noel, 54, 278, 328, 331,
    339
Crane, Cheryl, 161
Crawford, Cheryl, 190
Crocker, Harry, 7–8, 41, 59, 157, 175
    on CC, 265
    CC's friendship with, 4, 115,
    264–65, 277–78, 281, 283–84
Crosby, Bing, 128
Crouch, Paul, 218
Crowther, Bosley, 10, 198
Cukor, George, 257, 274
Curtis, James, 281

Daily Worker, 198, 215, 217
Daniell, Henry, 108, 113
Danks, Florence, see Deshon, Florence
Dark Corner, The (film), 282
d'Arrast, Harry, 78, 265
Daughters of the American Revolution,
    125
Davies, Joseph, 129
Davies, Marion, 46
    CC's relationship with, 46, 60
Day, Richard, 206
DeHaven, Carter, 78
DeMille, Cecil B., 135
deMille, William, 57
Democratic National Committee, 275
Democratic Party, in elections of 1942,
    126
Depression Island (Sinclair), 59
Deshon, Florence, 52
    abortion of, 54
    CC's affair with, 53–54
    Eastman's affair with, 52–53, 54–55
    suicide of, 55
De Sica, Vittorio, 279, 331
Design for Living (Coward), 54
de Valera, Eamon, 166
Directors Guild, 216
Disney, Walt, 104, 128
Doctor Zhivago (film), 330
Dolce Vita, La (film), 328
Donen, Stanley, 331
D'Orsa, Lonnie, 263
Dr. Strangelove (film), 207
Dryden, Leo, 44, 246
    Hannah Chaplin's affair with, 24
Dryden, Spencer, 24, 157–58, 227
Dryden, Wheeler, 24, 157, 227, 246,
    303
    as general assistant on Monsieur
    Verdoux, 44, 191
Duel in the Sun (film), 223
Duke of York's Theatre, 248
Dunham, Katherine, 148–49
Dunn, Joseph, 168

Dunne, George, 165–66, 175, 178
Dunne, John Gregory, 117
Durant, Tim, 100, 138, 139, 158, 159,
    189
  on CC, 149–51
  FBI interview of, 148–49
  indictment of, 160

Eagels, Jeanne, 228
East End, London, 4, 293
Eastland, James, 221
Eastman, Max, 35–36, 161
  on CC, 52–53, 142–43, 149, 299–300
  CC's friendship with, 40, 51–52, 97,
    142, 299
  sedition trial of, 52
  as Socialist, 51–52
Education of a Prince, The (film), 47
Eglevsky, André, 260–62, 277
Eight Lancashire Lads clog-dancing
    troupe, 25, 27
Einstein, Albert, CC's meeting with, 66
Eisenhower, Dwight, 2, 268
  in elections of 1952, 285
Eisenstein, Sergei, 60, 93
  on CC, 60
Eisler, Gerhard, 182
Eisler, Hanns, 238, 269
  CC's friendship with, 125, 181–83,
    200–201
Eisler, Lou, 199
elections, U.S.:
  of 1942, 126
  of 1952, 2, 285
Eliot, T. S., 154
Elizabeth II, Queen of England, 348
Elsom, Isobel, in Monsieur Verdoux, 190
Epstein, Jerry, 272, 283, 284, 311, 350,
    355
  on CC, 157, 312, 345–46, 354,
    357–58
  as CC's assistant, 4, 26, 252, 253–54,
    259, 264, 308–9
  CC's friendship with, 323, 327

Circle Theatre and, 225–29
  Hopper and, 229
  on Keaton, 262–63
  as producer for A Countess from
    Hong Kong, 331, 332
Escape (film), 127
Essanay company, 42
  CC's contract with, 37
Eternal Jew, The (Nazi
    "documentary"), 100
Eternal Jew, The (Nazi publication),
    99–100
"Eternally" (song), 346
Ethan Frome (play), 226
European Film Fund, 125–26
Execution of Private Slovik, The
    (Huie), 294

Fairbanks, Douglas, 13, 45
  CC's friendship with, 38, 59–60, 63,
    324, 339, 340
  in Third Liberty Loan campaign tour,
    48–49
  UA cofounded by, 38
Famous All Over Town (Santiago),
    116–17
Famous Players-Lasky, see Paramount
    Pictures
Farrell, Frank, 267
Farrell, Raymond, 11, 270
Fascism, Fascists, 61, 67, 101, 132,
    235, 277, 279, 306
  see also anti-Fascism
Fay, James, 200
Federal Bureau of Investigation (FBI),
    320, 321
  CC investigated by, 14, 15, 58,
    128–30, 133–34, 138–39, 144–45,
    147–51, 158, 160, 215–22,
    238–39
  CC surveilled in Switzerland by, 299
  disinformation and lies about CC
    disseminated by, 15–16, 156, 158,
    159, 216, 220–21

Grey questioned by, 12
Hollywood surveillance of, 206
informants for, 133, 135, 202–3, 217–18, 238–39
INS and, 219, 221
Los Angeles office of, 135, 147, 156, 159, 195, 217, 238, 268, 270; *see also* Hood, Richard
New York office of, 147, 218, 299
Security Index Card on CC of, 219, 221, 240
see also Bureau of Investigation (BOI); Hoover, J. Edgar
Feuchtwanger, Lion, 3, 125, 181, 196, 217, 294–95
Feuchtwanger, Marta, CC's friendship with, 125–26, 295
Field, Phoebe, 41
Fields, W. C., 97
Film Culture, 325
film noir, 282
Film Society of Lincoln Center, 341
Financial Times, 334
First National:
  CC's contract with, 37
  CC's films for, 39
Fischer, Ruth, 182–83
Florey, Robert, as associate director on *Monsieur Verdoux*, 190–91, 193–94
Footlights (Chaplin), 259
  see also *Limelight* (film)
Force of Evil (film), 206
Ford, Henry, anti-Semitism of, 103
Ford, John, 104
Foreign Office, British, 102–3
Foster, William Z., 57–78
Fox West Coast theaters, 276
Frankau, Julia, 87
Freeman, Kathleen, 226
Frenke, Eugene, 155
Frenzy (film), 348
Freud, Sigmund, on CC, 62–63
Freuler, John, 37

Gallup polls, 105
Gandhi, Mohandas K., 66
Gardiner, Reginald, 110
Gardner, Hy, 267
Garfield, John, 129, 229
Gelardi, A. M. G., 311
General Della Rovere (film), 328
Genevieve (film), 308
Genthe, Arnold, 53
Gentleman Tramp, The (documentary), 337
German American Bund, 102
Getty, J. Paul:
  Berry's relationship with, 137, 138, 139, 140, 145
  FBI interview of, 151
Giesler, Jerry, 161–64, 165
Gillette, William, 30
Gilliat, Sidney, 86
Gilliatt, Penelope, 332
Goddard, Paulette, 89, 252, 275, 335, 342, 347
  on CC, 150
  CC's relationship with, 69, 83, 100, 112–13
  CC's split with, 127, 137
  in *The Great Dictator*, 69, 113, 118
  in *Modern Times*, 69, 72, 74, 82
  Paramount contract of, 127–28
  Stowaway written for, 65, 330
Goessel, Tracey, 26
Goldfinger (film), 330
Goldwyn, Sam, 128, 195
  CC defended by, 286
  Deshon hired by, 53
  United Artists and, 249
Gone With the Wind (film), 83, 119, 202
Goodman, Ezra, 251–52
Gorbachev, Raisa, 123
Gough, Lloyd, 276–77
Graduate, The (film), 334
Graham, Martha, 222
Grand Hotel (Baum), 181

Grant, Cary, 343
  CC defended by, 286
Grauman, Sid, 298
Great Depression, 14, 48, 61, 68, 104
Great Dictator, The (film), 128, 228, 279, 340
  ballet with globe scene in, 108, 110, 123
  Breen office and, 186
  casting for, 109
  CC pressured not to make, 102, 105–6, 122
  as CC's first fully talking picture, 100, 102, 112, 117
  commercial success of, 15, 115, 122–23, 133, 138, 204, 348
  cost of, 102, 110, 117
  critical success of, 15, 118–22, 138
  final speech in, 99, 112, 113–14, 116, 120, 123, 125, 129, 274, 355
  Garbitch character in, 108
  Goddard in, 69, 118
  Hopper and, 3, 114–15
  Hynkel character in, 107, 108, 110, 119–20, 123, 207
  inspiration for, 98–99
  Jewish barber character in, 99, 108, 121, 123, 207
  length of, 122
  Napaloni character in, 109, 110
  Oakie in, 109, 110, 192
  production of, 110–17
  reissue of, 348
  score for, 112
  script for, 100
  sets for, 106
  shifting political climate and, 126–27
  Struss as cameraman for, 107, 192
  Syd as associate producer of, 108
  underlying theme of, 16, 68, 134, 197, 207, 218–19, 282
Green, Adolph, 7
Greene, Charles, 100
Greene, Graham, 317

Grey, Lita:
  CC divorced by, 11–12, 46, 128, 224
  CC's marriage to, 46, 324
  children of CC and, *see* Chaplin, Charles (CC's son); Chaplin, Sydney (CC's son)
  FBI's questioning of, 12
  in *The Gold Rush*, 45
Gribble, Mary Louise, *see* Berry, Joan
Griffith, D. W., UA cofounded by, 38
Gross, Milt, 49
Group Theatre, 104, 190
Guilbert, Yvette, 62
Gyssling, Georg, 105–6

Hale, Georgia, 275
  on CC, 93
  CC's relationship with, 48
  in *The Gold Rush*, 48, 93
Hamilton, Lady, 87
Hammerstein, Oscar, II, 104
Hangmen Also Die (film), 182
Hanwell Schools for Orphan and Destitute Children, CC and Syd at, 24–25
Hardwicke, Cedric, 131
Harrington, Tom, 39
Harris, Frank, 87
Harris, Mildred:
  BOI interview of, 57
  CC's divorce from, 54
  CC's marriage to, 44–45, 53
Haven, Lisa Stein, 118
Havoc, June, 228
Hawkins, Erick, 222
Hawks, Howard, 82
Hayden, Melissa, 260–62, 271
Hays, Will, 58
Hays Office, 131, 167, 196
Hearst, William Randolph, 103, 157, 267
Heaven's Gate (film), 288
Hecht, Ben, 279
Hedren, Tippi, 333, 334

Hellman, Lillian, 130
Hemingway, Ernest, 154
Hepburn, Katharine, 274
High Noon (film), 288
Hill, Mary Ann, 24
Hirschfeld, Al, on CC, 64–65
Hitchcock, Alfred, 191, 333, 348
Hitler, Adolf, 100, 101–2
  CC's resemblance to, 98–99
Hitler-Stalin Non-Aggression Pact, 104, 116, 132
Hollywood:
  anti-fascists in, 105
  birth of film industry in, 135
  CC on, 5, 68, 93, 213, 335
  CC's absolute independence in, 38, 105, 209, 339, 354
  CC's return to for honorary award, 342–44
  CC's studio in, *see* Chaplin Studios
  Communists in, 104–5, 195, 215
  Eisenstein's sojourn in, 60, 93
  The Great Dictator and, 102, 122–23
  HUAC and, 3, 202–3, 205
  Jewish moguls in, 205
  labor unions in, 110
  Nazi Germany exiles in, 125–26, 181–82
  shifting attitudes toward CC in, 80, 128, 132–33, 286
Hollywood, CC's Summit Drive house in, 5, 12, 83, 149, 213, 253
  Berry's breaking into with a gun, 140–41, 169, 171
  CC's guests at, 189, 222–24, 230, 231–32, 262
  closing down and selling of, 284, 288, 296
Hollywood Anti-Nazi League, 61, 104–5
  financed by American Communist Party, 104
Hollywood Boulevard, CC's star on, 344

Hollywood Forever Cemetery, 41
Hollywood Reporter, 133, 197, 216, 308
Hollywood Strikers Defense Fund, 275
Hollywood Ten, called before HUAC, 203
Hood, Richard, 135, 144, 156, 158–59, 165, 219
  Hoover's communications with, 144, 159–60, 195, 217, 220, 221
  see also Federal Bureau of Investigation (FBI), Los Angeles office of
Hoover, Herbert, 166
Hoover, J. Edgar, 215, 218, 221, 238–39, 270–71, 282, 320
  at BOI, 58
  death of, 344
  Hood's communications with, 144, 159–60, 195, 217, 219–20, 221
  Hopper's letters to, 3, 195
  McGranery's meeting with, 268–69
  Thomas's meeting with, 202
  see also Federal Bureau of Investigation
Hopkins, Harry, 106–7
Hopper, DeWolf, 115
Hopper, Hedda:
  animus and vitriol towards CC of, 2, 3, 6, 9–10, 114, 229, 240, 273–74, 275, 293–94
  Berry and, 142, 144, 156, 167
  death of, 344
  FBI's leaks to, 216, 220–21
  gossip column of, 1, 115
  letters to Hoover by, 3, 195
  lies told to FBI by, 156
  Nixon's correspondence with, 1–2, 115, 268
Hopper, William, 115
House of Commons, British, 295
House of Representatives, U.S., 202
  election of 1942 and, 126

House of Representatives, U.S.,
Un-American Activities Committee
of, 115, 116, 182
CC and, 202–3, 205, 213, 239
Hollywood shaken by, 3, 115
Motion Picture Alliance and,
114–15, 130
Nixon as member of, 3
Hughes, Howard, 202, 251
Hughes, Rupert, 51
Hume, Benita, 328
Huston, John, 288, 292, 322
Hutton, Barbara, 161
Huxley, Aldous, 204

"Idea for the Solution of War
Reparations, An" (Chaplin;
unpublished), 68
Ikiru (film), 272
Immigration and Nationality Act
(1952), 270, 321
Immigration and Naturalization
Service, 11, 12, 269, 335
CC interviewed by, 233–38
CC investigated by, 221, 314
CC's return visa revoked by, 7, 272
FBI and, 218, 219, 220–21, 238, 270
Independent Theater Owners of Ohio,
204–5
Internal Revenue Service (IRS), 128,
314
CC surveilled by, 14
In the Heat of the Night (film), 334
Inukai Tsuyoshi, 67
Iron Curtain, 299
Irwin, John J., 159
Isherwood, Christopher, 232
Ivens, Joris, 182

Jaglom, Henry, 184
James, Dan, 153–54, 223, 357
blacklisted by HUAC, 116
on CC, 111, 115–16, 129, 324
in Communist Party, 100, 115, 116

death of, 117
hired to work on The Great
Dictator, 100–102, 106–8, 112,
113–14, 190
resignation from Communist Party
of, 116
James, Eric, 341, 346, 349–50
as CC's arranger, 318
James, Frank and Jesse, 100
James, Sid, 309
Jewish Encyclopedia, The, 99
Jews Are Looking at You (Nazi
publication), 99
Jew Süss (Feuchtwanger), 125
Jim Henson Company, 298
Johnson, Van, 328
Jolson, Al, 228
Joyce, Peggy Hopkins, 46
Justice Department, U.S., 276, 299
CC's U.S. return visa revoked by, 7,
8, 10–11
see also McGranery, James
Justice Department, U.S., Mann Act
case against CC of, 161–64, 210,
218, 220
CC's acquittal in, 164
Giesler's summation in, 163–64
indictment in, 160

Kamin, Dan, 73, 99, 247
Karno, Fred, 21
on CC, 31
CC's work for, 30–33, 42, 119, 318,
319, 346, 356
comedy troupe of, 30, 91, 308
Syd's work for, 30
Kaye, Danny, 272, 343
Kazan, Elia, 190
Keaton, Buster, 16, 257
CC defended by, 281–82
CC on, 97–98
in Limelight, 247, 259–60, 261,
262–64
Kehr, Dave, 36

Kelly, Arthur, 42, 250, 305
Kelly, Hetty, 41–42, 356
Kendall, Kay, 308
Kennedy, Ethel, 341–42
Kennedy, Joseph P., 103–4
Kennedy, Merna, 46
Kennington, London, 4, 356
Kenyon, Dorothy, 239
Keyes, Evelyn, 228
Keystone company:
  CC's contract with, 33–34
  CC's work for, 35–36, 51, 227
Keystone Cops, 111
KFWB radio station, 131
Khrushchev, Nikita, 296
Kid, The (film), 36, 45, 341, 356
  CC's editing of, 53, 54
  commercial success of, 348
  Coogan in, 89
  Redmond in, 57
  Riesner in, 89
  Tramp character in, 208
Kilgallen, Dorothy, 267
Kincaid, Clarence, 172
King, Queen, Joker (film), 108
King in New York, A (film), 16, 302
  Addams in, 308
  CC on, 312–13
  CC's ideas for, 287
  cost of, 308
  critical reviews of, 310–11
  distribution of, 307–8, 309, 311
  Epstein as producer of, 226, 308–9
  filmed at Shepperton studio, 308–9
  financial returns of, 311
  idea for, 307
  King Shahdov character in, 309
  left out of CC's biography, 312, 323–24
  length of, 312
  Michael Chaplin in, 308, 309
  Rupert character in, 308
  script for, 311
  Sid James in, 309

Kitchen, Karl, 75
Kleiber, Rudolf, *see* Arden, Robert
Knight, Goodwin, 178
Koch, Howard W., 342
Kohner, Paul, 125–26
Korean War, 282
Kramer, Karl, 189
Kramer, Stanley, 288
Krim, Arthur, 288
Kristallnacht, 105
Kubrick, Stanley, 38, 350

Labour Party, British, 295
Lady and the Tramp (film), 348
Lady Killer, see Monsieur Verdoux (film)
Lambeth, London, 4, 61, 356
Lambeth Infirmary, Hannah Chaplin admitted to, 24
Lambeth Workhouse, CC at, 24, 25, 61–62, 356
Landru, Henri, 184
Lane, Lauri Lupino, 308
Lang, Fritz, 61, 125, 182
Langdon, Harry, 272
Langer, William, 183, 218
Lasky, Jesse, 60
Lauder, Harry, 29
Laura (Caspary), 218
Laurel, Stan, 97, 319–20
  on CC, 31–32, 319
  in Karno's comedy troupe, 31, 97, 319
Laurents, Arthur, 252–53
LeBaron, William, salary of, 128
left wing, 55, 104, 107, 116, 234, 316–17
  CC denounced by Congress as, 8
  writers, 51–52; *see also specific writers*
  see also liberalism, liberals
Legion of Decency, 167
Leigh, Vivien, 83, 278
Lejeune, C. A., 122, 199, 278

Leno, Dan, 29
Lester, Eva, 28, 357
Lewis, Jerry, 272
Lewis, Robert, 197
  in *Monsieur Verdoux*, 189–90
liberalism, liberals:
  CC's sympathies toward, 61, 135,
    218, 233, 236, 237, 239, 240, 278,
    286, 293
  see also left wing
Liberator, The, 52
Liberty, Modern Times reviewed in, 81
Life, 117, 265, 285
Limelight (film), 1, 3, 16, 36, 72, 243,
    245
  as apolitical, 245
  as autobiographical, 245, 248, 249,
    253–54, 272
  ballet scene in, 260–62
  Bloom in, 252–57, 258–59
  Bruce in, 248
  Calvero character in, 245, 246–49,
    256, 259–60, 264, 355
  CC's novel written in preparation
    for, 243, 248–49
  commercial success of, 277, 279,
    291, 314
  cost of, 251
  critical success of, 271, 277, 278,
    291
  edited by CC, 263–64
  Epstein as CC's assistant on, 26, 226
  European premiere of, 277–78
  Keaton in, 259–60, 261, 262–64
  length of, 263–64
  London world premiere of, 4
  New York premier of, 271
  Paramount studio preview of, 3–4
  Postant character in, 248
  previews of, 264
  production of, 254–63
  public reception of, 3
  rehearsals for, 253–54
  score for, 251, 254

  script for, 246, 251, 263
  self-financed by CC, 251
  Sydney Chaplin in, 257
  Syd's opinion of, 298
  Terry character in, 246–47, 251, 252,
    256, 258, 264
  U.S. boycott and picketting of, 267,
    268, 276–77
  U.S. release of, 267–68
Lindbergh, Charles:
  anti-Semitism of, 103
  kidnapping of son of, 58
Lloyd, Frank, 131
Lloyd, Harold, 98
Lloyd, Marie, 29
Lloyd, Norman, 222–24, 257–58, 263,
    272, 318, 321
Lloyd, Peggy, 224
Lloyd George, David, 65
Loew's theaters, 202, 276
London:
  Blitz in, 121–22, 356
  CC's early years in, *see* Chaplin,
    Charles, early years of
  CC's films premiered in, 4, 61,
    121–22, 279, 311, 334
  CC's trips to, 6, 13, 61–62, 233, 272,
    279, 281, 307–8, 312, 316–17,
    331, 356
London *Daily Express*, 334
Longshoreman's Union, 116
Look, CC's interview in, 117–18
Loren, Sophia, 331, 333–34
Los Angeles, 49, 61, 116
  CC on, 335
  CC's 1972 return to, 342–44
  CC's films premiered in, 66, 185, 205
  Communists in, 203, 218
  FBI office in, 135, 147, 156, 159,
    195, 217, 238, 268, 270; *see also*
    Hood, Richard
  Nazi Germany exiles in, 181
  Riefenstahl's visit to, 104
  Scott statue in, 178

Los Angeles Herald-Express, 170
Los Angeles Times, 8, 10, 166, 173, 344
    CC's interview with, 194–95
    Hopper's gossip column for, 115,
        240; *see also* Hopper, Hedda
Lourie, Eugene, 254–55, 256
Lubitsch, Ernst, 125
Luce, Henry R., 285
Ludwig, Emil, 131
Ludwig, Julian, 227
Lumet, Sidney, 104
Lyons, Leonard, 267

MacDonald, Ramsay, 66
MacMurray, Fred, 128
Mahler-Werfel, Alma, 181
Mailer, Norman, 243
Maland, Charles, 206
Man Hunt (film), 127
Mann, Heinrich, 181
Mann, Thomas, 125, 181
Mann Act (1910), 160, 162
    see also Justice Department, U.S.,
        Mann Act case against CC of
Manoir de Ban, 287–88, 317–18, 323,
    327, 347
March, Florence, 104
March, Fredric, 61, 104
March of Time, The (newsreel), 101
Marnie (film), 333
Martin, Strother, 226
Marx, Groucho, 32–33, 117, 343
    on CC, 33
Marx, Sam, 140
Marx Brothers, 97
Mason, James, 201
Masses, The, 52
Matthau, Carol Marcus Saroyan, 153,
    154, 156, 343
    Oona's friendship with, 302, 337
Matthau, Charles, 337, 338, 343,
    351–52
Matthau, Walter, 302, 337, 343
    CC's friendship with, 337–38

May Company, 148
Mayer, Louis B., 167
McCarran, Pat, 221
McCarran-Walter Act (1952),
    269–70
McCarthy, Joseph, 183, 217, 221, 239,
    268, 282, 340, 354
McCormick, Robert, 156
McCoy, Horace, 272, 321
McDowall, Roddy, 326
McGranery, James, 2, 7, 10, 15,
    275–76, 283, 314, 320–21
    CC's reentry permit revoked by,
        269
    death of, 344
    Hoover's meeting with, 268–69
    see also Justice Department, U.S.
McGuinness, James Kevin, 130
McLaglen, Victor, 275
media, *see* press
Medical Aid to Russia, 275
Meighan, Thomas, 44
Meltzer, Bob, 114
    as Communist, 115
Menjou, Adolphe, 116, 205
Mercury Theatre, 222
Meryman, Richard, 178
Meyer, Baron de, 53
MGM, 59, 130, 140, 147, 215
Millikan, Charles, 165, 167–69,
    171–72, 173, 174
Modern Times (film), 115, 208, 252
    Breen Office and, 80, 117, 186
    CC's decision to keep as silent film,
        74–75
    CC's writing of, 71–73
    commercial success of, 81, 194
    Conklin in, 228
    cost of, 81
    critical reviews of, 81
    feeding machine sequence in, 74, 77
    Gamine character in, 72, 82
    Goddard in, 69, 72, 74, 82
    inspiration for, 61, 71–72

Modern Times (film) (*cont.*)
  political focus of, 14–15, 16, 61, 68,
    81, 82, 85, 93, 128, 134, 207, 276
  production of, 72–76
  reissues of, 329–30, 348
  set of, 75
  score for, 75–79
  Syd's views on, 84–85
  trailer for, 305
Moffat, Ivan, 231, 232–33
Monroe, Marilyn, 161, 272
Monsieur Verdoux (film), 16, 68, 181,
    203–4, 207–10, 282, 330
  Academy Award nomination of, 210
  Annabella character in, 185, 186,
    193, 207
  boycotts of, 205
  CC's press conference and, 199–200
  commercial failure of, 202, 204, 206,
    210, 219, 277
  critical reviews of, 3, 4, 196–202,
    207, 210
  Elsom in, 190
  Florey as associate director on,
    190–91, 193–94
  genesis of, 184–85
  The Girl character in, 187, 207
  Henri Verdoux character in, 185,
    186–87, 188, 193, 194, 201, 206,
    207, 208–9
  Lewis in, 189–90
  Lydia character in, 206
  Madame Grosnay character in, 190
  Nash in, 189, 193, 202, 207
  1964 rerelease of, 207
  PCA and, 186–88
  previews of, 196
  production of, 192–94
  Raye in, 186, 191, 192, 206, 207
  score for, 182
  script for, 185–88
  Welles's idea for, 184–85
Montagu, Ivor, 93
Monterey, Carlotta, 154

Mosk, Stanley, 165, 167, 178
Mosley, Oswald, 67
Motion Picture Alliance for the
    Preservation of American Ideals,
    114–15, 130, 276
Motion Picture Association, 58
Motion Picture Democratic Committee,
    61
Muir, Florabel, 144, 156, 159, 167,
    169, 173–74
  lies told to FBI by, 156
Mundt, Karl, 221
Murnau, F. W., 107
Mutual Film Corporation:
  CC's contract with, 37
  CC's films for, 39
My Autobiography (Chaplin), ix, 33,
    41, 44, 67, 86, 99, 138, 162, 316,
    323–25
My Life and Loves (Harris), 87
My Life in Pictures (Chaplin), 347

Nasaw, David, 103
Nash, Marilyn, 192, 193, 252
  in *Monsieur Verdoux*, 189, 193, 202,
    207
Nathan, George Jean, 199
Nation, 198
National Council of American-Soviet
    Friendship, 239
Nazis:
  artists expelled from Germany by,
    125, 181
  CC misidentified as Jewish by,
    99–100
Negri, Pola, CC's relationship with,
    46, 60
Nehru, Jawaharlal, 294
Neruda, Pablo, 305–6
New Deal, 115, 268
Newington Workhouse, 24
Newman, Alfred, 77, 79–80
New Masses, 275
Newsweek, 197

New York, N.Y., 54, 55, 283, 284
  Berry's trip to, 138–39, 140, 160
  CC's 1972 return to, 341–42
  CC's films premiered in, 103, 119,
    185, 196–97, 199, 205, 271, 276
  CC's speeches in, 130
  CC's trips to, 4–5, 46, 49, 130,
    138–39, 140, 185, 222, 249–50,
    253, 272
  CC's walks around, 5–7, 32
  FBI's investigation of CC in, 147,
    218, 299
  1963 CC retrospective in, 330, 336
  Oona's upbringing in, 153–54
New York *Daily News*, 144, 334, 340
New Yorker, The, 5, 51
New York Foundling Home, 277
New York Herald Tribune, 156–57, 197
New York *Sun*, 197
New York Telegram, 197
New York Times, The, 10, 11, 134,
    198, 296, 320, 330, 334, 341
New York *World*, 61
Nichols, Louis, 220
Nixon, Richard M., 178, 221, 268
  Hopper's correspondence with, 1–2,
    115
"Notes on Camp" (Sontag), 16
Novello, Ivor, 198
Nye, Gerald, 126–27, 218

Oakie, Jack, 111–12
  in *The Great Dictator*, 109, 110, 192
Observer, 275, 310
Odets, Betty, 300
Odets, Clifford, 104, 302, 317
  CC's friendship with, 300–301
Old Drury Lane (Stirling), 158
Olivier, Laurence, 83
One-Eyed Jacks (film), 330
O'Neill, Eugene:
  death of, 295, 345
  Oona disinherited by, 156, 295
  Oona's relationship with, 153–55

O'Neill, Eugene, Jr., suicide of, 295
O'Neill, Oona, *see* Chaplin, Oona
  O'Neill
O'Neill, Shane:
  disinherited by Eugene, 295
  suicide of, 295
Othello (Shakespeare), 228–29
Outlaw, The (film), 202
Oxford University, CC's honorary
  degree from, 320

Panacea (Chaplin's boat), 83–84
Pantages, Alexander, 161
Paramount Pictures, 38, 60, 107, 265
  Goddard's contract with, 127–28
Parker, Dorothy, 104
Parrish, Kathy, 351
Parsons, Louella, 156, 197, 204, 220
Partisan Review, 198
Patterson, Richard, 337
Pearl Harbor attack, 122, 127
Pearson, Drew, 221
Pegler, Westbrook, 9, 132–33
  anti-Semitism of, 215
  on CC's Mann Act indictment,
    160–61
  FBI leaks to, 221
  vitriol directed at CC by, 134–35,
    214–15, 274
People's Daily World, 240
Perry Mason (TV show), 115, 298
Photoplay, 157
Picasso, Pablo, 238, 278–79
Picker, Arnold, 307–8, 309
Pickfair, 5, 108
Pickford, Mary, 199
  CC's disagreements over UA with,
    249–50
  in Third Liberty Loan campaign tour,
    48–49
  UA cofounded by, 38
  UA share sold by, 288
Pinter, Harold, 330
Pitt, Brad, 100

Place in the Sun, A (film), 222
PM, 197–98
Polonsky, Abraham, 206
Popular Front, 82, 128
Postal Service, U.S., CC surveilled by, 14
Postance, William, 248
Powell, Edward, 79–80
Powell, Michael, *19*, 232
Pravda, 220, 269, 279
press, 87, 103, 132, 150, 160, 232
    CC assaulted by, 9–10, 164–65,
        171, 181, 199, 201, 213, 216–17,
        273–74, 286, 287, 293–94, 304,
        308, 313, 340, 344
    CC's relationship with, 55–56, 150,
        199–201, 203, 235, 256, 265
    FBI's collusion with, 159
    Hearst and, 103, 267
    right-wing, 10, 132–33, 216, 217
    see also specific columnists and
        writers
Priestley, J. B., 307
Production Code Administration
    (PCA), 105, 167
    The Great Dictator and, 103, 117,
        186
    Modern Times and, 80, 186
    Monsieur Verdoux and, 186–88, 208
Progressive Party, 275
Pryor, Thomas, 134
Punch, 254
Purviance, Edna, 33, 189, 190, 274
    alcoholism of, 47
    CC's correspondence with, 43–44,
        47–48
    CC's relationship with, 42–45, 46,
        47–48, 303–4
    death of, 304
    hired by CC at Essanay, 42
    Squire's marriage to, 48
    in *A Woman of Paris*, 205

Quarry, Marcus, 29
Queen Elizabeth, RMS, 4, 6, 9, 13

Radio City music Hall, 260
Rain (Maugham), 228
Raksin, David, 80
    on CC, 354
    The Great Dictator and, 112
    hired, fired, and rehired by CC,
        77
    Powell's telegram to, 76
    work on score for *Modern Times* of,
        76–79
Rankin, John, 183–84, 202
    racism of, 183
Rasch, Ray, 254
Raye, Martha, 210, 343
    in *Monsieur Verdoux*, 186, 191, 192,
        206, 207
rbc films, 337
Rebecca (film), 223
Rebel Without a Cause (film), 115
Redmond, Granville, 56–57
Red Scare, 16, 282
Reeves, Alf, 81, 106, 117, 158
    as adept at Cockney rhyming slang,
        79
    CC's loyalty to, 92
    as Chaplin Studios general manager,
        47, 69, 71, 77, 90, 91, 101, 109
    death of, 227
    FBI interviews of, 147–48
    Syd's letters from, 71, 83
Reeves, Amy, 227
Reeves, May, 65
Regent Films, 47
Reinhardt, Max, acting school of, 138,
    140
Remarque, Erich Maria, 335
Renoir, Jean, 222, 258
Republican Party, in elections of 1942,
    126
Rice, Elmer, 226
Richardson, Ralph, 231
Riefenstahl, Leni, 104
Riesner, Dean, in *The Pilgrim*,
    89–90

right wing, 14, 51, 122, 130, 135, 205, 209, 285
  press, 10, 132–33, 216, 217; *see also specific journalists*
  writers, 51
Roberts, Richard M., 208
Robeson, Paul, 305
Robinson, Carlyle, 65
Robinson, David, 246, 355
Robinson, Edward G., 104, 218
Rockefeller, David, 341
Rodgers, Mary, 153
Rogers, Ginger, 128
Rogers, Will, 51
Rohauer, Raymond, 297
Romanoff, Gloria, 350
Romanoff, Mike, 350–51
Roosevelt, Eleanor, 214
Roosevelt, Franklin, Jr., 119
Roosevelt, Franklin D., 49, 103–4, 119
  CC's donation to, 60
  The Great Dictator supported by, 106–7
  third inauguration of, 125
Rose, Joel, 277
Rosen, Alex, 165
Ross, Lillian, 5–6
Rossellini, Roberto, 328
Rothman, Mo, CC film library lease deal of, 336–37, 338
Royal Ballet School, 315
Royal Society for the Blind, 277
Rubinstein, Arthur and Nela, 7
Runser, Miss, 302
Rushmore, Howard, 238–39
Russell, Jane, 202
Russia, Ukraine invaded by, 355

Sadoul, Georges, 206
St. Johns, Adela Rogers, 157
Salinger, J. D., 153
Sanders, George, 328
Sandford, Tiny, 72
Santiago, Danny, *see* James, Dan

Sargeant, Howland, 10–11
Saroyan, William, 51
Sartre, Jean-Paul, 278
Saturday Evening Post, 286
Saura, Carlos, 347
Schallert, William, 225, 226–27, 229–30, 343
Schenck, Joe, 60, 69, 167
Schlesinger, Arthur, Jr., 123
Schneider, Alan, 322
Schneider, Bert, 336–37
Schoenberg, Arnold, 182, 225
Scott, Joseph, 305
  anti-Semitism of, 167
  as Berry's attorney, 165–66, 167–75
  death of, 177–78
  statue of, 178
Screen Actors Guild, 216, 225
Script, 51
Sea Gull, The (film), 47
Sears, Gradwell, 203–4
Seck, Russell, 175
Selznick, Daniel, 223
Selznick, David, 3, 128, 195
  CC's spat with, 223
  UA and, 249
Selznick/Pathé studios, 256, 260
Sennett, Mack, 30, 33, 35–36
Shadow and Substance (Carroll), 138, 302
  film rights to, 138, 140, 147, 155
Shaw, George Bernard, 65
Sheekman, Arthur, 117
Sherman, Bob, 229
Shostakovich, Dmitri, 296
Sifton, Paul, 61
Simon & Schuster, 323
Since You Went Away (film), 223
Sinclair, Upton, 59, 61, 75
  CC's correspondence with, 322–23
Skelton, Red, on CC, 97–98
Skin Game, The (Galsworthy), 226
Skolsky, Sidney, 3
"Smile" (song), 346

Smith, Gerald L. K., 183
Smith, W. Eugene, 265, 285
Sobeloff, Simon, 11
socialism, Socialists, 51, 55, 59, 75, 104, 299
    CC's disavowal of, 237, 317
Sokolsky, George, 221
Solidarity movement (Poland), 355
Song of Bernadette, The (Werfel), 181
Sontag, Susan, 16
Southerner, The (film), 258
Spectator, 98
Spellman, Francis Cardinal, 268, 277
Spies, Walter, 63
Squire, John, Purviance's marriage to, 48
Stagecoach (film), 104
Stalin, Joseph, 115–16, 122, 129, 182, 205
Stanwyck, Barbara, 128
Star Is Born, A (film), 223
State Department, U.S., 270, 271
    CC surveilled by, 14
    see also Acheson, Dean
Stephen Acrobat (ballet), 222
Sternberg, Josef von, 47
Stevenson, Adlai, 285
Stewart, Donald Ogden, 104–5, 107, 197, 316–17
    as Communist, 104
Stirling, Edward, 158
Stokowski, Leopold, 341
Stone, I. F., 130
Stowaway, see Countess from Hong Kong, A (film)
Strand, 254
Strange Love of Martha Ivers, The (film), 195
Stripling, Robert, 205
Strong, Anna Louise, 239
Struss, Karl, 116, 296
    as cameraman for Limelight, 255–56
    as cameraman for The Great Dictator, 107, 112–13, 192, 255

Sullivan, Ed, 10, 164–65, 201, 267, 274, 283
Sunrise (film), 107
Sunset Boulevard (film), 186
Supreme Court, California, 168
Switzerland, CC and Oona's home in, see Manoir de Ban

Taft, Robert, 2
Taking of Pelham One Two Three, The (film), 338
Tamm, E. A., 148
Taradash, Daniel, 342
Taylor, Frank, 215
Terkel, Studs, 294
Terrail, Claude, 278
Tetrick, Betty and Ted, 227
Thalberg, Irving, 59
That Hamilton Woman (film), 127
They Shoot Horses, Don't They? (McCoy), 272
    movie rights to, 272, 318–19, 321–22
Third Liberty Loan campaign, 48–49
"This Is My Song" (song), 346
This Week, 304
Thomas, Dylan, 231–32
Thomas, J. Parnell, 202–3, 205, 221
Thompson, Dorothy, 10
Thomson, David, 310
Thonstein, Israel, Who's Who in American Jewry's misidentification of CC as, 99, 216, 220, 221
Tilden, Bill, 224
Time, 317
Time of Your Life, The (Saroyan), 226
Times (London), 334
Tinney, Frank, 246
Tolson, Clyde, 220, 320
Totheroh, Rollie, 91, 101, 107, 145, 191, 251–52, 255, 302–3
Touch of the Poet, A (O'Neill), 155
Tramp, the, 69, 134, 166, 206, 210
    animating principle of, 9, 14, 310, 353

CC's creation and development of, 35–36, 37, 208–9
CC's retirement of, 92, 329
in *City Lights*, 348
in *The Gold Rush*, 362
Hitler's resemblance to, 98–99
international audience for, 38
Jewish barber in *The Great Dictator* as, 99, 207
in *The Kid*, 45
in *Modern Times*, 72–73, 74–75, 82, 348
in *The Pilgrim*, 90
as symbol of Poland's Solidarity movement, 355
Verdoux character vs., 208, 209
Tramp and the Dictator, The (documentary), 110
Tree, Herbert Beerbohm, 223
Truman, Harry, 126, 268, 269–70, 282
Truman administration, 202, 354
Trumbo, Dalton, 51, 133
Truzzi, George, 308
Tully, Jim, 56
Turpin, Ben, 228
Tydings, Millard, 239
Tynan, Kenneth, 302, 310–11, 316

Ukraine, Russian invasion of, 355
Umberto D. (film), 272
Underwood, Agness, 170
Union for Democratic Action, 275
United Artists (UA), 42, 69, 81, 103, 106, 122, 195, 199, 202, 267, 276
CC's selling of his share of, 288, 307
CC's share of, 216
The Circus reissue and, 336
cofounded by CC, Fairbanks, Griffith, and Pickford, 38
financial difficulties of, 194, 250
High Noon and, 288

A King in New York refused by, 309
Limelight and, 267–68, 276–77
Pickford and CC's disagreements over, 249–50
Pickford's selling of her share of, 288
United States:
anti-Semitism in, 103, 105
CC barred from returning to, 1, 7, 11, 14, 270, 347
CC's cutting of his ties to, 283, 288, 292, 296–98
CC's decision not to seek citizenship in, 9, 75, 166, 178, 183, 201, 204, 236, 300
CC's evolving relationship with, 4, 7, 13, 32, 48, 61, 68, 71–72, 93, 178, 213, 236, 275, 287, 291, 293–94, 296, 299, 304, 312, 317–18, 347, 357–58
CC's first arrival in, 5–7, 32, 55
CC's return to, 338–39, 341–44
Eisenstein's sojourn in, 60
isolationism of, 100, 102, 126, 209
Karno's tours in, 30, 91
Limelight boycott in, 75, 267, 268, 275–77
political reversal following WWII in, 209–10, 318
post-WWI cultural and political shifts in, 166
Red Scare in, 16, 282
Unknown Chaplin (documentary), 297

Valentino, Rudolph, 161
Vanderbilt, Gloria, 153, 337
Van Vechten, Carl, 130
Variety, 10–11, 118–19, 194, 270, 337
CC's interview in, 120–21
Ventura, Michael, 98
Vidor, King, 78, 100, 151, 157–58
Viertel, Salka, 204, 291–92
CC's friendship with, 181–82, 217
Volkoff, Boris, 260

Wagner, Florence, 158
Wagner, Rob, 55–56, 57, 158
  as CC's secretary and ghostwriter, 51
  as Socialist, 51–52
Waiting for Godot (Beckett), 322
Walker, Danton, 267
Wallace, Henry, 270
Waller, Tom, 202
Wallis, Minna, 155, 158, 160
Walthall, Harris, 127
Wanger, Walter, 105, 195
Warner, Jack, 106, 167
Warner Bros., 195
  KFWB owned by, 131
  Syd signed by, 85
Warner brothers, 104, 105
Washington Post, The, 160, 198
Watson (CC's butler), 224
Watt, Lois, 303
Weisbrode, Kenneth, 282
Weissman, Stephen, 28
Welbourn, Phyllis, 223, 227, 275
Welles, Orson, 83, 130, 153, 222
  Monsieur Verdoux and, 184–85
Wells, H. G., 65
Werfel, Franz, 181
West, Nathanael, 107
Western Costume, 111
Westland School, 215
West Norwood Schools, CC at, 24, 25
What Every Woman Knows (Barrie), 228, 229
  CC's direction of, 229–30
Wheeler, George Dryden, *see* Dryden, Wheeler
White-Slave Traffic Act, *see* Mann Act (1910)
Whitman, Alden, 341
Wilder, Billy, 125, 186
Wilder, Thornton, 185
Wilkerson, Billy, 133, 216–17
Williamson, Lambert, 346

Willson, Meredith, 112
Wilson, Earl, 267
Wilson, Harold, 348
Wilson, Woodrow, 48–49
Winchell, Walter, 201–2, 221, 267, 274
Windsor, Claire, 46
Winnington, Richard, 198–99
Winter, Ella, 316–18
Woman's Home Companion, CC's articles for, 67–68
Woollcott, Alexander, 78, 185
World Peace Council, 296
World War I, 51, 116
  CC's Liberty Loan bond tour during, 48–49, 274
World War II, 116, 209, 214, 282
  America's political reversal following, 209–10, 318
  CC's support for a second front to aid Russia in, 4, 15, 128–30, 132, 171
  Charles Jr.'s service in, 12, 134, 274
  London bombed in, 23, 121–22, 356
  Sydney's service in, 12, 134, 224, 274
  war bonds bought by CC during, 274
Wright, Loyd, 164
  Berry's letters to, 175–77
  CC's correspondence with, 284, 304–5
  as CC's lawyer, 127, 174, 275, 277, 284, 292
Wright, Molly, Syd sued for assault, libel and slander by, 85–86
Wyler, William, CC defended by, 286
Wyndham, Francis, 339, 347

Yesterday, Today and Tomorrow (film), 331
Youngstein, Max, 267, 307–8

Zelensky, Volodymyr, 355
Zukor, Adolph, 167

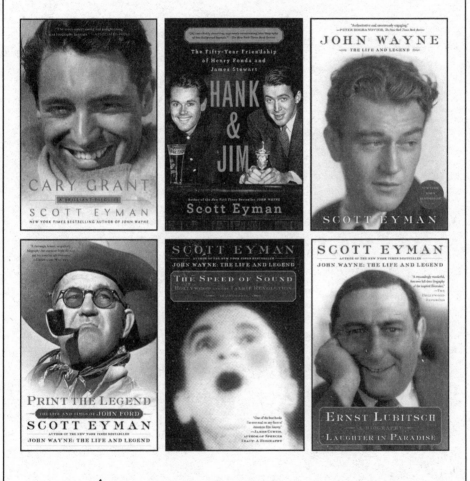